HEADS
OR TAILS

HEADS
OR TAILS

THE POETICS
OF MONEY

Jochen Hörisch

Translated by
Amy Horning Marschall

WAYNE STATE UNIVERSITY PRESS
DETROIT

Kritik: German Literary Theory and Cultural Studies
Liliane Weissberg, *Editor*

*A complete listing of the books in this series
can be found at the back of this volume.*

Originally published as *Kopf oder Zahl: Die Poesie des Geldes*.
Copyright © 1996 Suhrkamp Verlag.
Copyright © 2000 by Wayne State University Press,
Detroit, Michigan 48201. All rights are reserved.
No part of this book may be reproduced without formal permission.
Manufactured in the United States of America.
04 03 02 01 00   5 4 3 2 1

Library of Congress Cataloging-in-Publication Data

Hörisch, Jochen.
   [Kopf oder Zahl. English]
   Heads or tails : the poetics of money / Jochen Hörisch ; translated by Amy Horning
Marschall.
     p. cm.
   Includes bibliographical references and index.
   ISBN 0-8143-2754-0 (alk. paper)
   1. Literature—History and criticism. 2. Money in literature. I. Title.
PN56.M547 H6713 2000
809'.93355—dc21

                                                  99-054084

Die Herausgabe dieses Werkes wurde aus Mitteln von Inter Nationes, Bonn, gefördert.

[Grateful acknowledgment is made to Inter Nationes for its financial assistance in the
translation of this work.]

CONTENTS

Translator's Note 7

PART I
PROGRAMMATIC REMARKS ON THE POETICS OF MONEY

1. "For in This Sign All Now Can Find Salvation"—
   On the Problem and Theme of a
   Monetary Ontosemiology 11

2. "Aut Prodesse aut Delectare"—
   Literary History as the History of Problems 28

PART II
POETIC PHENOMENOLOGY OF MONEY

3. The Legibility of World and Money 41

4. The Materiality of Money (and of Literature) 58

5. "To Torment from Afar"—Money's Relational Mania ... 77

6. Money's Sex—Money Reproducing, Grandchildren,
   Compound Interest 91

5

Excursus: The Army, the Church, and the Alma Mater—
A Caprice on Corporate Bodies 117

7. "Time Is Money"—
The Time of Money/The Money of Time 127

8. Poetic Critique of Money—
On the Hermeneutics of the Deficiency 147

PART III
ONTOSEMIOLOGY OF MONEY

9. Equivalence, Indifference, Rings—
Summary and Transition 161

10. What Counts? Money and Validity 179

11. Money: Symbol, Allegory, Fetish—
Marx with Benjamin and Goethe 199

12. Schlemihl's Shadow—Nietzsche's Shadow 216

13. "The Source of the Center," or:
the Gift of Money, the Gift of Poesie 241

14. Deconstruction of Money 251

15. Ruin/Ruins 261

16. The Medial Blood of the Economy—
Klaus Heinrich or Dracula 276

Notes 287

Bibliography 321

Index 339

TRANSLATOR'S NOTE

Jochen Hörisch is not only a vastly erudite individual, he possesses a tremendous wit, and this combination of qualities makes reading his work a rare pleasure. His obvious delight in play with the German language—his use of dashes and slashes to allude to words sharing the same root but expressing additional meanings related sometimes through affinity, sometimes opposition—poses unique and interesting challenges for the translator. German and English being closely related, it was surprisingly often possible to capture both the wit and the serious thought behind a turn of phrase. There were times, however, where the sense of the passage required that I forgo the game, and there were others—passages where the sense of the argument relies on wordplay rather than logic—where I preserved what, in English, might seem like nonsense. At such points, I have added a note of explanation, which I hope will not be too cumbersome but will honor, instead, both the style and the substance of *Kopf oder Zahl: Die Poesie des Geldes*.

Quotations from other works abound in this study. I have, where possible, quoted from existing translations, so that interested readers may pursue the reference; in such cases I have referred in both text and notes to English titles. Occasionally, Hörisch's analysis of a passage required me to make slight alterations to these translations in order to capture that particular aspect of the text to which he refers. I do not mean to imply that these translations are flawed; inevitably translation requires that choices be made, and particular contexts require different choices. Where no translation is available, I have referred to the work in its original title and, where necessary for understanding the passage, have offered a translation of my own in brackets. Where no English title is otherwise mentioned, the translations are my own. Poetry is quoted in both translation and the original. I followed the author's lead in referring to works in languages other than German or English, offering them in their French or Latin originals when the author did so, and in English translation where the author referred to them in German.

For my own interpolations and explanations within the text I use braces. Where Jochen Hörisch adds statements to the text of quotations, his words are bracketed but not otherwise identified. In the notes section, my interpolations and explanations are bracketed and signed.

My sincerest thanks go to Jochen Hörisch for his unending patience with my myriad questions. I am also most grateful to North Carolina State University's outstanding reference librarians, in particular Bryna Coonin, and to Marihelen Stringham and Gary Wilson in the Inter-Library Loan Department. Gary was relentless in his efforts to help me track down numerous specific editions and rare translations. Were it not for the help of Ann Rothe and Melanie Norton of TripSaver, who helped me find and keep track of countless books and never once made me feel like a burden, this project would have taken much, much longer. Finally, I would like to thank my colleagues in the Department of Foreign Languages and Literatures, Helga Braunbeck, David Frauenfelder, Larysa Mykyta, Larry Schehr, and Mark Sosower, for their help with works and quotes in French, Greek, Latin, and Middle High German.

I

PROGRAMMATIC
REMARKS
ON
THE POETICS
OF MONEY

1

"FOR IN THIS SIGN ALL NOW CAN FIND SALVATION"—
ON THE PROBLEM AND THEME OF
A MONETARY ONTOSEMIOLOGY

> *Herald.* But tell us, also, what you are and do!
> *Charioteer.* I am that spendthrift, poetry;
> as poet, I augment my worth
> by squandering my very substance.
> I, too, am rich beyond all measures
> and count myself the peer of Plutus,
> add life and beauty to his revels,
> and give you what he can't bestow.
>
> *Herold.* Sag von dir selber auch
> das Was und Wie!
> *Knabe Lenker.* Bin die Verschwendung,
> bin die Poesie;
> Bin der Poet, der sich vollendet
> Wenn er sein eigenst Gut verschwendet.
> Auch bin ich unermeßlich reich
> Und schätze mich dem Plutus gleich,
> Beleb' und schmück' ihm Tanz und Schmaus,
> Das, was ihm fehlt, das teil' ich aus.
>
> Goethe, *Faust II*
>
> I am plagued by doubts. What if everything
> is an illusion and nothing exists? In that case,
> I definitely overpaid for my carpet.
>
> Woody Allen, *Without Feathers*

"The alphabet is really now superfluous, for in this sign all now can find salvation." Thus the Intendant, in Goethe's *Faust* (6081–82), speaks to the Emperor who, the night before, had "signed (the paper money {*Scheingeld*})" that was then "copied by conjurers before the night was over" {"durch Tausendkünstler schnell vertausendfacht"}. Now everyone may find salvation in this sign that is not exactly exclusive. The repeated use of "now" marks the line as a diagnosis of the times.

It distinguishes the present from the days when another sign, the sign of the cross, promised salvation: "in hoc signo. . . ." The doubled "now" points to the new present, or, more precisely, the historical philosophical moment in which, by the king's own signature, the decisive power of the king's word is replaced by the silent power of money as the social and national agency of governance. That he had approved this, the former sovereign forgot. For good reason: he ratified (which the drama of Goethe's old age hardly regrets) his document of capitulation as ruler by divine right. "Astonished as I am, I have to let it count" (6085)—the money, that is.

Yet when a sovereign allows money to be the medium of rule and control, he acknowledges at the same time (and this becomes the abyss of tremendous mourning in this work of Goethe's old age) the bankruptcy of powerful, sovereign language in favor of the numerical code, which has found its earliest and most powerful incarnation to date in money. The alphabet becomes superfluous in the face of (phantom/paper) money.[1] The medium of language transfers its predominance to money. No theory of communicative competence, no matter how optimistic, can take it back. And poetry, anachronistically loyal to the superfluous alphabet, observes the triumphant advance of money and numbers with ever increasing irritation.

The assignats that the emperor signed are only valid for a short time. Yet in this brief interval they allow old alchemical dreams of wealth to come true.[2] But then everyone (the fool first of all) makes an appalling discovery: the paper money is, or, the money papers are, not secured, not covered.[3] "In this sign," in the sign of the money, (nearly) everyone, if they did not find salvation, at least became rich, and then— poor: poor in metaphysical certainties, poor in sovereign guidance, poor in protection, comfort, and cover. Faust decides, on the basis of this insight into the dialectics of the modern age, on withdrawal. He is drawn from the superficial world of perfected appearance to the depths of being and matter—to the Mothers (cf. chapter 6); he escapes from modernity back into antiquity. But the modern age will not be evaded for long.[4] The conjuring of Helena has no more permanence than "phantom money" (6198).

Neither the modern age nor its main medium, money, can be negated. Both are, as Faust must learn, unavoidable and inescapable, their origins notwithstanding. Thus Faust's story can be read as an attempt to understand and survive the modern age in all its (un)beatifying signs. To live here on earth without security or cover, without metaphysical protection, and, though lacking salvation, nonetheless (or precisely: therefore!) at least happily enjoying the brief interval of existence[5]—that is the impudence and promise that the modern age offers its contemporaries. So far the human species has not quite convincingly mastered this task: to withstand the impudent demands and promises of the modern age. Therefore it is continually susceptible to headlong descents into fundamentalisms of all kinds.

Even the deposed emperor "fears some great and criminal fraud" {"ahnt Frevel, ungeheuren Trug" (6063)} when he perceives his signature[6] and likeness on the paper money. He who is used to justifying his legitimacy through transcendence, and relying on this godly guarantee of, or cover for, his earthly authority, is forced to let the legality of the money "count." Legality instead of legitimacy, functionality instead of transcendence and substantiality, self-reference instead of reference to the (fully) Other, the secondary instead of the (seemingly) primary, continual change instead of simple continuity: that is the formula for success and at the same time the impudence of the modern age. This ambivalence, these two sides of the coin, find(s) its/their incarnation in money. The children's game of "heads or tails" preserves an inkling of this.[7] Medals and coins, as is generally known, have two sides. In most cases the idealized image of a prominent ruler's head is to be found on one side; on the other the number, decorated with ornaments and state emblems, soberly announces the value of the coin. In the game, one can bet on one of the two sides, throw the coin in the air and then eagerly wait to see, after several flips, which of the two sides— "heads or tails"[8]—is up. This popular game justifies the alternative "or" in common parlance. This expression, however, is only justified when coins are misused for games. Otherwise, to be correct, one would have to say: "heads *and* tails." Obviously heads and tails make up two sides of *one* medal, *one* coin, which by definition could not possibly be one-sided.

Heads and tails: the psychology of the classical metal (and even of the paper) currency[9] is rather straightforward. Heads and tails complete each other in the embodiment of validity, they round each other out to embody value—in short: the two sides of the coin obviously belong and stick together. They cover each other. "Cover"— that is (like the corresponding German and French terms "decken" and "couverture," respectively[10]) an oddly ambiguous word.[11] A word that, despite its ambiguity and need for explanation, is slighted in the Grimms' dictionary:

> 1. zudecken {cover up}. 2. die decke, bedeckung {cover or ceiling, covering}, contignatio aedificii. . . . 3. uneigentlich, sicherung, die deckung einer festung, einer schuld, einer forderung {figurative, defense, the cover of a fortress, of a debt, of a demand}.

This threefold classification is astonishing. The first two fields of meaning are obviously very closely related. In both cases, "cover" means to cover something up, to keep something from being as visible to the eye as it has been. The third entry, however, is in itself twofold. Here, "cover" is introduced as a military term and as a concept of monetary policy, as a concept, in other words, from two completely different spheres. That they have something in common is nonetheless clear: in both cases "cover" refers to the attempt, always precarious, to ward off the danger that a fortress or a deed will become null and void, invalid, unprotected.

"Cover" is, moreover, a word that designates a central and strange problem common to a variety of discourses (such as law, science, religion, economics, and art): the problem of how to guarantee the truth, the appropriateness, and the value of oral and written statements, judgments, and claims. A promise is covered, for example, if the promised act or donation ensues. A proposition is covered if it corresponds to the facts.[12] A scientific assertion is covered if substantiated (for example with data, experiments, authority, or logical proofs) and thereby made incontrovertible. A judgment is covered if it arose within the framework of a legal process and conforms to the law. A document, in this case a draft or check, is covered if it can be converted into cash. Covered refers, accordingly, to judgments, assertions, claims, or promises (of payment) that can be redeemed in another medium and that can maintain their value in spatial and temporal contexts other than those in which they originated. Promises must become deeds; hypotheses, reproducible observations; checks, sums of cash; and coins or notes, goods; if verbal agreements, hypotheses, and checks are to be regarded as "covered."[13]

Now, one need not possess an uncommon penchant for sophistry in order to recognize how delicate the problems of cover are, and how naive the examples mentioned above. Any first-year student of law, communications, philology, philosophy, or business administration can reveal bewildering complications without difficulty. The general problems of cover in regard to money are particularly easy to detect. Money is always met, as the paradigmatic scene with the assignats in *Faust II* demonstrates, with suspicion. Notes can be fake or counterfeit, drafts and checks may not be covered, a currency can lose its value through inflation, the bank where the savings account is held can go bankrupt. Nonetheless, these widely known and historically well-documented risks have not hindered money's (modern) career. If the comparative form "more unavoidable" may be used: in modern times, despite the fact that it is regularly beset by structural crises, money is becoming more and more unavoidable; there seems to be no alternative for the medium of money (not only in modern, functionally differentiated societies).

The covering, validity, and authority of money is therefore dubious in every respect.[14] To a certain extent, money must procure credit and authority for itself. It does this in a rather suggestive way in its classical form of the coin. A ruler acquires credit for himself not least of all by creating and authorizing a valid currency. The head[15] lends the number on the other side authority and validity, which extends it to the head in return. And the number on the coin acquires validity and recognition not least of all through the authority of the one who issues it—a circular affair. The ruler's head secures the validity of the coin's number; the coin's number secures the authority of the head. Auctoritas, non veritas facit legem.[16] Money is, thanks to the authority of the ruler's head, the legal means of payment. Both sides of the coin have authority to the extent that they become one in the coin. Without validity no money, without money no intersubjectively binding authority. This means, however, that heads and tails obtain their authority, their cover and their validity from a third entity, into which they are synthesized: from the coin whose sides they are, from the money whose concept is, not coincidentally (note the economic valence of this expression[17]), closely related to the term "validity" {Geltung} or "reward" {Vergeltung}[18] (from Old High German geltan, Modern High German gelten; originally: to pay for, compensate, be valuable {now "to be valid," see note 17 to this chapter. Trans.}).

This means, furthermore, that money can (in defiance of all pro-hibitions against mixed metaphors), if not cover, at least grease almost anything. A declaration of love can become valuable and can be covered by a shockingly expensive piece of jewelry; expert opinion and the practice of science are expensive after all; similarly rights to which one is entitled; churches need money and impose taxes,[19] and so on. Money can cover almost anything; but great importance is generally attached to keeping this a secret. Money plays into all areas, or, to offer a theoretical formulation: even love, science, law, and religion participate in the economic system and its code. They look for cover there—although, or perhaps because, money itself is not covered by anything other than itself. It is just that it may not proclaim this all that triumphantly if it wishes to maintain its value. It must therefore seem to be covered (for example by God—"Vergelt's Gott," "In God we trust"—by the gold in Fort Knox, or by the GNP). And it is/seems to be covered, if its apparent cover is generally regarded as authentic. A simple game introduces discord into this agreement between heads *and* tails, united to form a coin and stick together: heads *or* tails. Everything has two sides; and not just things but absolutely everything has (at least) two sides: heads or tails. Not only coins, but money, too, actually has (at the very least) two sides: heads or tails. The circular affair that money seems to be, is (at the very least) ambivalent, even multiply divided within itself. Money and language are unreliable media per se—as Goethe's *Venetian Epigram* points out:

> So often on copper just silver-plated a prince
> Stamps his important face; the folk is long deceived.
> The fanatic stamps lies and nonsense with the mark of the spirit;
> The one without touchstone takes them for genuine gold.
>
> Fürsten prägen so oft auf kaum versilbertes Kupfer
> Ihr bedeutendes Bild; lange betriegt sich das Volk.
> Schwärmer prägen den Stempel des Geists auf Lügen und Unsinn;
> Wem der Probierstein fehlt hält sie für redliches Gold.[20]

It is not exactly easy to find the "touchstone" for genuine gold and verifiable speech. Whoever looks for it through or in literature must be profoundly desperate indeed. For nothing has less cover than poetic speech. Yet for this very reason literature is in a position to pursue a line of questioning normally shunned, the question of the validity {*Geltung*} and cover {*Deckung*} of other codes. Thematizing the pitfalls of monetary coverage cannot be the focus of discourses relevant to the economy. No minister of finance, banker, professor of economics or business administration, industrialist, legislator, or trade unionist involved in contract negotiations can be (under normal conditions) intent on thoroughly demonstrating the unfathomable depths of money and the problems of covering it. For money is extremely dependent on being generally regarded as covered. If it is met with collective mistrust and disbelief, it collapses immediately. One must believe in it precisely at those times when one should not believe in it. In *Fortunatus*, the very first great novel of money in the German language as well as the first "modern German prose novel" of any kind, appearing in Augsburg in 1509 (it was most likely penned, as Hannes Kästner[21] has demonstrated, by the Franciscan Stephan Fridolin, who was in close contact with two men from Augsburg who traveled to the Orient, Hans Tucher and Sebald Rieter), the word "faith" is used as a synonym for "credit."

> Now that the lad (named Andrean) no longer had anything at all
> and had lost his faith, too, among the merchants
> and among the whores and scoundrels
> no one would lend or give or vouch for him.

Do nun der bub (hieß Andrean) gantz nicht meer (= überhaupt
  nichts mehr besaß)
vnd auch den glauben verloren hett vnder den kaufleuten
auch vnder huren vnd buben
das jm niemand weder leuhen noch geben noch borgen wolt.[22]

In this context, "he has lost his faith" does not mean something like
"a certain Andrean has lost his faith in God," but that he has lost
his ability to borrow from creditors. Money may not lose this trust,
this authentication, if it is to maintain its threefold function—to be a
medium of exchange, a unit of arithmetic, and a means of storing value.

To problematize and analyze money seems, therefore, to be a
de(con)structive and at best unnecessary business. Nonetheless, ever
since theology essentially gave up its traditional critique in the late
Middle Ages,[23] the discourse of the modern age and of modern literature, though far removed from economics, has believed itself capable
of carrying out an unrelenting, literally careless study of money. The
reasons for this are obvious. Belles lettres is always surrounded by the
suspicion of being functionally superfluous—"I am that spendthrift,
poetry." That which is superfluous lives on excess and can therefore
afford what others must renounce. Literature began to perceive itself
early, and has continued to do so with increasing intensity since the
sixteenth century, as the medium that does *not* require cover and is
therefore all the more qualified to observe these problems. Literature,
after all, does not even claim to validate its statements. Literature is
fiction, which means, precisely, that it does not have to be covered by
actual events or realities.

Fortunatus offers clear evidence for this as well. It treats nothing
less than one of its two central figures with irony, indicating that
she simply does not exist.[24] "Lady Fortune" {"jungfraw des gelücks"},
who presents Fortunatus with a magic sack that continually dispenses
money, does not exist (any longer), as the conclusion of the text
illustrates with subtle hyperbole: Lady Fortune is "banished from the
land"; that is, she is no longer to be found in "this world"—doubtless,
however, in the other world, that of literature:

It is to be feared
Lady Fortune . . .
Is banished from the land
And no longer to be found in this world.

Aber wol ist zu besorgen
die jungfraw des gelücks . . .
sey auß vnseren landen veriaget
vnd in diser welt nit mer tzufinden.[25]

Lady Fortune is not of this world, but that which she gives Fortunatus is thoroughly at home here. (Novelistic) literature has a comparable double status: its assertions do not need to be covered by events of this world, and yet for this very reason its task in this world (where else?) is to offer alternative visions of this world. From the perspective of the history of genres, this means that the story of *Fortunatus* is situated on the frontier between the contentedly factual "historia" and the eagerly inventive "novel." As "historia" it attempts to establish and substantiate its story through, for example, precise geographical and historical details and specific references to currency.[26] As a novel, however, it also tells of things it would never claim to be true—of the maiden Fortuna for example. Even the money of which this early modern historical novel tells is characteristically ambiguous: nothing immediately significant can be done with the coins and notes (just as with literature); their existential status (like that of stories in books) is peculiar; money (like belles lettres) has precisely no intrinsic value and is therefore simply superfluous. At the same time, however, money (in contrast to literature) is in many contexts the absolute necessity, the very thing that may not be in short supply.

The affinities and differences between money and literature constitute the theme of this book. It treats, as the subtitle indicates, the "poetics of money"—or literature that has money as its theme, but also, as the ambivalence of the possessive preposition "of" suggests, the poetic qualities that distinguish money or threaten it. (Modern) literature, according to one leading theory, discovers in money a hostile (and unquestionably more successful) brother. Money is the theme and problem of early modern, modern, and postmodern literature (e.g., of *Fortunatus*, Shakespeare's dramas, Baroque poetry, the works of Lessing, Goethe, and the Romantics—*Schlemihl!*—, the novels of Gotthelf, Keller, Freytag, Dickens, Flaubert, Dostoyevsky, Fontane, and the brothers Heinrich and Thomas Mann, the works of Brecht, Döblin, and Dürrenmatt, new prose works such as *Im Operncafé* by Bodo Kirchhoff,[27] *Headhunter* {*Kopfjäger*} by Uwe Timm, or *Gutes Geld* by Ernst Augustin—to name just a few) to such an overwhelming extent, that one can hardly express enough surprise at how rarely it is the subject of scholarly investigations in the German-speaking world (in the English-speaking world this is not the case[28]).

This conspicuous avoidance, distinctly bearing the signs of taboo, is easy to explain, and stems from reasons more banal than anything else. German scholars of literature are in most cases civil servants. Money is received, if not in great amounts, at least regularly and reliably, giving little cause for inquisitive investigations. In addition, humanists, who not coincidentally call themselves scholars of the spirit in German,[29] would rather side with the spirit than with unrefined, spiritless, even filthy, mammon.[30] Hegel, whom one does not suspect of slighting the spirit, drastically surmises:

> It is a stroke of genius, the way people in Germany disparage *money*. The Germans attribute an origin to it that could not be more despicable. It is represented by figures that are called money-sh-ers. This is supposed to have a mythological basis. It is hard to imagine associating a sausage or whatever one might think of with a more lowly mode of origin.

> Es ist ein schöner Zug, welche Verachtung man in Deutschland gegen das *Geld* hat und zeigt. Die Deutschen dichten ihm einen Ursprung an, der nicht verächtlicher sein kann. Man stellt ihn fürs Auge in Figuren dar, die Geldsch-r genannt werden. Es soll eine mythologische Beziehung zugrunde liegen. Eine Bratwurst oder was es sei mag man nicht mit einer so niedrigen Entstehungsart zusammendenken.[31]

Of course, simple matters of competence impede the "scholar of the spirit" in the business of tracing the theme of money in literature. The fundamentals of business administration and economics are not discussed in seminars on German literature, even though they can more legitimately claim to answer the Faustian question of "what, deep within it, binds the (modern) universe together"[32] than philological interpretations of the scene in which this question resounds.

It may also seem as if a literary criticism that does not even ignore the poetics of money can cite literary trends that demand that money be ignored. Figures who are particularly indifferent to money have a certain (if also at times precarious) prestige. *Locus classicus* for such a confrontation between the beautiful and the base is the harpist's first song in *Wilhelm Meister's Apprenticeship*,

> What do I hear outside the gate,
> Resounding on the drawbridge?
> Bring your song into the hall
> That we may hear it better!

> Was hör ich draußen vor dem Tor,
> Was auf der Brücke schallen?
> Laßt den Gesang zu unserm Ohr
> Im Saale widerhallen.

Thus speaks the wealthy king, who immediately invites the poor old singer to perform at court, delights in his song, and, "in payment for the song,[33] / A golden chain had straightaway brought" {"ihm zum Lohne für sein Spiel / Eine goldne Kette holen" (läßt)}. But the singer does not want this "payment" (the song conspicuously avoids the closely related word "gift"):

> . . . give it to your chancellor
> That he may add its golden weight
> To all his other burdens.

> Gib sie dem Kanzler, den du hast,
> Und laß ihn noch die goldne Last
> Zu andern Lasten tragen.

The singer, free of wants, is not dependent on a degrading "payment" for work, but he does claim a right to hospitality. He proudly points out that his "music coming from the throat / Rewards itself right richly" {"Lied, das aus der Kehle dringt, / Lohn (ist,) der reichlich lohnt"}, and asks for a "draught of your best wine" {"Trunk des besten Weins"}—in other words, an offering (not a payment) whose intrinsic value and ability to give pleasure are not seriously contested.

By avoiding the obvious sharpening of the conflict, the ballad-like song outlines a highly stylized historical scenario of aesthetic indifference vis-à-vis the sphere of money. This scenario stands, however, in sharp contrast to the context in which it is embedded. The passages that surround the harpist's song, in other words, center on the power of money and the powerlessness of poetry. In Wilhelm's room, the merchant's son and title character of the company read from "a play about medieval German knights" until the listening "company" is so "transported" that the gathering ends in a powerful, shared "intoxication" that turns destructive. The night watchman insists on stepping in, and Wilhelm has "his work cut out, by words and money, and with some assistance from the innkeeper, to quieten people down," and (once sober again) to think about the "sad results" "which a stimulating, spirited and well-intentioned work of literature had produced."[34] Wilhelm "had the cost of the party and the damage put on his account." That is worth noting: a good literary work has (according, in any event, to a good literary work of Goethe's) sad results; filthy money, on the other hand, has good, calming effects.

This balancing of accounts that precedes the harpist's song, this exchange that ends the ecstacy, is followed, right after the voice of the harpist fades away, by a "handsome recompense" for, of all things, the very song that so decisively rejected the art of compensation. This time, however, Wilhelm pays before "a stimulating . . . work of literature [produces] sad results"—even the harpist's song has not unsuccessfully earned him a draught of wine. "Since the bad effect of such behavior was still all too vividly present in our friend's mind, he tried to break up the proceedings, giving the old man a handsome recompense for his labors."[35] This gives rise to the vicious comment by Melina, the leader of the company, that the harpist is able "to extract money [from us] . . . for one little song." So enigmatic can texts look, when they attempt to prove their aesthetic indifference vis-à-vis the economic sphere.[36]

The author of this text, too, none other than Johann Wolfgang von Goethe himself, brilliantly understood how "to extract money for a song."[37] It is part of Goethe's greatness to have made no secret of what would otherwise be awkward to discuss. On the contrary, he acknowledged this state of affairs remarkably openly, even commenting on things, frankly and in a businesslike manner, that convention would leave unmentioned: "Your Royal Highness, accept today, as, to my good fortune, you have so many times on this occasion, the warmest declaration of unswerving loyalty and devotion as well as my honest efforts to be, to the extent that disposition and vigor permit, of further use to you in your private and in your public affairs. Preserve for me, Your Majesty, that long maintained capital of goodwill and mercy that has always born such abundant interest."[38]

Thus writes the rich, best-selling author of wealthy patrician family, the ennobled privy councillor and well-endowed minister, property owner and art collector—thus writes Johann Wolfgang von Goethe, carefully observant of etiquette, to his patron on New Year's Day, 1821.[39] And the patron plays, ironically and jovially, the role he has played for decades, replying,

> To you, my dear, old friend and comrade in arms in this stormy world, I wish a New Year that is easy and pleasant to live through, and I thank you for the expressions of your constant friendship for me, also especially for the beautiful and gratifying enclosures. Vulpius did me a great favor by collecting and organizing Jacquin's peculiar oeuvre so carefully that we are now convinced it is complete. Binding and layout are very tasteful. Here is a seal for old Blumenbach, a New Year's gift and memento from me. Write him something nice and farewell. Carl August.[40]

This book will resist the temptation to lay out how authors dealt with the money that they had (or with the problem of having no money), with the exception of a few irresistible documents, such as the following:

> The artist's afflictions are many.
> Money asks him: do we have something going?
> There will never be anything between us, he responds curtly,
> links arms with money and together they take off.
> . . . .
> Sex, sense, nature and art

you change into commodities,
complains the artist.
My trade has always served
the Beautiful, the Good, the Pure,[41]
laughs money.

Groß sind des Künstlers Leiden.
Das Geld fragt ihn: Wie wär's mit uns beiden?
Mit uns wird das nie was, erwidert er knapp,
hängt sich beim Geld ein und zieht mit ihm ab.
. . . .
Geschlecht, Gefühl, Natur und Kunst
verwandelst Du in Waren,
klagt der Künstler.
Mein Handeln diente immer schon
dem Schönen, Guten, Baren,
lacht das Geld.[42]

It reconstructs, instead, the perspectives from which literature itself observes money. And whoever observes these literary observations of money will quickly notice that belles lettres perceives in money a horrible-beautiful and fascinating medium of competition that carries out, in calm anonymity, that which strictly speaking only God (or poetic art-religion and especially post-religious literature) ought to do and be permitted to do: rule the world and determine its meaning and sense (of direction). The conjecture to which this book (as well as many of the poetic works that it analyzes) is dedicated is also easily named. It links up with my previous study *Brot und Wein—Die Poesie des Abendmahls*[43] and spins it out further. The main hypothesis is this: "The Sacrament of Communion, money, and the new electronic media form (following one upon the other and overlapping one another) the ontosemiological frame of our so-called Christian-Western-Rational culture."

The technical term "ontosemiology" may refer to the problem that countless religions, philosophies, theories, and worldviews expressly or implicitly claim to solve, and which every social formation (if in very different ways) actually assumes to have mastered: how to prove or establish a correlation between being {*Sein*} and meaning {*Sinn*} in such a way that the question of whether this established view has in fact intersubjective validity does not come up at all. Since the decline of religiously grounded worldviews, literature feels a greater and greater responsibility for the question of how the logic of being {*Sein*} and of that which is {*des Seienden*}, ontology in other words, and the logic of meaning {*Sinn*} and signs, or semiology, can arrive at ontosemiological agreement. It will have to learn that it is precisely the eternal and the authentic which it cannot create. Unless, of course, one understands as eternal merely the experience that there is nothing unchanging and eternal. Communion, money, and the new media are nonetheless—in contrast to belles lettres—major media {*Leitmedien*} that span epochs (and increasingly cross cultures). They may be characterized as ontosemiological major media because, firstly, they fundamentally relate being {*Sein*} to meaning {*Sinn*} and vice versa, and make grasping for the scarce resource of meaning possible. Secondly, they allow a "synthesis of the manifold" (Kant's "Synthesis des Mannigfaltigen")—they provide viewpoints from which "everything" can be understood, evaluated and thematized. Thirdly, they make social cohesion possible. In High Christian times one could not bypass Communion without very serious threat of sanction. In modern times, one can be a critic of money and yet one cannot avoid the medium. Similarly, one cannot escape radio and television shows today without penalty. In short, ontosemiological major media organize intersubjective ties; they are simply unavoidable. Fourthly, they conform to systems theory's concept of media—in other words, they systematically transform improbability into probability. The improbability that God has an only-begotten son whom he sacrificed for the salvation of humanity, the improbability that anyone would leave his valuable goods to anyone else, and the improbability that this event, and not the countless other events, has occurred in a way worthy of being entered into the books, are made "more probable" through the Eucharist or money or the AV-media. Finally, these ontosemiological major media homogenize the dimensions of time and space, and for that very reason make distinctions possible. Communion is a meal of remembrance; it takes place in the present; and it refers eschatologically to future redemption and other worlds. Money can preserve past values; exchanges are always events of the present; and one can get credit on the future and entrepreneurially be there, where one is not, too. Radio and television also organize and synthesize the experience of time and space in a new way.

In short, the ontosemiological major media interweave. They give rise to a sociocultural tapestry that provides every individual event with an orienting framework. They determine a "collective conscience"—a collection of "available and unauthorized, shared ideas, assumptions, feelings of belonging that are polymorphic and changeable but not arbitrarily disposable."[44] That the "shared symbolic systems" (Talcott Parsons) are "woven," put into text, controlled, and therefore, if not exactly anonymously, certainly artificially, created—ontosemiological major media do not like to think about that. As for the literary texts that consciously observe them, one hardly needs to be reminded of the literal meaning of their conception. The Latin "textere" means, as is generally known, "to weave, to braid, to join"; "textum" is the weaving, "textor" the person who weaves the different strands into one—and "Textor" is also the name of Goethe's maternal grandfather. The German word "Dichtung"[45] (to the extent that one forgets its straightforward etymological origin in the Latin word "dicere") is increasingly closely related to the field of meaning of text and textile. The German "dichten"[46] means, precisely in modern times: to speak so densely, so condensed, with so much meaning, in a way that everyday speech (*dicere*) would not allow. To weave being and meaning, soma and sema, *physis* and significance into each other, to interweave words and things, *les mots et les choses*[47] in such a way that they will be experienced as a reciprocal unity, this is the project that literature works on incessantly. Literature would like to compose experiences in such a way that being as meaningful and meaning as being (at least previously or in the future) can be articulated and written down. Literature would like to cover the nakedness of an exposed and empty experience of being and existence {*Seins- und Daseinserfahrung*} in such a way that it can warm a freezing human life.[48] Literature knows at the same time (the more modern, the more clearly and in increasingly striking contrast to religious or theoretical texts) that it is poetics; in other words, that it is made, manufactured, produced, constructed, that it is art, that it is artificial.

For this reason poetics observes, with irritation, religions and social institutions that act as if there were binding (obvious or objective) algorithms that relate being and meaning to each other. The monotheistic world religions solve the fundamental ontosemiological problem in a structurally similar way. Jewish, Christian, and Islamic theology proceed from the doubled authorship[49] of God (a notable point of agreement which, precisely because of this corresponding claim, unleashes militantly enacted differences)[50]: He wrote the Book of the World and the Book of Books (the Torah, the Bible, the Koran). According to the edict of the Council of Lyon: "Unum esse auctorem."[51] Whatever meaning that which is, has, is to be gleaned from the Book of the one who created that which is. A simple and suggestive construction which, to be sure, loses plausibility in proportion to the extent that the different religions' claims of revelation enter into competition with each other. Revelation cannot be so evident, as Lessing's *Nathan the Wise* paradigmatically establishes,[52] if it immediately reveals itself in three different ways (or, if one includes other religions, in hundreds of different ways). Economically schooled rationality—as Lessing's *Nathan* and long before that Shakespeare's *Merchant of Venice* represent it—puts revealed religions in the embarrassing position of having to swear an oath of revelation: their declarations are not evident, cannot be translated into the language of evidence that demands agreement and is obvious, and they are therefore not covered. (Religions of) revelation are revealingly not so clearly revealed.

The Christian religion has developed (and this has surely contributed decisively to its success throughout world history) a particularly suggestive liturgy (and one most easily appended to pre-Christian theophagy rituals) that brings the meaning of being {*Sinn von Sein*} and the existence of meaning {*DaSein*[53] *von Sinn*} into the realm of experience: in bread and wine, the two spheres unite with each other in a substantial way. Since the sixteenth century, literature has been able to watch with curiosity as this suggestive religious solution to the fundamental ontosemiological problem falls apart. Religious statements are in no way binding, covered statements; one can believe in them— or not (the latter in modern times increasingly without sanction: one no longer has to suffer or die if one does not believe). (Not only) poetics is able to ascertain over and over again that, with continually growing decisiveness, money, and not God, rules the world. The substantial ontosemiology of Communion is replaced by the functional ontosemiology of money.[54]

The conflict-laden conversion—moneylenders were denied Communion in many communities until well into the seventeenth century[55]—was attentively registered by literature (and, primarily in its moral aspects, by philosophy as well[56]). A valuable literary document in this respect is Niklaus Manuel's Shrovetide farce, *Der Ablaßkrämer* {The Indulgences Peddler}, written in Bern in 1525. It is about a seller of indulgences, with the apt name Richard Hinderlist,[57] whose deceits are discovered by the peasant woman Zilia Nasennutter:

> I shit on the false ban of your Pope.
> You won't get my money for this dirty and tricky indulgence
> —not even a louse.

> Ich schiss dir uf ein ietlichen bagkenzan
> Und uf din falschen nidigen bäpstleban!
> Ich geb dir nit ein böse krumme gufen,
> Ja nit ein lus us einer grinden rufen
> Um din falschen ablass und ban![58]

Voltaire and Samuel Butler analyzed the encounter between money- and God-orientations more elegantly. Thus in the sixth of his *Philosophical Letters*, Voltaire, in view of the denominational disputes of his time, called upon the antagonists to go together not to church, but to the London Stock Exchange, for that is where the real Catholic-ecumenical cult of integration for the salvation of all takes place:

> Go to the Exchange in London, that place more venerable than many a court, and you will see representatives of all the nations assembled there for the profit of mankind. There the Jew, the Mohametan, and the Christian deal with one another as if they were of the same religion, and reserve the name of infidel for those who go bankrupt. There the Presbyterian trusts the Anabaptist, and the Church of England man accepts the promise of the Quaker. On leaving these peaceable and free assemblies, some go to the synagogue, others in search of a drink; this man is on his way to be baptized in a great tub in the name of the Father, by the Son, to the Holy Ghost; that man is having the foreskin of his son cut off, and a Hebraic formula mumbled over the child that he himself can make nothing of; these others are going to their church in order to await the inspiration of God with their hats on; and all are satisfied. (p. 26)

Expressly with respect to London, Schiller's poem "To My Friends" {"An die Freunde"} proclaims: "And the earth-god, Mammon, reigns supreme" {"Und es herrscht der Erde Gott, das Geld"}.[59] German literature, as is generally known, resisted the conversion from God to money particularly stubbornly.

Of course, the history of the conversion from religious to monetary formulae for integration can be told less frivolous-pacifistically than it is in Voltaire's account. An example would be Samuel Butler's:

> No Jesuite ever took in hand,
> To plant a church in barren Land;
> Or ever thought it worth his while
> A Swede or Russe to reconcile;
> For where there is not store of wealth,
> Souls are not worth the charge of health
> Spaine on America had 2 designes
> To sell their Ghospell for their mines;
> For had the Mexicans been poore,
> No Spaniard twice had landed on their shore.
> 'Twas Gold the Catholick Religion planted,
> Which, had they wanted Gold, they still had wanted.[60]

Stephen Greenblatt explains the fact that the blatant break from the primarily religious to the monetary worldview around the year 1500 was only possible through the internal logic of the central sacrament of Christianity. That the blatant injustice in the exchange of Spanish trinkets for Indian gold did not pose irreconcilable conflicts for Columbus and his religiously inclined Christian descendants is explained by its connection, according to Greenblatt, to the familiar miraculous transubstantiation of the worthless into the most valuable. "The conversion of commodities into gold slides liquidly into the conversion and hence salvation of souls,"[61] and it is only in this cultural horizon converti- and "conscionable."

The possibilities for connecting coins to the Host are overly evident, and for that reason gladly made invisible. The stamped Host will be inherited by the stamped coin.[62] Those two, the Host and the coin, resemble each other, not coincidentally, in their design; both must be issued by an authority; both have two sides; both raise the Faustian question of whether the thing is sacred or profane. For money, too, functionally produces correlations between abstract values and concrete goods, between meaning and that which is {*Sinn und Seiendem*} (for more detail on this point, see chapters 9–11). The cover for this monstrous achievement that transcends narrow economic functions in every way moves money, as a rule, out of that sphere for whose erosion it provides—out of the religious: "In God we trust," "Vergelt's Gott," as we say.

The medium that trusts in the possibility of the existence of a cover for religious, metaphysical, and ontosemiological declarations least of all, the medium that cannot (and does not even want to!) make the claim that its own statements are covered—the poetic medium— observes these transitions and declines with anxious attention. Always under the suspicion of being useless and therefore superfluous, belles lettres lives in superfluity. It can afford observations, assessments, and commentary that seem at first glance dysfunctional and that must be forbidden other discourses. But that means: literature interferes, literature makes observations that more likely disturb, literature irritates accepted codes, literature interrupts and disturbs communications and common figures of speech—for example those of finance and business administration (to the extent that these fields take note of literature and literary criticism at all). Because the assertion that the specific accomplishment of superfluous literature lies in disrupting communication and understanding is, firstly, accurate and, secondly, by no means commonly accepted in the field of literary criticism, a second preliminary reflection on the modernity of an old poetological saying is now due: "Aut prodesse aut delectare."

2

"AUT PRODESSE AUT DELECTARE"—
LITERARY HISTORY AS THE HISTORY OF PROBLEMS

> Beauty, which endures, is an object of knowledge.
>
> Schönheit, die dauert, ist ein Gegenstand des Wissens.
> Walter Benjamin

And who wants poets at all in lean years?[1] The question from Hölderlin's elegy "Bread and Wine" is often quoted in literary histories, but only rarely answered convincingly. Very rarely posed, not to mention answered, is the question of the purpose of literary history/ies in an age one could characterize, depending on the perspective of the observer, as "lean" or as an epoch of excess. In an age, moreover, that certainly does not know one thing: a quantitative dearth of literature and literary histories[2]—though definitely a dearth of literary histories that know what they want to know, when they reconstruct literary history.

Hermeneutists' current answer to the question of the purpose of literature (assuming here modern, and therefore functionally differentiated societies)—that it facilitates understanding and communication —is, at least in this simple formulation, clearly implausible. Those who wish to make themselves understood, to communicate successfully, to propagate their worldview convincingly, are obviously poorly advised to write esoteric poems like Hölderlin's or Celan's,[3] impenetrable novels like Jean Paul's or Arno Schmitt's, or overly complex dramas like Goethe's and Heiner Müller's. These texts are obviously disturbing because they are less conventional, more complex, more demanding, less accessible than, say, everyday conversation, front-page articles, business correspondence, and diplomatic negotiations—all tested and accepted forms for arriving at an agreement and communicating. Poetic texts do not function, by any standard, as strategic solutions to problems in communicating and making oneself understood; they are, on the contrary, particularly intricate components of these problems.

This is true in small as well as in large contexts. Authors' readings in Klagenfurt and other cities, large and small, cannot be counted on to contribute to intersubjective understanding, as is suggested by Rainald Goetz's bleeding forehead at the Ingeborg Bachmann Competition of 1983,[4] or forcefully illustrated by a scene from Klaus Modick's novel *Weg war weg* about a lost (in every sense of the word) manuscript: "I regard these stories [that had just been read in his literary circle] as the ultimate shit. I can't recall ever having listened to such lying filth, let alone having read it. If that's literature, then I'll win the Nobel Prize this year. Outrageous! . . . —the audacity! . . . —a provocation! . . . — I'm out of here!"[5] Surely this represents, despite its perfect clarity and intelligibility, no literary ideal of the art of communication, even in small circles. On a larger scale, the paradox of poetic communication, which explicitly disrupts accepted communication, intensifies accordingly. Novels such as *The Satanic Verses* or autobiographical texts like *Not without My Daughter* in no way contributed to cross- or intercultural understanding.[6] They led, on the contrary, to a notable break in communication.

This break in communication (which in the case of Salman Rushdie is a death sentence and thus implicitly an intent to silence) is noteworthy for the boundless profusion of nonpoetic responses it unleashed. That this exchange was intended to bring about unifying, perhaps even reconciling, communication, not even the most mealymouthed observer will seriously assert. The Salman Rushdie affair will play a decisive role in future literary histories (and not only there, but in general historical accounts and in sociological, political, and religious-philosophical analyses as well): as a paradigm for the communication problems and the difficulties of making oneself understood that literature creates, or, at the very least, accentuates, intensifies, provokes, and certainly does not solve. Thus, on many levels and in many contexts, the observation is born out that poetic texts specialize in blocking understanding, in disrupting successful communication, and precisely thereby in stimulating an ongoing, frustrated exchange that is enamored of uncertainty and conflict. It is not, then, just priests, politicians, and ayatollahs who experience a strained relationship with literature. Poets, readers, critics, and literary scholars live in ongoing arguments over texts—for example, by Goethe and Kleist, Wagner and Rilke, Handke and Grass, Christa Wolf and Hermann Kant. And that means: they do the same thing—they fight and argue with one another.

This obviously unavoidable paradox—that poetically induced disruption in communication provokes an ongoing exchange, and the conflict that cannot be resolved unites the antagonists irreconcilably[7]—takes place in a society that, with friendly militance, perceives and casts itself with increasing clarity as "the communication and information age."[8] "Communication" and "understanding" are concepts that have been nothing short of fetishized in the last two decades. In a libertarian society that has freed up nearly everything that has ever been held sacred (e.g., rulers, confessions, institutions, ways of life and love) for communicative negation, the protoliberal categories of "communication" and "understanding," of all things, are held to be non-negatable. In universally open societies, even the express wish not to communicate is interpreted as a message. Non-negatability (of a god, a king, an institution, and so on) or the immunization of central, leading concepts against negation, is, however, a most conspicuous characteristic of pre-liberal, stratified societies.

Failure to pay homage to the liberal and enlightened idols of communication and understanding, especially in the context of an academic study, is an extremely delicate enterprise. One risks (paradoxically or tautologically, depending on the perspective of the observer, the fulfillment of a self-fulfilling or self-destroying prophecy) the immediate confirmation of the outsider's assertion[9] of the negatability of communication. One risks excommunication from the scientific community (generally with the argument that one has indulged in a paradox or even a contradiction, and contradictions are scientifically unacceptable).[10] Interpretative sociology,[11] philosophical hermeneutics, analytic linguistic theory, Habermas's critical theory, and even Luhmann's systems theory[12] (to name just the extremes) operate to the same extent with these a priori, positively applied concepts—and then argue about their meaning. The statements, "meaning" is not negatable,[13] and one cannot not communicate,[14] insist (institutionally quite successfully!) on one's being undeniably and unavoidably communicative.

Now, according to a plausible assumption of systems theory, "the function of art lies in the *confrontation of the reality (accessible to everyone) with another version of the same reality.* Art allows the world to appear in the world. . . . Therein lies an indication of the contingency of the normal view of reality, an indication that things could be different. More beautiful, for example. Or less random. Or pervaded with still more hidden meaning."[15] Luhmann's examples are obviously taken from the reservoir of classical works and aesthetics. A cumulative scholarly observation specific to modern literature (since about 1850) allows, on the other hand, the suspicion discussed above to take hold:

the modern poetic "other version of reality" in an "information age" does not aim for more of the Beautiful, the True, and the Good, but makes its point, on the contrary, in the unfathomable suspicion that communication and understanding are, firstly, unavoidable apriorities and, secondly, not necessarily "good" but "bad"—that it is therefore (even beyond diplomatic and strategic calculations) worthwhile to disrupt communication and cause it to fail in order to achieve, for example, a silencing of all communication, or to put an end to previously held assumptions. Because this intuition can hardly be communicated other than communicatively, the prototypically modern mode of poetic communication is "the disconcerted communication" {"die verdutzte Kommunikation"}.[16]

Modernity doubtless offers numerous reasons for being disconcerted and disoriented and for communicating in a similar manner (or even for breaking off communication); hence the paradox of the normal chain of events in modernity: those who have wanted to do good have brought about catastrophes of unheard-of dimensions; politically conservative forces have changed forms of communication and production more than progressive ones have; institutions like the Stasi[17] that set out to protect their state forcefully, thoroughly ruin it (simply because of the costs involved); the radically enlightened world seems (at least in individual sectors, such as modern commerce and advertising) more irrational than the pre-enlightened one; what is new changes faster than what is old; human beings are getting older and older and—*sit venia verbo*—more and more finite—they lose their faith in their immortality; modern medicine does not just decrease, it also increases, suffering; with increasing knowledge secrets grow and proliferate; revolutionaries prove to be the real bureaucrats, and bureaucrats revolutionize society from the bottom up; nationalists destroy their fatherland, and so on. Modern society is not a risk society[18] simply because of its nuclear energy, pollution, military buildup, and traffic fatalities, but also because paradoxes control the possibilities of communication within it and about it.

The modern world, bereft of magic, appears to poetic observation as one radically bewitched. In contrast to scientific or everyday communication and as a result of its release from utility, poetic communication can afford to scrutinize paradoxes and dissonances attentively.[19] Yet literature cannot observe and communicate paradoxes of this kind without penalty: it becomes, as a result, more difficult, darker, more complex, even more off the beaten track. This (as well as its uncertain utility) is the price that belles lettres has to pay in order to have less trouble dealing with paradoxes than, say, scientific discourses, which restrict themselves to contradiction-free statements, or everyday speech, which generally has to pay homage to common sense. Literature specializes more and more in idiosyncratic and therefore (with respect to the natural order of things as well as to intersubjective acceptance) highly improbable observations on and interpretations of communication, being, consciousness, and presence.

To give a relatively harmless example, the observation, "war, trade and piracy together are / a trinity not to be severed" {"Krieg, Handel und Piraterie, / dreieinig sind sie, nicht zu trennen"}, made in lines 11187–88 of *Faust II*, is unlikely to find acceptance in economics, business administration, sociology, or everyday parlance. And the statement, "Philologists, I see, have led you (Faust), as they have themselves, astray" {"Ich seh', die Philologen, sie haben dich so wie sich selbst betrogen"}, as line 7426 proclaims, stands little chance of becoming a commonplace among philologists. Literary scholarship and history tend to neutralize the first statement by characterizing it as Mephistophelian and therefore inapplicable, and to grant the second validity only in its specific context: it has to do with the era of Helen alone, and the notion that the drama of Goethe's old age characterizes the philological endeavor as fundamentally fraudulent is off track.

In view of the above-mentioned paradoxes, at least one purpose of literary historiography cannot be overlooked: it generally tends to defuse the paradoxes literature observes and to ignore poetically induced disruptions in communication. One can accentuate the negative in this observation and emphasize the old enmity between poets and interpreters (e.g., Goethe's maxim, "Kill him, the dog! It's a critic"). Interpreters, reviewers, critics, hermeneutists, and literary scholars often enough perceive their task as cultivating a "rage for understanding" {"Wut des Verstehens"}[20] that makes demanding literature unreadable. They turn disturbing, emphatically different, belligerent, unwise, unintelligible, idiosyncratic, in short, diabolical communication back into symbolic communication[21] (and the Greek "Symbolon," as is well known, refers to a fragment that fits together with other fragments to form a whole—cf. chapter 11). Literary historiographers tend to achieve this reintegration of unruly communication by using history to defuse that which appears to be new: they redefine the presumably revolutionary as evolutionary:

> Farewell, *Original*, you pompous ass!—[22]
> How greatly would you be offended if you heard me ask:
> can anyone have wise or stupid thoughts
> that ages past have not already thought?—
>
> Original, fahr hin in deiner Pracht!—
> Wie würde dich die Einsicht kränken:

Wer kann was Dummes, wer was Kluges denken,
Das nicht die Vorwelt schon gedacht?
(*Faust I*, 6807–10)

One can of course also accentuate the positive in the observation of the strained relationship between diabolical literature and symbolic literary historiography (that is, that which trusts in the power of communication) and emphasize the scientific interrelatedness of improbable statements (for example, following Luhmann's systems theory). Poetic statements are not required to be correct, or even plausible. That poets lie has been a fixed component of traditional European common knowledge since Hesiod and Plato; and poets are for that very reason free of the imposition to tell the objective truth.[23] Modern literature's sometimes highly unlikely worldviews and versions of reality can turn this deficiency into a means of productivity. They can afford to observe that which eludes other observers[24] (for example that humanism, and above all Goethe's humanism, is "devilishly human").[25] And these poetic observations can, in turn, observe, articulate, devise a theoretical formula for, and redirect literary scholarship and literary history to specialized disciplines. Literary scholarship can then (though it refuses to do even this remarkably often) proliferate in its findings (and that consists of the literary observations that it observes). It does not have to make its statements plausible with regard to suitable (e.g., economic, sociological, historical, biological, and so on) observations of complex circumstances. The criterion of the validity of its statements is, on the contrary, a literary second encoding of such observations— scholars of literature must "prove" their interpretations of primary texts that are objectively more than difficult, but discursively often extremely stimulating, with these same texts (rather than with large quantities of empirical data, laboratory findings, or similar material).

Scholarly statements on literature are proved with or covered by literary figures of speech. They may be more anarchically, more arbitrarily, even more capriciously {*willkürlicher*}[26] produced than, for example, scientific, juridical, or journalistic statements, but they fulfill nonetheless the criteria that systems theory has established for defining autopoetic systems. Poetic primary texts can certainly be understood as communicative elements of the system art. "Systems need problems"[27]—otherwise they would not exist. Without the problem of shortages there would be no system of economics, without the problem of conflicts there would be no system of justice, and without the inevitable problem of abundant versions of one and the same reality there would be no system of art. Art, frankly and systematically, produces semantic excess; it is (precisely for functionally differentiated societies) a necessary luxury, and for this very reason it specializes in paradox and dissonance. It stockpiles alternative versions and interpretations of the very same reality that is the subject of other discourses—of those discourses that claim to observe and express this reality from entirely different perspectives. Literature can therefore (in contrast to moral discourses) view, for example, the Mephistophelian evil from a new perspective, as the principle that creates good (and, vice versa, the will to goodness as the foundation for producing evil, as in Goethe's Faust poem); it can see the politburo of the German Democratic Republic as a senile Round Table around the King of the Holy Grail who has lost the grail (as in Christoph Hein's *Ritter der Tafelrunde*); and it can identify Germanists as "nistgermans" {nesting Teutons} who are no longer capable of correctly differentiating between "minne" {love} and "sang" {song}—as in the anagram poem by Kurt Mautz:

germanisten	germanists
germanisten	germanists
nistenmager	nestingmeagerly
manistgerne	oneisgladly
nistgermane	nestingteuton
sagterminne	hesayslove
meintersang	hemeanssong
sternmagien	magicofstars
stangenreim	amessofrhymes
rastimengen	restconfined
arminsegnet	poorinblessing
amensingter	hesingsamen
geistermann	manofthespirit
samegerinnt	semencongeals
imargennest	inthedreadfulnest
nagermisten	rodentsdung
greinenmast	whimperingmast
grastmeinen	grazemy
magernstein	meagerrock[28]

The extreme form of the anagram also throws light on the code specific to the aesthetic subsystem, literature. Systems differ in their genuine (binary) codes: thus the economic system and its code pays/does not pay, the justice system and its code lawful/unlawful. The aesthetic code is certainly more complicated than these poor semantic systems, working as it does with a code attenuated by real relativities: appropriate (or intelligible)/inappropriate (unintelligible). A poem that works can, and may, sacrifice correctness to a good, appropriate, phonetically true rhyme. The anagram game that has Germanists nesting meagerly and confounding love with song or saying with meaning, does not have to be factually true. Well-said, clever, immanently appropriate, and (according to the rules of anagrams!) correct it is, indeed. And so may it seem, in a strange way, as if there is, objectively, "something to" this anagrammatically produced, highly idiosyncratic version of the Germanist's existence.

Conflicts of interpretation[29] are provided for through the methodical privileging of the improbable. (N.B. to evade them, as does the Popper School, by resorting to the notion of falsification and declaring those interpretations that do not correspond to an empirical reader psychology to be inappropriate, would obviously be unproductive. It cannot be ruled out that scholars of literature perceive more dimensions of meaning in a text than, for example, critics or avid readers, and vice versa.) The philological temptation to resolve conflicts of interpretation quasi-totemistically is great: one can, for example, honor Goethe or Thomas Mann, in proportion as one obliterates their works interpretatively, by adapting them to the standards of normal versions of reality. Philology is also quite capable of taking it into its head to collect biographical and publication data, and thereby modestly forgo suggesting differences between poetic and other texts (or making observations). It can also, however, approach literary history as a history of problems, which entails switching to discursive differences in view of the thematization of tangible issues. The methodological assumption of such a procedure is as simple as it is far-reaching. A history of problems with a literary focus assumes "that there is nothing of beauty which does not contain something that is worthy of knowledge."[30]

Unquestionably, poetics and knowledge separated themselves from each other very early (with Plato's *Ion* at the latest) in the so-called Western tradition.[31] This differentiation (which would have been technically impossible without the medium of writing) makes, first of all, the observation of discrepancies between various writings and books possible—and thereby the perception of the discrepancy, too, that the writing of the Books of the World does not always coincide with the observations of writers of books. Observations of this kind achieve increasingly higher status in the modern age. This is ensured by the breakdown of taboos surrounding positions of authority, presumed to be all-powerful, that have themselves now become, unexpectedly, objects of scrutiny. Since the erosion of the belief in absolute (= ab-solved/dissolved) theological-political ultimate positions, literature and philosophy specialize, in different ways, precisely in observing, thematizing, and articulating problems of world and presence.[32]

Such texts are regarded in common parlance as primary literature. Interpretations or reconstructions of these poetic or philosophical observations observe and evaluate these texts and are regarded ac-cordingly as secondary literature. Primary literature can feel flattered by these secondary observations, but it can also defend itself against them. The quantities of primary and secondary texts are not dimin-ished by such mutual references. For it quickly becomes apparent that interpretations, meanings, and reconstructions of texts do not necessarily bring about the solution to the problems embedded in the primary texts in question, but are themselves (at times highly) problematic. Whenever it is not clear what constitutes a solution and what a part of the problem (of understanding), a pressing need arises for a renewed distancing and an analysis that takes everything into account. Numerous literary histories or histories of philosophy would like to satisfy this need. And their observations can be, once again, observed, commented upon, and evaluated. Thus histories of literary histories or of histories of philosophy emerge.[33] All these observations face (if not always explicitly) the dilemma of whether they should construct "diabolical" difference or "symbolic" uni/formi/ty.

The basic form of expressing symbolic uni/formi/ty is simply a matter of averaging: texts are related to texts, rather than intertexts to subjects, problems and motifs that are communicated, in them, in vari-ous ways.[34] This book attempts an alternative method: it is guided (even in its structure) not by literary *history*, but by the complex association of subjects, motifs, and problems (having to do with money). A literary history that proceeds as *problem* history must suspect in literature a storehouse (even if a bizarre one) of knowledge. Precisely because lit-erature proceeds via the immanent code appropriate/inappropriate or intelligible/unintelligible (and not, for example, by the scientific code right/wrong), it can know things that elude extra-literary discourses. Walter Benjamin, who discovered in the beauty of poetic texts its means of covering up its shocking knowledge, defined the specifically poetic form of knowledge as an interplay of historical content and philosophical truth.[35] "The object of philosophical criticism is to show that the function of artistic form is as follows: to make historical content, such as provides the basis of every important work of art, into a philosophical truth."[36]

One need not be captive to the melancholy of Walter Benjamin's writings in order to recognize how compelling this conception of literary scholarship is. In a (surely problematic) paraphrase of systems theory, it aims at allowing the emergence, through second-order observation, of that "ideal representation of the problem"[37] that eludes individual disciplines. Literature's knowledge, for example, of money, language, institutions, the logic of the psyche, commerce and media techniques is so different from knowledge of economics, linguistics, management theory, psychology, and communication theory that a historically systematic correlation of these differences would unquestionably be worthwhile. For such a correlation can prove, for example, that it is not entirely implausible to look for the basic form of validity in money (and not, say, in logic or religion) and to expose the fact that money is as little or as securely covered as literature is, or that institutions (like central banks or churches) are capable of spreading the anxiety they were founded to calm.

In the conscious linking up with and radicalizing of Aby Warburg's *Mnemosyne* project,[38] Walter Benjamin tried to elicit the philosophical truth of historical content. His interest in Goethe's *Elective Affinities* as well as in Baroque and specifically modern literature has its basis not least of all in the fact that these groups of works constituted, in their allegorical forms, a dissident storehouse of knowledge. The allegory is the poetic manifestation of that excess of knowledge that bursts the boundaries of the symbolic forms of the beautiful as well as the commonly accepted versions of reality. A literary history that proceeds as a history of problems[39] will bring together not just knowledge of literature, but literature's knowledge, and knowledge in literature. And it will have to devote itself with particular attentiveness to allegorical texts.

This is clear in *The Man without Qualities*, for whose protagonist, significantly, at least one problem does not exist: a lack of money. He can afford to take a vacation from life, and he can afford reflections that accentuate difference as well as essayistic attentiveness (for example, even to the abysses of money). And it becomes clear to him that

> What is so striking about all this [the new dance fanatics, abstract painting, current film and literature] is a certain tendency to allegory, if this is understood as an intellectual device to make everything mean more than it has any honest claim to mean. Just as the world of the Baroque saw in a helmet and a pair of crossed swords all the Greek gods and their myths, and it was not Count Harry who kissed Lady Harriet but a god of

war kissing the goddess of chastity, so today, when Harry and Harriet are smooching, they are experiencing the temper of our times, or something out of our array of ten dozen contemporary myths, which of course no longer depict an Olympus floating above formal gardens but present the entire modern hodgepodge itself.[40]

It is one of the paradoxes of money that it plays a decisive role in the thoroughly modern hodgepodge, and that this hodgepodge would certainly not grow simpler—on the contrary it would become incomparably messier—if money were to lose its value (the historical periods of inflation drastically confirm this). In the current age, the legibility of the world is no longer to be had without the legibility of money. Literature makes it possible to discover more than one meaning in money. Its true ambition, however, is to discover the currency of meaning itself. Heads or tails, heads and tails.

II

POETIC
PHENOMENOLOGY
OF
MONEY

3

The Legibility of World and Money

World and money {*Welt, Geld*}—those are well-known, beloved rhyming words, devalued, meanwhile, through inflation. Whoever would like to make a rhyme with world {*Welt*} will have to orient themselves to the vault of heaven {*Himmelszelt*} or, well, money {*Geld*}. And whoever sets out into the wide world with no money and returns with a sack full of it has proved, in the most convincing of all codes, that he, the successful hero, still knows how to read the most peculiar ciphers in the Book of the World. The critique occasioned by the impudence of this most accessible of all German rhymes, the critique, that is, of an orientation to the world based on the major medium of money, is old—almost as old as money itself.[1] On the threshold of modernity, the critique of this theme swells to a shout of rejection. Humanist scholars and Baroque poets, virtuosos in the reading of the Book of the World, are seized by utter horror at the realization that they are contemporaries of a monetary, inexplicably successful, yet highly problematic second encoding of the entire (and that includes its salvation) world.

"Nothing, I say, is more harmful than money," says Erasmus of Rotterdam in "The third elegy, against a greedy rich man." "No crueler affliction has been sent forth by the darkness of hell. She is the very mother and nourisher of evils, the fomenter of vice, the cruel stepmother of virtue." For it obstructs the fitting and obvious reading of the book of nature, the book of absolute truth, which gave

41

a decisive and easily understood suggestion when it hid metal, from which money, as the embodiment of the second nature, is made, deep in the earth, while kindly offering the real treasures, "yellow grain," golden apples, and "grapes flowing with wine," for gathering.[2]

> Greed alone is the abyss of all crime, the gateway to hell, the road to death. We can also learn this lesson from Nature, who shut up harmful riches behind such formidable barriers. The yellow grain has been taught to spring up in the open fields; so too the happy grapes on the tendrilled vine-stalks are flowing with wine, and the soft, yellowing fruit ripens on the spreading branches. The rich ground openly pours forth thousands of gifts. But Nature, who long ago knew all things in advance, commanded that her harmful gifts be hidden from the children of earth. She hid the heavy mass of gold, which would do harm, in the bowels of the earth, and she sunk ill-omened riches down into the lower world.[3]

Erasmus's argument has been a stock image of popular philosophy since antiquity. Horace, Seneca, Pliny the Elder, and a poem in hexameter by Tiberius on the ruinous effect of gold wrung from the interior of the earth—all warned against bringing that which nature, in its wisdom, has hidden, to the light of day, and letting oneself be dazzled by it.[4] The Christian interpretation of the ancient motif easily links up with this tradition. Anyone who knows how to read the book of nature at all would therefore have to realize that the material from which money is made originates, not without reason, from the depths of hell and death; the monetary second encoding of the divinely created world is satanic. On the basis of such readings of nature, the founder of Strasbourg's "Aufrichtigen Gesellschaft von der Tannen" ("Upright Society of the Firs"),[5] Jesajas Rompler von Löwenhalt (1605–74), melancholy in the way of the Protestant, offers the following rhyme in his poem "Reichtum in Armut" ("Wealth in Poverty"):

> Pious heart
> forgo desire
> to be of high position in this world:
> Satan cements birds' perches
> with honor-apparent
> and with money.

> Frommes Herz
> hab kein Verlangen
> hoch zu sein in dieser Welt:
> Satan leimt die Vogelstangen
> mit dem Ehr-Schein
> und mit Geld.[6]

Three centuries later, with the formula of the "satanic rule of money,"[7] the Jesuit Naphta in Thomas Mann's novel *The Magic Mountain* summarizes his militantly gnostic private lecture on the history of the monetary division of God and world. Money is not a part of the divine plan for the creation. On the seventh day, as is well known, the God of the Old Testament declared his work finished and rested—without having created money.

The poets of the sixteenth and seventeenth centuries, on the threshold of modernity, remember the epochs in which the world that has grown old and decadent still seemed new and innocent. And they feel pressure to rhyme world with money {*Welt/Geld*} in order to reject this rhyme with the assertion that it only holds "these days" {"jetzo"}, thus in the epoch remote from salvation. Thus says Friedrich von Logau (1604–55): "The spirit and lifeblood of man these days is treasure and money; / he who does not have these, is a corpse to the world" {"Der Menschen Geist und Blut ist jetzo Gut und Geld; / Wer dies nicht hat, der ist ein Toter in der Welt"}.[8] (This is early evidence of the association of blood and money—see chapter 16). In modernity, whoever is bloodless, because without money, is dead in the topsy-turvy world that is ruled not by God but rather by satanic mammon. In the Book of Life, however, an entirely different order of debit and credit reigns, namely an order based on the Passion and Salvation of Christ, and one that puts the monetary (dis-)order of poor and rich right. The monetary encoding of *this* world is, however, disturbing, precisely because it encroaches upon *that* world: the disturbance occasioned by the conversion of the Book of the World to the code of money encroaches even on the peace of death. It prevents the wealthy man who, in contrast to the poor man in Logau's verses, was not "a corpse to the (earthly) world," from finding peace of mind, even in the other world. Thus Logau's "Grabschrift eines Reichen" {"Rich Man's Epitaph"} reads:

> Here lies a rich man; do you think
> that he lies in peace at last?
> I think he worries still about money
> how to scrape it together in the other world.

> Hier liegt ein Reicher; meinest du
> Daß er nunmehr liegt in der Ruh?
> Mich dünkt er sorgt wie er noch Geld
> Zusammen kratzt in jener Welt.[9]

In short, with an almost banal consistency, literature at the start of modernity characterizes money as the medium that undermines

God, transcendence, religiosity, and morality.[10] All theologically based objections to the monetary second encoding of the divine world remained nonetheless remarkably ineffective. For—to use another one of Friedrich von Logau's formulations: "The fifth monarchy is *now* resurrected, / Money alone is *now* ruler in all lands" ("Die fünfte Monarchie ist *nunmehr* auferstanden, / Das Geld ist *jetzt* allein ein Herr in allen Landen"). As early as 1494 Sebastian Brant, in his *Ship of Fools*, can attest to the thoroughgoing failure of the critique of money. It is dashed on the sheer numerical superiority of those who are "now" fools for imprinted metal and disdain the traditional ideal of poverty.

> Of money-fools there's never dearth,
> One could not count them all the earth,
> . . . .
> Which *now* is common here on earth,
> All evil's done for money's worth.
> . . . .
> Stark need, which *now* has little worth,
> Once bore a name upon the earth,
> To Golden Age it *once* was dear,
> No money-lovers were there here.[11]

With the success of the modern major medium of gold or money, the end of the world that was itself once golden, the end of the golden age begins. It loses its principles, its grounding; through the success of money it experiences an inflationary loss of value, and so the ages and eons of silver, bronze, paper, and, all told, of mere appearance, begin. A straightforward dialectic ensures that, with the logic of this world and its satanic medium, the critique of money also suffers inflation. The poetic critique of money is quickly cheapened, meets with general approval, and is thereby cheap in every way. To condemn money becomes a potentially boring poetic commonplace. Not just in the sphere of economics, but also in that of poetry, the law of the increasing value of that which is rare, in short supply, uncommon, reigns;[12] indeed, modern literature specializes precisely in improbable observations that are beside the point and incapable of finding widespread acceptance. Thus literature, at the beginning of the eighteenth century, is forced to recognize, and does so with a certain amount of irritation, that philosophy (primarily under the rubric "ethics") pulls away from its critique of money and with increasing willingness creates figures of speech that compromise with the satanic medium. It is not money as such, according to the basic argument (of Thomasius, for example), that is satanic. Much more worthy of criticism are the mistaken ways of handling money, such as greedily and wastefully. Hence a remarkable dialectic takes shape that efficiently reverses the traditional critique of money. Money does not simply ruin the divinely created golden age, according to the argument; on the contrary, though a problematic and deficient medium, it contributes to the improvement of the world's problematic and deficient arrangement (for which human beings are responsible).

Johann Georg Walch's *Philosophische Lexikon*, which appeared in 1775 in Leipzig, the city of trade fairs and books, raises money to a principle possessing philosophical dignity. The entry includes not only conversion tables for all the current European coins, but also describes in detail, in a separate article titled "Geldkunst" ("The Art of Money"), the "talent for handling oneself reasonably with respect to money."[13] Johann Gottlieb Krüger (1715–59), "Professor of Worldly Wisdom and the Scholarship of Medicine" at the University of Halle, would like to provide a philosophical foundation for such maxims. He has forsaken, as befits his position, a theological-fundamental concept of truth in favor of an "apothecary" one, according to which, not "what has been proved to be theoretically the most logical, but rather what best proves itself within the context of a successful life" emerges as true.[14] That money has proved itself brilliantly in the wicked world is hard to contest. In the "Preface on Money" that Krüger wrote for his student Johann August Unzer's *Neue Lehre von den Gemütsbewegungen* of 1746, he legitimizes money as the medium that slyly keeps human beings on the straight and narrow, something nature itself fails to do. "If humanity had more than human reason, we would not need money." However, because of the deficiency of the human makeup, particularly with respect to morals and reason, it is necessary. Only money can do what reason and a sense of duty cannot achieve of their own accord: "To urge human beings on to fulfillment of those duties prescribed by reason, to which, however, reason is not violent enough to force them. For reason is indisputably a righteous lawgiver, but it does not force anyone to accept its laws."[15] Money translates, in other words, the strict and, because of this strictness, rather impractical moral law, into small and fluid coins. With gentle pressure, it sees to it that reason is put into practice. Money is reasonable in a sly way, for it brings, as Barthold Heinrich Brocke's practically psychoanalytical saying shows, pure reason and dirty desire to the intersubjectively acceptable inclination to increase wealth without resorting to theft and murder, thereby contributing indirectly to the welfare of the entire society: "A worm delights a child, a yellow turd the adults" (an expression that certainly would have delighted Freud, if he had run across it).

Criticizing the yellow turd of money on the basis of insights into the dialectical power of the filthy medium to bring success to the golden virtues is in danger of being trivialized. Enlightened literature can still, nonetheless, respond to the power and ubiquity of money with irony. Money obviously achieves the status of inevitability, and as such is no longer up for discussion, let alone at one's disposal. One can fight, to be sure, all the more fiercely over the just distribution and appropriate use of the medium:

"How very, very odd it is,"
Said Clever Hans to Cousin Fritz,
"The wealthy of the world alone
Nearly all the money own."

"Es ist doch sonderbar bestellt,"
Sprach Hänschen Schlau zu Vetter Fritzen,
"Daß nur die Reichen in der Welt
Das meiste Geld besitzen."[16]

Literature's stinging critique of money was as little able to disturb the yellow turd's power of inertia as a critique of feces would be able to put a stop to digestion. Money establishes itself in modernity as a nearly omnipresent second nature. So literature, in view of the immovable strength of the money it has criticized, sets out to find its own exclusive areas that are beyond the influence of money. It quickly becomes a poetic commonplace to agree, with a sigh of resignation, that "money rules the world,"[17] and then immediately to add the qualification that the iniquitous mammon has, however, no power over . . . —followed by, depending on one's culture, confession, and mentality, a reverential naming of the spheres that are immune to money. The continuing popularity of Matthias Claudius can most likely be attributed to the fact that he named those inner regions (but also the outer one: health!) that appear to be beyond the reach of money. Money, according to the pathos of the famous poem "To sing everyday" ("Täglich zu singen"), is and remains secondary—for it presupposes the divinely created existence. What really matters in life (to avoid, at all costs, the expression "what really counts"), is beyond the influence of money:

I thank God, and am as glad
    As a child with a Christmas present,
That I am, I am! And that I have you,
    Fair human countenance!

. . . .

And also worship him from my heart,
    That I on this earth

Am not a great and wealthy man,
  And likely won't become one.

For wealth and honor drive and bloat
  And bear all kinds of danger,
And have turned the hearts of many men,
  Who formerly were upright.

And all the money and all the things
  Afford a lot it's true;
But health, and sleep, and cheerful heart
  They still cannot provide.

Ich danke Gott, und freue mich
  Wie's Kind zur Weihnachtsgabe,
Daß ich bin, bin! Und daß ich dich,
  Schön menschlich Antlitz! habe

. . . .

Auch bet ich ihn von Herzen an,
  Daß ich auf dieser Erde
Nicht bin ein großer reicher Mann,
  Und auch wohl keiner werde.

Denn Ehr und Reichtum treibt und bläht,
  Hat mancherlei Gefahren,
Und vielen hat's das Herz verdreht,
  Die weiland wacker waren.

Und all das Geld und all das Gut
  Gewährt zwar viele Sachen;
Gesundheit, Schlaf und guten Mut
  Kann's aber doch nicht machen.[18]

The critique of the monetary second encoding of the world could console itself with this compromising gesture. And common sense, in addition, has developed a view that is drastic yet nonetheless compels acceptance: money, power, technology, and media are in and of themselves theologically, ethically, and politically innocent, and everything depends on the proper use of these means and instruments, which furthermore do not touch the essence of the human being and of being. This beloved rhetorical figure lasted for a long time. It is to be found, to name just one more example—and one that spills over into the American milieu—in Lion Feuchtwanger's book of poetry of 1928 titled *Pep: J. L. Wetcheek's American Songbook*, in which is to be read:

His dollars would have paved his house for him—
ten bedrooms, seven baths, all told—

and yet they could not buy what would not bore him:
sunshine when he was cold.

At fifty-six he needed little sleep.
Digestion poor, he couldn't eat.
Had twenty good teeth, which he hoped to keep—
preserved from sweet, or meat.

What should he buy, now that he owned all things
Mountains, and sea, and sky, and God?
And the wind's flute sounds, and the thrush that sings?
His checks came back. How odd.

He opened up his checkbook to the sky
but the sky showed no expression.
Between the clouds there peeped no envious eye.
Great was Smith's depression.

See him sitting there, with twenty good teeth,
and six porcelain—five gold,
chagrined and disappointed, underneath
a sun not bought nor sold.

Als er so viele harte Dollar gemacht hatte,
daß er alle Böden seines Hauses damit zudecken konnte,
sah er, daß er bis jetzt nichts bedacht hatte,
was man kaufen könnte, das wärmte und sonnte.

Er brauchte wenig Schlaf und war 57 Jahre,
sein Magen war schlecht, sonst eigentlich war er ganz gesund,
auch hatte er noch 26 Zähne, gute, schwer zerstörbare;
höchstens um die Taille war etwas rund.

Er sah mit Verdruß, daß man ihm nicht entgegenkam,
als er sich jetzt Meer, Himmel, Berge und Gott kaufen wollte.
Er sah mit Verdruß, daß man hier seine guten Schecks nicht nahm
und seiner Unterschrift nicht die gehörige Achtung zollte.

Er zeigte seine Schecks den Bergen, ihren Gleichmut zu brechen,
allein die Berge schauten nicht einmal her.
Er hatte nur gelernt von Geschäften sprechen,
doch Gott sprach nicht von Geschäften, und der Himmel blieb leer.

Da saß er jetzt mit 26 Naturzähne und sechsen von Golde,
ein erstklassiger Bursche, mit Bankkonto, eine Pracht,
und konnte nicht kriegen, was er doch bezahlen wollte.
Wozu also hatte er die vielen Dollar gemacht?[19]

Making money, making dollars: the potency of money (for more on
this subject see chapter 6) is enormous, and it goes far—but not exactly

everywhere. And not at all into transcendent spheres. This rhetorical figure, to be found in the work of authors as different as Matthias Claudius and Lion Feuchtwanger as well as many, many others, has, nonetheless, one drawback: it is hardly a sound argument. Money, in other words, does reach into all spheres of the economy, and beyond. To stick with the areas named by Matthias Claudius, "health, sleep, and cheerful mood": those who have money can afford better doctors and a longer stay at the spa; those who have no financial worries sleep more peacefully than those who expect the sheriff in the morning; and a full wallet doesn't hurt one's mood.

The critique of money that followed theology's fundamental money-critique is particularly applicable, given the fact that the medium of money reaches beyond the system in which it is undeniably functional, that is, the economy, into other systems. Thus, for example, into the justice system, as none other than Matthias Claudius, who wanted to put money in its place, notes:

> Hinz and Kunz (Dedicated to the Sheriff of ———.)
> K. Hinz, is there justice in the world?
> H. Not justice, Kunz, but money.
> K. But there are so many involved in administering justice!
> H. You got it.

> Hinz und Kunz (Dem Gerichtshalter in ——— gewidmet.)
> K. Hinz, wäre Recht wohl in der Welt?
> H. Recht nun wohl eben nicht, Kunz, aber Geld.
> K. Sind doch so viele die des Rechtes pflegen!
> H. Eben deswegen.[20]

The insight, acknowledged with fury, that not only systems such as justice, education, and science, but also the very institutions that concern religion, are susceptible to the functional imperialism of money (because they, in the jargon of systems theory, cannot not participate in the economic system and its code, money), stands not coincidentally at the beginning of Luther's Reformation. The argument surrounding indulgences, and thus the brusque criticism of the church's sanction of an equivalence of money and time (to be more precise: of money and years of release from purgatory) brought about the Reformation. Moreover, the Protestant band of theologians, poets, and thinkers has worked incessantly since then to immunize the sphere of human longing for salvation against the temptation of money. There are surely many reasons why the rhetoric of the true, inner human being, who is free of external ties ("and even if he had been born in chains!"[21]) has developed with particular success in Germany. The Protestant tradition of the internalized and personalized anticipation of salvation, but also the establishment of an economically secure bureaucracy, have doubtless contributed to it.

Perhaps it is more than just the whim of a Germanist to suspect, beyond such sociological data, that a remarkable circumstance of poetry shares the responsibility for the emphatically exceptional position of the true human being in the repository of German culture: there is nothing in German that rhymes with the word for human being, *Mensch*. It is, poetically, as singular and incomparable[22] as that which it designates. "Geld," "Welt," "Zelt," "Feld" and even "Held" {money, world, vault, field, hero} enter into a game of rhymes with other words that hardly knows an end. *The* singular *Mensch* can create a far-reaching rhyme and thoughtfully hint at this correlation, without having to suffer the indignity of entering into assonance or harmony with other notables.[23] Money makes everything compatible with everything, but the human being is downright incompatible, without rhyme. The one exception, the poetically self-referential rhyme (by Peter Rühmkorf) that rhymes *Mensch* with an adjectival form of the name of the inimitable poet, Gottfried Benn, proves the rule. It celebrates an unrivaled genius:

> The most beautiful poems of the *Menschen*—
> Now find a rhyme for that!—
> Are those of Gottfried Benn*schen:*
> Brain, learnaic glob.
> Sinking throne of Euphrates,
> Roses on bark and trunk—
> Epigon slips
> Into the sweet Benn-agram

> Die schönsten Gedichte der Menschen—
> Nun finden Sie mal einen Reim!—
> Sind die Gottfried Bennschen:
> Hirn, lernäischer Leim.
> Sinkende Euphratthrone,
> Rosen auf Rinde und Stamm—
> Gleite Epigone
> Ins süße Benn-Engramm![24]

In spite of all the geniuses who despise money, the code/turd {*Code/Kot*} of money finds universal acceptance in modernity. The monetary second encoding of the world leaves little semantically unoccupied and no unexplored territory behind. But that means: the modern age succeeds, under the sign of money, at the project at which the old metaphor of the Book—and the legibility—of the World failed. Money produces, in contrast to the medium of the book, intersubjectively binding readings of the world; money cannot, in contrast to books, be avoided; money has at its command that functional authority that books increasingly lose in proportion to the extent to which they are mass-produced; the information that money passes on is, in contrast to that of books, immune to the most thoroughgoing abysses of interpretation; and money has at its disposal, in contrast to books, a clear digital code (payment/non-payment, or debit/credit[25]), amenable to verifiable bookkeeping and precise reckoning. This is already evident in the fact that someone else's dollar is money I do not have, unlike information and culture, which can be shared without relinquishing them.

No wonder the metaphor of the book suffers crises and irreversible losses of credibility to the same extent that the code of money covers more and more ground. And the code that is more valuable, because it is more limited in supply, extends itself universally, while there are belletristic books in such excess that they soon seem functionally superfluous. None other than Goethe took careful note of this development. He has Wilhelm Meister experience both the excess of books and the lack of money, as the complementary data under whose sign the modern age stands. Wilhelm Meister is forced to realize, even as he writes his dramas, that "the *golden* age of authorship, . . . when the printing press had not yet deluged the world with so many useless writings," is definitely over when even beautiful spirits {*Schöngeister*} like himself recognize "the value and worth of money."[26] That profane money usurps sacred writing and advances to the center of the modern world, indeed that money is the real key to understanding the modern age, Goethe has already emphasized in the early burlesque *Fellow Culprits* {*Die Mitschuldigen*}. As the tremendously indebted actor Söller, a mask in every sense of the word, forces his way into the room of his wife's lover at night in order to pick the lock of his safe, he speaks the truly golden key words:

> Come, sacred thing, container of my god and hero!
> Without you any king is nothing but a zero.
> (*He draws a picklock from his pocket and goes on speaking
> while he is breaking into the strongbox.*)
> Ah, jimmies open paths to lands of milk and honey;
> With little jimmy's help I get Big Jimmy—money.
>
> O komm, du Heiligtum! Du Gott in der Schatulle!
> Ein König ohne dich wär eine große Nulle.
> (*Er zieht die Diebesschlüssel aus der Tasche und
> sagt unter dem Aufbrechen.*)
> Habt Dank, ihr Dietriche! ihr seid der Trost der Welt!
> Durch euch erlang ich ihn, den großen Dietrich, Geld![27]

Now the metaphor of the book and its legibility is not exactly one among many metaphorical traditions. It is, on the contrary, the metaphor that made metaphors possible to begin with, and legitimized them—it is, purely and simply, the meta-metaphor. Metaphors translate, to work toward a minimal definition, an element of a text that is difficult to understand into another, illuminating context, in the hope of increased intelligibility and more concise expression. Those who cannot quite understand how the Holy Ghost came to dwell on earth may be helped by a supplementary text that describes a white dove gliding from the heavens down to earth. Those who do not know what a sovereign has to contend with in eventful times can visualize the challenges faced by the captain of a ship rocked by the sea. And those who see no rhyme or reason in the Book of the World or of nature, can find it in the Book of Books.[28]

Such a translation, such a metaphor, is only useful if there is reason to believe that the unfathomable logic of the one domain is the same as that of the well-known, obvious, other domain. The fundamental figure of speech of this assumption (in the cultural traditions of scriptural religions, in any event) is that of the doubled authorship of God (see the remarks in chapter 1): He wrote the Book of the World and the Book of Books (the Torah, the Bible, or the Koran); He gave being and signs their homologous forms; He composed the real as well as the symbolic. Hebrew, Arabic, and Greek are therefore not just a few languages among many; they are sacred languages: their syntax and semantics are that of the divine creation itself.

The basic paradox of all scriptural revelations is, to be sure, that they are not, in the end, so unambiguously revealed: otherwise they would not exist in the dissonant plural as, now that cultures are coming into closer contact with each other, is noted with increasing consternation. Lessing's Nathan {the Wise}[29] is able to make sense of this plurality in a liberal (and functional!) way: he answers the question about truth not with the help of books, but through recourse to the expressive power of a valuable ring and its simulacra. The Caliph Omar II, in contrast, after capturing the library at Alexandria—according to an anecdote that is hardly authentic—had all its books destroyed, with the justification that either they agree with the Koran and are therefore superfluous or they do not agree with the Koran and are therefore dangerous. The *one* godly world is compatible with only *one* Holy Book. With the invention of the printing press, at the latest, the Christian tradition made this traumatic discovery: there are, once and for all, books in the plural (including the many translations of and commentaries on the one Holy Writing!) and these books often contain completely different, indeed often conflicting ideas. Thus the metaphor of the book, as a result of the sheer quantity of books,[30] plunges headlong into its deep crisis: because of the many books, the Book loses its authority altogether. "Les mots and les choses" have been drifting apart ever since. Hamlet, who no longer fathoms the one meaning of being in books and in the one Book, but reads only "words, words, words," and Don Quixote, who becomes a laughing-stock because he accepts the authenticity of the many books, are the melancholy heroes of this crisis of the metaphor of the book.[31]

This crisis is shocking to the core because it makes it quite clear that we are no longer reliably at home in a world committed to writing. Books, including Holy Scripture, that are entirely of profane origin (as historical scholarship on the Bible quickly discovered), do not reveal (the) meaning (of being); they produce, on the contrary, only a series of letters that become systems of symbols and linguistic cages—even when they claim to be something different. If they speak of more, they misspeak. Books, empirically inflationary ever since Gutenberg, automatically lose authority. Money, on the other hand, has (to a certain extent by definition but also qua etymology[32]) authority; indeed, money is authority, for it authorizes its own reading of the world authoritatively. And it owes this authority to the scarcity by which it functions. If one prints it (like books, and with the same technology as books) in excess, it simply stops being money and becomes wastepaper. The other side of this functional scarcity of money (which duplicates and balances the scarcity of goods[33]), however—as literature, with the attentiveness of a rival, notes—is the scandalous semantic poverty of money.[34]

Money tells how solvent its owner is, and about the exchange value of goods; that is (just about) all. As for the character and intentions of its owner, its heritage, its further use as well as its effects on the psyche and the living world, money has as little to say as it does about the intrinsic value of a commodity or the damage that economic processes cause to the ecosystem.[35] Money is of a monstrous, indeed "degenerate"[36] indifference, and its heart is as cold as stone.[37] This structural character weakness is to some extent the price that the medium of money has to pay for its bewildering ability to function—to make it possible, in other words, "to ignore . . . when something is bought, what is bought, and the persons involved in the exchange."[38] This indifference is the necessary condition for the ongoing second encoding of the world through money. It is characterized, however, by a deep paradox: the paradox of the unnecessary necessity of this code/turd. If money were to disappear all of a sudden, everything would remain just as it was: no house, no fruit, no goods, no wares, nothing that exists (except of course for coins, bills, checks, drafts, passbooks, stocks, and so on) would be missing. And yet everything would immediately be completely different. The world would have become entirely illegible, and would vanish in the pandemonium of a universal loss of structure and orientation.

Thus money makes the world legible. For money rules and structures the world: it orients it toward that which is limited, efficient, and expensive. And money also makes the world frankly, coldly, and indifferently legible. Money does not hide the fact that it organizes, produces, establishes, and thus simulates the legibility of the world with one and just one focus. But this monetary second encoding, this simulation of the legibility of the world, has one inestimable advantage: it functions (if not always free of crisis—how could it?). For it stimulates traders, producers, and those who amass wealth tremendously. Poets as different as Novalis and Brecht have thematized the "stimulating impact of money" {"belebende Wirkung des Geldes"[39]}. This s(t)imulation naturally leads to new and irritating crises in the world—for example, to the paradox that scarcity becomes scarce, that there are crises of overproduction, and that overproduction can lead to ecological difficulties (for example, the economic system displaces its own specific scarcity and turns the original elements of water and air—and peace!—into rare resources).

The monetary s(t)imulation of a complex, utilitarian, value-laden world makes it clear, in hindsight, that simulation (in the broadest sense of the production of alternative realities that bear plausible and suggestive resemblances to the world[40]) was also the norm in the reading of the world in premodern times. Heidegger's thesis that modernity is the first age of the worldview, because the "basic process of modern times is the conquest of the world as picture,"[41] has also quickly gained acceptance among postmodern media theorists over the last few years. It relies on the hardly tenable suggestion that premodern times were less oblivious to being and able to cope without worldviews. Even cultures that knew no subject that imag(in)ed[42] (pictures of the world) have tried to make their world legible (or perceptible {vernehmbar}, to use Heidegger's antithesis of "imag(in)e" {"vor-stellen"}) via their simulations: via rites, stories, myths, soothsaying, books, theologies, and so on. The age of the s(t)imulation of worldviews most certainly did not begin with modernity and its new media (including the medium money!).

On the contrary, it is clear that the modern age, armed with media, attempts to put a stop to the simulation of worldviews (in writings, rites, signs, liturgies, and so on) that proceed symbolically. With the invention of photography, film, and the gramophone, modern society has finally acquired the means of driving patiently lying paper, with its extremely confining symbol-cage of twenty-six letters, out of its millennial monopoly on information. Writing can do nothing besides simulate—it admits it, too, so one does not overestimate it and take it to be sacred. Film and television can actually contribute, on the other hand, to the "redemption of physical reality," to borrow Siegfried Kracauer's apt battle cry.[43] "Indeed, along with photography, film is the only art which exhibits its raw material. Such art as goes into cinematic films must be traced to their creators' capacity for *reading the book of nature.*"[44] The new media have not merely put an end to the age of books; they have also fulfilled the promise of the Book—in other words, they have made nature and the world legible. It is simply untenable to assume that a newspaper report of a parliamentary debate or soccer game is authentic while a recording or direct transmission of these events is, in contrast, simulated.

The currently fashionable debate over the new media's powers of simulation will only become productive when they are viewed before the backdrop of the simple fact that the new media (in contrast to the medium of the book and also the utilitarian medium of money) can, in fact, avoid simulation—but they do not have to. The truly exciting fact of our media-saturated contemporary age is not that it has become difficult to differentiate between feature films and news reports, and that some may experience life as a television show. Forgery was commonly practiced even in the highly Christianized Middle Ages (for example by the Vatican); and Don Quixote was a prominent figure right from the start of the Gutenberg Galaxy because he became ensnared in the undifferentiablility of book and real world.[45] It is not the eternal problem of the confusion between being and appearance that is confoundingly modern, but rather the insight that the modern age, armed with the technology of the media, is capable of achieving what was merely a promise under the sign of writing and of money: "to read the book of nature." And this in a sense that exceeds the metaphorical remnants of Kracauer's insight to the same degree that the reading of nature has become the thoroughly unmetaphorical practice of research: the genetic code and the law of nuclear energy are available, literally, for the reading.[46]

Money forms the ontosemiological vertical structure of the second nature that we have grown used to calling society. Money structures this second nature; money reduces many of the overly complex decisions that enter the realm of possibility in this second nature to comprehensible dimensions; money facilitates simple approaches to complex societies; in short, money makes this second nature legible. And money stimulates efforts to reach out of the dimensions of this second nature over and into those of the first (compare the comments on Chamisso's story of Peter Schlemihl in chapter 12). All of this suggests that overarching attempts to infer the perfectibility of societies on the basis of the legibility of the second nature have failed. However, there are many indications that there are, currently, militant attempts not just to read the book of first nature, but to rewrite it.

The legi- and (re)constructibility of the genetic code and the nuclei of atoms put an unmetaphorical end to all metaphorical talk of nature's writing in ciphers that speak to us figuratively in their beautiful forms, or to numbers and figures that hold the key to all creatures. Not, however, to just the logic that informs the metaphor of legibility alone—to the logic of two worlds. It seems to be the case that the two-world model of being and appearance (that is in its basic structure originally Platonic), of the real and the simulated world, or of the world of things and that of monetary values, is being dramatically displaced at present. The imitation, second(-ranking), derivative nature is replaced by manufactured nature, which is supposed to demonstrate what the first nature should look like. "Nature appears to some in lyrical intensity, to others in logical clarity, and they are the masters of the world," as Chargaff says in his *Vorwort zu einer Grammatik der Biologie* {"Introduction to a Grammar of Biology"}.[47] The decoded, the deciphered, the fully revealed divine nature is the necessary condition for the second nature, literally made (and certainly "better" made, made complete) by master human beings. But is revelation not a synonym for apocalypse? And is "complete" not an abysmal word? It is worthwhile, even in times when one can read the Book of the World without metaphor, to read "words, words, words."

Then one can see, namely, that the history of the reading of the book of nature has a purpose that is hardly a secret anymore: to compose it anew, to turn from the reader into the author of this book. Money is the most important intermediate medium on the way from the earliest reading (of the stars and of viscera) to the reading of the one Holy Scripture and the many books to the reorientation of reading from the first to the second nature, and beyond that to the capital-intensive attempt to write the first nature anew. No longer to read in the book of nature, no longer to long to hear the song that sleeps in all things {"das Lied . . . das in allen Dingen schläft"}, but rather to decipher the genetic code in order to create a new version of the book of nature, and to become the author of being: that is the truly postmodern imperative. It is connected to the oldest impulses:

Eritis sicut Deus. This prophecy is the hot core of the Faustian project. The few who still read and write, who still cling to the world of books, fear they will have to pay dearly for this attempt at writing, this fickle author's ambition that moves from the playground where letters are combined onto the playing field of the real.

4

THE MATERIALITY OF MONEY
(AND OF LITERATURE)

> Money is what words are.
> Words are what money is.
> Is money what words are,
> are words what money is.
>
> Gertrude Stein

Reading Notes

Money and language, coin and word: Gertrude Stein stands in a long tradition in which their use in analogy borders on direct identification.[1] This analogy was developed theoretically (after many forerunners: Locke, Hamann, Goethe, and Novalis among others) along with the structural linguistics of value of de Saussure (who, as is generally known, hailed from a family of bankers). Poststructuralism (so-called, above all, in Germany) initially gets involved in this intersection of language and money marked by de Saussure. Only a reading intended to cultivate its image of the enemy (poststructuralism = new French Irrationalism, uninterested in sociological Enlightenment) could miss, in the fight for presumably pure reason, how intensively theoreticians as different as Lacan, Foucault, Deleuze, Derrida, and Baudrillard concentrated their investigations on the meaningful intersections of the old (basic) code of language and the slightly newer but hardly less secondary code of money.

In his most famous essay on Poe's short story about the purloined letter, Lacan characterized money as the "most annihilating signifier"—and Lacan knew, as a practicing and expensive analyst, what he was talking about. Foucault showed, in *Les mots et les choses*, how the functional encoding of money at first confirmed the order of representation and then desiccated it. Deleuze traced, together with Guattari in *Anti-Oedipus: Capitalism and Schizophrenia*, the meandering river of money as it intrudes into the thinking, living, and wishing of identities and substance. Derrida showed (whether in early texts such as *Economimesis* or in more recent investigations such as "Counterfeit Money" ["Fausse monnaie"]) that money is the paradoxical incarnation of the deconstructive movement. And Baudrillard left nary a doubt that the (anti-)foundation of all despair/doubt in reality lies in the ir/reality of money.

The reference to this theoretical tradition, but also to the last two hundred years of literary history, can make it likely that the seemingly fashionable talk of simulation, deconstruction, and the end of the referential order finds an overwhelming testimonial in the logic of money's development. Those who take note of this will also realize that those who do not wish to speak of the medium of money should not speak of media at all.

Literary scholarship has considerably broadened the concept and understanding of the texts for which it feels responsible in the last couple of decades. It is hardly disputed anymore that popular literature, comic books, and pamphlets deserve scholarly attention. Instructions, cookbooks, advertisements, and graffiti have long been, no doubt for good reason, approved objects of inquiry for a methodologically ambitious comparative literature. And yet those printed papers, of all things, that have determined, as no other texts, the ordinary as well as the heroic life of the educated and propertied citizenry of the modern, high modern, and postmodern era, and practically cry out for intercultural analysis, exceed the limits of even a substantially broadened conception of the text: banknotes.

At the same time, the value, the dignity, the influence, the power, the enormous amount printed (well beyond the reach of books), and the functional strength of this monetarily imprinted paper cannot seriously be doubted. If that which is available for reading on this paper is nonetheless hardly ever read in detail, the reason for this disregard is easy to name. Banknotes have no significance to be hermeneutically revealed—they function.[2] What counts are the numbers, not the words. "The alphabet is really now superfluous. . . ." Nonetheless it is worthwhile to pay attention to the words and images that surround the numbers. For money has a unique, functional, surplus value. It serves not only as the code that shapes the communication specific to the highly functional system of the economy.[3] It infringes upon other semantic spheres as well. Literature, which for its part wants to join in the discussion and meddle in everything, is particularly interested in these intrusions.

In particular, theological and erotic references on coins and bills have always been unavoidable. And the function of these functional intrusions is hardly a riddle. They are supposed to help "cover" the paper appearance of money, the value of the notes.[4] For money (and especially paper money) is obviously without value in and of itself. It is free of any intrinsic value whatsoever. Now and then a coin may come in handy in changing an AA battery, and a note can always be used to light a cigar and impress onlookers with the wealth of one who dares to use money in a way so alien to its purpose.[5] Because of its material poverty, money, in order to function well, is forced to refinance in noneconomic systems (such as religion, art, and love). Such inspiration must back up the note's appearance of being "covered" by more than just itself.

The brilliant swindler in Uwe Timm's novel *Headhunter* knows this too. He, who can make gigantic and, in every sense of the word, abstract, sums of money disappear into a "black hole,"[6] has the most sensual and hands-on relationship to money imaginable. His involuntary stay in Brazil while fleeing the police is ruined for him by a number of things, among them the poor quality of the banknotes. "Something I usually enjoy, paying, dipping into my pocket, pulling out a bundle of notes, counting them and adding a good tip, disturbs me here; in fact, I feel aversion every time, more than that, revulsion when out of my pocket I pull these limp, yellow-brown notes that absorb the humidity."[7] The trustworthiness of the Brazilian currency is not, however, undermined solely by the poor quality of the paper, but also by the fact that, imprinted on the back of the note with the highest denomination, is, of all things, a poem: "A poet unknown to me, a man with glasses, sits [as the obverse of the note would have it] at a desk. On the reverse side of the note a poem is printed. The note had been stuck together three times with tape, but a part of the poet's desk is still missing."

National banks that wish to "cover" paper money with poetically inscribed paper are obviously ill-advised—both types of paper lie like a rug. The Swiss solution is surely cleverer: "It's not by chance that in Switzerland . . . you get the impression that you're always getting freshly-printed money for change. The size of the institution that withdraws and destroys old money in a country also informs you about its creditworthiness. And the ant depicted on the thousand-franc note reveals every bit as much about the mentality and economy of Switzerland as the notes of printed poetry about Brazil."[8] The simplest and yet most suggestive form of extra-monetary "cover" is promised not by the Swiss, however, but by the prototypically modern currency, that of the United States. The brief and suggestive "In God we trust" is there for the reading, and pregnant with meaning, on all its coins and bills. Theological explanations for this monetary confession of faith can hardly be deduced from the coins. These are delivered only by the bills: the defiant motto is semantically "covered" by the bills, which are of higher value. There is, after all, more room for thoughtful entries on bills than on coins.

The theological spheres of imagery into which the American coin's inscription points are present on the bills in all their emblematic-esoteric weightiness.[9] The profane face of the one-dollar bill has a sacred soberness about it: Next to the portrait of George Washington are to be found (as on the bills of all the countries of gentlemen) the indication of value, the serial number, the signature of the secretary of the treasury, and the name of the country of origin. These functional terms are covered, conveyed, and well-grounded by the esoteric politico-theology that the back of the bill concisely propagates. On its left half is a thirteen-tiered pyramid awaiting completion, on whose base the founding year of the USA is engraved in Roman numerals: 1776. The pyramidal structure reaches toward a triangle that is surrounded by a halo and encloses a godlike eye. Around this obvious symbol of Freemasonry, an inscription that welcomes and celebrates future works winds its way: "Annuit coeptis." This is from Virgil's *Georgics*, and it corresponds to the motto on a banner below the emblematic pyramid: "Novus ordo seclorum." Like Virgil's Fourth Eclogue, the dollar bill promises a new golden age, which the right side of the bill bespeaks. The two emblems are connected through the central phrase, "In God we trust." The word "ONE" is arranged beneath it in such a way that it reads as if the one-dollar bill trusts in God. The monotheism that resurrects "E pluribus unum" is the flip side of the national treasury's money.

The God in whom the United States' gold trusts is the God of the typological fulfillment of the ancient syncretic promise of a redemptive rebirth that occurred in the year 1776. The image on the right side points to it as well. It has an eagle on it. An eagle already appears in *Physiologus* as an image of rebirth. A shield with thirteen horizontal and thirteen vertical stripes (like the thirteen steps of the pyramid on the left side) protects the eagle. Thirteen is also the number of arrows that the eagle holds in its left talon, and there are thirteen leaves on the olive branch held in its right. A banner (a late form of emblematic representation and an early form of the comic strip) unfurls from its beak, on which can be read: "E pluribus unum." That out of the thirteen states that declared their independence—out of the many, the scattered, the chaotic, the disparate, the polymorphic—

an incomparable unity would form as a result of future works, is the promise of the dollar. It domesticates the recalcitrant prime number thirteen,[10] it provides the new, young nation with an ancient prehistory (reaching back to Solomon's temple and the high culture of Rome), and it integrates that which even the esoteric tradition is unable to bring together—just as the thirteen five-pointed stars that are encircled by light come together to form a hexagon.

Thus the esoteric promise of a rebirth of Solomon's Temple out of the spirit of Freemasonry is to be found on the most profane of all papers, standing in the political-theological-economic-semantic center of "God's own country." Lawrence Ferlinghetti dedicated a remarkable poem to this constellation (which proves once again that the ontosemiological series Communion-money-new media must be more than the idée fixe of a literary scholar: it can be seen over and over again, though seldom as transparently as in this literary statement of the deep structural correlations between being and meaning:

> I am waiting for my case to come up
> and I am waiting
> for a rebirth of wonder
> and I am waiting for someone
> to really discover America
> and wail
> and I am waiting
> for the discovery
> of a new symbolic frontier
> and I am waiting
> for the American Eagle
> to really spread its wings
> . . . .
> I am waiting for the Second Coming
> and I am waiting
> for a religious revival
> . . . .
> and I am waiting
> for them to prove
> that God is really American
> . . . .
> and I am waiting
> to see God on television
> piped onto church altars
> if only they can find
> the right channel
> to tune in on

and I am waiting
for the Last Supper to be served again

. . . .

I have read the Reader's Digest
from cover to cover
and noted the close identification
of the United States and the Promised Land
where every coin is marked
In God We Trust
but the dollar bills do not have it
being gods unto themselves.[11]

More sober than the dense politico-theology of the dollar, and less profound than the poem's ontosemiology, which can hardly be regarded as implicit anymore, is the ornamental quality of the new German banknotes. It is certainly noteworthy that, years ago, the Federal Bank of Germany (and it alone among the large institutions![12]) had a presentiment that October of 1990 would be a historic date and issued new banknotes precisely at the time of the German reunification. Nonetheless, the new notes are not, on the whole, a pathetic document, but rather a caricature of late modern balance.[13] The Federal Bank must have been concerned about feminist criticism, otherwise the (nearly) exact parity between the sexes is difficult to explain: exactly the same number of women's as men's heads adorn the new banknotes. The masculine notes are nonetheless worth twice as much in each case: Bettina von Arnim is valued at five German marks, Carl Friedrich Gauß at ten; Annette von Droste-Hülshoff is worthy of a 20-, while Balthasar Neumann a 50-mark note; Clara Schumann brings it to 100, but Paul Ehrlich to 200; Maria Sibyll Merian can be had for 500, the brothers Grimm (of course, one gets two likenesses for the price of one) for no less than 1000 marks.

"In the choice of the 'areas of activity and inquiry'—in connection with the heads—an old prejudice, believed overcome, shines through with new intensity. Hard science is the province of men, the arts— obviously conceived of as softer—are delegated to the women."[14] On the other hand, the appropriate proportion of northern to southern Germans as well as that of Protestants to Catholics (4:3, and with Paul Ehrlich, a Jew is represented on the notes) is for the most part preserved. And so one could hardly praise the sense of justice and the sobriety of the Federal Bank enough, were it not for the fact that, on the most valuable note, of all places, a downright unreasonable motif is to be found. The finishing touch on the 1000-mark note is the eccentric, extremely poor, and extremely rich "Star-Coin girl,"[15] whose economic behavior is simply not sensible, and whom the brothers Grimm have made immortal through their collection of fairy tales.

The girl is surrounded by a garland that adorns the lowest denomination as well, the five-mark note. On the face of this cheap note "the graphic artist placed, next to the youthful beauty (=Bettina von Arnim) looking enthusiastically and expectantly into the future, a horn of plenty—as a sign of her many talents. No matter how honorable the intention—the artist's unconscious guided his hand in creating a horn that is more likely to be interpreted as a phallic symbol; it lends Bettina's longing a concrete emphasis."[16] On the most valuable note, this phallic horn of plenty unloads its gifts, so to speak, into the lap of the Star-Coin girl, turning its immense privation around and recalling the ancient myth of the godly shower of gold in whose shape Zeus pours himself into the lap of the beautiful Danae. Thus the 1000-mark note, explicitly reminiscent of a fairy-tale miracle, belongs to the land of the economic miracle as well, and can be understood as the typological fulfillment of its poor five-mark forerunner. For on the five-mark note, the garland surrounds an empty space; on the highest denomination it radiantly encircles immense, unearthly riches. The old pattern of expectation and fulfillment still rules the postmodern banknotes. Money breeds money; money increases wondrously; money is of phallic potency (see chapter 6); money is full of a godlike joy in creation—why shouldn't it be covered?

The Im/Materiality of Money

Money has not always been as eloquent as the highly functional legal tender of modernity. The coins of antiquity simply do not offer enough space for the references, so rich in allusion, that are supposed to secure extra-monetary authority in paper money's classic game. They are therefore content with drastic references to their origins in the contexts of theological-erotic sacrifice.[17] The most common motif on early coins is the sacrificial animal, in whose place the means of payment stands. The etymologies of the concept of money make no secret of its religious origin: "pecunia" (from "pecus," "sacrifical cow"); "obolos" ("sacrificial spear"); "Moneten" (from Juno Moneta, the goddess of fertility).[18]

The history of the materializations, the embodiments of the abstract, the wondrous, the godlike value of money can thus hardly be clearer.[19] In place of obvious values (1) that, precisely because of their unquestionable intrinsic value (and their religious function as well!), are capable of functioning as a general standard of exchange (the cow is the usual unit of measure), enter (2) coins, that are then (3) devalued to small units by paper money, just as (4) the centrally issued paper money is pushed aside by self-issued and signed promissory notes. "Just pay with your good name"—says an advertisement for a credit card. A professor of German who advises firms on questions of style and a nobleman who is a Social Democrat, among many other prominent individuals, have had no qualms about lending their names to this ad, thus exchanging them for money. Perhaps they need it. There was a time when such a thing would have been considered bad form in these circles.

It is an openly acknowledged goal among those who currently manage financial transactions, to check the "paper flood" of checks, transfer forms, drafts, and credit card receipts through electronic banking. Monitor-money is quite plausibly the logical conclusion of the development from concrete value via minted gold and assignats to the check and from signed paper on into the sphere of the fully immaterial. It is not just information that counts that is taking leave of the Gutenberg Galaxy at this point—money is too. The consequences of money's protean change of form are difficult to gauge. It is, however, already clear that money is becoming less and less poetic. Plastic,[20] magnetic stripes, electronic PIN-numbers, and the columns of figures on the monitor leave little room for thoughtful mottos and emblems, for ornamental excess, for aesthetic, theological, and mythological attempts to guarantee the value of money extra-monetarily.

The aesthetics of the classic paper money might not have been so thoroughly superfluous. It contributes to nothing less than the functioning of the illusion of money—the illusion that is, that money is a (covered) value in and of itself that can be converted into other things of value at any time. This illusion is dependent on its ability to free itself, through general acceptance, from its illusory character. Along the way toward the cashless society,[21] however, that part of money that is pure illusion will become more and more evident. "Of all the financial transactions in the Federal Republic of Germany today, only about 5% of the value of all the exchanges, according to reliable estimates, are carried out in cash."[22] Money we can be sensually certain of—like the kind hoarded by Uncle Scrooge McDuck so that he could swim in it, rump in the air—is visibly disappearing. And with real, tangible money, faith in its reality vanishes—as well as faith in the reality of reality at all. It is a melancholy thought that, in the age when everything is suspected of being fraudulent, the new German banknotes have abandoned the familiar pronouncement that lent the old bills the aura of the original manuscript: "Whoever counterfeits or falsifies banknotes, or acquires counterfeited or falsified banknotes and enters them into circulation, will be punished with a minimum of two-years' imprisonment." The omission of this well-known pronouncement must have had an animating effect on the friends of forgery. For the new notes, presumably impossible to forge, are eagerly being robbed of their aura thanks to modern and inexpensive techniques of color copying. According to a statement (slightly ambiguously worded and for that very reason ingenious) by Munich's chief investigator for crimes of forgery, "Unfortunately, the modern color copier makes it possible for anyone to create their daily need for money [!] themselves."[23]

Money has always been accompanied by the suspicion that something about it is not quite right. Money is, for once and for all, a medium of duplication—and this duplication is not less problematic as a result of the fact that limited money duplicates and balances the limited supply of goods. Because money is a simulacrum, it is surrounded by latent irreality. If one questions money all too forcefully, asks what it is really all about, whether it is in fact covered, whether it actually indicates a "real" price, it collapses with amazing rapidity. Money has to pass if all depositors storm a bank at once in order to withdraw their deposits, if everyone wants to exchange their foreign currency at a fixed rate of exchange tied to gold,[24] if all creditors of supposedly completely safe government bonds want to appraise the national wealth they presume to be in the finance minister's vault (how does one bunker the Gross National Product?). Just as the value of one and the same painting can shrink to the value of the canvas it is painted on in no time at all if it emerges that it has been falsely attributed to Rembrandt, so can money itself—as the dramatic stories of tremendous inflation[25] have demonstrated on the world's stage many times—deflate to the value of wastepaper.

The irreal[26] and the irrational aspects of money are the other side of its reality and rationality. Latent irreality continually surrounds it. And the very medium that has always (even prior to money—the *Odyssey* is older than the coin) been suspected of having a troubled relationship to the real has keenly observed the irreality of money: literature. The connection between money and information is especially susceptible to crisis. The prototypically modern example of susceptibility to crisis is the institution that feeds bits of information from around the world into the specific code of the price of stock (and beyond that into the code of money itself): the stock exchange. Heinrich Heine described this crisis, in his *French Affairs (Französische Umstände)*[27] of 1832, as the crisis of orality, transferred to, or better yet transubstantiated into, the written medium of government stocks and bonds.

Heine characterized the Paris Stock Exchange as a "great temple of marble where Perier [the French minister of finance] was honoured like a god and his word like an oracle."[28] The voices that buzz throughout the hall try to interpret the oracle and bring together unearthly amounts of information in order to distill from it a rate that can be fixed in print and considered valid for a short time, only to be renegotiated immediately and thus indicating, in all its variation, that the only constant is the continual state of crisis. "Here, in the vast space of the high-arched hall, here it is that the swindlers in public funds, with all their repulsive faces and disagreeable screams, sweep here and there, like the tossing of a sea of egotistic greed, and where, amid the wild billows of human beings, the great bankers dart up, snapping and devouring like sharks—one monster preying on another; and where, in the gallery, like birds of prey watching on a cliff, even speculating ladies may be seen."[29]

This temple is especially susceptible to crisis because (despite the theological implications of its architecture) all "faculties are directed to the practical," and yet there is no method for separating fact from fiction, true from false information, and thus for allowing only relevant world news in. In order to characterize the touchy status of information relevant to the stock exchange, Heine develops an attractive theological-monetary fantasy: "Should there be suddenly received on Change a telegraphic message stating that M. Talleyrand believed in retribution or reward after death, French funds would at once fall 10 per cent, for it would be felt that he would attempt to reconcile himself with God, and renounce and sacrifice Louis Philippe and the whole *Justemilieu*, and set at stake the admirable tranquillity which we now enjoy. Neither existence nor non-existence, but peace or disturbance is the great question of the Bourse."[30]

Similar characterizations of events on the stock exchange as one of unexpectedly unsettling background noise can be found in Zola's novel of 1891, *Money*. It discusses another possible scenario for putting an end to this hullabaloo and its irrational effects: by adding a religious dimension to the socialist and communist critique of capitalism and stylizing Marx into the Jesus who throws the traders and the money out of the temple: "I must apologize for sitting down," said the young socialist, Sigismond, to the banker, Saccard, in this novel,

> "I remained up all night in order to read this book, which I received yesterday. A masterpiece . . . ten years of the life of my master, Karl Marx. It is the treatise on Capital which he promised us so long ago. So now we here have our Bible. . . ." "Then this is the sweep of the broom?"

asked Saccard, still jesting. "In theory, yes," answered Sigismond. "It only remains for us to carry it out."

Which would lead of course, as the discussants quickly recognize, to the abolition of money. No longer would a perverse code, says Sigismond, distort the path to the wealth of being. A crazy idea, according to the Catholic banker, who is convinced that it is impossible to do without the churchly as well as the economic means of grace.[31]

Both Heine and Zola sharply accentuate the religious dimension of the stock exchange, but also its critique. Capitalists, like communists, cannot so easily dispense with God, the Bible, and the means of grace. Both face the problem of filtering out, from the noise of modernity, the information about the world that really counts. In fact, as Heine clearly shows, the stock exchange, in that moment of truth that counts (because in it one faces the decision "to buy or to sell"), is incapable of deciding the status—"to be or not to be"—of the news it receives (which consists of "words, words, words"). The Count of Monte Christo takes advantage of this (in Alexander Dumas's novel of 1845–46), as the author drastically spins out Heine's telegraph motif. The count has understandable reasons for wanting revenge against the banker Danglars. And he carries out his revenge, not anachronistically with poison or stiletto, but with the help of the most modern of media technologies, the one that makes the intersection between the general code of news and the specific code of money even more effective and more susceptible to crisis.

For 25,000 francs he bribes an official of the telegraph service to feed the following wire into the news service:

> "The king, Don Carlos, has escaped the vigilance exercised over him at Bourges, and has returned to Spain by the Catalonian frontier. Barcelona has risen in his favour." All that evening nothing was spoken of but the foresight of Danglars, who had sold his shares, and of the luck of the stockjobber, who had lost only five hundred thousand livres by such a blow. Those who had kept their shares, or bought those of Danglars, considered themselves as ruined, and passed a very bad night. Next morning *Le Moniteur* contained the following:—"It was without any foundation that *Le Messager* yesterday announced the flight of Don Carlos and the revolt of Barcelona. . . . A telegraphic signal improperly interpreted . . . was the cause of this error." The funds rose by double the amount of the fall. This, reckoning his loss and what he had missed gaining, made the difference of a million to Danglars.[32]

The idea of transferring, with the help of the telegraph, not merely information relevant to the stock exchange, but money itself as well, quickly became imperative. The hundreds of billions of dollars that are transferred across the ocean daily at present are obviously not transfers of cash. They are, for anyone who cannot or does not want to give up thinking in terms of tangibles, particularly suspiciously abstract. They are free of any remnant of materiality; they are pure book-money: *nomen est omen*. Even the term book-money is a euphemism. Book-money has been surpassed by monitor-money. Marshall McLuhan pointed out long ago that, "Today, electric technology puts the very concept of money in jeopardy,"[33] because it deprives money of its last remnant of substantiality. Naturally, one could also turn this around and say: Electronic money brings the code of money to a certain extent back to itself by freeing money of its mistaken identity as something substantial. Money can be electronically digitalized these days[34]— to the point where the difference between information and money implodes. New digital media are not simply new protean forms of the same old money; they achieve, on the contrary, supremacy over money.[35] When money is transformed into the pure signs 0 and 1, this change of form implies "that the bits not only encode money in the same way they encode television or the telephone, but that they themselves *are* money and that money is a *code*. The exchange of commodities and of information, money and media merge, under these circumstances, into the language of machines. The economic category of value is absorbed by information value."[36] Small wonder that this is possible: value is always information as well. Valuables that are not known to be valuable are not, in fact, valuable.

How consequential such a transformation of the material of money, which itself is a simulation of limited goods, into the immateriality of its simulation can be, was demonstrated forcefully by the stock market crash of October 19, 1987. It was, as is well known, induced by computers. Computer trading has recently made it possible for Wall Street to establish the smallest variation in rates in real time, and, preprogrammed for particular changes, to react immediately with orders to buy or sell. The accumulation of preprogrammed orders led to recursive chaos effects. The stock exchange, an institution with a rich tradition of transforming chaos into structure,[37] experienced meta-chaos. It thereby became evident that stock prices increasingly react autopoetically to stock prices, and not directly to information from the "real world." In addition to that, however, another, more fundamental problem became evident:

> The relationship between "reality" and simulation achieves another vec-
> tor if we realize that the *real system*, to which the simulation refers as a
> *substitute*, is not the kind of "reality" we might think it is, not something
> we can touch or deal with in a material sense, but another "simulation,"

since it is something "untouchable," and there is only reference but no materiality. This "immateriality" of money, all the more the case without a gold standard, has its pendant in stocks and obligations of and for corporations whose value seems to be represented by the individual values of their distributed stocks. But this representation is only one of the market's perspectives on this particular business. This aspect of the market, being in itself constituted by a configuration of signifiers, is even more obvious in the dealing of futures of, for example, bananas that have not yet been grown. If this market is automatically handled with the help of simulation programs, we are finally confronted with the question of the constitutive gap between "reality" and simulations.[38]

This boundary, this gap, this intersection, or, platonically, this *chorismos* between reality and its simulation, or between being and appearance, vanishes vertiginously. On the day after the stock market crash of October 19, 1987, the world was not any poorer in real goods—though in unimaginable, unthinkable, and thus sublime (in the Kantian sense) sums of money, it was. It is surely no coincidence that the most famous theoretician of simulation, Jean Baudrillard, began his analyses as a theoretician of exchange and money. For in the medium of money, the two most important aspects of the concept of simulation coincide. Money is, firstly, an inconvertible copy of the world in terms of the scarcity of goods; the circumstance emphasized repeatedly by culture critics, that the confusion of the simulacrum of money with the real value of the desired commodities has become thoroughly common, offers compelling evidence for the thesis that there is a modern, exponentially growing problem of differentiating between being and appearance. Money is, secondly, quite apart from the problem of the fetishistic confusion of the literal and the figurative, the genuine, because calculable, object of computer simulation. The traditional medium of literature, which understood itself (with the help of the concepts "mimesis" and "ut pictura poesis") as a copy of the world and/or unpredictable simulation of the world, observes both rivals with as much attention as antagonism. Money and the new media, in close alliance, enchant the world more powerfully than poetry would ever be able to.

The Counterfeiters or the Money of Literature

Literature has always regarded money (and the new media in any case) with distrust. Indeed, rivalry rules the relationship between the media of money and literature (or, according to the early observation of one cynical contemporary of the postrevolutionary machinations after 1789, a disconcerted complementarity: "Poverty is the primary cause of the Germans' incredible desire to write."[39]). The rivalry between money and literature is a result of the closest, almost sibling-like proximity. The zenith of paper money and the zenith of literature in the epoch of the educated and prosperous middle class are of a piece. In his study *Money and Fiction*, John Vernon stressed this alliance. Money is not merely, more so even than love, the preferred and most common theme of the "realistic" literature of the nineteenth and twentieth centuries (thanks, above all, to mystery novels that never do without money, though occasionally without the intrigues of love, while the massive love literature almost always shares its focus with money—for example in the configuration poor servant girl/lord of the manor or modest nurse/well-established hospital administrator). Classic paper money is also closely tied to poetically imprinted paper through a deep structural cross-referentiality. "The transition from metal currency to paper money indicates a more general cultural shift that submitted immediate reality to a kind of semantic coding. . . . As money was becoming more fictional, fiction was becoming . . . more mediated, more representational, more omniscient—in a word, more realistic."[40]

Simultaneously with and yet independently of Vernon, Jean-Joseph Goux developed, on the basis of the French literature of the last two centuries, a similar (and yet in one important point precisely opposed) thesis. "There is a close sociohistorical correlation between the painterly or literary aesthetic founded on representative realism and the type of monetary circulation in which gold, as general equivalent, circulates in person— . . . the comparison confirms likewise the equally close correlation between the new aesthetic based on nonfiguration or abstraction and a type of economic circulation in which money is reduced to a 'token' that lacks any intrinsic value."[41]

The structural similarity of the arguments is obvious; the difference between the theses all the more penetrating. Vernon conceives of realistic literature as cultural compensation for the demands increasingly abstract (paper) money brings with it. Goux on the other hand understands money tied to the gold standard as the foundation of realistic European literature—he diagnoses "the strict correspondence between realistic literature and the circulation of gold."[42] Identity and difference of both theses can nonetheless be explained in terms of the two different intercultural contexts. England, quite simply, had more positive experiences with paper money than France did, where a fundamental distrust of money's illusion developed as a result of the quick collapse of John Law's experiment in paper money (1716) and the brief phase of the assignats following the French Revolution. On the basis of these experiences, the essentialist money-and-gold

paradigm persisted much longer in France (on into the times of de
Gaulle) than in the financial metropolises of London and New York.[43]

This circumstance surely contributed to the fact that literary sub-
versions (as in Gide's novel *The Counterfeiters* and even as early as
Zola's *The Money*) of the paradigm of substantial coverage (not just
of money but also of meaning and authority altogether) were more
militantly developed in France than in the Anglo-Saxon world, where
it has generally been the pragmatic preference to avoid the question of
adequate cover. In fact, Anglo-Saxon literature has tried to compensate
for the insufficient realism of paper money with its realism; French
literature, on the other hand, repeatedly points to the illusory quality of
the gold standard. Not without reason is Gide's novel *The Counterfeiters*
the terminus ad quem of Goux's brilliant analysis. It calls attention to
the fact that, not least of all because of the collapse of an essentialist
concept of value and money in nihilistic modernity, and given all the
questioning of a true correspondence between being and meaning,
forgery is unavoidable.

This insight—reluctant though one may be to acknowledge it—
cannot be escaped, even by a poet as conscious of tradition as Hugo
von Hofmannsthal. He composed, in 1890, "Verse, auf eine Banknote
geschrieben" {"Verses Written on a Banknote"}, with its many meanings. Hofmannsthal took the title and the money motif of his poem
from the deeply indebted Scottish poet Robert Burns, who, in 1786,
cursed money and actually wrote this poetic curse on a banknote:

> Wae worth thy pow'e, thou cursed leaf!
> Fell source of all my woe and grief!
> For lake o' thee I've lost my lass;
> For lake o' thee I scrimp my glass.[44]

There are many reasons why Hofmannsthal did not publish his
verses—one being that the title is literally nonsense. A poem with
so many letters would not fit on the largest of banknotes.[45]

> What you call mood, I know not
> And I am silent when someone speaks of it.
> There may be a surge of spring
> When verse weaves into verse and image into image,
> When deep in the heart it glows and froths and loves. . . .
> For me, it is never so good. Like froth, vanishing
>
> In the sunlight, my every dream image,
> Leaving a dull trembling from the force
> Of the melody I have heard in a dream. . . .

Was ihr so Stimmung nennt, das kenn ich nicht
Und schweige still, wenn einer davon spricht.
Kann sein, daß es ein Frühlingswogen gibt,
Wo Vers an Vers und Bild an Bild sich flicht,
Wenns tief im Herzen glüht und schäumt und liebt. . . .
Mir wird es nie so gut. Wie Schaum zerstiebt

Im Sonnenlicht mir jede Traumgestalt,
Ein dumpfes Beben bleibt von der Gewalt
Der Melodie, die ich im Traum gehört. . . .

Now and then it seems that literature, in this vanishing rapture, leaves us with something. In order to preserve in song and rhyme that which threatens to be lost in the "bustle of everyday life" with its "bewildering chaos," meaning needs a material form and substance that makes sure it does not, like speech and voice, scatter and vanish in the wind. And so Hofmannsthal develops a brief phenomenology of the materiality of poetic communication: one can write verses on wooden walls, on the bark of trees, in the margins of newspapers, on beer coasters and on unpaid bills. The most enigmatic surface, however, is a banknote:

And so I embrace inspiration's timid pledge
And it holds fast, the occasionally colorful trifle
A worthless toy, sometimes—rarely—more,
And write it, anywhere, in the newspaper's margin
On an empty page of Homer,
In a letter—(it is rarely very heavy). . . .

I have also written on a park bench,
On a stone by the spring from which she drank,
On colorful bows, sheer colorful verses,
On the trunk of a birch tree, shimmering white, shiny,
And most recently on a crumpled piece of paper
With matter-of-fact inscription, crinkled curlicues:

A scrap of debt, piled up by the state,
As it runs through thousands of hands,
Acquires bread for one, for another, pleasure,
And wine for one in which to drown his sorrow;
Longed for with everyone's first, last strength,
With cunning, in work, agony, passion.

So faß ich der Begeisterung scheues Pfand
Und halt es fest, zuweilen bunten Tand,
Ein wertlos Spielzeug, manchmal—selten—mehr,
Und schreibs, wo immer, an der Zeitung Rand,

Auf eine leere Seite im Homer,
In einen Brief—(es wiegt ja selten schwer). . . .

Ich schrieb auch schon auf eine Gartenbank,
Auf einen Stein am Quell, daraus sie trank,
Auf bunte Schleifen buntre Verse schier,
Auf einer Birke Stamm, weißschimmernd, blank,
Und jüngst auf ein zerknittert Stück Papier
Mit trockener Inschrift, krauser Schnörkelzier:

Ein Fetzen Schuld, vom Staate aufgehäuft,
Wie's tausenfach durch alle Hände läuft,
Dem einen Brot, dem andern Lust verschafft,
Und jenem Wein, drin er den Gram ersäuft;
Gesucht mit jedes erster, letzter Kraft,
Mit List, in Arbeit, Qualen, Leidenschaft.

This material, of all things, presumably so far-removed from poetry, permits the flash of insight that even the requisites of pantheism such as wood, leaves, and stone cannot offer. Money has, at the very least, this in common with literature: It condenses the infinite to one expression. It is "crystal clear" that nothing less than "human existence" lies before the poet, who, in order to grasp the meaning of this existence, turns a banknote with his verses into a particularly modern palimpsest and learns, in the process, that the banknote destroys the authority of his rhymes.

As if illuminated by a flash of the spirit,
I saw a wealthy throng, a world.
Crystal clear lay human existence before me,
I saw the magic realm, whose gates close
Before the accursed formula,
Of wealth's boundless, opulent hunting ground.

I thought of books, heavy with deep wisdom,
Wrenched from life's sea of anguish,
Of sounds, overheard from the spheres of dance,
The color glow of pictures, host of forms,
The goblet of wine from which inspiration rushes,
All traded in for the magic scrap.

Submissive strength, bent to hard work,
The kiss and passion of false love,
The hymn of joy and the arrow of wit,
What art and nature create in the contest
For sale! Everything for sale! Honor itself for sale!
For a note, a piece of privilege!

And my multitude of verses, so triflingly trite,
On this permit for boundless pain,
They strike me as sculpture and bough
On a sword's deadly polished steel. . . .

Und wie von einem Geisterblitz erhellt,
Sah ich ein reich Gedränge, eine Welt.
Kristallklar lag der Menschen Sein vor mir,
Ich sah das Zauberreich, des Pforte fällt
Vor der verfluchten Formel hier,
Des Reichtums grenzlos, üppig Jagdrevier.

Der Bücher dacht ich, tiefer Weisheit schwer,
Entrungen aus des Lebens Qualenmeer,
Der Töne, aus der Sphären Tanz erlauscht,
Der Bilder Farbenglut, Gestaltenheer,
Der Becher Weins, daraus Begeistrung rauscht,
All' für das Zauberblättchen eingetauscht.

Der harten Arbeit untertän'ge Kraft,
Erlogner Liebe Kuß und Leidenschaft,
Die Jubelhymne und des Witzes Pfeil,
Was Kunst und was Natur im Wettkampf schafft,
Feil! alles feil! die Ehre selber feil!
Um einen Schein, geträumter Rechte Teil!

Und meiner Verse Schar, so tändelnd schal,
Auf diesem Freibrief grenzenloser Qual,
Sie schienen mir wie Bildwerk und Gezweig
Auf einer Klinge tödlich blankem Stahl. . . .

The poet's horror at the power of paper money is the horror of the recognition of one's own distorted expression in the other's. Both the paper written on by the poet and the paper imprinted by the state have more in common than their authors would prefer. Neither is covered, both rely on appearance, both condense, both drive a morally questionable enterprise and a universal exchange of essentially everything (money turns everything into a commodity, literature thematizes everything, regardless of its knowledge of the subject matter), both simulate (or pretend), both are elements of the Gutenberg Galaxy, and both are becoming anachronistic epiphenomena in the age of media. Of course, money is money, even in electronic or plastic form. Literature, however, when it leaves its paper medium, stops being literature; it rediscovers itself (or not) in the form of a television program, radio show, or film.[46] Information that counts, and payments that count, (are) no longer fit for/on paper. The museum of paper money and the museum of poetry can be cost-effectively brought under one roof and preserved by a computer. This museum will pay tribute, however, not just to paper money and to literature but also to the epoch of the transcendental authority (of words) and the authority of the transcendental.

5

"To Torment from Afar"—
Money's Relational Mania

As Hofmannsthal's "Verses Written on a Banknote" illustrates, money and literature maintain strange relationships to and with each other. What they have in common, once one begins to examine this question, is limitless; their rivalry just as much so. Gottfried Keller's fantastically clear-sighted story *The Misused Love Letters* {*Die Mißbrauchten Liebesbriefe*} established this even earlier and more forcefully than Hofmannsthal's subtle verses. Literature and money also share something that became fashionable in nineteenth-century realistic literature: they establish and regard relationships in ways that can stop common sense in its tracks. In his piece "Nur keck!," Johann Nestroy coined the famous expression the "categorical imperative of money," by which "even you are forced to marry Fräulein von Jahrzahl, a distant relative of your uncle."[1]

To have an affair or affairs—that is (like the similar formulation "to have relations or a relationship") a phrase of many meanings. In the singular it usually means an erotically exciting connection, in the plural on the other hand, an economically worthwhile one. The two conceptions, according to a literary motif that is as old as it is widespread, tend to be mutually exclusive. He who is involved in an erotic affair must be able to afford it psychically, socially, and of course economically as well. For he will neglect, for the sake of a love that requires expenditures, those useful connections that further him professionally and financially. In view of this incompatibility between expenditure and profit-producing affairs, even a hero as lovable as Botho von Rienäcker (in Fontane's novel *Delusions, Confusions* [*Irrungen, Wirrungen*]) must renounce his affair and come to terms with the web of relationships that money, in all its cold objectivity, establishes. "Rienäcker," as the Prussian officers debate his case at the club, "[is] in a tight corner." "What kind of a corner?" "He's supposed to get married." "You call that a tight corner? Come on, Wendell, Rienäcker's in a much tighter corner than that. He gets nine thousand a year and spends twelve. That's the tightest corner of all, at least tighter than the marrying corner."[2]

In a class-conscious marriage the corners lose their edge. For in such a marriage, the value systems inherent in the two conceptions of affairs coincide: within this framework, relations that do not exclude profitable relationships are preferred. Admittedly, this is at the price of establishing an exclusive relationship that is based not on love but on the spirit of money, and thus one that is not really so exclusive. Botho's future mother-in-law's letter to his mother leaves no doubt about this, and his mother, quoting it extensively, makes numerous references to these relationships in a letter to her son, who is not favorably inclined toward marriage:

> Does the House of Rienäcker . . . perhaps believe that a fortune, which is constantly decreasing like the Sibylline Books (where she got that simile, I'll never know), is getting more and more valuable? Käthe is going to be twenty-two, has become quite the sophisticated young lady, and with the help of an inheritance coming from her Aunt Kielmannsegge, has at her disposal a fortune whose interest is probably not considerably less than that of the entire principal of the Rienäcker heaths, their Eel Lake included. Such a young lady is not to be kept waiting. (p. 90)

Botho von Rienäcker does not keep her waiting long. For if he were to refuse such an advantageous relationship, he would soon have to declare bankruptcy and lose his property, because the value of the commodity physical labor, which would then be all he had to offer, would never in the world be enough to balance his annual discrepancy between debit and credit: "Who am I? An average person from the so-called upper sphere of society. And what am I capable of doing? I can break in a horse, carve a capon, and know how to gamble at cards. That's all. And so I've got a choice between a circus rider, a headwaiter, or a croupier. At best you can add on a trooper, if I feel like joining some sort of Foreign Legion. Then Lene can come along as Daughter of the Regiment" (pp. 90–91).

Even a fine Prussian nobleman like Botho von Rienäcker is forced to see that he is not master of, but rather a pawn in, his relationships, that his way of life is not just dependent on his affair but also on his affairs: confusions, delusions. Of all the forces that are capable of establishing relationships, money (in the so-called modern age) is the most profane, most common, and most powerful. Money establishes intersubjective relationships that would otherwise never come about. Money establishes in addition relationships that, even if not desired by both sides, have authority. Friendships can be withdrawn, relationships with relatives can be neglected, relationships with colleagues may be stabilized by maintaining distance. Relationships, in contrast, that are established by money and money alone cannot simply be broken off. Legal persons are free of business associates and relationships with creditors once they have declared bankruptcy; for natural persons, as everyone knows, there is (as of yet[3]) no right to declare bankruptcy. Middle-class (legal) subjects cannot go bankrupt: that would contradict their idealistic self-concept much too crassly, and shamefully call attention to the fact that the transcendental subject is disguised in the form of a commodity.[4] That one can dissolve a marriage but not a debtor-creditor relationship; that money dictates whom it is that one simply cannot escape; that money, in spite of or because of its personally indifferent objectivity, establishes relational mania between life histories, ways of life and entire cultures, and does so in truly psychotic dimensions—that is a major theme of the great prose literature of the nineteenth century, if not its central one.

Madame Bovary has two brief affairs and a good, long-term relationship with the merchant and moneylender Lheureux. The unfortunate debts that bind her to Lheureux (*nomen est omen*), who specializes in the business of good business, correspond precisely to the debt of good fortune she incurs through her extramarital relationship.[5] Emma Bovary, or her lovers, are thoroughly capable of breaking off her erotic affairs, but they cannot put an end to her financial dependence. To the horror of the readers of the time, the adulteress is ruined not by her sins but by her debts. No passionate lover but instead an utterly improbable man whom she has never even met personally, to whom Lheureux has nonetheless sold her promissory notes, and whom she will meet for that reason, breaks her heart: "One day, however, she was visited by an ill-kempt individual, red-faced and bald, who said he had been sent by Monsieur Vinçart of Rouen. He pulled out the pins fastening the side pocket of his long green frock coat, stuck them in his sleeve, and politely handed her a document. It was a note for 500 francs, signed by her, which Lheureux, despite all his promises, had endorsed over to Vinçart."[6] When Emma Bovary seeks out Lheureux, questions him, and finally begs him for some time to pay off her debts, he appeals to the authority of money's objective and unrelenting obligations—he, too, has financial obligations:

> Lheureux sat down in his broad, rush-bottomed armchair. "What's new?" he asked her.
> "Look!"
> And she showed him the document.
> "Well, what can I do about it?"
> She flew into a rage, reminding him that he had promised not to endorse her notes. He admitted it.
> "But my hand was forced: my creditors had a knife at my throat."
> "And what's going to happen now?" she asked.
> "Oh, it's very simple: a court warrant, then execution; there's no way out." (p. 270)

The reordering of personal relationships in accordance with monetary obligations fascinated the realistic literature of the nineteenth century to an immense degree. Debts and the chain of relationships they engender constitute the focus of novels as different as Keller's *Der grüne Heinrich* {*Green Henry*}, Dostoyevsky's *Crime and Punishment*, Gustav Freytag's *Soll und Haben* {*Debit and Credit*}, and Jeremias Gotthelf's *Geld und Geist* {*Wealth and Welfare*}. These novels also share a tendency to stylize money's web of relations into a specifically modern equivalent of traditional religious ties. The protagonists of these novels are forced to learn that their release (absolution) from the binding power of the absolute is counterbalanced by money's powerful entanglements. In the nineteenth century, money finally achieves the status of modernity's god and becomes the primary medium of social synthesis (in small as well as in the largest contexts: personal, institutional and intercultural contacts and obligations have been mediated ever since, one and all, by money). Money's power to bind and relate replaces, from this point on, religion's power to do so. Sinful believers turn into creditors and debtors.[7] "With God" reads the motto at the front, not of the hymnal, but of the private book of the firm T. O. Schröter, into which, in the end, the middle-class hero of Freytag's *Debit and Credit* marries. The last sentence of this book of success, transforming the traditional book metaphor of the Holy Scripture into that of the business- and passbook, carefully fashions the economy of debit and credit as the authentic heir of theology. "The old diary of his life is at an end, and henceforth, ye gracious house-sprites, in your private book will be inscribed, 'With God, his future career of Debit and Credit.' "[8]

In assessing the profits and losses of modernity, freedom of belief surely belongs in the profit column. Forced religious affiliation is, all in all, no longer a problem of functionally differentiated societies but rather an individual issue. Whenever societies that have been violently forced into the process of modernization (whether Iran, Serbia, or the Soviet Union) collapse, however, the collective religious orientation makes an oddly inflated resurgence. After the collapse of currencies and states, people, particularly those who have never seen the inside of a church or mosque and have nearly forgotten that they were orthodox Christians, Catholics, Shiites, Druze, and so on, discover their confessions once again. A mild case of such a new orientation to one's confession could be observed in the collapsing German Democratic Republic. For a few months during the changeover, it was governed by pastors and members of the Presbytery (Stolpe, Eppelmann, Schorlemmer, de Maizière, Gauck among others). The *anschluss* to a territory with a functioning currency put a quick stop to this form of politico-theology and the politics of confession.

There are many indications that in functionally differentiated societies, overly complex secular sets of relationships that engender the universal monetization of modern societies have replaced relationships required by religion (for example that of the Trinity). As early as 1784, in his "Ideas for a Universal History with Cosmopolitan Intent," Kant made reference to the interweaving of time and space that arises with the expanding circulation of money.

> Eventually, even war will become a very dubious enterprise, not only because its result on both sides is so uncertain and artificial, but because in its aftermath the state consequently finds itself saddled with a growing debt the repayment of which becomes undeterminable. At the same time the effect of each impact of a government upon other governments in our continent, where the states have become so very much linked through commerce, will become so noticeable that the other states, compelled by their own danger, even when lacking a legal basis, will offer themselves as arbiters and thus start a future great government of which there is no previous example in history. (pp. 128–29)

Kant's postbellum Maastricht dream of a monetarily interwoven order is much more to the point than Georg Simmel's quasi-pantheistic philosophy of money. Simmel speaks, in language full of religious undertones, of the "all-embracing teleological nexus" in which the "various elements of our existence" are "placed" and in which

> no element is either the first or the last . . . since money measures all objects with merciless objectivity, and since its standard of value so measured determines their relationship, a web of objective and personal aspects of life emerges which is similar to the natural cosmos with its continuous cohesion and strict causality. This web is held together by the all-pervasive money value, just as nature is held together by the energy

that gives life to everything . . . [and this] results in a relationship between all [forms] and makes each of them a condition of any other.[9]

In a natural cosmos ordered by a strict causality, everything stands in relationship to everything else; in the second nature, "each form with every other" and every individual with everyone else—and precisely with those, too, with whom one would rather not associate. Money establishes impartially coercive relationships between all elements of a society as well as among societies as a whole. In contrast to the natural web of relationships, nonetheless, the monetary chain of relationships is characterized by a delusional impulse. The term relational mania {*Beziehungswahn*} was, if not coined, at the very least defined as a distinct diagnosis by Ernst Kretschmer in 1918: patients who compulsively and "inflatedly" relate neutral events to themselves. This is in fact the case with monetary sets of relationships. The events of New York's, Tokyo's, or Frankfurt's stock exchanges, in and of themselves neutral (they did not happen expressly to annoy or unsettle every single one of us), may not involve one from the start—and yet these events stand in an obvious and perceptible relationship to each and every individual, who therefore has good reason to feel expropriated. In the case of relational mania, according to Kretschmer, there is an unhealthy, if "relatively benign"[10] increase in sensitivity of reaction that can, of course, escalate to paranoia. In the case of the relational mania of money, there is (in comparison to pre-modern mass psychoses such as witch mania {*Hexenwahn*}) a relatively benign increase in intersubjective and intercultural interconnectedness—a unique escalation without a subject, of which the subject does not exactly know how it should, can, and will end.

There is an outstanding poetic illustration of Simmel's philosophical-monetary thesis of the "continuous cohesion" that money engenders. It is by Gottfried Keller and might be superior to the philosophical text in complexity, as it associates the internal dynamic of monetary connections with misuse right in its title: *The Misused Love Letters*. The story, which was published in 1874 in the cycle of novellas *The People of Seldwyla*[11] {*Die Leute von Seldwyla*}, treats misuse in its many aspects. Misuse occurs because, firstly, a hard-pressed wife forwards her husband's love letters to another man, secondly, because the husband had written the letters not out of love for his wife but as a means of her aesthetic education to become his muse, and, thirdly, because the frugal correspondent and salesman appended to his pseudo love letters downright profane postscripts whose sole purpose was bill collection.

The story of relational mania, as it unfolds at the intersection of the erotic, aesthetic, and monetary flow of information, is suggestive and yet highly complex. The very first sentence leaves no doubt as to the protagonist's priority in economic and erotic relationships: "Viktor Störteler, known to everyone in Seldville as Viggi Störteler, lived a comfortable, methodical life as the proprietor of a profitable freight forwarding and general goods agency and the possessor of a pretty, healthy and good-tempered wife. The latter, apart from her very pleasant person, had brought him quite a fortune, . . . her money had been a great help to him in expanding his business" (*The Misused Love Letters*, p. 13). Wider and broader yet than the world of money he comes to know so well during his business trips is the world of the poetic spirit. In order to make his earthly fortune complete, the successful and victorious salesman (Viktor-Viggi) has pledged himself to literature and, under the pseudonym of "Kurt of the Forest" {"Kurt vom Walde"} has written himself into the network of relationships in a bustling literary industry.

Highly characteristic of this poetic world is that its poets reject the profane interrelationships established by money—and that which is rejected reasserts its authority all the more forcefully. The salesman gives himself over to his passion for beautifully arranged letters in order to rise above the profane logic of the numbers found on coins and notes. Yet the logic of money catches up with him over and over again—and particularly when, during business trips, he enters into that other, more distant sphere and visits, as is his habit, a café frequented by literati. The colleagues whom he meets there one day are easy to identify as literati because they are talking about the poetic spirit's Other, namely, the poetic spirit of trade:

> For it was not long before the conversation was dominated by words like royalty, publisher, clique, coterie, and all the other things that arouse the wrath and occupy the imagination of such people. There was a booming and buzzing as though twenty people were speaking, and a glorious mutual recognition could not be long delayed. Then this one turned out to be Guido von Strahlheim, that one Oskar Nordstern, and a third Kunibert vom Meere.[12] Then Viggi . . . hesitated no longer and shyly slipped into the conversation the fact that he was known as Kurt vom Walde. He was known to everyone . . . for these gentlemen . . . devoured on the spot everything written by people like themselves . . . —not out of sympathy, but out of a strange watchfulness. (p. 16)

Strange watchfulness is in any case required whenever relation-ships are controlled in ways other than as they appear to be. An active relational mania characterizes the new poets' association that those present agree to form, and its members carefully observe each other: everyone is someone other than he seems to be, every has a name different from the one found in his identification, and everyone is out for something other than what he says he is. Faced with such poetic-economic enchantments, the poetic dilettante and salesman Viktor, too, decides to enter into another relationship to himself and to become someone definitively other than himself. In order to do this he needs another, a muse. And since muses are not available in abundance, he decides to make his "good-natured" wife into another, into a, into his, muse. He therefore subjects her to a program of aesthetic education that is supposed to turn her into his "inspiration," who thereafter will urge him on to unheard-of acts of writing. The requirements of this program, which Gritli perceives as degrading, do not even stop when Viktor goes on an extended business trip. For Störteler invents a "splendid way of tormenting her from a distance" {"aus der Ferne zu quälen"}: he forces a sentimental exchange of letters on his wife. "Instead of his trip setting her free from a nightmare—an idea that was new and confusing for her—she had a new bogey to expect in the shape of the mailman" (p. 29).

The first letter that the postman of her nightmares hands over is evidence of the fact that the poetic salesman has not only split his wife's personality in two, but that he, as his self's Other, is condemned to live in two worlds. "Dearest friend of my soul, When two stars kiss two worlds perish" (p. 29), his horrified wife is forced to read right at the start of the letter. That two worlds are not destroyed, that on the contrary one way of life and one individual is splitting in two when a salesman decides to take Schiller's program of aesthetic education seriously and become a whole human being, is made clear by the similarly doubly split letter. Its boundaries, moreover, are burst by no less than two postscripts. In the first, Viggi develops the program of aesthetic education and therefore the rules that mass-produce letters like the present one: "P.S. . . . You can see that one single motif runs through these lines: the idea of separation. Now express your feelings on this subject and introduce a new theme . . ." (pp. 29–30). The second postscript reacts to the fact that, without notice, the aesthetic program has turned into an economic one. "N.B. We will write about business and domestic matters on a separate sheet like this, so they can be kept apart" (p. 30). The message to be detached from the rest was all too profane as well: "I met young Müller from the Burggasse and he asked me to lend him 40 francs, in the presence of other passengers and so casually that I couldn't refuse point blank. I know his parents still have a batch of rapeseed, so send our clerk over to buy the rapeseed on account. But do it right away, before they know the lad owes me money, otherwise we shall get neither rapeseed nor money" (p. 30).

Gritli, after a brief shock, reacts to the love letter that is split and misused in so many ways with her own rupture—and in perfect correspondence to the economy of her strength. She feels herself incapable of bringing love, the aesthetic education of a muse, and economics under one cover. She will not, however, allow two worlds to be destroyed as a result of this calamity. In the good, Swiss way, she takes account of her assets. And with relief, she remembers her neighbor, a visionary with a passion for looking at women. She hands lightly edited transcriptions of her husband's letters over to this schoolmaster, who is considered rather dim-witted by the people of Seldville. "So she went and copied out her husband's letter, changing the words as though a woman were writing to a man" (p. 32). Everything goes as planned. The schoolmaster believes his quiet love requited, gives up his long-held atheism based on the wickedness of women, and does his part—he answers with enthusiasm.

Gritli's deception works (at first!) splendidly. She forwards the schoolmaster's letters intended for her to her distant husband, not without the obligatory split, namely, the economic postscript from her own hand: "Our clerk went to Müller's on the Burggasse right away today and bought the rapeseed; but scarcely two minutes later, before we had time to bring them here, they sent for a delivery of 100 blue whetstones. In the meantime they must have heard from their son that he borrowed 40 francs from you; because when we sent for the rapeseed they apologized and said that without her husband's knowledge the wife had sold it to a farmer two days ago. So now they have the 40 francs and the whetstones as well" (p. 35).

Viktor is so intoxicated by the erotic-aesthetic part of the letter with its simulated authenticity, that he is hardly annoyed by his wife's sober, thus all the more authentic, postscript. The boundaries between authentic and fake blur from the very beginning: "I forgot to sign the first letter. Write under it very carefully Kurt v. W." (p. 36). The wife, who is supposed to sign for her husband using his pen name, and, also at his behest, give up her "prosaic domestic name" (p. 38) and sign the misused love letters with "Alwine," is now punished for her small transgression. She becomes, that is to say, the secret secretary for two men who exchange letters with each other in a mad rush, wounding both her soul and her writing hand: "Therefore letter after letter was written so that the quills flew. Gritli grew pale and ailing, because she had to write like a court clerk; and the schoolmaster became as thin as a lath and didn't know whether he was standing on his head or his heels, because on top of everything he was still writing with deep passion and could not figure out what was happening at all" (pp. 40–41). Thus unfolds a postal love-madness, a word Heinrich Heine insightfully called a pleonasm: "Love-madness! Pleonasm! Love is madness" {"Liebeswahnsinn. Pleonasmus! Liebe ist doch schon ein Wahnsinn."}. The love-madness of Seldville, however, may be so called without suspicion of redundancy, because it corresponds precisely to the economic madness that the postscripts record. The point of comparison for the two forms of madness is easy to find: the love letters have as little backing as the demands for money (and delusions in general). For this very reason, an ever-accelerating accumulation of debits and credits is necessary in order to make their backing seem secure. It is not long before Viktor realizes that he will not be able to collect his debts. This, however, brings him down just a little; his poetic productivity and the aesthetic development of his fine-tuned interiority seem more than adequate compensation for the growing liabilities.

Too steep a rate of growth and acceleration, however, can come to no good end. And so it is here. The postal-economic-aesthetic-erotic productivity with its recursive slides cannot stave off the collapse of all involved. Despite his pleasure in the business of tormenting from afar, Viggi cheerfully returns home one day, dreaming of the fame the publication of his mad correspondence will bring him. He has a title in mind, one more appropriate than he could imagine. "Fundamentally . . . it doesn't need any particularly ingenious title. The simplest will be the best. A combination of two names produces a fine-sounding word: *Kurtalwino, Letters of Two Contemporaries.* That's good, very good" (p. 41). The joke is, in fact, a good one: in contrast to neurotics, the paranoid tend not to disguise their compulsions completely but to distort them into images that are very close to a transcription of the truth.[13] Viktor/Viggi/Kurt vom Walde writes Gritli/Alwine/Wilhelm. The masculine form of the title hardly disguises the homosexual implications[14] of this exchange of love letters between two men who are (unknowingly) using a (female) go-between: the art-pair Kurt and Alwine combine to create a single (grotesquely productive and yet unfruitful) hermaphroditic salesman, Kurtalwino.[15]

Upon his return to the place of his origin, this happy pen-hermaphrodite sees, with horror, how completely he, the thoroughly deceived deceiver, has been misused. He runs into Wilhelm, who, hurrying to avoid him, leaves a stack of letters under the fir tree that had provided shade for his dreams of love. Indiscreetly Viggi leafs through Wilhelm's letters, which seem uncannily familiar to him. Nothing is incorrect in the analysis that he then carries out (except perhaps that Viggi has not yet taken cognizance of insightful publications in gender studies and thus confuses sex and gender). Viggi recounts (almost) as if he were reading:

> "[A woman] takes pure and honest expressions of feeling, her husband's letters, twists the sex and juggles the names and, parading in stolen feathers, uses them to incite her infatuated comrade in sin. Thus she elicits from him similar outpourings burning with sinful ardor and wallows in them. Her poverty of spirit lives like a vampire on alien riches.[16] But, not content with that, she twists the neck of the sexes again, changes the names once more and craftily deceives her unsuspecting husband with the newly acquired love letters, once again decking out her hollow but cunning head with alien feathers. Thus two unacquainted men make fools of themselves. . . . I believe that any outsider who could look at this fine story objectively would say he had come upon good material for—"
>
> Here he broke off and shook himself, because he began to get the feeling that he himself had become the subject of a real story and he didn't want that. (p. 44)

The author senses that he, himself, is becoming a character in a story in which he has become entangled and whose author he does not know. The telling subject (*sujet de l'énonciation*) has become the subject under discussion (*sujet de l'énoncé*);[17] the despotic master of the discourse has become the object of Seldville's gossip. The end of the story is quickly told (though only by overlooking many noteworthy motifs). Viggi seeks comfort from and falls for an artistic figure who possesses just one attractive attribute: her name—Käthchen Ambach. Her real name (if names can be real at all[18]) is irresistibly close to the pseudonyms of the literati circle: Ambach = am Bach, or by the brook. The couple Kurt vom Walde and Käthchen Ambach are the joke of Seldville, whose citizens, in addition, invent a masculine form of Käthchen's name: Kätter. This men-pair succumbs completely to the madness of poetry without backing, or cover, and coauthor books no one wants to read: libri. Gritli, however (after the divorce and a long moratorium rich in privation), gets together with Wilhelm who, for his part (a remarkable motif!) stops teaching, stops introducing children to literacy, stops worshiping "the alphabetic gods in his encyclopedias" (p. 34) and, in general, taking books so seriously, in order to devote himself to farming and having children: liberi instead of libri.[19]

Naturally, the fruitful pair prospers economically, since they live for the most part in economic self-sufficiency and can therefore avoid debts. The other pair, however, is ruined by its poetic-economic relational mania. In the end, Viggi cannot even afford the postage stamps necessary for continuing his poetic and universal correspondence:

In secret they (Viktor and the literati) despised each other, and Viggi, who had formerly led such a simple and carefree life, was now plagued not only by worries and complications, but also by absurd passions and the torments of aroused and impotent ambitions. He was already having difficulty in paying the postage on all the meaningless letters, the printed or lithographed circulars, manifestos, and prospectuses that daily flew hither and thither and were worth less than nothing. (p. 61)

The "meaningless," uncovered paper of those literati who see themselves as the avant-garde in the second half of the nineteenth century (thus at the time when *Fleurs du mal* and *Madame Bovary* were scandalous new publications) is worth "less than nothing." Literature that is worth less than nothing is damaging. It robs even men named Viktor of their victory and of their varied good fortune: that is, of their financial fortune, of their potency (admittedly, the marriage to Gritli was also childless), and even of their capacity for reasonable acknowledgment of the reality principle and the boundaries that separate being from appearance. In the intoxication of a postal-poetic-economic rush approaching an all-encompassing mobilization, the salesman and poet's ability to make distinctions vanishes. The lovers, in contrast, who narrowly escaped the victory march of money and books, opt for a return to the land with their "well-brought-up children" (p. 94), for a slow pace and "enthusiastic tranquility"[20]—an option for the atheist and enlightened ex-schoolmaster that makes no secret of how provincially Swiss an answer to modernity it is.

The novella of the 1848 revolutionary and archliberal Gottfried Keller is brilliantly constructed and remarkably aggressive, even contemptuous of a literature that sees itself as progressive. The sarcastic critique of a self-referential and autonomous literature is particularly noteworthy because it criticizes, as early as 1874, tendencies that are only fully developed in the avant-garde literature of the twentieth century. An unpretentious waiter (Keller![21]) with a poet's past, in one of the literati cafés that Viggi likes to visit so much, did more than just play with his own name, Georg Nase, permutating it into Georg d'Esan. He revolutionized poetry as well by turning it into something completely self-referential: "I had nothing to write about except writing itself, so to speak. When I dipped the pen in the ink I wrote about this ink. . . . I wrote about the word writer itself; I was dissatisfied with it and, not knowing it was an old and genuinely German word, proposed all sorts of better alternatives, such as inkman, pen artist, bookman, bookmaster and so on" (p. 20).[22]

The ex-writer who delights in confession is—like Viggi and his colleagues—an "utter scoundrel" because he repeatedly takes out loans that he cannot cover (p. 21). One provocative aspect of Keller's novella is that it does not hesitate to use culturally conservative clichés, and yet cannot repress the insight that it is futile to expect words and coins to be covered. It is especially surprising that Keller's novella does not simply (in the Romantic and critical-enlightened tradition) oppose beautiful poetry and the prose of economic obligation, but rather (in opposition to conservative *and* progressive repressions) reveals the economic, the aesthetic, the postal, and the enlightened endeavors (literacy!) to be elements of a modern project of universal mobilization. This modern mobilization leads to a "reign of interdependency" {"*Verflechtungsordnung*"} (Norbert Elias) that simply demands too much of the antiquated human being.

This universal mobilization of modernity stands under the sign of money. It is difficult to dispute that money makes more rational and less bloody forms of management, exchange, calculation, and analysis possible than other forms of the exchange of goods (such as plundering, theft, sacrifice, extortion, and even potlatch). It is difficult to dispute though easy to repress the insight that the flip side of the form of rationality induced by the medium of money[23] is nothing other than the overly complex relational mania that money, in spite or because of its systematic indifference (with respect to partners, the timing, and the objects of an exchange), establishes. Money interweaves individuals, groups, cultures, regions, religions, epochs, and economic patterns that might be better off interacting with each other as little as possible. The simple ideal of leaving each other alone (like neighbors who do not like each other but still offer the conventional greeting), and, when coming into contact with something foreign, acknowledging its rules and experiencing it as something "wonderfully foreign" {"schöne Fremde"}, is impossible to achieve under the conditions of an extensive circulation of money.

To offer an illustration for this thesis: It is an effect of a relational mania that invades everywhere, when in all corners of the earth (regardless of cultural, religious, ethnic, or other characteristics) the economy must be managed according to the imperatives of one unified world market. And to have experienced, for the first time, the (temporary) superiority of the Japanese economy on a large scale, may help the western European states as well as the USA to understand what it means to be economically and monetarily dominated on the world market. It is a monetary relational mania that brings antagonistic cultures such as the American and the Iranian into contact with each other at all. Tranquil poverty of association could even be the slogan of a politics and an economy that is slowly realizing that internationalization, far from the solution to all problems, is the main component of major political and economic problems. Reduction of the paranoia-inducing intensity of interaction or radical exclusion from world society (with unpredictable, for example, radicalizing, effects of terrorism)—this seems to be the alternative of choice. In a confounding way, total isolation is emerging the world over as an unintended consequence of the international monetary connection mania—in the form of slums. The slums of large South American cities and the slums of the world's metropolitan areas are without relationship in every sense of the word: they have no administration, no system of education or of justice, no currency, and so forth. If it did not sound so cynical, one would have to say they do not even stand in the relationship of exploited-exploiter to the rest of the world. In these areas that are literally cut off from the world there are no natural or human resources worth exploiting.[24] The desert grows.

To personalize the thesis of the relational mania of money: It is a temporary relational mania when large numbers of people, in spite of the obviously fragile state (or, as one says, precisely because of this fragility) of the world (of the states, the currencies, the joint-stock companies, and so on), purchase life insurance beyond their thirtieth year—and thereby not only fail to recognize that one simply cannot be sure of one's life, but also make large amounts of capital available that can hardly be sensibly controlled and that possibly induce the very insecurities for which it was purchased to guard against. Beyond the boundaries of space, time, and culture, money sets a "compulsion of connection" {"*Verknüpfungszwang*"} in motion[25] that surpasses the mantic compulsions of connection of premodern cultures in every way. Money is, in its hardly escapable ambivalence, ir-/rational.

6

Money's Sex—

Money Reproducing, Grandchildren,
Compound Interest

Kurtalwino, the ex-salesman and neo-writer with the androgynous name from Keller's wonderful novella *The Misused Love Letters*, remains barren. Neither is Kätter am Bach or Käthchen Ambach, despite her flowing *locus-amoenus*-name, fit to be the maternal source of a family tree. And the two comic figures leave neither prosperity nor posterity behind. They do leave a pile of letters that come together in senseless and insensate signs. Gottfried Keller has interwoven the motifs of barrenness, the impoverishment of the initially well-off salesman, and the inflationary quantities of signs intricately, if not without malice (which can be tolerated because he did not except himself). In doing so, he revived and skillfully modulated an old but somewhat obscure motif: the one that expresses the alternative "aut liberi aut libri / et liberi et libri." Whether a man should make books *and* children or books *instead of* children—this question haunted monks and scholars, and not just them.

Today this alternative is as out-dated as the Latin language in which it was given its classic formulation. In its specifically modern incarnation, the alternative is whether a productive man should make money or children. The exalted, realistic prose of Charles Dickens and Fyodor Dostoyevsky have, despite many differences, one motif, repeated to the point of mannerism, in common: many of their protagonists' obsession with money is the flip side of their antagonism toward children. Mr. Quilp in Dickens's serial novel *The Old Curiosity Shop* (1840–41) can

91

only conceive of procreation as a financial event. Postmodernism can easily be conceived, from an erotic-economic perspective, as the epoch in which not only men but also women face the question: money or kids. According to one malicious comment,[1] the ancient Greek ideal of pederasty finds its postmodern incarnation in the "cool, slender, pin-striped" type of woman targeted by an ad for the German Federal Bank. Anorectically free of all the attributes of the potential mother, steeled in body-sculpting studios, boy-women, too, make money these days, instead of children. If they hook up with men who want the same thing, these universally emancipated Kurtalwino-couples of postmodern renewal are called "dinks": double income no kids.

Making children, making money: the sexual and specifically phallic connotations of the fiscal abstraction cannot be overheard. Those who have a pile of money are potent and solvent and can indulge themselves in an injection of money. Those who have a fat wallet can get back on their feet and satisfy creditors after their enterprise goes belly-up. When the going gets rough, they are ready: their business runs as if greased. The bull market is on their side and at their command. As early as 1509, the novel of *Fortunatus* gives broad and extreme shape to the motif of the phallic power of money. It couples the sexual and financial potency of its protagonist closely. Just three of many relevant instances will be mentioned.

Firstly, his phallic vigor is more important to the young Fortunatus than money. Because he is threatened with castration, entangled as he is in the intrigues of the court and the darling of the women, he flees the count's castle.

> For he well knows that no woman would love
> a castrated man,
> since it is entirely against her nature

> Wann er wisse wol das kain frauw kainen verschnitten oder
>   hodenlossen man
> nit lieb müg gewinnen
> wann es gantz wider ir natur ist.
> (*Fortunatus*, p. 400).

Secondly, the woman he meets deep in the forest after his escape, the very Lady Fortune {"iunckfraw des glücks"}, loans him a magic sack and obligates him, on each anniversary of his receiving it and with the help of its unceasing monetary potency, to bring about a good marriage for a "poor virgin" (p. 431). The inexhaustible potency of the sack has just one limitation. Lady Fortune tells Fortunatus that the sack will lose its magic if there are no male heirs.

Thirdly, the novel invokes the traditional Danae motif twice. Both Fortunatus's loyal servant as well as Fortunatus's son Andolocia pour a shower of coins onto the lap of a woman:

> Now the countess was angry that Fortunatus was taking her
>   youngest daughter,
> who was her favorite,
> but when {Fortunatus's servant} poured a thousand crowns onto her
>   lap, she got over her anger.

> Nun was die graeffin unmuotig das Fortunatus die jüngsten tochter
>   genomen het
> wann sy ir die liebste was
> do ir aber lüpoldus die tausend ducaten in iren geren schutt do ließ
>   sy den unmuot faren.
> (p. 474)

Fortunatus's son behaves similarly. In order to convince the princess Agrippina of his financial potency, Andolocia bids her lift her skirt and then proceeds to pour one thousand crowns right out of his sack and onto her lap:

> to keep his word, Andolocia said to the beautiful lady,
> "now lift your skirt," and he pulled his sack out,
> let Agrippina see it and said,
> as long as I have this sack
> I will never lack for money, and he poured a thousand crowns onto
>   her lap and said,
> these are a gift for you,
> and if you want more I'll give you more."

> auff die guotte wort sprach Andalosia tzu der schoenen junckfrauwen
> "nun heben auff eüern geeren" und zoch herauß seinen
>   glückhafftigen seckel
> lyeß den Agripina sehen und sprach
> die weil ich disen seckel hab
> so gebrüst mir kains gelts vnnd zalt ir also tausent Cronen in ir
>   schoß vnnd sprach
> die seyen eüch geschenckt
> und wellen ir mer haben ich zel üch mer.
> (p. 522)

With the sons of Fortunatus, the family will die out and the power of the sack will expire. To make a giant leap from the first great modern novel of money to late modern cartoon characters: Uncle Scrooge Mc-Duck has no problems with heirs or offspring. Nonetheless, Walt Disney saw the kinship between money and potency clearly and expressed it with powerful effect. He shows, with remarkable regularity, the childless and money-hungry multi-billionaire Uncle Scrooge, ducktail erect, diving into the pool of his treasury. Refreshed, Scrooge McDuck then gets to work on his one and only, infinite project: to turn a lot of money into even more money. Where the children come from, with whom he occasionally comes into contact, is not quite so clear. In the world of ducks the avuncular advances to the fundamental ethnological structure. Since cartoon characters are timeless and immortal, profound questions such as where babies come from are irrelevant. When everyone lives forever, human procreation is unnecessary. But that of money obviously not. It multiplies without limit.

The widely evident phallo-monetary semantics and iconography are joined by another, more perverse—the anal semantic field surrounding money[2]: *pecunia olet*, the shitter of ducats {*Dukatenscheißer*[3]}, to do his business, to have a pile of money, to be filthy rich, and so on. The two semantic fields seem to contradict each other. Yet they come face-to-face with a *logos spermaticos* essentially incarnate in money, which creates splendid wealth from that which is the most worthless and despicable of all. The brilliant code of money and the filthy turd: their point of comparison resides in the paradox, as Freud's brief but highly controversial study "Character und Anal Erotism" illustrates, that intrinsically worthless money has become the most valuable thing there is. In Freud's words: "It is possible that the contrast between the most precious substance known to men and the most worthless, which they reject as waste matter ('refuse'), has led to this specific identification of gold with faeces."[4]

Freud and the psychoanalytical tradition refer only implicitly to additional correspondences: both gold and excrement are at home under the earth. Plutonian caves are obviously indispensable in histories of money.[5] Whether Fortunatus, the Romantic visitors to mines, Richard Wagner's Alberich, or Goethe's Faust, they all—and many, many others in search of gold and money—must descend into caves and the domain of the Mothers. There lies the shining gold that must be brought to the surface, there lies the Plutonian-uterine secret; and that is where earthly remains, complete with excrement and filth, must disappear in order to avoid offending the senses. Freud likes to point out that in ancient Babylonian mythology, the concept "mammon" meant nothing other than "excrement of hell." What actually constitutes wealth, what and when something is really valuable ("my kingdom for a horse"), whether something shall be the very last or the very first, where wealth originates, how to explain increase (whether of a population or a pile of money), how to find rhyme or reason in the phenomenon of increase: these are the questions that have animated myths, stories, and theories from the beginning. Whoever wishes to answer them must also answer the question of how it is that something (whether a life span, a population, or a fortune) decreases, ends, stops, disappears. And they will have to investigate caves: a cave is, after all, both place of birth and grave.

Surely the most ambitious attempt to answer these questions in their entirety is Goethe's *Faust*. To praise it (especially among Germanists) is not particularly original. To suggest that Goethe interwove the oldest layers of Plu- and Platonic cave mythologies with modern money motifs[6] is less common. Even the newer and highly productive turn to the theme of money in *Faust*,[7] however, has failed to note that Goethe offers a psychosexual and historical theory of money that deserves attention not only for its poetic charms, but for its profound diagnostic acuity as well. Goethe's drama of Faust modulates the question, original in every sense of the word, of "what, deep within it, binds the universe together" toward the belated question of the sex of the money that binds the modern world together, by continually teasing it apart/differentiating it.

To open up this dimension, one need only review the basic plot of the drama of Faust, often enough overlooked in favor of the countless thematic subtleties. A clever mind, not completely satisfied by the study of science, has turned to the magic of alchemy. He has a burning interest in the question of what binds the universe together and, more precisely, where wealth originates. The attempt to answer, at any price, this most basic question of all (mythological-metaphysical, psychological-sexual, and sociological-economic) Enlightenment, leads the childless Faust away from the world of scholarly books and, via the stations of drunkenness (Auerbach's "Wine-Cellar") and orgy ("Walpurgis Night"), to Gretchen. To be more precise: to Gretchen's dungeon-cave and, previous to that, to Gretchen's bosom and to Gretchen's lips that speak the golden words,

> Wealth is what's wanted,
> only gold counts.
> And if we're poor—too bad!

> Nach Golde drängt,
> Am Golde hängt
> Doch Alles. Ach wir Armen!
> (2802–4)

and ask the Gretchen-question of how the rich lover regards religion.

Liberi/libri: Faust and Gretchen do not, as everyone knows, become parents. An attempt follows, in *Faust II*, to fathom the essence of origin and propagation. And look at that: the alchemical promise of turning something worthless into something of the highest value is economically-fiscally fulfilled. Not fulfilled, however, is Faust's wish that the propagation of a child follow the propagation of increased economic value. No convincing success is granted the movement toward the Mothers. Things are even more troublesome for the only other two children who turn up in this powerful drama than they are for the child of Faust and Gretchen. Homunculus and Euphorion are in each case testimonials, but they are not, as is the usual way of testifying, begotten.[8] And they who appear, until it seems that they are truly becoming, are sentenced to a swift end. Faust, his ambition to become a father once again thwarted, throws himself all the more obsessively into the one project that offers reliable prospects for increase: the economic-monetary endeavor. Goethe's *Faust* is the drama of a man with a fast-paced career (from scientist via manager of finances and the military to infrastructure industrialist), who, instead of books, wanted to create creatures and become creator, and who nonetheless leaves just one thing to posterity (to whom?): money.

Just how drastic and sarcastic this plot is would be even more glaring if Goethe had dared to publish the addenda to the "Walpurgis Night" scene in *Faust I*. They leave no room for doubt that the "double theme . . . of gold and sexuality rules the 'Walpurgis Night' scene."[9] Mephistopheles promises Faust "a bit of theft or lechery" {"Ein bißchen Diebsgelüst, ein bißchen Rammelei"} (3659),[10] thus Faust knows what awaits him on the mountain with the eloquent name of "Brocken" {crumb, piece, mouthful}. The following lines from the version printed in 1808, too, which Albrecht Schöne's groundbreaking study on the "Walpurgis Night" scene inexplicably does not comment upon, maintain a systematic sexual-monetary double entendre. Faust, who is on the way to Gretchen during the satanic prophecy of a "glorious Walpurgis Night" and will be stopped by her brother Valentine, wants to bring his beloved an expensive gift. And so he asks Mephistopheles:

> *Faust.* Perhaps by then that treasure will have risen
> whose aura I see gleaming, off back there?
> *Mephistopheles.* It won't be long before you have the pleasure
> of raising that small pot from out the ground.
> I happened to peep into it the other day
> and saw some fine Bohemian dollars.
> *Faust.* No piece of jewelry, no ring,
> with which to prettify my mistress?

> *Faust.* Rückt wohl der Schatz indessen in die Höh',

Den ich dorthinten flimmern seh'?
Mephistopheles. Du kannst die Freude bald erleben,
Das Kesselchen herauszuheben.
Ich schielte neulich so hinein,
Sind herrliche Löwentaler drein.
Faust. Nicht ein Geschmeide? Nicht ein Ring?
Meine liebe Buhle damit zu zieren.
(3664–71)

Instead of jewelry, Faust comes across "Bohemian dollars" {"*Löwen-taler*"}—silver coins with a coat of arms of the lion, of which Goethe had read, in Praetorius's *Anthropodemvs Plutonisvs* of 1666, that they glimmer from within the earth and emerge from its secretive depths already bearing imprints.[11] This idea bears the stamp of Pluto—he is, after all, considered the god of the wealth that is secured and hidden in the underworld. Already in the first part, Goethe's *Faust* drama shifts from jewelry, or gold, to Bohemian dollars, or money. Nor is this the end of the chain of substitutions.

Mephistopheles answers Faust's question, "No piece of jewelry, no ring?" as follows: "I think I did see something in it / that rather looked like strings of pearls" {"Ich sah dabei wohl so ein Ding, / Als wie eine Art von Perlenschnüren"} (3672–73). A truly diabolical remark. Faust of course will see a "dead-pale lovely girl" that "looks like my own dear Gretchen" on whose "lovely neck / there is as ornament a single scarlet thread" {"schönen Hals / [muß] ein einzig rotes schnürchen schmucken"} (4203f.). "It is a magic image, a phantom without life" {"Es ist ein Zauberbild, ist leblos, ein Idol"}, replies Mephistopheles, using the very words that later, in *Faust II*, will characterize Helena as well. As an apparition, Gretchen is a typological prefiguration of Helena. The "string of pearls" suggests the words that Mephistopheles, singing in front of Gretchen's window, adds to his "song of morality." "Rather . . . like [a] string of pearls," the words of the song replace the Bohemian dollars, which had in their turn replaced the piece of jewelry Faust had wanted. A substitution with an increasing degree of abstraction and a deadly concrete result: jewelry, Bohemian dollars, Mephistophelian verses, a string of pearls of sorts, Gretchen's execution—the "scarlet thread" of the magic image is "no thicker than a knife."

The restrained sexual allusions of the words that accompany Faust, with his treasure to his treasure, in the pleasure of the anticipation of something rising and gleaming, become more pronounced in the "Walpurgis Night" scene. Mephistopheles and Faust join the crowd that orgiastically rushes toward the mountain peak and Satan's mass.

The words signaling the obscene (the "gaping whole" {"ungeheuren Loch"} which calls for a "fitting cock" {"rechter Propf"}) cannot be overheard, even in the printed version.[12] The riddle, too, that is supposed to be solved during the Walpurgis Night is clearly named. It is the riddle of propagation and reproduction. It is a question, after all, of how "to make your own small worlds inside the great one":

> *Faust.* Those crowds are surging on toward Satan;
> the answer to many riddles is surely there.
> *Mephistopheles.* But many riddles, too, are set.
> Great folk may like the noisy life,
> we'll be quite cozy in this quiet spot.
> Besides, it is an ancient practice
> to make your own small worlds inside the great one.
> I see some nice young witches over there,
> stark naked next to elders wisely veiled.
> Be pleasant to them, simply for my sake;
> a little effort gets you much amusement.

> *Faust.* Dort strömt die Menge zu dem Bösen;
> Da muß sich manches Rätsel lösen.
> *Mephistopheles.* Doch manches Rätsel knüpft sich auch.
> Laß du die große Welt nur sausen,
> Wir wollen hier im Stillen hausen.
> Es ist doch lange hergebracht,
> Daß in der großen Welt man kleine Welten macht.
> Da seh' ich junge Hexchen nackt und bloß,
> Und alte die sich klug verhüllen.
> Seid freundlich, nur um meinetwillen;
> Die Müh' ist klein, der Spaß ist groß.
> (4039–49)

In order to participate orgiastically in the rite that solves this riddle, Faust and Mephistopheles forge ahead, in male-bonding unity, toward the Brocken. Thus the first part of the *Faust* drama emphasizes, subtly yet clearly (though not clearly enough for the all too chaste philological admirers of Goethe's, with their scholarly disdain for despicable mammon), a motif that the second part then draws out: the motif of the homosexual aura of money, which reproduces itself through interest, without having to get (heterosexually) involved with the Other. In the words of Heinrich Mann in his novel *In the Land of Cockaigne*, "So your bank note has had little ones."[13] Not for the first time, in his enamored homage to the angel at the end of *Faust II*, do Mephistopheles' homosexual inclinations (which find an illuminating parallel in that of Peter Schlemihl and the "gray man" of Chamisso's narrative—see chapter 12) become obvious, when it is said:

I love to look at them, these loveliest of youths;
what makes me hesitate to curse them?
And if I let myself become infatuated,
who will be henceforth called a fatuous fool!
Confounded rascals—though I hate them,
I find them only too attractive.

· ·

Another thing! Without offending decency
you could wear less; long pleated robes are prudish—
They're turning—see them from the rear!—
the rascals really whet my appetite!

Ich mag sie gerne sehn die allerliebsten Jungen;
Was hält mich ab daß ich nicht fluchen darf?—
Und wenn ich mich betören lasse
Wer heißt denn künftighin der Tor?
Die Wetterbuben die ich hasse
Sie kommen mir doch gar zu lieblich vor.

· ·

Auch könntet ihr anständig-nackter gehen,
Das lange Faltenhemd ist übersittlich—
Sie wenden sich—Von hinten anzusehen!—
Die Racker sind doch gar zu appetitlich.
(11762–68; 11797–800)

This final outing of Mephistopheles is not all that surprising. Homogamous kisses and other anal travesties of Christian liturgy play a decisive role in Mephistopheles' enthusiasm as early as the Walpurgis Night.[14] Mephistopheles' homosexuality would hardly deserve more than passing interest if it were not so closely tied to mammon. Mephistopheles characterizes "the immortal part of Faust," in utter profanation, as the "prey" and the "treasure" of whom the angels who "dallied at the graveside" have robbed him {"an dieser Gruft genascht"} (11827–29). Mephistopheles, if not a second Pluto, is at the very least (as in other contexts the Romantic investigators of caves, with their interest in the world of mining) highly fascinated by the modern underworld of money, the foundation of the world. He is driven to the heights of the Brocken because he hopes to be able to fathom the profound riddle of this underworld there. The words with which Mephistopheles leads/(seduces) Faust to the Brocken are also of similar phallic-Plutonic ambiguity:

Get a good hold of my tail![15]
Here's a sort of half-way peak
that affords a marvelous sight:
mammon glowing in the rocks.

Fasse wacker meinen Zipfel!
Hier ist so ein Mittelgipfel,
Wo man mit Erstaunen sieht,
Wie im Berg der Mammon glüht.
(3912–15)

Thus says Mephistopheles to Faust. Even such a sovereign commentator as Albrecht Schöne takes refuge with respect to these lines in a question mark: "*Half-way peak*—for mid-mountain range?" "Tail" and "half-way peak" can hardly be misunderstood if they are identified with the phallic tail and the occasionally towering male mid-body.

Schöne passes over Mephistopheles' "tail," unlike "half-way peak," without comment for a good reason: it needs no explanation. Yet the circumstance that tail, half-way peak, and mammon are brought and thought together in these verses, and not just here, requires explanation and interpretation. The motif is obviously important to the text, as the following verses demonstrate: "Lord Mammon has, you must admit, illuminated / his palace lavishly for this occasion!" {"Erleuchtet nicht zu diesem Feste / Herr Mammon prächtig den Palast?"} (3932f.). Schöne's commentary is typically prudish here as well: "*Lord Mammon:* here personified, in contrast to 3915 (as in Matthew 6:24 and elsewhere), illuminates the *palace* of mountains for the celebration of the witches arriving in flight. The common reference, since Morris, 1901, to Milton's *Paradise Lost I*, 670–717 (where Mammon directs the devils to expose veins of gold, melt them down, and erect the scaffolding for a palace for Satan out of it) contributes little to an understanding of the text." Exactly. One only need remind Albrecht Schöne of his own thesis, that the "double theme . . . of gold and sexuality rules the 'Walpurgis Night' scene" in order to understand the function of this motif. Mephistopheles' tail leads Faust to the peak, since not just witches and devils, but Lord Mammon and Dame Baubo have also arranged a meeting.

A Voice. There's ancient Baubo coming alone,
she's riding on a mother sow.
Witches. All honor, then, where honor's due!
Dame Baubo, come and lead our crew!
A good fat sow with dame on her back,
and witches will follow all in a pack.

Stimme. Die alte Baubo kommt allein;
Sie reitet auf einem Mutterschwein.
Chor. So Ehre dem, wem Ehre gebührt!
Frau Baubo vor! und angeführt!

Ein tüchtig Schwein und Mutter drauf,
Da folgt der ganze Hexenhauf.
(3962–67)

The ancient Baubo and personified mythical Vulva (she is to be found remarkably often on early coins[16]) leads the Nordic witches in their dance. This feminine group lines up with the one-half of the choir on the peak and, together with the other, masculine half of the choir, pays homage to Satan. This motif of the unity divided into the two halves of the sexes, so clearly enacted, alludes to Aristophanes' well-known story in Plato's *Symposium*,[17] according to which the initially androgynous human being was split into man and woman by jealous gods, and they have longed to reunite as the animal with two backs ever since (N.B. a motif that Goethe often adapted in esoteric ways, above all in his *Wilhelm Meister*, which not coincidentally has so many Amazon figures: the initials of the hero, W and M, already mirroring one another, point to woman and man[18]). Schöne's cleverly reconstructed Walpurgis Night addenda, hardly publishable during Goethe's life, make it clear where the climax of the scene lies: in the Satan worship that is spelled out and the orgy into which it develops. The actual point of this composition, however, consists of the two choir halves, the billy goats and the nanny goats,[19] not merely because they desire the opposite sex, but because they desire gold and money orgiastically as well. This lesson stands in the middle of the Satanic liturgy that celebrates "The trace / of everlasting life / of deepest nature" {"Spur / Des ewigen Lebens / der tiefsten Natur"}:

> *Satan turned to the right* [thus to the he-goats]
> To you it [the life of the deepest nature] gives two things
> So splendid and great
> Gleaming gold
> And the womanly womb.
> One procures
> The other devours
> Thus happy is he who
> Wins both.
> ·
> *Satan turned to the left* [thus to the she-goats]
> For you there are two things
> Of delightful glory
> Glowing gold
> And a gleaming tail
> Thus you women know
> To delight in gold

And still more than the gold
To treasure the tails.

Satan rechts gewendet [also zu den "Böcken"]
Euch giebt es [das Leben der tiefsten Natur] zwey Dinge
So herrlich und groß
Das glänzend Gold
Und der weibliche Schoos.
Das eine verschaffet
Das andre verschlingt
Drum glücklich wer beyde
Zusammen erringt.
. . . .
Satan lincks gewendet [also zu den Ziegen]
Für euch sind zwey Dinge
Von köstlichem Glanz
Das leuchtende Gold
Und ein glänzender Schwanz
Drum wißt euch ihr Weiber
Am Gold zu ergötzen
Und mehr als das Gold
Noch die Schwänze zu schätzen.[20]

What flows from Goethe's pen here is surely unusually drastic—and
unusually sharp-witted. For a significant asymmetry is built into these
satanic words. The men are supposed to desire the gleaming gold *as
much* as the womanly womb: "Thus happy is he who / Wins both."
The "women," on the other hand, are advised, "still *more* than the
gold / To treasure the (glowing) tails." Gleaming gold serves the men
as a phallic medium that "procures" and creates when it gets involved
with a womanly womb that devours it. It does not serve the "women"
as a "procuring" medium, but rather as "delightful" ornamentation
that deserves less attention than the phallus, which, as a result of its
power of procreation, truly deserves to be "treasured." In short: the
relationship of the sexes to gold and money is completely different. So,
too, is it more than just one more effrontery when Goethe has, of all
people, a "young girl" fail to understand this satanic lesson, so obvious
to the he-goats sitting to Satan's right.

> *Girl.* Oh no! the gentleman there speaks so curiously,
> Of gold and tail and gold and womb,
> And it seems that everyone is happy!
> Do only grown-ups understand?
> *Mephistopheles.* No dear child, just don't cry.
> For if you want to know what the devil means,
> Just reach into your neighbor's pants.

Mädchen. Ach nein! der Herr dort spricht so gar kurios,
Von Gold u Schwanz von Gold u Schoos,
Und alles freut sich wie es scheint!
Doch das verstehn wohl nur die Großen?
Mephistopheles. Nein liebes Kind nur nicht geweint.
Denn willst du wissen was der Teufel meynt,
So greife nur dem Nachbar in die Hosen.[21]

. . . and not into his wallet. For the "women," gold remains a second-rate attraction; they are attracted above all to the first nature. For men, in contrast, gold and mammon are (at least) as important as the womanly womb. Not just the phallus, money/gold, too, procures—if the phallus or the money/gold get involved in the womanly womb or the matter (mater) in mammon's cave, respectively.

The point of comparison between the womanly womb and mammon is not difficult to determine. Both are cavities of increase, of procreation, or of payment of interest. He who as a man/he-goat wins both money and the womanly womb may therefore count himself lucky. He will be lord of the miracle[22] of wealth and increase. With these motifs, Goethe takes up the strands of an old theological-monetary discussion (that surely evokes mythological images as well: Zeus pouring himself onto Danae's lap in the form of a gold rain). The theological point, in the meantime, is that the satanic words addressed to the "women" thoroughly correspond in content (naturally not in style) to elements of the theological tradition. It is, to be precise, firmly established in this tradition that the natural power of propagation takes absolute precedence over that of money—indeed, that money, when it seems to propagate itself, makes a mockery of the divine creation, and of the procreative power of the human being as well.

"Nummus nummum non gerit" or "Nummus non parit nummos": with these apodictic forumlae, Thomas Aquinas long ago summarized a long discussion on money and interest.[23] Money cannot beget money. Scholastic theology can appeal to canonical biblical passages in its judgment of interest. The famous prohibition against interest in Deuteronomy 23:19–20 provides an example: "Thou shalt not lend upon usury to thy brother; usury of money, usury of victuals, usury of any thing that is lent upon usury. Unto a stranger thou mayest lend upon usury; but unto thy brother thou shalt not lend upon usury: that the LORD thy God may bless thee in all that thou settest thine hand to in the land whither thou goest to possess it." There is another in Exodus 22:25: "If thou lend money to *any of* my people *that is* poor by thee, thou shalt not be to him as an usurer, neither shalt thou lay upon him usury."

The difficulties occasioned by the prohibition of interest (quasi-"officially" rescinded for the first time in 1543, when Karl V allowed merchants of the Netherlands loans with interest) as economic forms became more complex, as well as the ways implicit in it for getting around the dysfunctional precepts, are skillfully portrayed by Thomas Mann in *The Holy Sinner.* In the chapter that plays with the child/interest motif with virtuosity, precisely titled "The Money-breeding" {"Das Heckgeld"}, it is evident that one can charge interest, if not to one's fellow believers, at least to "others," in full knowledge of its perverse implications:

> "Brother, I, your Abbot, have here fairly rich capital and orphan-money in gold marks, seventeen in number; it has been given over to me for safe keeping not that I should merely put it in the chest as caput mortuum, but in order to make profit from it. Now it is said a pious servant shall not bury the pound God entrusted to him, but rather make it fructify. And yet, when one thinks twice, usury is not the Christian's business and is a sin. In this dilemma, what do you advise me to do?"
>
> "That is quite simple," replied Chrysogonus. "You give the money to the Jew Timon from Damascus, with the beard and pointed hat, an exact and reliable man, well versed in usury. He deals with nothing but money in his bank of exchange, and has a look-round in the money world you wouldn't believe. He will send your sum if possible to Londinium in Essex, that it may work there and make profit, interest and compound interest; if you leave him your capital long enough, he will make you a hundred and fifty marks out of your seventeen."
>
> "Is that sooth," asked the Abbot, "does he know how to milk time like that?" (Thomas Mann, *The Holy Sinner,* pp. 104–5)

One can describe modernity, from this perspective, as the epoch that, in an economic-monetary sense, no longer recognizes the difference between ethnic or religious "brothers" on the one hand and all "others" on the other. When "all men become brothers," all men become others.

There are prohibitions against interest in Islam that are structurally similar to those of Judaism and Christianity. The Koran forbids "living off interest" in part 3, section 2, verse 275: "Those who live off the interest on loans will never stand up, except in the way those whom Satan knocks down with a fit rise up again. . . . Yet God has permitted trading and forbidden taking interest." Whether the Arabic word for interest, *riba,* refers to all interest or just usurious interest, is a matter of controversy. The passage in part 4, section 3, verse 130 can be understood as a prohibition not against interest altogether, but against the usurer: "You who believe, do not live off usury which is compounded over and over again . . . ,"[24] thus warning against high interest and compound interest. Section 102 warns against acquisitiveness in general, or "piling up":

> The mutual rivalry
> For piling up diverts you
> Until ye visit the graves.

In many Islamic countries yet today, large amounts of wealth (such as bridal gifts) are kept in jewelry in order to avoid the accumulating and trading of capital.

The themes of the Jewish-Christian-Islamic critique of interest are quite similar. Thomas Aquinas summed it up: "Now money, however . . . was invented chiefly for exchanges to be made, so that the prime and proper use of money is its use and disbursement in the way of ordinary transactions. It follows that it is in principle wrong to make a charge for money lent, which is what usury consists in."[25] The exchange function of money is never criticized in the theological tradition. On the contrary, Aristotle celebrated it as a guarantor of fairness and social reciprocity.[26] Money's participation in preserving and increasing value is rejected by the religious tradition, with particular objections; firstly, that money that restlessly breeds money fails to observe the Sabbath; secondly, that money loaned in exchange for payment of interest appropriates time and therefore God's property (insofar as money, to use the words of Thomas Mann's abbot once again, "milks time"); and, finally, that artificial money as the essence of the second nature is "unnatural" when it propagates itself.

This argument does not originate with psychoanalysts and psychohistorians prone to overinterpretation, but with Aristotle: "For money was intended to be used in exchange, but not to increase at interest. And this term interest, which means the birth of money from money, is applied to the breeding of money because the offspring resembles the parent. That is why of all modes of getting wealth this is the most unnatural."[27] The theological tradition is closely tied to Aristotle's argument: "Money cannot bear fruit in and of itself, the fruit originates elsewhere," according to Bonaventura, and Thomas von Chobham completes the thought: "Sleeping money bears no *natural* fruit, the grapevine is *naturally* fruitful."[28] If money seems, nonetheless, to multiply, this increase must be "contra naturam"—just like homosexuality. "The fruit originates elsewhere. . . ." Interest is, according to the classical association that has now been for the most part driven into the unconscious, the (perverse) offspring of money that becomes perverse when it is presumed to be more than a medium of exchange, when it is presumed to multiply.[29] The Japanese language makes no secret of these associations: the word "rishoku" (earning money) stems from "shoku" (procreation), thus "rishoku" means the sexual event in the procreation of money; "kinyu" (the circulation of money) means erotic "merging" ("yu") through "money or gold" ("kin"); the Japanese word for phallus ("kintama") means literally "money or gold-ball"; in a novel by Ihara Saikaku from the late seventeenth century there is repeated play with the alternatives of generating children or money.[30]

Goethe is not the first to offer a literary adaptation of the theological tradition of rejecting the (homosexual) money-breeding money. One need only remember the thirtieth song of the *Inferno*, in which the liar Sinon, who convinced the Trojans that the wooden horse was a sacred relic of the gods, and the counterfeiter Master Adam, who counterfeited Florentine coins for the Lords of Romena, bait one another. "My words were false—so were the coins you made" ("S'io dissi falso, e tu falsati il conio," XXX, 115),[31] shouts Sinon at Master Adam, master of coins, and hits him on the roundly swollen belly that has turned the counterfeiter and reproducer of money into a caricature of a pregnant woman. Gide's novel *The Counterfeiters* takes up this Dantesque motif and skillfully highlights the homoerotic components of the reproduction of money, or counterfeiting. In a lyrical outburst of contempt, Ezra Pound less ingeniously highlights the "contra naturam" motif of money's increase: interest, for him always usurious (*usura*), is the perverse child of perverse money, which dries up the true fertility of the first nature.

. . . .
with usura
seeth no man Gonzaga his heirs and his concubines
no picture is made to endure nor to live with
but is made to sell and sell quickly
with usura, sin against nature,
is thy bread ever more of stale rags
is thy bread dry as paper

. . . .
Usura is a murrain, usura
blunteth the needle in the maid's hand
and stoppeth the spinner's cunning.

. . . .
Usura rusteth the chisel
It rusteth the craft and the craftsman
It gnaweth the thread in the loom
None learneth to weave gold in her pattern;

. . . .
CONTRA NATURAM

They have brought whores for Eleusis
Corpses are set to banquet
at behest of usura.[32]

Pound intensifies Shakespeare's ingenious motif to the point of crude militancy. For Shakespeare had already provided Shylock, in *The Merchant of Venice*, with an antinatural aura of the perverse[33] in that he acts as if "barren metal" could propagate itself. Says Antonio to Shylock:

If thou will lend this money, lend it not
As to thy friends—for when did friendship take
A breed for barren metal of his friends—
But lend it rather to thine enemy
Who, if he break, thou may'st with better face
Exact the penalty. (1.3.127–32)[34]

"A breed"—this is a "hatch, brood, increase;" "to breed" means "to hatch out, to have offspring." This is precisely what money cannot do. The idea that something is not right when cold metal propagates itself is firmly anchored in popular belief as well. Names such as "Brütpfennig" {breeding penny} and "Heckpfennig" {hatching penny} are revealing. "Wechseltaler, Teufelsgeld, Hecktaler, Brütpfennig, Heckpfennig" {changing talers, devil's money, hatching talers, breeding penny, hatching penny} are mentioned in the *Wörterbuch der deutschen Volkskunde*, where it is written that, as early as the tenth century, "There is evidence of a widespread belief in money that never runs out, but miraculously propagates itself (breeds). The devil, a water sprite, or the Wandering Jew procures it during the first night of the New Year. Money capable of breeding must be old, found, or it must carry the number seven. Following every payment and exchange, it returns to its owner. Changing talers bring good luck."[35] And later disaster—they cannot be kept free of satanic associations.

None other than Mephistopheles, whose interest in mammon and money is already established in the first part of the *Faust* drama, hatches the plot at the beginning of *Faust II* to have money turn into hatching money (it is well known that this is one of Marx's favorite expressions) and thereby overcome the serious crisis of state, finance, and debt. He does this with striking emphasis on the men "that nature has endowed with mighty intellect."

Mephistopheles. Where in the world is something not in short supply?
Someone lacks this, another that, but here the lack is money.
Of course you can't just pick it off the floor,
but Wisdom's skill is getting what's most deeply hidden.
In mountain veins and in foundation walls

you'll find both coined and uncoined gold,
and if you ask who will extract it, I reply:
a man that nature has endowed with mighty intellect.

Mephistopheles. Wo fehlts nicht irgendwo auf dieser Welt?
Dem dies, dem das, hier aber fehlt das Geld.
Vom Estrich zwar ist es nicht aufzuraffen;
Doch Weisheit weiß das Tiefste herzuschaffen.
In Bergesadern, Mauergründen
Ist Gold gemünzt und ungemünzt zu finden,
Und fragt ihr mich, wer es zutage schafft:
Begabten Mann's Natur- und Geisteskraft.
(4889–95)

The arrangement of motifs is related to that in the first part of the *Faust* drama.[36] There, too, the discussion is about that which "the earth coughs up," "Bohemian dollars," about procuring and creating. Paper money {*Scheingeld*} is supposed to find cover in the essence of profound existence: in the riches that have not yet been raised or born, in mountain veins and foundation walls. When appearance corresponds to being, when paper money is covered by matter or at least seems to be, it is because the principle of reproducing being and appearance has not been discovered. In order to gain credibility for his suggestion for increasing wealth miraculously through the invention of paper money, Mephistopheles prompts the court astrologer to say the following golden words that culminate in notable homage to "erudite" men with productive and creative powers:

Astrologer (with Mephistopheles prompting).
The Sun himself is gold without alloy,
his herald, Mercury, will serve if kindly paid;
Dame Venus has already cast her spell upon you,
who see her lovely face at dawn and dusk;
chaste Luna, who's erratic, does have whims;
Mars's power threatens you, although he does not smite.
And Jupiter is still the brightest star,
while giant Saturn seems remote and small.
The latter is, as metal, not much venerated
and has, despite its density, but little value.
What's certain is that skies will shine
when Sol and Luna, gold and silver, are conjoined;
all other things are then obtainable,
palace and park and rosy cheek and pretty breast,
and they will be provided by the erudition
of one with power none of us possess.

Astrolog spricht, Mephistopheles bläst ein:
Die Sonne selbst sie ist ein lautres Gold,
Merkur der Bote dient um Gunst und Sold,
Frau Venus hat's euch allen angetan,
So früh als spät blickt sie euch lieblich an;
Die keusche Luna launet grillenhaft;
Mars trifft er nicht so dräut euch seine Kraft.
Und Jupiter bleibt doch der schönste Schein,
Saturn ist groß, dem Auge fern und klein.
Ihn als Metall verehren wir nicht sehr,
An Wert gering, doch im Gewichte schwer.
Ja! wenn zu Sol sich (Luna fein) gesellt,
Zum Silber Gold, dann ist es heitre Welt,
Das übrige ist alles zu erlangen,
Paläste, Gärten, Brüstlein, rote Wangen,
Das alles schafft der hochgelahrte Mann,
Der das vermag was unser keiner kann.
(4955–70)

Those are remarkable words. The erudite man, the very one who is an expert in the quasi-alchemical art of making worthless paper breed real assets, appearance breed being, and banknotes true wealth, "provides" it all: palace and park and rosy cheek and pretty breast. There is a strange philosophical peculiarity about the central verses quoted here that name the economic conditions for a world in which "skies will shine." "What's certain is that skies will shine / when Sol and Luna, gold and silver, are conjoined" (4965f.). Thus Mephistopheles, through the mouth of the astrologer and with recourse to an anachronism, makes sense, for himself and his audience in the throne room, of the prototypical modern event: the marvelous propagation of wealth. The highly praised *Faust* edition of Albrecht Schöne, which follows the manuscript not of Goethe's hand (such a thing does not exist), but of his copyist John's, and to which Goethe occasionally made corrections, reproduces the version that at first and second glance makes little sense: "What's certain is that skies will shine / when Sol and Jupiter, gold and silver, are conjoined."

Peter Michelsen's excitement over this unorthodox (or perhaps philologically all too orthodox, because all too constrained by principle) reproduction of the text is understandable:

You cannot believe your eyes; there [in Schöne's edition] it stands [Jupiter instead of Luna]![37] In his annotations to this passage, Schöne explains that the last authorized edition and all subsequent editions, in "unnecessary deviation from H" [the manuscript], print "Luna" instead of "Jupiter."

Who can have occasioned this deviation? It is certainly unthinkable that Göttling or Riemer interfered with the text to this extent behind Goethe's back. The "deviation"—that is to say the correction . . . — originates from Goethe himself of course! And now Schöne—true to his principles of editing, according to which the version as it stands in the manuscript must somehow be forced to make sense—continues, in explanation of his perplexing version: Like the moon ("Luna"), "Jupiter" was associated (besides with tin) with "silver" in the alchemical doctrine of correspondences. When the latter, as well, conjoins itself with "Sol" (with "sun," with "gold"), then "gold and silver are conjoined." An inquiry to Joachim Telle, an expert on alchemy, established that this explanation is off track. In the usual allegory of Sol (man/gold)-Luna (woman/silver), a substitution of the masculine Jupiter for Luna would be unthinkable. It is also contradicted by the context that makes it obvious that Goethe was playing with the sequence of correspondences between the seven planets/metals. ("Diplomatik als Editionsprinzip," p. 703)

Michelsen's objections to Schöne's reproduction of the text and the commentary that explains it away by virtue of a truly forced twist of logic is obviously justified (though not, as a consequence, his defense of an edition of texts based on combinations of different manuscripts). Indeed, there is more to the philologists' argument than Michelsen explains. It is admittedly difficult for Schöne's critics to explain why it says "Jupiter" instead of "Luna" in the hand-written text. "Now one can always speculate on how John could have stumbled upon the non-sensical transcription 'Jupiter.' " Michelsen forgoes, true to the spirit of the philologist, this speculation. That John, Goethe's loyal copyist, so thoroughly misunderstood Goethe as to hear "Jupiter" instead of "Luna" from the divine mouth of the master is, in view of the great phonetic difference between the names, hardly a plausible explanation. All the evidence suggests, instead, that Goethe in fact preferred, at first, the semantically highly improbable text variant that has Jupiter and Sol conjoining, and then—much more conventionally—let sun and moon, Sol and Luna, find each other.

The difference between these two variants is obvious: in one two men conjoin (Sol and Jupiter), in the other a man (Sol) and woman (Luna). *Die Sonne, der Mond, le soleil, la lune, solus, luna,* Mr. Sunshine and Mrs. Moon: as everyone knows, German grammar deviates in gender attribution of sun and moon from practically all other languages. Goethe's original dictation confuses accepted gender assignments; it deviates from convention to a high degree (and obviously not just from those of the alchemists) and is for that very reason highly and provocatively enticing—and immanently appropriate. For the men-pair Faust-Mephistopheles, initiated on the Brocken into the deep secrets of Baubo and mammon, and complaining on the way to the top that the moon was shining imperfectly—

> How drearily with its belated glow
> the red moon's crescent now is rising
> and gives us such poor light . . .

> Wie traurig steigt die unvollkommne Scheibe
> Des roten Monds mit später Glut heran,
> Und leuchtet schlecht . . .
> (3851–53)

—tried out, here, that which was learned among the she-goats and he-goats. And this means Mephistopheles, who whispers his wisdom to the astrologer, advocates in fact a theory of purely masculine money-procreation. "Don't lay your hands on me, disgusting females!" {"Vom Leibe mir, ekles Weibsgeschlecht!"} (5646).

This masculine fixation on money finds its embodiment in the figure of Sir Greed as portrayed by Mephistopheles.[38] It leaves no room for doubt as to its gender identity and sexual disposition. Once again "barren metal," speaking in plain language, is quoted: "Don't lay your hands on me, disgusting females!" For Mephistopheles, the only object of desire that counts is "the lure of gold" {"des Goldes Reiz"}— with which the next line, in the original, rhymes: "I am Sir Greed, am masculine" {"Bin männlichen Geschlechts, der Geiz!"} (5664–55). This masculine-phallic identity of greed is overestimated. For the money-phallus of greed has no object. Obviously, the last thing the Mephistophelian money-phallus has in mind is to squander itself on "females" or, worse yet, to impregnate them. He would much rather drive "the females" away, and is satisfied with his unconnected erection.

> *Sir Greed.* I'm not so far gone yet as not to find
> a pretty woman beautiful,
> and since the entertainment's free today,
> there's nothing to prevent my picking up a girl.
> Still, in a place so overcrowded,
> my words cannot be heard by all,
> I'll take a prudent course, and hope I can succeed
> in being pantomimically explicit.
> My purpose can't be served by gesture, hand, or foot,
> so I shall have to try a prank.
> Gold can be converted into anything,
> and so I'll use this metal just like clay.
> *Herald.* What is our thin fool up to now!
> Can he be both a hunger artist and a comic?
> He's kneading all the gold into a dough

that in his hands becomes quite slack
and stays a shapeless mass
no matter how he molds or pummels it.
He's turning toward those women there,
who scream and try to get away
and act as if they all were much disgusted;
our clown turns out to be a mischief-maker,
and one of those, I fear, who think it fun
to cause offense to decency.

Geiz. Noch bin ich nicht so völlig eingerostet
Ein schönes Weib ist immer schön,
Und heute weil es mich nichts kostet
So wollen wir getrost sponsieren gehn.
Doch weil am überfülltem Orte
Nicht jedem Ohr vernehmlich alle Worte,
Versuch ich klug und hoff' es soll mir glücken,
Mich pantomimisch auszudrücken.
Hand, Fuß, Gebärde reicht mir da nicht hin,
Da muß ich mich um einen Schwank bemühn.
Wie feuchten Ton will ich das Gold behandeln,
Denn dies Metall läßt sich in alles wandeln.
Herold. Was fängt der an, der magre Tor!
Hat so ein Hungermann Humor?
Er knetet alles Gold zu Teig,
Ihm wird es untern Händen weich,
Wie er es drückt und wie es ballt,
Bleibt's immer doch nur ungestalt.
Er wendet sich zu den Weibern dort,
Sie schreien alle, möchten fort,
Gebärden sich gar widerwärtig;
Der Schalk erweist sich übelfertig.
Ich fürchte, daß er sich ergötzt
Wenn er die Sittlichkeit verletzt.
(5772–94)

This sarcastic joke deserves attention. For it aims at a notable amalgamation of phallus and gold or money. This passage, moreover, makes it clear that it is not just permissible, but even obligatory, to hear the word "money" along with the word "gold" ("Geld," "Gold") in *Faust II*: the recognized difference, by definition, that a specific amount of gold stays the same without accruing interest, while money can "turn into anything" and yields interest, is expressly invalid in this context. In addition to that, the pantomimic prank—in this scene, too, "the alphabet is really now superfluous" and the dumb language of phallic money capable of expression—prepares the way for a deeply earnest motif. Sir Greed is not the only one who behaves phallogocentrically and transgresses taboos. As a result of the stunning success in increasing money and wealth, the Emperor begins to have fantasies of omnipotence. He desires the impossible and transgresses nothing less than the divine temporal order when he asks to see Helena and Paris—in other words, to go back two-and-a-half millennia in time or to have the "paragons" of antiquity transported two-and a-half millennia forward.

Even Mephistopheles reaches his limits with this wish. For Helena is "not so easily conjured up / as phantom money" {"nicht so leicht hervorzurufen / wie das Papiergespenst der Gulden"}, which, to the extent that it is covered and promises to preserve past assets, easily rearranges the temporal order. Nonetheless, the wish for a fundamental revision of irreversible time can be accomplished in the phallogomonetary age. Even if only via a detour to the realm of the Mothers and of Matter. In short, the sequence of scenes that causes difficulties for so many interpreters, with the invention of the assignats and the collective fantasy of the omnipotence of money ("High spirits and a merry life for me!" "The wines I drink will now be twice as good," "The dice have started dancing in my purse," "Tonight I'll dream of my estates") {"Ich lebe lustig, heiter, guter Dinge," "Von nun an trink ich doppelt bessre Flasche," "Die Würfel jucken mich schon in der Tasche," "Heut abend wieg ich mich im Grundbesitz"} (6145ff.) followed by the journey to the Mothers, is eminently correct. From paper money to being, from phantom money to the embodiment of the real, from the surface to the deepest depths, from the phallic prank to the awe-inspiring Mothers: this is the path of the first act of *Faust II*.

The actual point of this arrangement of scenes, however, resides in the fact that Goethe's drama conceives of this turn from appearance to being, from money to the Mothers in such a way that the man "that nature has endowed with mighty intellect" acquires, literally, a key position. A key is necessary in order to enter the realm of the Mothers. Mephistopheles can provide it—he has kneaded it out of gold, after all, in the previous scene. Entry into the realm of the Mothers is made possible by yet another overly obvious masculine requisite: a key that has a particular, again phallic, metamorphic peculiarity.

Mephistopheles. Here, take this key!
Faust. That tiny thing!
Mephistopheles. Just grasp it, and remember what it's worth!
Faust. It's growing in my hand—it shines and flashes!
Mephistopheles. You're quick to see that it has special properties!
It has an instinct for the place one wants to be;
follow its lead down to the Mothers.

Faust (shuddering).
The Mothers! It's a shock each time I hear their name!
What is this word I so dislike to hear?
Mephistopheles. Have you some prejudice against new words?
Must you hear only what you've heard before?
Nothing you are about to hear should cause dismay
to one so long inured to all that's strange.
Faust. I do not seek salvation in mere apathy—
awe is the greatest boon we humans are allotted,
and though our world would have us stifle feeling,
if we are stirred profoundly, we sense the Infinite.
Mephistopheles. Well then, descend! Or, if you wish, ascend—
it makes no difference which I say. From finitude
escape to realms where forms exist detached,
where what has ceased to be can still afford delight.
There shapes will crowd and swirl like clouds—
brandish your key and keep them at a distance!
Faust (with enthusiasm).
I hold it tight and feel new strength, new courage.
Let the great enterprise begin!
Mephistopheles. A glowing tripod, finally, will let you know
that you have reached the deepest depth of all.

. . . .

and go directly to the tripod
and touch it with your key!
(*Faust, with the key, strikes an imperious pose as* MEPHISTOPHELES
    watches.)
Yes, that's the way!—
It then will be your faithful follower.

Mephistopheles. Hier diesen Schlüssel nimm.
Faust. Das kleine Ding!
Mephistopheles. Erst faß' ihn an und schätz' ihn nicht gering.
Faust. Er wächst in meiner Hand! er leuchtet, blitzt!
Mephistopheles. Merkst du nun bald, was man an ihm besitzt?
Der Schlüssel wird die rechte Stelle wittern,
Folg ihm hinab, er führt dich zu den Müttern.
Faust schaudernd. Den Müttern! Trifft's mich immer wie ein Schlag!
Was ist das Wort das ich nicht hören mag?
Mephistopheles. Bist du beschränkt daß neues Wort dich stört?
Willst du nur hören was du schon gehört?
Dich störe nichts wie es auch weiter klinge,
Schon längst gewohnt der wunderbarsten Dinge.
Faust. Doch im Erstarren such ich nicht mein Heil,
Das Schaudern ist der Menschheit bestes Teil;
Wie auch die Welt ihm das Gefühl verteure,
Ergriffen, fühlt er tief das Ungeheure.

Mephistopheles. Versinke denn! Ich könnt auch sagen: steige!
'S ist einerlei. Entfliehe dem Entstandnen,
In der Gebilde losgebundne Räume,
Ergötze dich am längst nicht mehr Vorhandnen,
Wie Wolkenzüge schlingt sich das Getreibe,
Den Schlüssel schwinge, halte sie vom Leibe.
Faust begeistert. Wohl! fest ihn fassend fühl ich neue Stärke,
Die Brust erweitert hin zum großen Werke.
Mephistopheles. Ein glühnder Dreifuß tut dir endlich kund,
Du seist im tiefsten, allertiefsten Grund.
. . . .
Und gehe grad' auf jenen Dreifuß los,
Berühr ihn mit dem Schlüssel!
Faust macht eine entschieden gebietende Attitüde mit dem Schlüssel.
  Mephistopheles ihn betrachtend. So ists recht! . . .
Er schließt sich an, er folgt als treuer Knecht.
(6258–84; 6292–94)

These words and requisites (phallic key, feminine tripod) absolutely
demand allegorical interpretation. Even the realm of the Mothers,
even the sphere of the platonic "paragons" and ideas, even Matter that
appears to provide a foundation for appearance, even the "deepest
depth of all" stands under the domination of that which is established,
of the second nature, of the secondary—that is, of money, which
has obtained, in modern times, the position of the master key. Not
for nothing did Faust, "with the key," strike "an imperious pose."
The second nature has become so omnipotent that it reclaims even
the genuine achievement of the first and "deepest" nature: to ensure
reproduction and procreation. The scene of the Mothers is followed
by the Homunculus-scene. "Old-fashioned procreation / is something
we reject as folly" {"Was sonst das Zeugen Mode war, / Erklären wir
für eitel Possen"} (6838–39) says Faust's amanuensis. The historical-
philosophical perspective of this drama is monstrous: after modernity,
with its medium, money, has mobilized so "contra naturam" that it
imitates the fiery nucleus of nature, it moves on to the book of first
nature, to the rewriting of the book of the creation (see chapter 3).

The precondition for this project is the abstraction, far-removed
from Matter/the Mothers, under whose sign the modern age stands.
The phallocratic principle of abstract paternity, proclaiming its supremacy over sensually certain maternity, amalgamates with the medial
principle of the validity of money as the universal equivalent superior
to all concrete values, and, moreover, it seems to increase in value in
and of itself. Goethe did not just bring the motive of the (phallic) key
and the key function of money together in *Faust;* he did so in his early
burlesque *Fellow Culprits* as well (see chapter 3).

Where there is a key or, respectively, money, a safe or a cav(e)/ity is not far. Both motifs (cav[e]/ity and safe) {*Höhle* and *Schatulle*} are condensed in the motif of the little box that fascinated Goethe his whole life (like Shakespeare before him). Goethe's interest in the motif of the little box started early. The primal scene of this fixation on a dark and secretive box can be—thanks to *Poetry and Truth* {*Dichtung und Wahrheit*}—reconstructed with precision. The ten-year-old Johann Wolfgang enjoyed a child's friendly companionship with the French Count Thoranc, who was quartered in his parents' house. In his room, the young prepubescent Goethe found

> a small black box behind the stove. Immediately I wanted to see what might be concealed in it and, without much hesitation, drew out the bolt. The picture it contained was not one of those usually exhibited openly! Though I tried to push the bolt right back in again, I was not quick enough. The count walked in and caught me in the act.—"Who gave you permission to open this box?" he said with his king's lieutenant expression. I did not have much of an answer to that, and he gravely pronounced my punishment at once: "For a week you will not enter this room." I bowed and left. I obeyed his command very punctiliously, too.[39]

Of course nothing is more enticing than that which is forbidden. Goethe immediately created his own little mythology about the bolt and the box that easily links up with the great mythology and especially the fertility symbolism of the Eleusinian *cista mystica*.[40] The symbolism of the little box weaves its way through Goethe's oeuvre like a red thread. Whether in the *Journeyman Years* (see chapter 11), in the "Neue Melusine," or in the twelfth of the *Roman Elegies* (to name just a few of the most famous texts): the little box always serves a highly ambivalent function. It symbolizes the place of fertility and of wealth as well the place of death. Goethe's specific coloring of this motif consists of its monetization: from the Eleusinian *cista mystica* he creates a safe in which money reproduces itself. Astoundingly, monetary conceptions predominate even in Goethe's most private uses of the motif of the little box. Thus he writes to Charlotte von Stein on March 10, 1781: "Anyway, I am as quiet inside as a little box, full of all kinds of jewelry, money and papers, that is sinking down into a well."[41] The erotic motif of the key, too, finds its way into another letter, of December 6, 1781, to Charlotte von Stein: "Send me, dearest, my key that I left yesterday. But the key with which you lock my entire being so that no one besides you can get in, guard it well and keep it for yourself alone." The master key of money is different from this most private of keys. It fits in all boxes. Indeed, it is the "Big Jimmy" that appears to grow and become so valuable that it believes it no longer needs fruitful boxes and cavities.[42]

EXCURSUS: THE ARMY, THE CHURCH, AND THE ALMA MATER—

A CAPRICE ON CORPORATE BODIES

"I am Sir Greed, am masculine!" (*Faust II*, 5665). It is not always so easy to identify sex. With the sex of money things are more complicated. According to the bold diagnosis that Goethe's *Faust* drama offers, the neuter money, the cold, coined metal, the abstract paper asset is of perverse sexuality when it seems to reproduce by yielding interest. A neuter thing, in other words, that homosexually mingles only with its own kind, and yet reproduces. This perverse aura of the pecuniary may have contributed to the culturally conservative distance that old and honorable corporate bodies such as the army, the church, and the university maintain from the medium of money. Nor are these corporate bodies, as is obvious, free from the pleasure and fascination of allegorical mystifications of their sex.[1] What they have to hide is an open secret. But let us take a detour before this secret gives itself away as directly as that of greed.

The polis is a *body* and may be only *one* body. This is how one of the oldest, most effective and suggestive, and least original, political metaphors would have it. And because of this—according to Menenius Agrippa's incredibly effective fable—the members may not revolt against the stomach. "And, as in a body which is diseased," as it says paradigmatically in Plato's *Republic*, "the addition of a touch from without may bring on illness, and sometimes even when there is no external provocation a commotion may arise within—in the same way wherever there is weakness in the State there is also likely to be illness,

117

of which the occasion may be very slight, the one party introducing from without their oligarchical, the other their democratical allies, and then the State falls sick, and is at war with herself; and may be at times distracted, even when there is no external cause."[2]

The success of this widespread political metaphor of antiquity was not to be stopped, in part because (Pauline) Christianity took it over unconditionally. Reworking the metaphor platonically, the apostle with the talent for organizing characterized the entire church explicitly as a corpus, as the Body of Christ (Ephesians 1:22f.). Corinthians I, 12:19 clearly alludes to Agrippa's fable as well: "For as we have many members in one body, . . so we, *being* many, are one body in Christ, and every one members one of another" (Romans 12:4f.).[3] It was Paul, too, who consciously conceived of the church in the image of the military and armed it rhetorically. The metaphor of the *militia* for the relationship of the congregation to its leader was one of his favorite turns of phrase (see Corinthians II, 10:3, Ephesians 6:10–17 among others).[4] The state is a body that consists of countless bodies; the congregation is a body that consists of countless inspired members—a model with an incredible capacity for oral transmission. The frontispiece that Hobbes placed at the beginning of his book *Leviathan* in 1651, three years after the end of the Thirty Years' War, represents the classic combination of the two traditions. This "masterwork of Baroque imagery" shows "an enormous man consisting of many small human beings, holding the Bishop's crosier and sword protectively over a city . . . nothing but a metaphor for the state in charge of politics and theology."[5]

With the Pauline adaptation of the model of the state's body to the body of the believing community, and with Hobbes's emblematic combining of many individual bodies into one politico-theological body with two extremities bearing symbols, however, a problem becomes quite obvious that is already virulent in the basic metaphor itself. When several (natural) bodies combine to create one corporate body, they immediately come up against other (corporate) bodies that they— see Plato's warning—experience primarily as challenge and threat, but possibly also as an object of the desire for incorporation and the will to power. How state and church or parties and associations or joint-stock companies and churches can and should conduct themselves toward one another is obviously the problem. The variety of bodies cannot be driven out by an ultimate meta-body. Even the Christian God itself is threefold and has more than just one body.

Despite the difficulties, the conception of the congregation and the state as a body is not an exquisite metaphor that occupies philosophical heads full of political ambitions alone. It is, rather, a model of such obvious and great suggestiveness that it still leaves its imprint, more than a couple of millennia later, on the matter-of-fact constitution itself. It conceives of the Federal Republic explicitly as a corporate legal person that, through its "organs," exerts legislative, executive, and judicial powers (Article 20.2).

"Corporate body," "organs," "the hand of government," "corpo-ration," "member," "head," "political body": seldom have metaphors managed to persist through the ages and beyond the borders of lan-guage to such a degree that they—from Roman Law to the Code of Civil Law {*Bürgerliches Gesetzbuch*}—obtain continual juridical enno-blement. Seldom, however, have metaphors been able to immunize themselves against the questions that are so close at hand, and that they really ought to provoke. If corporate bodies—from the associ-ation to the joint-stock company to the university—are bodies that unite many bodies to form one legal person: which sex does this body then have? And which desire do these bodies have, or, which is valid for them?[6]

The first question is easy to answer. Yet the urge to clarify it is not particularly well-developed. Erotic associations flood the corre-spondingly risky expression of the Apostle Paul's that says that Christ, in loving the church, loves himself, just as a man yearns for himself in a woman: "Husbands, love your wives, even as Christ also loved the church. . . . So ought men to love their wives as their own bodies. He that loveth his wife loveth himself, . . . even as the Lord the church. For we are members of his body . . . This is a great mystery: but I speak concerning Christ and the church" (Ephesians 5:25–32). The secret is tremendous and yet obvious: the church is a woman.

Those who, like the first Social Democratic president of the Fed-eral Republic, Heinemann, speak this simple truth, however indirectly, immediately find themselves in the realm of scandal and taboo. "I love my wife and not the state." This statement assumes, unless it is to become immediately engulfed in the abysses of psycho-pathology, that the body of the state is feminine and therefore capable of binding men passionately. Passionate objections to the sober statement from the mouth of the president were certain. If two things compete with each other, then, obviously, they do the same thing. And the irritated objections to Heinemann's courageous words fundamentally prove what they intend to challenge: corporate bodies are women, and more precisely, mothers. Thus the imperative under which corporate bodies place their masculine members: Before one may love *one* woman, one has to desire *the* motherly corporate body absolutely.

Such primordial desire is incomprehensible, like all that is allegedly primeval. This is made fully evident by a brief dispassionate
look behind the veil of the three great corporate bodies that—in contrast to associations and joint-stock or "mother" companies that often
spawn "daughter" companies[7]—have held on through the disruptions
of the ages with admirable stubbornness: *the* army, *the* church, *the*
academy or university. They are all mothers. And mothers, moreover,
that hardly veil this quality of theirs. The university calls itself, with
disarming openness, the "alma mater"—the nourishing mother. The
church, too, likes to be addressed as the "Mother Church." Only
the army gives itself airs. It certainly knows—metonymically and due
to the remarkable grammatical ambivalence of subject and object in
possessives, as in "the mother of the company"—yet it only unwillingly
discloses the feminine quality of its body (army corps).

Without question, corporate bodies, and especially these three
archetypal corporate bodies, are obviously motherly. Yet no open and
public speech reflects this open secret. On the contrary, Mephistopheles' conviction and Faust's reply are closer to the norm:

> To speak of them I find embarrassing—
> these are the Mothers!
> *Faust.* (*startled*) Mothers!
> *Mephistopheles.* What? Afraid?
> *Faust.* The Mothers! "Mothers" sounds so strange!
> *Mephistopheles.* And it is, too.

> Von ihnen sprechen ist Verlegenheit.
> Die Mütter sind es!
> *Faust, aufgeschreckt.* Mütter!
> *Mephistopheles.* Schaudert's dich?
> *Faust.* Die Mütter! Mütter! -'s klingt so wunderlich!
> *Mephistopheles.* Das ist es auch.
> (6215–18)

The path to the institutional mothers is also paved with embarrassment. For the mysterious commonalities of these three mothers cannot
be overlooked. They act in each case in the name of a strikingly abstract
and therefore incorporeal but powerful father: in the name of the
fatherland, of God, and of the mind. And they celebrate the absent
father with extreme rituals. These rituals are of tremendous daring and
are as a rule only observed by the innermost circle of the hierarchy of
the sons. The army tends to ruin the fatherland it is supposed to serve.
In his novella *A Man of Honor*, Fontane has a prominent member of
Prince Louis's *cercle intime* express the simple insight that "the state of
Frederick the Great is not a country with an army but an army with

a country. Our country is no more than a military base and supply center."[8] The Christian church is similar. She continually celebrates— locus classicus of the insight into this paradox is Dostoyevsky's *The Legend of the Grand Inquisitor*—the God to whose absence she owes her power and whose only-begotten son she offers for consumption. And wagging tongues proclaim again and again that the university's real mission is to drive out far too much intellect.

The three motherly corporate bodies have one more thing in common that is, on the surface of it, striking. They have, in principle, only sons. Certainly loyal, devoted, reverent, and—after having endured extravagant rites of initiation in the commissioning of an officer, ordination, and the granting of tenure—spoiled mama's boys. Even in post-(uni)(re)formed times, clergywomen and women professors are now as before the exception that strikes one as odd, causing embarrassment. Tradition-conscious corporate bodies like the Catholic Church and the army, which know that it pays to keep the treachery from getting started, militantly refuse to allow women to serve in the motherly corporate bodies at all. That has—why shouldn't it?—considerable consequences. The army, the church, and the alma mater are not exactly corporate bodies whose members practice liberated forms of heterosexuality. On the contrary, these members fancy themselves in a male-bonding cult of the mother whose exclusivity is more likely to obstruct the inclination toward other women.

Homosexual latencies and an overly strong attachment to the mother are—as Freud forcefully showed in "Neurotic Mechanisms in Jealousy, Paranoia and Homosexuality"—often enough one and the same disposition. It is the breaking point of military psychology. From the wish of the Shakespearean Caesar to have only particular types of men around him, to the misogyny of the great Frederick and the scandals surrounding Wilhelm II and Count Eulenburg, to the Wörner-Kießling affair,[9] a bow of taboo is drawn that ultimately none other than Franz Josef Strauß, in his memoirs, overloaded to the point of release:

> One of the most scandalous incidents since the change of government in 1982 is the affair surrounding General Günther Kießling of the German Federal Armed Forces. When I think about the fact that I had to resign as minister of defense because I allegedly gave false information to Parliament! That Wörner stayed in office despite the Kießling affair betrays a thoroughly unimaginable capacity for scandal. A minister of defense relies on the most dubious reports of agents from the demimonde, regards them as trustworthy, begins proceedings against the general in question, the loathesomeness of which cannot be surpassed, then has trouble finding

evidence, invites, at the expense of the taxpayer, a scintillating, appropriately notorious "writer" from the homosexual milieu in Switzerland to Bonn, a colonel gives the gentleman an escort, the minister spends hours talking to the "witness," listens to detailed reports on the alleged offenses of the general—and at the end of this unspeakable campaign with its unspeakable chief witness the entire edifice of accusation collapses.[10]

The edifice of accusations may collapse—but a part of the psychostructure of the feminine corporate body army[11] bursts forth in affairs like this. Similarly, much of the profane secret of the churchly corporate body becomes manifest in the report of an acolyte who has become psychotic and who—an authentic case of clairvoyance—reveals the psycho-structure of the apparently so patriarchal and yet so motherly church. With ethnographic precision he shares observations of many years that can hardly be contested: in mass the women, and above all the old women, would sit in the foremost and most renowned seats and watch approvingly as a man prepares the table and performs what is specifically women's work. For this kindness he will then be rewarded with the privilege of being permitted to wear women's clothing.

Professors no longer wear women's clothing, ever since the criticism of the mustiness of a thousand years under the robes became loud enough to do some harm.[12] Similarly the university, among the traditional corporate bodies, has distanced itself the most from the matriarchal paradigm. At the same time, the university was without question the most motherly of the motherly corporate bodies. Her very name gives away her secret: alma mater. It is not enough to read Latin; one must also be truly able to read in order to grasp that the university was in fact an alma mater: a large, benevolent mother who dispenses nourishment. She nourishes the misfits, crazies, and misguided in the *societas magistrorum et discipulorum*, who in turn worship her as if she were a cult figure. This mother did not ask, in contrast to, for example, the fatherland, whether it is socially useful or productive to research the Indo-Germanic roots of language, to memorize the lascivious exploits in Ovid's *Metamorphoses* or to feel at home with Leibniz's monadology. On the contrary, she took pleasure in the brooding earnestness of her academic children, whom she often enough, through her generosity, may have spared psychiatric marginality. The same can be said, however, for other professions: since the electrification of the railway lines, the extinguishing of the home fires, the remote control of blast furnaces, the number of pyromaniacal arsonists is supposed to have climbed dramatically. Since the replacement of fire with electricity, those who love to light fires no longer have a professional field of activity, only a criminal one.

Mothers must have children, otherwise they are not mothers—that is their defining feature. Now the means by which motherly corporate bodies and churches acquire their children—to put it delicately—is highly disturbed. They do not give birth; rather they recruit sons through force, in order, then, to send them in many cases to an early and gruesome death or have them kill themselves. Or, given the express insistence on a celibate way of life, they procure children for themselves through systematic adoption: sons of the church, who alone are permitted to prepare the Lord's Supper, and brides of Christ, who for their part may not have any natural children.

The alma mater does not bear natural children. Yet she knows a method of procreation that has always been regarded as the equivalent of the production of children: the generation of books. It can hardly proceed without a touch of the uncanny when the alma mater, with one of her sons, who then advances explicitly to *Doktorvater*,[13] makes a "liber": a book, a child. "Libri sunt liberi." Play with the polysemy of the Latin word "liber" (book, free, the free) is old; and old, too, is the play with the assonant plural forms "liberi" and "libri" (children or books).[14] Hesiod already grasps poets as sons of muses: "for by the power of the Muses and far-shooting Apollo men who sing and play on the lyre exist on the earth."[15] It is not long, then, before this poetic-genealogical diagram is filled out in a new and remarkable way. Early in the fifth century B.C.E., Pindar turns the motherly muse into the beloved, and the poetic son into her lover. The child that arises from this affair is literature. Books and children have this in common as well, that one reproduces on into eternity through them: "Liberos nullos, sed libros plures reliquit, cum et liberis et libris aeternitas propagetur."[16] With this, a realm of associations opens up that stimulates the topos of the poet who, with his beloved, produces a child, and often enough, with precise intensification, instead of a mortal child, an immortal book.

It is of course striking that in the history of the child-book metaphor, the mother is increasingly absent. "Books, who are you? What do you bring?—The daughters of the father Homer / are we," says Antiphilus of Byzantium[17] at the turn of the millennium, naming of course the poetic father while simply suppressing the mother. And the virile Virgil is obviously willing to risk the suspicion of effeminacy when he, according to his biographer Suetonius, describes the creation of the *Georgics* in a daring image: "He bears his poem in the manner of a mother bear, and licks it into shape."[18] Not just children, books, too, need transforming, reworking, and molding. In Book III of his *Tristia*, Ovid ultimately understands the process that sets his works free as an explicitly motherless parthenogenesis: "Palladis exemplo de me sine matre creata / Carmina sunt; stirps haec progeniesque mea" {"My poems spring from me, in the pattern of Pallas, without a mother: they are my children, my posterity"}.[19]

It was reserved for a bishop of early Christianity to resexualize this topos that had been increasingly taking shape as parthenogenetic. As Synesius (who lived from about 370–413) says with cheerful ease: "I have generated some writings as sons, with the highly holy Philosophy and her temple-mate, Poetry, to be sure; the others, however, with that prostitute, Rhetoric. Yet it is plain to see that they all have the same father." This bishop was obviously neither a prude nor monogamous; nonetheless he may have lived in celibacy. Faced with the decision circumscribed by the monk's saying "aut liberi aut libri" (either children or books) stood—and stand often enough even now— those who choose the spiritual or intellectual career. Virtuosi of this fruitful game with the letters and the spirit of the beautiful word with two meanings were—to make a tremendous leap into the modern age, jumping over such important authors obsessed with children and books as Ronsard, Shakespeare, Bacon, and Cervantes—Goethe and Gottfried Keller.

As is generally known, Goethe was not, despite the children's cult surrounding the *Werther*-novel, successful as a real father. All the more insistently did he mold his work according to the child-book metaphor. Thus he says of the sacred Ottilie, the site of whose cult he sought out from Strasbourg, in *Poetry and Truth*, "I formed a mental picture of her which, together with her name, made a deep impression on me. For a long time I kept them both in mind, until I bestowed them on one of my later, but no less beloved, 'daughters'" (368–69). Goethe did not need to endow his real and beloved daughter-in-law with this name—she had carried it since her christening. Goethe did not, however, merely lend his beloved creation of *Elective Affinities* this name, he also refused her a child. Instead of her own, Goethe's fictive daughter Ottilie takes care of the child of her aunt.

Yet she neglects it, too—naturally in favor of a book. In one scene in which the precision of the choreography catches the eye (how is one supposed to hold a rudder, a child, and a book all at once?), Goethe lets both book and child slip, if not into a well, into the deceptively reflective element of water.

> She leaps into the boat, takes hold of the oar and pushes off. She has to push hard, and push again; the boat sways and drifts a little way out into the lake. On her left arm the baby, in her left hand the book, in her right hand the oar. She loses balance and topples into the boat. The oar

slips out of her grasp to one side, and just as she tries to right herself, the child and the book slither off to the other, all of them into the water. She manages to grab hold of the baby's clothing; but her uncomfortable position prevents her from even getting up. With only her right hand free, she cannot turn and sit up. Finally she does manage; she pulls the child out of the water, but his eyes are closed and he has stopped breathing.[20]

Thus, at the end of an important book, a child of peculiar parents and a book share a common end.

The bachelor Keller, short of stature, molded the topos of the fictive book-child more aggressively—and applied the old maxim of the uncertain father ("pater semper incertus est") to the problems of authorship as well. The story of the "Schmied seines Glückes"[21] who finds and invents a novel-father for himself (who is only too willing to become his coauthor), is forced to recognize, upon his return from his travels as a journeyman, that this father now reclaims the child he had produced as his own. Thus the book-son has disinherited himself. This story is too wonderful to paraphrase in earnest, and almost as melancholy as the *The Misused Love Letters*, in which the category of authorship becomes as muddled as the childless marriage which, following elective affinities-like reorganization, becomes fruitful because the new husband devotes himself to producing real children instead of poorly conceived books, while the divorced husband continues with his hack writing that no one wants to read.

The mother university does not treat her sons who only create books no one wants to read as maliciously as does the author Keller. On the contrary, she takes joy in her horde of strange children and grandchildren who furnish their books with dedications that are not always as clear as Paul Rée's to Nietzsche, to give one example: "To the father of this text most gratefully, its mother." And even Freud gave thanks to the father of his "dream child": "The period of gestation is almost over," he wrote to his friend Fließ shortly before finishing the *Interpretation of Dreams*. Paul Rée, Nietzsche, Freud: all are great outsiders of the university before and around 1900. Their relationship to the alma mater is a fundamentally disturbed one, or, more precisely, one imprinted with erotic disappointment. In this century and more pronouncedly in the last two decades, the university has lost her body and her sex; she has become, in a diffused manner, bodiless and sexless. This is why no one loves her anymore. "What amazes every member of my generation," says the scholar of religion Klaus Heinrich, who, as a student, helped to found the Free University in Berlin, "is the complete de-eroticization of the relationship between the members of the university and the institution."[22] The university of today is no

longer an alma mater at all. She is not, however, its simple opposite—
she has not become a strict father university. On the contrary, she has,
to stick to the ethnological metaphor (is it really "just" a metaphor?),
skipped over the revolt of the patriarchs in a ghostly way in order
to become a fatherless university as well. A university that has no
personal authority against which it would be worthwhile to fight, just
governing boards. A de-individualized and disembodied university in
which, according to a puzzling one-third to one-ninth parity "formula"
that does not really represent parity, nothing is really decided, it is
merely governed. A university to which no minister of science, no
professor, no graduate student, and above all no student has desire and
impulse to pay homage.

That the university was once an attractive and erotic, desirable corporate body is recognizable yet today, if only by its uniquely anachronistic, irritating attribute: now, as before, women have it remarkably
hard at the alma mater. Appointed women must see to it that women
in the domains of this once feminine-maternal and currently neutral
corporate body are received and initiated into the higher callings.
Women who are called must generally make a commitment: they may
not become mothers. The still rare women's careers in the university
function by virtue of—be it lamented or welcomed as emancipatory—
a renunciation of children. University women produce books instead
of children. Yet perhaps this mutually exclusive relationship is not
so troublesome anymore. For all three are losing importance, power,
respect, and influence: mothers, children, and books—along with the
churches and universities. Banks, whose boards of directors protect
themselves even more successfully from infiltration by women than
the classic corporate bodies, are made of tougher stuff. What they
issue, increase, and pay cultic homage to, counts, now as before.

7

"TIME IS MONEY"—
THE TIME OF MONEY/THE MONEY OF TIME

> Thanks to the mysterious potential of my purse . . .
> we succeeded in overcoming time.
>
> Chamisso, *Peter Schlemihl*

Money establishes relationships across the greatest distances—and across the widest expanses of time. Indeed, money even binds the Plutonic realm of the dead with the earth and the heavens. The social (and the transcendental as well!—see chapter 10) arrangements of space and time are, to an extraordinary degree, determined by money. Those who take out a life insurance policy with a term of more than thirty years get involved in a remarkably complex set of assumptions. He, the insured, who truly puts a possessive pronoun in front of his life (my life is my possession, as proven by my possible demise—it is worth 300,000 German marks), he, who wants to be insured, not only promises to make regular payments but offers a number of additional assurances (among others, to be healthy, not to want to commit suicide, and so on), and he depends on (too) much: among other things, that the first general assurance of reciprocity on the basis of which he agrees to a policy lasting longer than the average marriage is not one of those peculiar, third-class uninsurance policies with a 100 percent commission. He assumes that the system of justice that will help him put through his claims for payment will still have authority in thirty years, that insurance will still exist in the next millennium even if the super powers with nuclear weapons are still in decay, that a new currency (such as the Euro) will be compatible with the currency named in the policy, and that he or his beneficiaries will still be alive in thirty years.

Those who place so much trust in money and time may by all rights be called gullible—and distrustful. Distrust with respect to being and time first motivates the need to insure oneself or one's life. So distrustful in ontological and so gullible in monetary respects are, at present, so many millions of citizens of the (rarely so-called) first world. So much gullibility and willingness to believe, or bear witness, among critical, secularized, enlightened consumers is bizarre, exotic, and strange. People who, despite their A-13 salary,[1] drive ten kilometers to the next supermarket because coffee is 49 pfennigs cheaper there than it is in the shopping center five kilometers away, pay hundreds of German marks monthly for thirty years, often reaching a total sum of six figures—for, literally, nothing, for an abstraction, for a pledge, for a future promise that, like all promises, threatens to be an empty one. In any event, for thirty years and for considerable sums of money, the insured receives annually, assuming "his" insurance company—the possessive pronoun might even be more euphemistic in this case than in the combination "his/my" life—is willing to reveal the (usually startlingly low) amount to his credit, a piece of paper and, occasionally, a frugally prepared customers' newsletter. This piece of paper does not just contain the sender's promise of payment, but also an implicit obligation for the recipient: he who has signed a contract for a life insurance policy will hardly continue to take an interest in economic-political-social changes that threaten the existence of "his" insurance. Life insurance has therefore always been insurance for insurance. Against what does one insure oneself at so great an expense with such apotropaic fantasy? Against what one simply cannot ward off: finiteness, time, and death.

These honest remarks obviously flow from the pen (or, more precisely, from the keyboard) of a writer who, firstly, has not taken out a life insurance policy and, secondly, though not particularly pious, regards the project of insuring life as at the very least a stylistically problematic sacrilege, and who, thirdly, as a philologist, allows just one objection to his otherwise thoroughly sound remarks: what he describes should not be called simply life insurance, but capital-life insurance—for it is capital, and not life, that is insured. Such an objection is seductive in its precision. It provokes, however, another question which, despite first impressions, is not merely of a philological-aesthetic nature: is the monster-phrase "capital-life insurance" a metaphor, a metonymy, or a synecdoche?

The last is the most plausible solution: capital and life stand in a *pars-pro-toto* relationship to one another. What counts in life is that for which one is willing to pay; what remains of the finite life is the immortal capital that this life leaves behind. What is entered into the Book of Life (or the life insurance policy) is the sum of its existence.

The capital of the life insurance policy occupies precisely the place once occupied by an immortal soul insured by sacraments. Capital is timeless and yet has an (at times downright suspenseful) history—like the soul. Capital is liquid and assumes different, aging forms and embodiments—like the soul. Capital is payable to a name—like the individuated soul. Capital is marked—like the soul pledged and vowed to God (or the devil). For the preservation of capital one makes commitments—as one does for the preservation and salvation of the soul. Capital survives and transcends its earthly remains—like the soul. Capital is a means. Whoever possesses it is potent; whoever is truly potent has the means of outwitting time and death.

Economic takeovers of the theological structure according to which a finite life is condensed into an immortal soul can be accomplished with elegance, otherwise they would not have been so successful. In the furious words of the converted, militant Catholic Léon Bloy, who, in his *Exégèse des lieux communs* {Interpretation of Platitudes} of 1902, writes: "Is it not crystal clear that money is one and the same with the God who requires one to consume him, who preserves life, who is the living bread, the redeeming loaf,[2] the wheat of the chosen, food fit for angels, but also the hidden manna that the poor seek in vain?"[3] In order that money or, more precisely, capital, which seems to be immune to and insured against the abyss of time, can become the supplement to the immortal soul, the following, among other things, must occur:

—the hope of salvation must be replaced by the telos of the final rest, the endless vacation ultimately reached by virtue of generously paid-out life insurance (annuity, pension);
—the principle that one must atone for everything must be replaced (and this occurred in the nineteenth century in Europe) by the tenet that one must pay for everything;
—(religious) debts must be traded in for (economic) debts;
—money must become the "god term" of modern societies, and intersubjective and transcendent(al) authority must be transferred from God to money;
—the theological taboo (last but not least) against the possibility of buying and selling time must be removed. With the sale of indulgences the history of the slow erosion of the Jewish, Christian, and Islamic prohibition against trafficking in sacred time reached its preliminary high point within the framework of the culture of the so-called Christian West. The Lutheran protest against this erosion contributed, ironically, to the increasing tempo of the process, at the high point of which a worldly ascetic Protestant coined the classically spare identificatory formulation under whose sign high modernity stands: "Time is money."

"Remember, that *time* is money," Benjamin Franklin says in his "Advice to a Young Tradesman." His essay "The Way to Wealth," which appeared in 1758 in his successful annual *Poor Richard's Almanac*, served Max Weber (next to Baster's *Christian Directory*), as is well known, as the main source of his thesis on the birth of capitalism out of the spirit of Protestant asceticism.[4] "He that can earn ten shillings a day by his labour, and goes abroad, or sits idle, one half of that day," continues Benjamin Franklin, "{though he spends but sixpence during his diversion or idleness,} ought not to reckon *that* the only expense; he has really spent, or rather thrown away, five shillings besides."[5] The analogous conclusion as to the productive power of work with respect to the "reproductive power of money" follows immediately. Yet this conclusion instantly loses sight of the fact that it ensues from an analogy: money itself is declared to be a source of productivity, indeed, of reproductive power. "Remember, that money is of the prolific, generating nature. Money can beget money, and its offspring can beget more, and so on." The revocation of the scholastic decree could not be made clearer. "Nummus nummum non gerit," said Thomas Aquinas; "Money can beget money," indeed, says Benjamin Franklin. Both thinkers, despite the direct contradiction of their statements, are pious. "This Doctrine {of honoring work and the increase of wealth}, my Friends, is *Reason and Wisdom;* but after all, do not depend too much upon your own *Industry*, and *Frugality*, and *Prudence*, though Excellent Things, for they may all be blasted without the Blessing of Heaven; and therefore, ask that Blessing humbly."[6]

To many, and especially artists, this mercy—to receive the gift of time on loan in order to work and allow money to increase and multiply—is not merciful enough. That Faust, at the dawn of the age that did away with the principle "nummus nummum non gerit," sold himself to the devil, is not so incomprehensible or scandalous. The devil, after all, has assumed the place of the Lord, who has more to offer than empty hours of work and borrowed time. "We sell time"— so succinctly does the devil sum up his offer to Adrian Leverkuhn in Thomas Mann's novel *Doctor Faustus*. The time that the devil sells is of course not empty, abstract time to be used at will, but rather specified, devilishly good, materialized time.

> Wheresoever the houre-glasse is set up and time fixed, unthinkable yet measured time and a fixed end, there we are in the field, there we are in clover. Time we sell. . . .
> *I.* "So you would sell time?"
> *He.* "Time? Simple time? No, my dear fere, that is not devyll's ware. For that we should not earn the reward, namely that the end belongs to us.

What manner of time, that is the heart of the matter! Great time, mad time, quite bedivelled time, in which the fun waxes fast and furious, with heaven-high leaping and springing."[7]

Thomas Mann's devil is only partially appropriate for the twentieth century, but brilliantly so for the sixteenth, in which he recognizes his specifically modern opportunity. He is anachronistically stylized for good reason. He would hardly do as a life insurance salesman. For he sells materialized time and not, say, indeterminate time. And Adrian Leverkühn pays for it not with money but with his soul, and the renunciation of love. Philosophically and systematically more exciting[8] than even this premodern, thus pre-monetary, offer is the modern and monetary possibility of selling (empty, unspecified) time. This possibility requires more complex structures than that of the simple exchange to which Doctor Faustus and the devil agree. If time and money are supposed to be so easily converted into each other that even their precarious identification can become proverbial ("time is money"), then the hardly common reversal of Benjamin Franklin's concise formula must also be true: "money is time." Those who are experiencing cash flow problems buy, with a loan, the time needed to reorganize their household or business. Those who take out a mortgage purchase the opportunity to acquire the house of their dreams right away rather than twenty years hence. The formula "money is time" logically and chronologically precedes the formula "time is money."

The condition that makes this equation, equivalence, point of comparison, indeed, identification of money and time possible is obviously the scarcity of both resources. Time and money grow scarce in modernity, because two long-standing taboos were lifted: to doubt eternity in conjunction with doubt in the existence of God, and to buy and sell life's time in the form of labor and work hours. A life that can no longer be sure of its perspective on eternity must experience life's time as menacingly limited, and this limitedness becomes even more dramatic as a result of the fact that life as a rule can only be maintained through the sale of work hours. Time and money can be converted into one another. Precisely because, under such structural conditions, there is a shortage of both, the shortage of money counterbalances the shortage of time and vice versa. Both resources have a characteristic paradox in common. With respect to every single life story or every single *homo economicus* they are always limited; "in and of themselves," however, they are infinite. The fact that time passes does not decrease its supply; money ("as such") does not become more limited because it leaves safe A for safe B. Time is primed by (the fantasy of) eternity, against which finiteness stands out dramatically; money is, as an artificial medium, virtually infinite, but would, were it not artificially limited, dramatically lose its value. Pure time and pure money are, moreover, peculiarly abstract and indifferent; in both cases what matters is "what one makes of it."

There is no such thing as *the* time pure and simple—just as there is no such thing as *the* money. There are coins, notes, checks, drafts, but not money. There are points in time, spans of time, epochs, biographical dates, terms of loans, investment periods, but "there is" no time as such (in any event, not in the way that there are entities {*Seiendes*}). That which does not exist, that which is neither at nor in hand and yet without a doubt determines our fate is uncanny per se. The uncanniness and strange insubstantiality of time as of money has certainly simplified their convertibility. In the face of all these characteristic monetary-temporal commonalities, however, it should not be overlooked that conversions and transactions only make sense if they offer advantages to those who enter into them. No one would make an exchange if the goods received did not provide something that the goods traded in could not.

Social forms that very systematically exchange a (theological) fix-ation on God, time, and eternity for a (monetary) fixation on money, time, and eternity must perceive an advantage in the exchange. What shift does the identification of time and money undergo that makes this trade-off worthwhile? What are the contours of the deep structural shift from (theologically primed) (experience of) time on the one hand to monetary possibilities for making time tangible on the other? What makes the shift from God to money so irresistible? It obviously is worthwhile—it pays—beyond all its pragmatic aspects, for the addi-tional reason that money, for all its compatibility with time, is, in at least one way, the radical counterpart to the image of (the experience of) time that is condensed in death.

Death is, as Heidegger demonstrates phenomenologically in *Being and Time*, the most personal, isolating, impossible to supersede, certain and indeterminate eventuality of existence {*Dasein*} (the philosophical tradition, in contrast to Heidegger, would have formulated this in the plural, depending, of course, on the particular perspective—of the subjects or of the individuals). It is the most personal eventuality: it cannot be changed, it is always already and unsubstitutively my death. It is the isolating eventuality: it can only be experienced as a rupture in all communication. It is the eventuality that cannot be superseded: one cannot speak, without destructive paradoxes, in the future perfect about one's own death (whoever attempts to supersede it temporally in

sentences like "I will have been dead" has described not death but life).
It is the most certain and yet indeterminate eventuality: *mors certa, hora incerta*, and finally, the *eventuality*: my death cannot be experienced as a reality during my life; however, possibly real is the experience with other dead, with corpses.

Money, which has united itself with time so successfully in modernity, is now the counterpart to death in every single respect: it is the least personal, a purely social medium, existing precisely in order to change and move from one person's wallet to another. It is universally connected (to things, to points of time, and to natural as well as legal persons whom it unites through exchange). It can be "superseded" (one can treat it, in contrast to one's own death, in the future perfect: I will have survived the term of my capital-life insurance). It is uncertain (because it can be changed into anything and is thoroughly unspecific and indifferent materially, personally and temporally). It is determined to a high degree (for example, with respect to rates of exchange, term and maturity dates, legal obligations, political and psychological contexts, and so forth). It is, last but not least, not an existence {*Dasein*} but, if the serious joke may be permitted, something that is gone {*Fortsein*}; not a subject but a semantic object (Heidegger would have been compelled to regard it as an "indicator" {"*Zeigzeug*"} if he had not been so rigidly disinterested in everything sociological); not an individual but a medium.

Time and money are thus compatible for the very reason that a worthwhile shift is inherent in their identification. Money has put death to death; but the dead remain. It seems to offer a force that is more capable, more potent, and more liquid than death. Thus the experience of time that is given with money, or that is given money, is different from the experience of former times, which knew neither the universal exchange of money nor life insurance. By the end of the nineteenth century at the latest, the theologically explosive identificatory formulation "time is money" had gained general acceptance. In the years around and after 1900, neo-Romantic literature registered, with remarkable attentiveness, this monetary reorganization of the traditional experience of time.

The Chiasma of the Present:
The Silver, the Silver-Plated Rose

Time is a strange thing.
While one just lives for the moment, it is nothing.
But then all at once
we feel nothing else but it,

it's all around us, it's right inside us,
it trickles away in our faces, it trickles in the mirror,
in my temples it flows away.
And between me and you there it is flowing too.
Soundless, as an hour-glass.
Ah Quinquin!
Often I hear it flowing incessantly.
Often I get up in the middle of the night
and stop all the clocks.

Die Zeit, die ist ein sonderbares Ding.
Wenn man so hinlebt, ist sie rein gar nichts.
Aber dann auf einmal,
da spürt man nichts als sie:
sie ist um uns herum, sie ist auch in uns drinnen.
In den Gesichtern rieselt sie, im Spiegel da rieselt sie,
in meinen Schläfen fließt sie.
Und zwischen mir und dir da fließt sie wieder.
Lautlos, wie eine Sanduhr.
O Quin-quin!
Manchmal hör ich sie fließen unaufhaltsam.
Manchmal steh ich auf, mitten in der Nacht,
und laß die Uhren alle stehen.[9]

Thus muses the Princess {*die Marschallin*} in Hofmannsthal's *The Cavalier of the Rose* {*Rosenkavalier*}. Yet she interrupts herself immediately, as if she were shocked at the paradox that she has heard the "silent" slipping away of time. And she who, inexorably aging, would like to be youthful, a child again, encouragingly adds while regarding the abyss of temporality:

Only we must not be afraid of it.
Time too is a creature of the Father
who has created us all.
(p. 429)

Allein man muß sich auch vor ihr nicht fürchten.
Auch sie ist ein Geschöpf des Vaters,
der uns alle geschaffen hat.

Flowing time as a creation of the eternal godly Father who created us all—this is the traditional ontotheological answer to the riddle of the essence of time. The creator is eternal, his creatures are temporal; the prime unmoved mover is infinite, the moved are finite; God is absolute, the created are contingent. When the contingent, finite, temporal things return home to their maker, they will partake of his eternity.

"Today you speak like a priest {*Pater*},"[10] Octavian interjects. How subtle and smoothly composed that is. The Princess, who is no longer young and who ponders this fact—

> but can it really be true
> that I was that little Resi
> and that it's I who will one day be the old woman?
> (p. 423)

> Wie . . . das Wirklich sein (kann),
> daß ich die kleine Resi war
> und daß ich auch einmal die alte Frau sein werd! . . .

—the Princess calms her dread in the face of time with a reference to the eternal godly Father. Of course she must immediately endure her young lover's ridicule as a woman who speaks like a "priest"—that is, as one who denies his own name and brings no creatures into the world yet always speaks in the name of the heavenly Father who created without limit. At this, she has the horses harnessed—Hofmannsthal spares nothing to show that he means to avoid exaggerated profundity—and goes, in order to dispel her melancholia, to the "Prater,"[11] which so doggedly rhymes with the unfatherly "Pater," that is, with the priest that speaks in the name of the eternal Father, the one responsible for temporality and transience.

Hofmannsthal's "Comedy for Music" was written in 1910; the story, however, takes place "in Vienna, in the first decade of the reign of Maria Theresa," thus around 1745. The piece is not only characterized by a fissure in time, by a temporal gap, because its author is an unnerved contemporary of the theory of relativity while his protagonists move in the pre-Kantian epoch with its theological confidence in time. A rupture in time rends this magnificent opera for the added reason that it, as a musical event, is timely art in the eminent sense of the word and yet attempts to immortalize the moment—the moment in which Octavian, not as himself and not for himself, but as a suitor "in the name of {his} cousin Lord of Lerchenau,"[12] hands Sophia the silver rose and their eyes meet. Yet this celebration of the eternal moment is mysterious, like the identity of those who experience it. For the rose of the cavalier who woos in the name of another is an ancient symbol of transience that liberates beauty, and at the same time (in this particular context—it is of course a silver rose), a highly paradoxical allegory of permanence. Its bedazzling charm, the "strong smell" that makes it, the artificial, silver-plated, dead rose of art seem "like roses, like live ones" is a result of a technical trick—"a drop of Persian attar of roses," whose scent quickly dissipates. This scent unleashes the pull of the past[13] to which Sophia and Octavian fall prey, and they, though they are indeed together at the moment, are drawn back into their own separate pasts. The scent "draws one after, as with cords about one's heart. / Where I have been once before . . ." (p. 438). In the very moment of their imaginary union, in the blink of an eye, the lovers are separated in the present.

Hegel thought about the paradoxes of the moment that seems to go on forever and to pull away at the same time, and he captured it (alluding to Rosicrucian esotericism) in the marvelous formulation of the "rose in the cross of the present." The cross that we must bear and that carries us, the finite, runs counter to the present. The cross of the present is that the present is not. It passes in the movement of the cross, in the chiasma of elapsing temporality that knows the present not as the Faustian eternal tarrying of the moment but only as the "fury of the disappearance."[14] The present is, as the Cavalier of the Rose must learn, never the presence of the present but always the presence of the past and the future, or the future of the always already past present.[15] The future perfect of the future that has passed is the genuine grammatical tense-mood of the ecstatic present: "I will have lived."

The fury of the destruction of the present, however, and this is the point of Hegel's thought and Hofmannsthal's art, is significant and beautiful. "Out of the fermentation of finiteness that evaporates into nothing, the spirit wafts forth."[16] The fury of destruction is terrible-beautiful, and the rose in the cross of the present is beautiful for its transience. The rose that loses its petals makes it possible to experience, to regard, and to interpret the final withdrawal of permanence as the fulfillment of a meaningful being and existence. The gift of being is one with the withdrawal of time. Not for nothing do the death that takes *and* the love that gives have the power to strip, to defoliate the moment and dispel its momentary presence. Without the terror (of time), that beauty (that being is at all and is not on the contrary not/hing) is not to be had; and for this reason beauty can hardly be defined except as the onset of terror. And so the "fury of the destruction" is beautiful—beautiful like a rose losing its petals, beautiful like the music of *The Cavalier of the Rose*, beautiful like the melancholy "Stanzas in Terza Rima—On Transitoriness" of the early Hofmannsthal.

> Still on my cheek I feel their warm breath fall:
> How can it be that these near days are spent,
> Past, wholly past, and gone beyond recall?
>
> This is a thing that mocks the deepest mind

And far too terrifying for lament:
That all flows by us, leaving us behind.

Noch spür ich ihren Atem auf den Wangen:
Wie kann das sein, daß diese nahen Tage
Fort sind, für immer fort, und ganz vergangen?

Dies ist ein Ding, das keiner voll aussinnt,
Und viel zu grauenvoll, als daß man klage:
Daß alles gleitet und vorüberrinnt.[17]

That everything slides and slips away, the lovers in Hofmannsthal's libretto do not want to acknowledge. They act, on the contrary, as if they had an Apollonian right to repression, misunderstanding, and transfiguration when they act as if they wanted everyone to forget that even the most present and successful evening of opera eventually will have faded away, leaving once again and quite literally the last word[18] to "eternity." "Always together, you and I / to all eternity," Sophia and Octavian sing without embarrassment at the banality, in German, of the rhyme, *Zeit* and *Ewigkeit*, and, so to speak, against their better judgment. They grasp the moment, true to tradition, as the temporal brink of eternity. And they do everything—no: they let everything go—in order to slow down the experience of time slipping by. Their final duet is intended to transfigure what can only be endured on the basis of aesthetic-religious transfiguration: the "too dreadful" flow of time.

Monetary Coverage of Time

Those who are suspicious of such Apollonian transfigurations and insist on being enlightened as to the significance of temporality and finiteness can, as of 1900, hardly avoid the hideous discovery which the lovers can still skillfully and lovingly hide in the sign of the silver rose: that the experience of earthly life and finiteness is no longer covered, that it is on the contrary groundless and unfathomable, that the experience of temporality (and surely of time itself) suggests an eminently secular point of reference and thus has time at its core. Literature, too, hardly ever attempted, in previous epochs, to clarify the puzzling essence and the secrets of time as such. Questions of the type "What is time?" do not fall under the auspices of literature. Theology, philosophy and (as of 1900 to a greater extent) physics feel responsible for this. Literature, however, does attentively register the ways in which the ones wise to the experience of time change.[19]

The years after 1900 have required of their contemporaries a revolution in the conception of time, the monstrous dimensions and dislocations of which cannot be overlooked: the theory of relativity. Above and beyond its view of the physical and cosmological world, it has a descriptive value that cannot be overestimated. "Relative"—this stands above all (and most assuredly for Einstein himself as well) in contrast to "absolute." And "absolute" is the traditional philosophical concept not only (as for Kant) for absolute forms of perception (that is, prior to all concrete apperceptions), but also for God, for the ab-solved, the set-free, the entity independent of all relations and feedback loops, the sublime entity above all finite conditions and thus the unconditional. A theory of relativity therefore means, even for those who cannot read mathematical-physical formulae, that no Absolute lasting from eternity to eternity catches, redeems, consolidates, and covers elapsing time.[20]

During the years after Einstein's epoch-making publication (of 1905) and contemporaneous with the composition of the *Cavalier of the Rose*, Rilke was working on *The Notebooks of Malte Laurids Brigge* {*Die Aufzeichnungen des Malte Laurids Brigge*} (published in 1911). This most comprehensive prose text of Rilke's more than adequately lives up to its matter-of-fact title. Rilke offers no new worldview and does not attempt to establish something that promises to survive Einstein. Instead he notes the ways in which the modern age attempts to react to the relativity of an experience of time that is no longer covered by an absolute.

Rilke, too, stylized the rose as the terrible-beautiful incarnation of the pure contradiction of the present, even in the epitaph he stipulated in his testament of October 25, 1925. On the gravestone next to the church's wall facing the valley in Raron is to be read:

> Rose, oh pure contradiction, joy
> of being No-one's sleep under so many
> lids.

> Rose, oh reiner Widerspruch.
>   Lust,
> Niemandes Schlaf zu sein
>   Unter soviel
> Lidern.[21]

Rilke's lyric, too, strives incessantly to make the hideous retreating of time experienceable as the fulfillment of meaningful and beautiful being and existence.[22] This genuinely aesthetic experience mobilizes the dream, sleep, and the transfigured night against the "suffering under the domination of time."[23] Rilke's work, however, knows that this aesthetic attention to the terrible or perhaps beautiful paradoxes of earthly life—that it is threat and gift, that it gives and takes, that gift without giver precludes its existence, for there "is" no time[24]—are all the more founded as the modernity of this post-theological discovery of time sets up a specifically new form of cover: namely, the monetary.

Monetary problems play a role in Hofmannsthal's libretto that could hardly be more central. To replenish his meager finances, Baron Ochs hopes for an alliance with Sophia Faninal, the daughter of wealthy middle-class parents. Octavian's silver rose ostentatiously keeps its aesthetic distance from both Ochs von Lerchenau's and Faninal's inclinations to turn everything (including the bride or daughter, respectively) to silver, in other words, to use everything for financial advantage. Sophia is not so far off when she thinks the Baron imagines "he has bought {her}" (p. 443). Baron Ochs exhibits the efficiency of the businessman when he, during his rendezvous in the private room with Octavian, who is dressed as a girl, makes a case with threefold temporal-erotic-economic ingenuity for putting out the candles: firstly, as burning candles have always indicated, time is always limited; secondly, darkness makes erotic advances easier for less attractive builds and figures; and thirdly, candles are, as the baron's orders to the waiter to put out the light indicates, expensive. "You're a good fellow. If you'll help me knock a bit off the bill, / there'll be a little something for yourself. Sure to cost a fortune here."[25]

Even beautiful and profound silver roses, however, are not immune to being turned into cash. Indeed, even the eminent symbol of time, the silver rose, can be recast in monetary terms. For "time is money"; time, as a limited resource, is not only compatible with the limited resource of money, time itself *is* money to the extent that it (like and together with money) represents the highest value. Because time and money are the values pure and simple, limited money in its scarcity can counteract limited time. One invests time for the sake of atemporal money, gains in money compensate for the loss of time, money accumulates the past and passing time, money is virtually eternal, a fortune outlives the mortal one that has it, and to make a will and thus to remain a legal subject beyond death makes sense only for those who have something to bequeath and hand over in the future. In short, money cannot die; a well-worn coin that looks old is not worth less nor is it less legal than a newly minted one: "Time is money," because the meta-temporal medium money is permitted to reign over time.

Though not in his lyrics, Rilke pursues the displacements in the experience of time ushered in by post-religious times in his prose work *The Notebooks of Malte Laurids Brigge*. When trust in the eternal

Father, whose passing creation time is, no longer seems indicated, time, which, as one discovers, is no longer covered, must be experienced and appraised as a limited resource. The story of the short and youthful bureaucrat Nikolai Kusmitsch, which is scattered throughout the *Notebooks*, tells of one who tries to make do with his limited and precisely calculated remaining time. He generously estimates the rest of his life at fifty years, and he breaks this span down into days, hours, and seconds remaining to him. And he, the calculator and, with respect to his temporal fortune, the calculated, "put on his fur coat, to look a little broader and more imposing, and presented to himself the whole of this fabulous capital, ... he calculated and calculated, and a total resulted such as he had never seen before. It made him giddy."[26] This giddiness never leaves Nikolai Kusmitsch, who no longer conceives of himself as a gift of creation, but rather as a united-divided giver and given.

The giddiness in which all of his future ideas threaten to vanish undergoes a decisive change without ceasing to be giddiness. At first it is the giddiness of pure, "fabulous" excess that puts Nikolai Kusmitsch "in an almost exuberant humor." This exuberant champagne-mood nonetheless disappears quickly, giving way to that dizziness that makes the life of those who are seasick a hell. For the fullness of time is one with the fullness of its disappearance; Kusmitsch plays his part on ground that is not just swaying but disappearing, on ground that is merely "fabulous": "He now employed his Sundays in putting his accounts in order. But after a few weeks it struck him that he was spending an incredible amount. I will retrench, he thought. He rose earlier; he washed less thoroughly, he drank his tea standing, he ran to his office and arrived much too soon. He saved a little time everywhere. But when Sunday came there was nothing of all this saving. Then he realized that he had been duped" (p. 149).

In contrast to the lovers in *The Cavalier of the Rose*, Kusmitsch does not try to stop the experience of passing time. Kusmitsch mobilizes and accelerates the time that is granted him on earth. He recognizes the situation without repression; he takes account of the time, given the loss of eternity, that he has. And he practices that rational interaction with time in whose sign modernity stands. For first the modern age and then modernity, which can no longer summon up the binding, obliging belief in the immortal soul, conceives of time as the limited resource par excellence. Yet this rationality in interaction with the limited resource of time is tantamount to a dizzy swindle; it rests on a deception, a (self-)deception, that makes one dizzy.[27] It rests on the illusion, the fraud, that limited and therefore valuable time—since its disconnection from eternity—can be covered by limited money. To cover finite time, however, is not even possible through the medium of time itself. Its small units cannot be converted into great epochs and vice versa.

> How long one can live on just one year. But then, this confounded small change, it disappears, one doesn't know how. And there came an ugly afternoon, which he passed sitting in the corner of the sofa and waiting for the gentleman in the fur coat, from whom he meant to demand the return of his time. He would bolt the door and not allow him to depart until he had produced the amount. In notes, he would say, of ten years, if you prefer. Four notes of ten, and one of five, and the remainder he could keep, in the devil's name.

But the giving Kusmitsch in the fur does not appear; "probably his defalcations had been traced" (pp. 149–50).

The semantic field in which Rilke places the monetary anchor of time is free from ambiguity in one respect alone: A "deception" is a deception, and this alone, among the major concepts around which the story of Nikolai Kusmitsch revolves, is unambiguous. The other major concepts are, in contrast, of notable ambiguity: a *Schwindel* {dizziness/swindle} can arise from an excess of joy but also from a mysterious threat, and it can be, moreover, synonymous with "deception"; an event that exceeds all expectations may be called "fabulous," but so can one that takes place in the realm of the fable; and Kusmitsch becomes familiar with the many meanings of *Schein* {shine/appearance/banknote} to the extent that he intends to convert his dwindling trust in the dwindling stature of being and time into trust in large *Geld"scheine"* (money/banknotes). "And so, this slight confusion had taken place, out of pure absentmindedness: Time and Money, as though the two could not be kept apart" (p. 150).

This "slight confusion," this little exchange, this conversion from time to money rests on a promissory note that is no longer covered. One could characterize Rilke's sovereign play with ambiguity as a "merely" poetically interesting pleasure if it were not so obvious that the crisis in the experience of time after 1900 coincides with the crisis in the experience of language.[28] Hofmannsthal's "Letter of Lord Chandos" {"Chandosbrief"} and Rilke's numerous notes revolving around the insight that we are no longer reliably at home in a world put into words and endowed with meaning, together with the crisis in the experience of time, participate in a thoroughly unmediated economy of exchange: both time and language appear (in literature—and certainly not just in Hofmannsthal and Rilke), as of 1900, as uncovered entities.

Dis-covered time (and dis-covered language) cause traditional forms of intimacy with the world and life to lose their footing.

Kusmitsch, felled by this dis-covering of time, finds himself no longer on solid ground but on a swaying deck no longer, as before, brushed by the gentle breath of Hades, but pounded suddenly by a time-snatching storm:

> He suddenly felt a breath on his face; it blew past his ears; he felt it on his hands. He opened his eyes wide. The window was securely shut. And as he sat there in the dark room with wide-opened eyes, he began to realize that what he now sensed was actual time, passing by. He recognized them concretely, these tiny seconds, all equally tepid, one like the other, but swift, but swift. . . . He leaped up. . . . Beneath his feet as well there was something like a movement, not one movement only, but several, curiously interoscillating. He went stiff with terror: could that be the earth? Certainly, it was the earth. And the earth moved. . . . He staggered about in his room as if he were on deck and had to hold on right and left. Unluckily something else occurred to him, about the oblique position of the earth's axis. No, he could not stand all these movements. He felt wretched. Lie down and keep quiet, he had once read somewhere. And since that time Nikolai Kusmitch has been lying down. (pp. 151–52)

Temporal Mobilization

"As if on deck"—Nikolai Kusmitsch is horrified by his discovery of non-covered time. It literally throws him over. No silver rose, no transfigured love, no Apollonian celebration of the moment can dispel his horror at the thought that passing moments are no longer covered by an eternity, the flowing chain of signifiers no longer by a transcendental signified. But Kusmitsch's search for "a kind of time bank, where he might exchange part at least of his shabby seconds," is in vain.[29] Banks would not earn enough by exchanging small change for large notes and vice versa, even if they earned a commission for this exchange. For banks do not trade in coincidental coincidences of time but in money *and* time, in the intersection of payments and points of time, in the "risks of promissory notes."[30] Time is the embodiment of risk, but it is also the medium for mitigating it. Those who cannot meet their financial obligations at the moment they come due can buy themselves time at banks, and thus for a certain span of time remain solvent. Solvency means that the flow of payments and the flow of time continue to synchronize and do not come apart, even if individual debtors cannot pay at the moment.

Thus banks make it possible to count on more than just that which is currently at hand. For banks buy and sell "promissory notes" (promises to pay).[31] Promissory notes systematically bind temporal to monetary perspectives. If the financially obligated borrower has paid off his debts with the interest due, the bank can sell this influx of money once again to others who have paid off promissory notes, or to others who cannot pay at the moment but promise to pay in the future and are able to make it credible that this promise is covered. Banks shift problems of coverage to the long bank,[32] to the infinitely long, to the eternal bank. That does not exclude the possibility that individual participants in the commerce of payments who are unable to make their future ability to pay credible to the creditor come to grief. It is nonetheless fundamentally true that the circulation of promissory notes is infinitely prolonged by banks. Anachronistic questions about covering money at all and in particular promissory notes can be defused in all their awkwardness by temporalizing them. Money is the medium that, in times that no longer ask about the cover for metaphysical statements, nonetheless provides authority.

A promissory note will have been fulfilled, money will have been covered—the future perfect is the temporal medium that banks sell. Banks in fact always will have been time banks. In order that they can be this, they have a noteworthy privilege at their disposal: they may sell their debts.[33] Deposits in banks are, at the same time, the bank's debts to its depositors. The bank must therefore give the depositor a promissory note—a promise to pay that the bank, however, can turn around and sell when it grants someone else credit, thereby accruing a promise to pay the bank. When banks sell their debts at a profit (from interest), they understand this profit as the price for their performance: they are never immune to the awkward discovery that their promises to pay are not covered.

Time banks play their part (almost) on the profound *niveau* of the Anaximandrian principle: "Whence things have their origin, there they must also pass away according to necessity; for they must pay penalty and be judged for their injustice, according to the ordinance of time."[34] And they make it abundantly clear that, when they maintain the liquidity of promissory notes and uphold the order of time, they take possession of a theological legacy and arrange for temporal as well as metaphysical profundity: in their temple architecture, in the priestly, strict dresscode for their employees, in the altar-like quality of their windows, in their safes that resemble tabernacles, in the basic terminology of debtor and creditor,[35] in the ornaments and epigrammatic truths of the banknotes with which they deal ("in God we trust"), in the pauper's oath that they insist upon when things get serious. These temporal-ontotheological references that are very pronounced but rarely clearly thematized surely have apotropaic components as well: to conjure up cover for the monetary and temporal rivers that they administer and to disguise the fact, through cryptotheological show, that in the religious tradition, trade in time was regarded as a satanic business.[36]

Yet everything, even the dialectical forms of bank organization, has its price. Everything must be paid for. That money and time should remain liquid—even this has its price. You can't get something for nothing. So, as Rilke illustrates through Nikolai Kusmitsch, the temporal mobilization of modern times costs, in addition to many positions (such as theological and ecological foundations), a great deal of space above all: "The expansion of the consumption of space is . . . still the most tested remedy for the shortage of time. Essentially all production and transportation operations can be accelerated with the help of additional space and spaciousness. Level building methods in production and warehousing, wider streets and larger airports, denser networks of roads and additional corridors for air traffic—the list goes on and on—save on limited time."[37]

Those who save, do without. Societies and cultures that save time systematically do without space, indeed, they approve of taking the destruction of space into account. "To do without," however, is the rational and economic form of the (religious) sacrifice. And Walter Benjamin, in his *Passagen-Werk*, searches the modern ways of systematically accelerating time for its religious or theological implications. He suspected "that the acceleration of traffic, the tempo at which news is conveyed, the rapidity with which newspaper editions follow one another is moving towards the elimination of all interruption, all abrupt endings."[38] That is the cryptotheological core of the project of modernism: At its very core this project intends to keep time flowing, unending, free of rupture; at its very core it intends, specifically, to guarantee the very eternity it had theologically desiccated. Cash flow, together with the points of intersection for the accumulation of capital, then assumes the place of the religious connections between finiteness and eternity.

In a poem with the lapidary title "Das Geld" {"The Money"}, Hans Magnus Enzensberger captures this incessant transcendence of money in dense verse:

It isn't that way at all, as if it could be gathered into a bundle,
reined in with rosy ribbons,
rolled, stuffed into a mattress
forever; so that
you could sleep easy

and dream of it, how you inherit it,
print it, pour it down the drain,
distribute it, destroy it, have it;
how you stand there with hands raised
and tremble, and someone hollers:
Undress for twelve marks
For twelve million lay down,
either die or else fight for it,
until it gets outside;

no, it isn't that way; it isn't
that way at all, as if you could have it,
not have it, grasp it, grab it;
it doesn't smell, doesn't crackle,
has no essence; but it trickles
psychically, is gone, of its own accord, collects
itself within, flows, sets; thickly
floods while setting
everything that telephones;
and it rises of course so that
only corpses do not drink from it;
but then it recedes again, is gone,
evaporates and trickles, anew,
economically, and of its own accord.

Es ist ja nicht so, daß es sich bündeln,
mit rosigen Banderolen bändigen,
rollen ließe, in die Matratze stopfen
für immer; dergestalt,
daß du einfach einschlafen könntest
und davon träumen, wie du es erbst,
druckst, aus dem Fenster wirfst,
austeilst, vernichtest, hast;
wie du dastehst mit erhobenen Händen
und zitterst, und einer brüllt:
Zieh dich aus für zwölf Mark,
für zwölf Millionen, leg dich hin,
stirb entweder oder kämpfe darum,
bis es wird draußen;

nein, so ist es nicht; es ist
ja nicht so, als ob du es haben,
nicht haben, fassen, anfassen könntest;
es riecht ja nicht, knistert nicht,
hat kein Wesen; sondern es tropft
psychisch, fehlt, von selber, sammelt
sich innen, rinnt, gerinnt; dickflüssig

überschwemmt es beim letzten Fixing
alles was telephoniert;
und zwar dergestalt steigt es, daß
nur die Leichen nicht davon trinken;
doch dann fällt es wieder, fehlt,
verdunstet und tropft, von neuem,
wirtschaftlich, und von selber.

8

POETIC CRITIQUE OF MONEY—
ON THE HERMENEUTICS OF THE DEFICIENCY

To Negate or Critique

To critique money is not the exclusive right of literature. Political parties, churches, and associations also have an interest in particular ways of critiquing money (for example, in their claims that one can bribe politicians of the other parties with money, that the other religions or confessions forget God over money, and that the other associations, with their assets and the contributions of their members, run things just as one would expect). In the chorus of the critiques of money and in the rustle of the numerous arrangements with this medium, it is not so easy to isolate the voice of literature. Is there such a thing as a specific, unmistakable, genuinely literary, poetic critique of money at all? A critique of money that can be distinguished from the discourses of sociology, psychology, theology, and philosophy?

The pluralistic point of view is of course correct in this respect as well. Accordingly, there are as many forms of a poetic critique of money as there are poetic works that treat the theme. Nonetheless, the less judicious search for a cumulative perspective from which it would become clear whether there is a view of money common to modern literature in all its individual works, thus constituting a specifically aesthetic-poetic observation, is seductive. What is it about money, then, from a genuinely literary perspective, that is so sorely in need of critique? And is it even remotely possible for a utopian negation of money to grow out of this critique?

One can criticize—where things are sufficiently liberal, even publicly and without retribution—everything, as is well known: the weather, society, characters, those in government, those governed, events, structures, meals, even being and time. On the other hand, not everything can be unproblematically negated. Those who stubbornly negate something run the risk, and not just since Freud's essay on negation,[1] of affirming the very thing they negate. Those who negate a negation must take into account, and not just since Hegel, that they have constituted rather than repudiated that thing: *duplex negatio est affirmatio*.[2] Those who negate being, time, world, or meaning lay claim to time and meaning and presuppose being and world. In this sense concepts like being, time, world, and meaning can certainly be criticized, but they cannot be negated without contradiction. One can lament that being is rather than nothing, that time passes, that the world is falsely organized, and the meaning of the universe and all that is (or is in it) is not manifest enough. Yet one cannot avoid these concepts (or the experiences that are—however unclearly—indicated by these concepts) outright.

That which cannot be controlled can in any event be experienced very differently. Whether a glass is half full or half empty is, as is well known, less an objectively decidable controversy than an illustration of two incompatible ways of experiencing the world and existence {*Dasein*}. The curmudgeon's paradise is different from the hedonist's; and the world of the fortunate is—as the metaphysical logician Wittgenstein puts it—a different world than that of the unfortunate. This also means, however, that primary interpretations (statements like: existence is a burden, or a gift; being is good or, on the contrary, a disturbance of the purity of nonexistence) cannot be derived; they stand in unresolvable conflict—they arise from origins about which one could argue with compelling conviction.

Institutions usually like to forget that freedom (of underived interpretations) is the *reason for reasons* {*Grund des Grundes*}.[3] Indeed, Arnold Gehlen's less than charming anthropology that regards human beings as nothing but instinct-bound "deficient beings"[4] notwithstanding, it is precisely the task of institutions to ascribe to and inscribe in human beings capable of interpretation a hermeneutics of being, of the world, of time, and of meaning. Thus institutions or corporate bodies like churches, universities, prep schools, special interest groups, and central banks do not merely manage their specific set of tasks, they also necessarily interpret the world and existence in the process—e.g., as standing in need of salvation, education, representation, or money. The point of comparison of these institutionalized worldviews is usually the neediness of the deficient being, the human being, and the deficiency of the world as a whole.

Institutions must legitimate the obligations they impose (from school to military service to taxation) through the deficiencies they claim to redress. And at the same time they must hide this correlation. Otherwise the suspicion that they have an interest in the deficiency to which they, due to their claim to redress it, owe their existence, would become much too threatening.[5] Institutions share this structural interest in hiding this correlation with obsessive-compulsive neurosis {*Zwangsneurose*}. Neurosis, too, compensates for lacks, shocks, mistakes or transgressions that it wants forgotten with quasi-institutional coerciveness; the neurosis, too, has access to implicit knowledge of this correlation that must remain un-conscious/known.

Thus Ulrich Sonnemann defined "neurosis as the institution in miniature"[6] and suggested the inversion of this informative figure of analysis: institutions are obsessive-compulsive macroneuroses (and therefore often as prolifically productive as the individual neurotic in other contexts). Institutions make no secret of their neurotic constitution: the compulsory use of proof of delivery, transparent wrappings, printed forms, and the obligatory standard phrases of the bureaucrat's speech speak for themselves. To criticize the implicit worldviews of these corporate bodies, whose condition for and right to existence is deficiency and neediness, is the business of the critique of ideology. To take part in this critique—thank goodness!—is not, after an epoch of enlightened hermeneutics of suspicion lasting more than two hundred years, all that challenging. Especially because corporate bodies—*nomen est omen* (see chapter 12)—offer themselves for personal criticism in the form of their leaders and spokespersons (popes, boards of directors, party bosses, and so forth).

More intricate than the problem of obsessive-compulsive institutions is therefore that of the generalizable media. For they are uniquely anonymous, of indifferent ability to function, and empty of content. In contrast to corporations they have no recognizable and transparent business purpose. To criticize language, books, newspapers, television, or money pure and simple is not only possible, it is widely practiced, but it is relatively unproductive. It is widespread practice for good reason, on the other hand, to distinguish between languages that are easy to learn and those that are difficult to master, good and bad books, informative and tabloid newspapers, silly and serious TV shows, and helpful versus destructive handling of money. In the process it is easy to show that the profound structural interpretations that the generalizable media impose upon us are still much more far-reaching than the worldviews of institutions that are all too obviously influenced by vested interests. Much suggests, in fact, that the generalizable media congeal into the second nature that is as little up for negation as the first.

Of course, one can criticize *the* books, *the* television, or *the* money. But then one criticizes evolutionary, quasi-transcendental-historical apriorities of societies that are hardly to be negated, because they are no longer seriously (or perhaps only at the terrible price of fatal repudiation) up for discussion. To reject generalizable media as such thus means to risk a macropsychosis; to erect institutions means, on the other hand, to establish the neurotic, normal state of psychic systems in social macrodimensions.

In this sense, one can criticize or negate money as much or as little as one can the world with which money is so stubbornly consonant. Money is the world all over again; money is the medium of a remarkably successful attempt to simulate the world in toto. Attempts to negate money pure and simple and reject it (psychotically) as the source of all evil could not, therefore, succeed. We cannot afford, so to speak, to do away with money; it is not "in the picture." A world without money is nonetheless always aesthetically in the picture. And this is no doubt true for the simple reason that art has always provided alternative versions of reality (such as utopian or past) and because, as is generally known, there has not always been money. It makes no appearance in Homer's *Odyssey*—precisely because it was first "invented" in post-Homeric times. Although money undoubtedly does not belong to the first world (even in the monotheistic religions' accounts of creation it is not mentioned among the original works of God but is usually excluded as a product of a satanic second encoding of the world), it is *nearly*, it is *almost* as impossible to negate as the world with which it forms (at least in the German language) an uncommonly suggestive and plausible rhyme.

This "nearly" indicates a complex problem. According to an ingenious insight of Friedrich Schlegel, Kant neglected to include the category "almost" in the table of categories in his *Critique of Pure Reason*.[7] Money nearly/almost cannot be negated. Since, however, even high cultures have developed without money, it must be true that money is not the *conditio sine qua non* for a complex experience of world and existence. In any event, all the evidence suggests that money, once "invented," cannot be negated without the greatest of complications. And thus the suspicion arises that the medium of money itself is to be grasped precisely as a negation—as a negation, that is, indeed as a rejection of a world(-experience) that does not yet convey being, time, and world as limited and therefore dear resources, but instead as a gratuitous gift (of, say, the gods or of the emanating being) and as a gift of excess.

Scarcity

"The Phoenicians invented money—but why so little?" Nestroy's precise and therefore deeply comical question can be answered with precision. Money must be limited, otherwise it has no value. If everyone had unlimited access to the medium of money, if everyone had as much as they wanted at their disposal, if there were a superfluity of money, money would be superfluous. For a superfluity of money or superfluous money would not fulfill its essential function: to make the unlikelihood likely that one would relinquish his (limited) goods to another. The historical test of the thesis of the necessity of money's scarcity and of the functional superfluousness of a superfluity of money is provided by the numerous inflationary epochs (including the most recent experiences in the former Soviet Union). Money as such can without question be increased enough to make everyone a millionaire many times over, indeed even a billionaire. Then it stops being money, however, and that means it stops having value. No one will trade a loaf of bread or a pair of shoes for riches made of paper. Paper printed in mass falls back on its intrinsic value. And this is obviously so negligible that it is only fit for the most lowly of uses: "pecunia olet."

The paradox of the artificially achieved scarcity of money is psychically not always easy to accept. The temptation to compensate for public or private deficits with counterfeit money of all kinds is seductive—and under very trying circumstances almost irresistible. It certainly was for the pitiable employees of the German Federal Bank whose only responsibility was to destroy banknotes taken out of circulation. Years ago a group of such Federal Bank employees, poorly paid, of course, were unable to resist the temptation to refuse to destroy this money, and to return at least some of the notes removed from circulation to the active economy. The sentencing for this quickly discovered deed turned out to be difficult. After all, the perpetrators only—surely a pardonable misdeed—stole wastepaper that was earmarked for destruction.

Despite the psychological resistance, it is true that money must be limited. Only as a limited resource does money make sense as a medium. For limited money is systematically correlated to limited goods. Goods and services, of course, do not have to be limited. But they are—in any event when money puts them in perspective.

The post-paradisiacal world and in particular the world since the "invention" of money is marked by universal deficiency. The infinite deficiency of being, of existence, of time, of love, of fulfillment, of happiness, of recognition, and so on is obviously not to be permanently redressed. There is no deficiency of this deficiency that constitutes the world. This elemental, mundane lack is not lacking. This ontic, indeed ontological[8] scarcity will not become scarce. But the scarcity of the first nature can be answered with an artificial scarcity, with the scarcity of money, that is. Then there are

> two languages of scarcity—that of goods and that of money—which respond to different circumstances. In the modern economy, *all* economic operations are constrained to use *both* languages of scarcity *at once*, thus the complete code of the economy and only this code, in other words, to *pay* for *services*. The structure of the economy resides in the conditioning of this operative connection. Thus one can only reduce the shortage of goods, because it is accompanied by a simultaneous shortage of snatching them up.[9]

Those who hoard lots of money do not have the goods that they could have for this hoarded money. Those who, conversely, hoard goods, do not have the money that was spent for these goods. The very first sentence of Sohn-Rethel's *Exposé zum Plan einer soziologischen Theorie der Erkenntnis* calls attention to this binary logic of the shortage: " 'Society' is . . . an association of human beings with respect to their existence, and certainly on the level at which a piece of bread that one eats cannot satisfy the other."[10] Both shortages, that of money and that of goods, correlate to and in *one* encoding. And this encoding should be as stable as possible and may not, for this very reason, be completely stable. Prices have to fluctuate so that limited money can encode access to limited goods with relatively little violence: Desired goods must become more expensive, goods that are shunned must, via lower prices, be made "more reasonable," meaning they must be made into goods that one (if not for their outstanding quality, at least for their favorable price) can "reasonably" accept. The paradox cannot be overlooked: Inflation and deflation are mechanisms of stabilizing the code of money with respect to limited goods. For the sake of its ideal: namely, to avoid chaos, to establish reliability, to protect calculability and guarantee stability (not only of prices, but of the economic system, of institutions and of interactions) the code of money must fluctuate.

However fluctuating and unstable this monetary code may be, it imposes one perspective with the most highly stable force of obligation: precisely that of scarcity and deficiency. Since the medium of money cannot be avoided in modern times, and since it has advanced to preconscious and non-negatable self-evidence, its scandalous, deep hermeneutical implication is hardly judicious. Worldviews and experiences of being that take as their point of departure the glorious improbability that being is rather than nothing/ness, that existence in comparison with the normal case of nonexistence is pure extravagance, that among the millions of stars without life, our earth is an incomprehensibly splendid exception to the rule, and that life is a wonderful, incomprehensible gift rather than a debt whose term has been extended, have no real chance of prevailing in the market of free opinion and interpretation in view of the (religiously prepared for and) monetarily induced hermeneutics of universal deficiency, equivalence, and debt(s).

Aesthetic celebrations of the fullness of being do not stand a chance today. Modern literature that understands itself as beautiful, even transfiguring literature whose task it is to extol the fullness of being and the pleasure of life rather than to criticize the burden of it, exposes itself to a smile and mild ridicule at best, more often, however, to irritated critique. Goethe's late "Whatever the outcome, you have known beauty" {"Es sei wie es wolle, es war doch so schön"} (*Faust II*, 11302–3), the final sentence of *Memoirs of a Good-for-Nothing* (*Aus dem Leben eines Taugenichts*), "And all was right with the world!" (p. 120), or Rilke's "Praising is what matters!" {"Rühmen, das ists"[11]} can hardly find their sequel in contemporary literature. The most well-known exception to the rule, namely Handke's poetic art of the affirmation of being, meets with criticism that is downright rabid. That life-affirming art[12] cannot be unproblematic since the traumatic catastrophes of the twentieth century is obvious. That therefore, however, an aesthetic of praise, of extolling, and of transfiguration would be left, without competition, to advertising, did not even occur to Goethe.

Excess[13]

One cannot negate money (almost). And thus that deeply hermeneutical medium that systematically shapes scarcity and thus the experience of the fullness of being as the illusory, anachronistic-aesthetic exception is (nearly) incapable of being deceived. Not for nothing do aesthetics of abundance, of extravagance, of celebration, and of expenditure have the effect of seeming premodern (and thus premonetary). Goethe contrasts, in the Masquerade scene of *Faust II*, the carnivalesque forms of an antiquated economy of expenditure with the monetary forms of a specifically modern economy of equivalences. And in this theological-economic-dramatic tract, the chariot on which

Mephistopheles, as the personification of greed, and Faust, as the personification of wealth, sit is driven by the allegory of poetry, who says anachronistically:

> I am that spendthrift, poetry;
> as poet, I augment my worth
> by squandering my very substance.
> I, too, am rich beyond all measures
> and count myself the peer of Plutus,
> add life and beauty to his revels,
> and give you what he can't bestow.

> Bin die Verschwendung, bin die Poesie;
> Bin der Poet, der sich vollendet,
> Wenn er sein eigenst Gut verschwendet.
> Auch bin ich unermeßlich reich
> Und schätze mich dem Plutus gleich,
> Beleb' und schmück' ihm Tanz und Schmaus,
> Das, was ihm fehlt, das teil' ich aus.
> (5573–79)

Poetry has at its disposal that which even Plutus, the god of excessive wealth, lacks. Wealth as a concept is correlated to poverty; wealth indicates that one can afford what is not to be obtained by meager means. Extravagance and spending evade questions such as whether or not one can afford this or that to begin with. Economically senseless spending enacts that to which Bataille repeatedly refers—that life is an eccentric abundance: "The living organism . . . ordinarily receives more energy than is necessary for maintaining life; the excess energy . . . can be used for the growth of a system; if the system can no longer grow, or if the excess cannot be completely absorbed in its growth, it must necessarily be lost without profit; it must be spent, willingly or not, gloriously or catastrophically."[14]

Modernity, standing under the sign of the limited medium of money, is an expert in the catastrophic form of wasting excess, in that monstrous devourer of resources, war. Precisely to the extent that it fetishizes an economy of equivalence and reacts almost psychotically to an economy of splendid expenditure, it organizes orgies of warlike destruction. Compared to this systematic destruction of abundance, the impetuous economy of the potlatch is a charming as well as harmless show. In the wise and melancholy drama of Goethe's old age, the Masquerade scene with its uncertain memory of an aesthetic economy of expenditure is followed by the enactment of a violent war—and the analytical statement, "war, trade, and piracy together are / a trinity not to be severed" (11187–88).

Poetry, squandering and expending itself freely, stands not in the harmony of a trinity, but remarkably alone in the Masquerade scene. It offers a glaring contrast to the modern aesthetic of advertising as staged in the immediately preceding scene.[15] The two choruses "continue to set up the displays of their wares in gradually rising tiers and to offer them for sale."[16] And when they metonymically praise "what is sold and those who sell it" {"Krämerinnen wie die Ware"} (5115) and display the "ripe wares {they} offer" (5173 {"reifer Waren Fülle"}, 5172), they stage the unfathomable insight that, after the end of every unbroken aesthetic of praise, extolling, and affirmation, advertising, of all things, becomes the functional equivalent of this pre-monetary aesthetic of affirmation, of praise of being and of Dionysian thankfulness. It can be this, however, only as a result of a cruel paradox: Advertising systematically creates the perception of deficiency; it creates needs from which it, praising wares as the hymn once praised the all-powerful Lord and his kingdom, promises deliverance. In times when money is in fact the valid code, praise and transfiguration are hardly possible any longer, unless transfiguration and a conjuring up of the deficiency are a given.

Faust is the protagonistic arena of that hermeneutics of the deficiency that, in the unfolding economy of money, achieves power and universal authority. In the Masquerade scene, Faust disguises himself as Plutus, who is pleased with his wasteful son and enjoys his "abundance" (5699). Yet the sphere of beautiful appearance {*schönen Scheins*} and carnivalesque expenditure ends abruptly in the very next scene when Mephistopheles, present at the masquerade as the personification of greed, "invents" the assignats. Affected by the banknotes and the paper/illusory money {*Geldscheine und Schein-geld*}, Faust reels, more than ever, from desire to gratification, and he languishes, in gratification, more than ever before, from desire. For the one who enters the world's stage with a lament—"I've studied, now, to my regret . . ." {"Habe nun, ach . . ."} (354)—the pleasure of the Dionysian yea-saying has become ultimately impossible. Foundering, Faust is reminiscent of a depraved, monetarily overcome aesthetic of existence that could say to the moment, tarry a while, you are so fair {" 'Verweile doch, du bist so schön!' "} (11582). The drama of Goethe's old age constitutes the final refrain on a world whose praises Faust, as the prototype of a thoroughly monetized modernity, can no longer sing, something it is still possible for "Lynceus, the keeper on the palace watchtower," to experience:

Sight is my birthright;
assigned to this tower

to watch is my task,
and the world is my joy.
. . . .
In what I behold
there always is beauty;
content with it all,
I'm content with myself.
Oh fortunate eyes!
whatever you've seen,
whatever the outcome,
you have known beauty!

Zum Sehen geboren,
Zum Schauen bestellt,
Dem Turme geschworen,
Gefällt mir die Welt.
. . . .
So seh' ich in allen
Die ewige Zier
Und wie mir's gefallen
Gefall' ich auch mir.
Ihr glücklichen Augen,
Was je ihr gesehn,
Es sei wie es wolle,
Es war doch so schön!
(11288–91; 11296–303)

Goethe uses the past tense: a world not yet inscribed with the monetary hermeneutics of universal deficiency *was* beautiful. The song of the keeper ends (after a "long pause") with a lament that is (no longer) at home on the historical-philosophical boundary line: "What was once a joy to see / now belongs to ages past" {"Was sich sonst dem Blick empfohlen, / Mit Jahrhunderten ist hin"}. And soon after the end of these final verses "four gray women" appear, who prepare the way for the end of the economy and the aesthetic of plenty, of excess, of expenditure: Want, Care, Debt, Distress. They note laconically that Faust, who has participated so intensively in the modern mobilization of the world, "is starving though there is plenty" {"in der Fülle verhungert"} (11462).

The violent, indeed almost desperately imploring moment of Goethe's aesthetic of the expenditure of praise and of the praise of expenditure is probably nowhere more obvious than in the erratic-defiant closing lines of the poem "The Bridegroom" {"Der Bräutigam"}, which portrays all of the shortcomings, the cares, the afflictions of the middle-class hero's life, only to end by exclaiming: "Life's good, though worst

befall us, life is blessed" {"Wie es auch sei, das Leben, es ist gut"}.[17]
Without the surmounting of the hermeneutic of deficiency and without an aesthetic of existence {Daseins-Aesthetik} of pure expenditure, it
becomes impossible to sabotage fate. It is not only the old Goethe who
recognizes this, the young joker Johann Nestroy, wise beyond his years,
knows it too, having offered these great words: "Revolutions make
their assault . . . on earthly governments. That is too insignificant
for me. . . . I revolt against the government of the world, meaning
against that which is called fate . . . {and} in the process something
emerges that destroys the grizzled absolutism of fate, requiring destiny
constitutionally to take responsibility for squandering as well as for
denying its gifts."[18]

Among Nestroy's insights is his refusal to place the sabotage of
fate in the depths of metaphysics in which all essence is ostensibly
grounded but all groundings more likely to decompose.[19] Nestroy's
works are thus not given to the profound metaphysics of the search
for final causes, but prescribe on the contrary to a witty aesthetic of
superficiality. With downright stubborn regularity, this aesthetic takes
as its point of departure the greatest superficiality: filthy mammon. It
is the key to the deepest questions—such as the question of whether
being and presence are a gift or a debt, a celebration or a demiurgical
destruction of the purity of nonexistence.

A year after Goethe's death, Nestroy wrote a confused sequel to
Faust with his "magical burlesque" {"Zauberposse"}, Der böse Geist
Lumpazivagabundus oder Das liederliche Kleeblatt. That such a thing is
only possible as a farce and a burlesque was fully evident to Nestroy.
That Knieriem can only experience the fullness of being when he is
filled with the spirit of alcohol—thus (nearly) always—is among the
farcical elements. This fullness is balanced, however, by the experience
of extreme want. Even as he meets Fassel, the happy lottery winner at
the tavern who buys round after round, he comments soberly:

> What bad timing, to win something now.
> *Fassel.* Why?
> *Knieriem.* Because it's too late to invest it. In a year the new comet is
>   coming that will destroy the world, and afterwards my Lord is a
>   goner with all his winnings.
> *Leim.* Don't say such stupid things, nothing's gonna happen, a
>   professor told me so.
> *Knieriem.* Don't you think I know more than a professor? I learned
>   astronomy out of a book and make my own observations all the
>   time when I'm going home at night.
> *Leim.* Ya, when you're wasted.[20]

Knieriem, who always assumes that a comet will hit the earth, is not to be deterred from his melancholy perspective, even when he, too, hits it big in the lottery. For the final comet, which makes everything scarce at one blow—time, love, discourse, intoxication—fulfills Knieriem's unrelenting expectation. When Peppi, whose favor he courts with Viennese charm and (once again) little money as well as little effort, for it is not worth the trouble, points out: "He has to become upstanding. He has to better himself," and presses a banknote into his hand for this purpose, he answers curtly: "No, don't do that.—It isn't worth the trouble for this little bit of time. The comet is coming in a year, afterwards the world will be destroyed."[21] Precisely because of this elemental shortage, the newly rich cobbler (who had been poor before and would be again) gives himself over to an aesthetic economy of pure expenditure. And for this very reason he finds mercy from Amorosa, the powerful fairy and protector of true love. Redeemed are only those who, in the universal mobilization of modernity that stands under the triumphant sign of monetary equivalence, acknowledge this as a quasi-transcendental apriority, and nonetheless delight, unfathomably, in existence.

III

ONTOSEMIOLOGY
OF
MONEY

9

Equivalence, Indifference, Rings—
Summary and Transition

"Whatever the outcome, you have seen beauty." A lovely Goethe-phrase from those not yet thoroughly monetized times in which be-ing, time, and existence {*Dasein*} were still experienced as a gift and not merely as limited resources. In the last years of Goethe's life a revealing controversy arose in the *Morgenblatt für gebildete Stände* over the question of what time *was* and now (around 1830) *is*. The literati Wilhelm Wackernagel and Karl Simrock had argued over whether primacy is due the sword (for which Wackernagel pleaded) or the pen (Simrock's preference). The typical *querelle allemande* mingled high-spirited analytical claims with postulates. The arguments and adjurations flew thick and fast: Napoleon and Goethe were stylized into historical-philosophical background figures. And one writer, who knew France and Germany equally well and had made a name for himself as the Prussian Queen Luise's page, as a literary man of Ro-manticism, as a polyglot world traveler and as the author of one of the best-known novellas of the German language, was called upon to act as "judge": Adelbert von Chamisso. He published the following apodictic "judgment" in the *Morgenblatt* of June 3–4, 1831, which elegantly, and just as cynically, faults both contenders:

> Money is power and glory,
> Baron Rothschild is the hero of our age,
>   Only debt and debts are deadly.

Money alone creates peace and war,
Money, precious money alone determines who will triumph,
  While accepting the service of sword and pen.

And if you, gentlemen, care about my judgment,
  He who honors me most highly,
Gives me the most money, will receive, as is right and proper,
Justice from me, and that by all rights.

  Geld ist Macht und Herrlichkeit,
Ein Freiherr Rothschild ist der Heros unsrer Zeit,
  Verderblich sind die Schuld nur und die Schulden.

  Das Geld schafft Frieden nur und Krieg,
Das Geld, das liebe Geld bedingt allein den Sieg,
  Dem Schwert und Feder dienend sich gedulden.

Und ist euch, meine Herrn, an meinem Urteilsspruch gelegen,
  Wer mich am besten honoriert,
Das mehrste Geld mir gibt, behält, wie sichs gebührt,
Bei mir auch Recht und das *von Rechtes wegen*.[1]

Chamisso's judgment is clear: neither sword nor pen,[2] neither spirit nor power can lay claim to priority in the nineteenth century. The serene scientist, polyglot world traveler, aristocratic emigrant, page to Prussia's queen and Romantic poet states, rather laconically (as did Lyotard 150 years later), "the economic genre's hegemony over the others."[3] For "by all rights" functional primacy befits money. The emphasis in the last verse is Chamisso's. To understand this expression of the greater right of money simply as sarcasm or cynicism would miss the mark. It is far more important to Chamisso to emphasize, with an earnestness that does not preclude Romantic wit, the legitimacy of modernity along with the legitimacy of money: By the end of the age of Goethe and following the Napoleonic Wars, money has functional primacy over power and spirit—and not due to the normative force of the factual alone, but rather "by all rights."

It is also revealing to note which one of money's opponents does not present itself at all in the struggle for priority in the late age of Goethe: religion. Thomas Mann heard a "very good story" pertaining to this problem, which he immediately recorded in his diary: "Laurenz Müllner, clever Jesuit of the University of Vienna, says of Friedrich Jodl, the liberal and ethicist of the Enlightenment: 'Look, Jodl *really* believed that there is no God. I don't even believe that.'"[4] It was obviously clear to the author of the arguments between Naphta and Settembrini in the *Magic Mountain* that money may still stand in rivalry with pen and sword, but not with divine salvation, whose promises it has for the most part assimilated. The fight for preeminence is carried out solely in the inner world: sword and pen serve money, not God.

The profundity of this displacement becomes clear when one looks back 600 years via some late-Romantic lines of poetry and is reminded of one of the earliest tales of a fight between power, money, and salvation: Rudolf von Ems's *Der Guote Gêrhart* {Gerhart the Good} of 1220 (or perhaps of 1210, as claimed in an early study and made plausible once again by Sonja Zöller). The story of this courtly epic poet and world historian can easily be retold.[5] Emperor Otto prides himself on his generous donations, for which he expects, even counts on, heavenly rewards. Yet an angel shows him an international merchant from Cologne who has honestly earned the epithet "the Good" through impressive acts of generosity, and is thus far dearer to God. This piques the imperial curiosity; he travels to the Rhine in order to meet his financial-religious, middle-class rival. This salesman, Gerhart, has bought Christians out of Muslim captivity in Morocco—including Erêne, daughter of the Norwegian king—without regard for financial losses (admittedly not without money, but with goods of trade). At the request of Erêne's father, Gerhart renounces plans for a marriage between Erêne and his son when Erêne's intended, the English Prince Willehalm, believed dead, suddenly and apparently miraculously returns. Emperor Otto is not unimpressed by such magnanimity and generosity; he regrets his self-importance, and promises more humility and more gifts motivated by religion (including one for the writing of this story). That the events forming the basis of this epic of transfiguration occurred differently—that the Cologne merchant and financier of Otto's imperial policy was not given the epithet "the Good," but on the contrary was called "Gerhart the Unfair" ("Gêrhart Unmaze") by his contemporaries, and that Rudolf von Ems relied on a clerical source who stepped forward (in exchange for alms?!) to do PR work for the good merchant—all of this is recounted in another source.[6]

That an international merchant, in the year 1210, is fit to be an epic hero, and that the archaic scheme of give and take (as it is still portrayed in the *Nibelungenlied* and Parzival's *Wolfram*[7]) is reformulated in fiscal terms, is in itself an exception in literary history. That Gerhart does not, however, immediately establish his own kingly line but modestly withdraws, observing the demands of feudalism and allowing his wealth to flow into clerical institutions, makes this story by the ministerial[8] Rudolf von Ems (he refers to himself in *Willehalm von Orlens* as "a civil servant of Muntfort") possible at such a remarkably early point in time. That Rudolf von Ems was prepared to put pen to paper in order to ennoble merchants and their medium of money so decisively remains, for centuries, the crass exception. Stories about money, in an era where the need for recourse to the medium in order to arrange exchanges was the exception, are always exotic and adventurous. It was not until the nineteenth century that the universally established and coolly functioning code of money put an end to the historically true "extravagant stories from the economic life of Europe" of the Middle Ages and the early modern period. The Italian historian of economics, Carlo M. Cipolla, recounted three paradigmatic "money-adventure" stories[9] of the early modern period. They all revolve around the ways in which sword and pen (that is to say, PR campaigns avant la lettre) struggle in vain to prevent the triumphant advance of money. Thus the story of Piero di Gualterotto of the Bardi family of Florence, who openly proclaims that merchants may not become richer than warriors and therefore purchases the Kastell Vernio (!) as a stronghold from which to attack merchants passing by, to spare their lives for money, and then to shift to activities involving (the counterfeiting of) money. The warriors capitulate in the face of the superior force of money, which can no longer be restrained by the sword.

Whether the sugarcoated story of the good Gerhart or the unembellished stories from Europe's early economic life: there is no doubt that the medium of money is enjoying its victory lap. By the beginning of the nineteenth century, at the latest, the epoch in which sword and pen, power and spirit, reign supreme, ostensibly independent of the monetary sphere, ends definitively. The monetarily formulated "prose of relationships" takes the place of the religious-aesthetic "poetry of the heart,"[10] according to Hegel's diagnosis. In short, "it is all over"— everything, that is, which pertains to a pre-monetary order of things, power, discourses, and ontosemiology. A variant of the epochal arbitration poem in Chamisso's *Poetisches Hausbuch* makes an even more apodictic and laconic judgment than the published text:

> Gentlemen, it is all over,
> There was absolutely nothing to be done, frankly,
> About heroism, about sailing around the world.

> Absolutely nothing, I mean, absolutely no money to make.
> And now, as a man of the pen I try to make my way in the world
> Yet there is nothing to be gained from the pen either.

> So it may be that, free from undue influence of sword and pen,
> I stand in judgment of both
> That only money, though, and money alone
> Wins the prize remains uncontested.

Ihr Herrn, das alles ist vorbei,
Es war mit Heldentum, mit Weltumsegelei
Gar nichts zu machen, sag' ich unverhohlen.

Gar nichts, ich meine gar kein Geld.
Und jetzt als Federvieh versuch' ichs in der Welt
Doch mit der Feder ist auch nichts zu holen.

So mag ich von dem Schwert und von der Feder unbestochen
Ein Richter über beide sein
Daß aber nur dem Geld und nur dem Geld allein
Der Preis gebührt bleibt unwidersprochen.[11]

That Chamisso is serious about his apodictic formulation is substantiated by the fact that it can be judged a thinly veiled self-reference. For
the penultimate sentence of his "amazing story" of Peter Schlemihl
{*Peter Schlemihls wundersame Geschichte*}, first published in 1814, reads
as a *fabula docet:* "But you, my friend, if you wish to live among your
fellow men, learn to honor your shadow, and then, money." This is,
given that it brings an amazing story about a traumatic experience
with money to an end, a remarkable phrase. It involves the paradox
that characterizes money motifs and problems throughout most of
modern literature: regarding money as the medium equally deserving
of veneration and repudiation.

To analyze modern literature historically in terms of motifs and
ambiguities (as does the second part of this study with respect to poetic
representations of money) means: to do individual works an injustice.
For modern works of art usually conceive of themselves (and in fact
function, too!) as expressions of idiosyncratically dissident observations, insights, and values.[12] They deviate intentionally from standard
findings and observations, and they regularly produce and present
something akin to semantic excess. They overaccentuate peculiarities,
deviations, differences, violations of the norm, and particularities—for
the simple reason that these are more worthy of narration and preservation in print (it is currently acceptable to say that they have more
bite and more bits) than the routine normal case. It is therefore all the
more striking when literature, as it does in Chamisso's lines, believes
itself capable of announcing "uncontested" truths. "That only money,
though, and money alone / Wins the prize remains uncontested." An
ironic contradiction has inscribed itself into even this "uncontested"
thesis: the formulation "wins the prize" has a double meaning that is, if
not ruinous, at the very least remarkable. If money alone wins the prize,
then everything has its price. The functional primacy of the controlling
medium of money in modern societies can only be achieved at a price.

This primacy exists "by all rights." And yet, or precisely therefore, one must pay for everything. One must praise money and yet one may not forget the price of this praise. Brecht's "Song of the Stimulating Impact of Cash" {"Lied von der belebenden Wirkung des Geldes"} praises the medium of money as a vitalizing element—in melancholy verses that read as an express paraphrase of Chamisso's lines.

1

People keep on saying cash is sordid
Yet this world's a cold place if you're short.
Not so once you can afford it
And have ample cash support.
No need then to feel you've been defrauded
Everything is bathed in rosy light
Warming all you set your eyes on
Giving each what's his by right.
Sunshine spreads to the horizon.
Just watch the smoke; the fire's alight.
  Then things soon become as different as they can.
  Longer views are taken. Hearts beat harder.
  Proper food to eat. Looking much smarter.
  And your man is quite a different man.

2

O you're all so hopelessly mistaken
If you think cash flow has no effect.
Fertile farms produce no bacon
When the water-pump's been wrecked.
Now men grab as much as they can collect.
Once they'd standards they used not to flout.
If your belly's full you don't start shooting.
Now there's so much violence about.
Father, mother, brothers put the boot in.
Look, no more smoke now: the fire's gone out.
  Everything explodes, incendiaries are hurled.
  Smash-and-grab's the rule; it's a disaster.
  Every little servant thinks he's master
  And the world's a very bitter world.

3

That's the fate of all that's noble and splendid.
People quickly write it off as trash
Since with empty stomach and unmended
Footwear nobody's equipped to cut a dash.
They don't want what's good, they want the cash
And their instinct's to be mean and tight.

But when Right has got the cash to back it
It's got what it takes to see it right.
Never mind your dirty little racket
Just watch the smoke now: the fire's alight.
 Then you start believing in humanity once more:
 Everyone's a saint, as white as plaster.
 Principles grow stronger. Just like before.
 Wider views are taken. Hearts beat faster.
 You can tell the servant from the master.
 So the law is once again the law.

1

Niedrig gilt das Geld auf dieser Erden
Und doch ist sie, wenn es mangelt, kalt
Und sie kann sehr gastlich werden
Plötzlich durch des Gelds Gewalt.
Eben war noch alles voll Beschwerden
Jetzt ist alles golden überhaucht
Was gefroren hat, das sonnt sich
Jeder hat das, was er braucht!
Rosig färbt der Horizont sich
Blicket hinan: der Schornstein raucht!
 Ja, da schaut sich alles gleich ganz anders an.
 Voller schlägt das Herz. Der Blick wird weiter.
 Reichlich ist das Mahl. Flott sind die Kleider.
 Und der Mann ist jetzt ein andrer Mann.

2

Ach, sie gehen alle in die Irre
Die da glauben, daß am Geld nichts liegt.
Aus der Fruchtbarkeit wir Dürre
Wenn der gute Strom versiegt.
Jeder schreit nach was und nimmt es, wo er's kriegt.
Eben war noch alles nicht so schwer
Wer nicht grade Hunger hat, verträgt sich
Jetzt ist alles herz- und liebeleer.
Vater, Mutter, Brüder: alles schlägt sich!
Sehet: der Schornstein, er raucht nicht mehr!
 Überall dicke Luft, die uns gar nicht gefällt.
 Alles voller Haß und voller Neider.
 Keiner will mehr Pferd sein, jeder Reiter.
 Und die Welt ist eine kalte Welt.

3

So ist's auch mit allem Guten und Großen.
Es verkümmert rasch in dieser Welt
Denn mit leerem Magen und mit bloßen

Füßen ist man nicht auf Größe eingestellt.
Man will nicht das Gute, sondern Geld
Und man ist von Kleinmut angehaucht.
Aber wenn der Gute etwas Geld hat
Hat er, was er doch zum Gutsein braucht.
Wer sich schon auf Untat eingestellt hat
Blicke hinan: der Schornstein raucht!
  Ja, da glaubt man wieder an das menschliche Geschlecht.
  Edel sei der Mensch, gut und so weiter.
  Die Gesinnung wächst. Sie war geschwächt.
  Fester wird das Herz. Der Blick wird breiter.
  Man erkennt, was Pferd ist und was Reiter.
  Und so wird das Recht erst wieder Recht.[13]

Not just Brecht's lines that speak of justice but Chamisso's, too, look back on a long tradition of the poetic representation of money. At least two things are striking about this backward glance: that the intensity and breadth of poetic observations on the medium of money hardly ever captured the attention of German-speaking literary historians,[14] and that modern literature thematizing money (which it does with an almost forced regularity) revolves, again and again, around the same sets of problems. To summarize some of the results of the previous section—literary money-observation stands in rather sharp contrast to economic-theoretical money-observation:

Firstly, the monetary orientation to the world succeeds the religious and fulfills its functions precisely, and not metaphorically but analytically: the coin is heir to the Host, money becomes the "God term" of modernity.[15] The language of money (as well as the technological language of the media) links up with religious language for good ontosemiological reason: credit (credo), debtor, believer/creditor,[16] pauper's oath, praise/price,[17] Holy Mass or economic fair,[18] *obolus*, *pecunia*, and *Moneta*, or with respect to the concepts of the media, (trans)mission, destiny, (e)mission, good news/gospel, excommunication, communion, calling/kerygma.

Secondly, money expands the scope of thinking and of orientation beyond the demands for coverage (of values and statements) and referentiality. In order to function, however, it depends on a distortion of the "antimetaphysical" perspective; in other words, it must take cover from questions of cover.

Thirdly, money is of a scandalous semantic poverty, and for this very reason is a highly efficient and intersubjectively valid code. Its triumphant advance in modernity assures a radical conversion from an alphabetic to a numerical orientation to the world.

Fourthly, money is, despite its abstract qualities, an object of desire, and yet it also encodes desire in that it implements a logic of infinite deferral. As "money-hatching money," capital ambushes— and this has enormous psycho-historical effects—the feminine power of procreation. It works and increases parthenogenetically, without women, quasi-homosexually.

Fifthly, money regulates interpersonal relations; it makes the release of valuable goods without fighting, robbery, and war more likely. At the same time the medium of money[19] establishes an intersubjective, intercultural, and international interdependency that is highly complex and no doubt displays concrete manifestations of relational mania.

Sixthly, the controlling medium of money makes heretofore unheard-of economic wealth possible—and yet at the same time, as the medium of artificial shortage, it imposes a hermeneutic of want. It allows scarcity to become scarce only at the price of introducing a universal hermeneutic of scarcity.

Seventhly, time becomes especially scarce under the hegemony of money. Money, which not coincidentally carries Plutonic associations, has little patience for eternity. Money transforms divine eternal time into a limited resource whose limits, of course, can be balanced monetarily. One can store, call in, and manage time via money: time is money.

Eighthly, money displays an ineradicable ambivalence between rationality and irrationality (which the numerous novels about the figure of the gambler often thematize). Indeed, it is the medium, as the following remarks are intended to show, which creates the "Western" figure that is characterized by both rationality and an inherent irrationality.

Modern literature takes note of this ambivalent ir/rationality of money over and over again. The most prominent poetic foundation for the observation of the ir/rationality of money is Shakespeare's *The Merchant of Venice* (see chapter 6). Such widely varying works as Lessing's *Nathan the Wise*,[20] his comedy *Minna von Barnhelm*,[21] and Wagner's powerful *Ring* take up the theme of "ir/rational" money. The medium of money is above all ir/rational because it arranges for equivalence between the most varying goods and services. A sweater, a book, a daily special and a train ticket have little in common aside from the fact that they each cost, for example, 100 German marks. X, y, and z are not equal—yet their exchange makes them equal. It is not identical things that are equivalent but things that, despite obvious inequality, are of equal value or are declared to be of equal value. To determine or establish an equivalence is only worthwhile with respect to goods and services that are not equal. Those who get involved in the money-mediated exchange of equivalents (as exchange partners, and not as ludicrous and self-sacrificing collectors of, for example, old clocks) are therefore indifferent. Thus the literal meaning of equivalence in every act of exchange or payment remains intact: equivalence = equality = indifference. To emphasize the paradox and to paraphrase Hegel's famous formula of the identity of identity and difference in terms of the theory of exchange and money: Equivalent is (in the money-mediated exchange) that which ("in and of itself" {"an sich"} and in comparison with the other) is not equivalent; equivalence is the equivalence between equivalents and non-equivalents.

Exchange and money function so splendidly, too, because on the market, in the department store, in the bank, or on the stock exchange it makes no sense, in functional terms, to be a philosopher or, heaven forbid, a Hegelian who waxes profound on the abyss of the equating of the unequal. Precisely this wearing away, however, of the (depending on one's perspective and theoretical emphasis) paradoxical, irrational, or even contradictory dimensions of the money-mediated exchange is at the same time the very negation of the philosophical joy in profundity and the basic form of abstraction, without whose existence philosophy would not exist. For the birth of abstraction results from the (un-)spirit of the exchange. The exchange partner (as an exchange partner but not, for example, as a person suffering from hunger) apathetically disregards concrete objects which manifestly contradict the idea that apples and light bulbs, apples and tickets to the movies, or apples and travel insurance are equivalents and thus, with respect to their exchange value, identical, precisely alike (in value).

The fact that this exchange-abstraction, this disregarding and overlooking, this wearing away of the concrete has been as much an everyday as a delicate, consequential undertaking since, at the latest, the rise of coined money, has been more irascibly as well as more shrewdly observed by literature than by philosophy (precisely differentiated from pre-Socratic profundity), which, without that shift to abstraction caused by money, would not exist at all.[22] Among the gains in abstraction achieved with the "invention" of coined money in the Greek world of the seventh pre-Christian century may be counted the increasingly obvious differentiation of functionally closed social subsystems and their specific codes. This process of differentiation, too, with its characteristic moments of indifference and apathy, has been registered by modern literature. And it has found (or taken over from tradition and reformulated) a remarkably reliable and, for its part, already practically notorious and therefore to be regarded as unoriginal, *Dingsymbol:* a ring, or several (apparently) equivalent rings.

The Merchant of Venice, Nathan the Wise, Minna von Barnhelm, and *The Ring of the Nibelungs* (to name just a few)—these plays and musical dramas, respectively, in all their formal, rhetorical, and emotional variation—have in common that they revolve around the great themes of equivalence and the impudent differentiation of subsystems, and that they use the symbol of the ring to accentuate these themes. A pound of meat is a pound of meat, one ring is like another. Major von Tellheim must become Minna's financial equal before the marriage is deemed acceptable. Freia, pledged to the giants in exchange for the building of Valhalla, must be covered by the Rhine's gold. Despite their passionate insistence on non-equivalence, the protagonists of all these ring dramas are under the spell of equivalence. Equivalence, however, also means—indifference. In Kant's apt words: "Whatever has a price can be replaced by something else which is *equivalent;* whatever is above all price, and therefore has no equivalent, has dignity."[23] In this light, passion, too, has dignity. For passion precludes the indifferent wisdom that Adorno brings to a head in his *Minima Moralia:* "Underlying the property relation to human beings, the exclusive right of priority, is the following piece of wisdom: After all, they are all only people, which one it is does not really matter. Affection which knows nothing of such wisdom need not fear infidelity, since it is proof against faithlessness."[24]

Infidelity is an offense arising from passion, from suffering at the succession of time which refuses the timely meeting with a desired human being, thus a result of the passionate impulse not to omit the sin of omission; faithlessness, however, which Portia, Minna, and Brünnhilde fear, is an offense of indifference. Thus individual faithlessness corresponds to the universal principle of equivalence under whose sign modern, differentiated societies stand. And Shakespeare's colossal piece points paradigmatically to the apathetic, indifferent differentiation of subsystems. It demonstrates that justice is justice, a financial liability is a financial liability, love is love and belief is belief. And all these systems differentiate their apathetic, indifferent code: the code lawful/unlawful (to have or to get), the code pays/does not pay, the code "you and no other" and the code transcendent/immanent (or divinely ordained/contingent). A ring closed around itself is a suggestive symbol for autopoiesis and indifference toward the rest of the world. Lovers, exchanging rings, symbolize that their world no longer presents itself to them in bits and pieces but rather within that closed unity symbolized by the ring. "Marble, stone and iron breaks, / but not our love" {"Marmor, Stein und Eisen bricht, / aber unsre

Liebe nicht"}. The hit's refrain is so vehement about the unbreakable unity that it has forgotten elementary rules of grammar—it would of course have to be: marble, stone, and iron break.[25]

In contrast to the code of universal equivalence, the ring symbolizes that closed system of passion that is/seems not (to be) reliant on (ex-)change with the outside world. In contrast to the code of money, so scandalously and degenerately indifferent with respect to persons, things, and points in time of exchanges, the code of love defines the passionate difference: "you and no other"[26] are the one with whom I enter into that symbiosis that sets our love apart from all others. "Then would you be Siegfried and Brünnhilde" {"So wärst du Siegfried und Brünnhilde"}, says Brünnhilde to Siegfried after he places the ring on her finger, of which she says, "I shall hoard it as my sole treasure!" {"Ihn geiz' ich als einziges Gut"}. And Siegfried answers, "Where I am, both are sheltered" {"Wo ich bin, bergen sich beide"}.[27] For you are incomparable, incompatible, inexchangeable—for you are, as is evident in the symbiotic ring, the Siegfried who belongs only to me and not the interchangeable and replaceable Gunther, you are Brünnhilde and not Gutrune. One can say it in the words of Wilhelm Meister, who, upon meeting his future wife Natalie, was struck above all by her ring, which, although on the finger of someone else, mysteriously displayed his own initials, even if upside down: WM (and the letter W/woman/*Weib* is the reverse of the letter M/man/*Mann*—see chapter 6)—one can say it more poetically with Wilhelm Meister's closing words of the novel of his apprenticeship than in the concepts of systems theory: "I do know that I have found a treasure I never deserved. And I would not exchange it for anything in the world."[28]

Because the ring symbolizes non-equivalence, inexchangeability of lovers, and thus passionate non-indifference, it is the ultimate trauma for the lover(s) to see this pledge of love degraded to an object of exchange. For the ring is the one thing that one may not trade for anything in the world—"I shall hoard it as my sole treasure!" And yet it is a peculiarity of dramas as different as those of Shakespeare, Lessing, or Wagner that they use that very symbolic embodiment of inexchangeability as an object of exchange: it ends up on the wrong finger. Bassanio has given, if against his will, the ring that Portia gave him as a pledge of love to the wise judge who, through a procedural trick, rescues Antonio from Shylock's insistence that he fulfill the promise of equivalence: a pound of meat as the equivalent of a sum on credit. And so Bassanio sweats blood as Portia says the following words about exchange- and inexchangeability to Gratiano, who has likewise traded and given away his ring, the one thing which may not be sacrificed:

Portia. You were to blame—I must be plain with you—
To part so slightly with your wife's first gift,
A thing stuck on with oaths upon your finger
And so riveted with faith unto your flesh.
I gave my love a ring, and made him swear
Never to part with it, and here he stands:
I dare be sworn for him he would not leave it
Nor pluck it from his finger for the wealth
That the world masters. Now, in faith, Gratiano,
You give your wife too unkind a cause for grief.
An 'twere to me, I should be mad at it.
Bassanio. [Aside.] Why, I were best to cut my left hand off
And swear I lost the ring defending it.
Gratiano. My Lord Bassanio gave his ring away
Unto the judge that begged it, and indeed
Deserved it too; and then the boy, his clerk,
That took some pains in writing, he begged mine;
And neither man nor master would take aught
But the two rings.
Portia. What ring gave you, my lord?
Not that, I hope, which you received of me.
Bassanio. If I could add a lie unto a fault,
I would deny it; but you see my finger
Hath not the ring upon it—it is gone.
Portia. Even so void is your false heart of truth.
By heaven, I will ne'er come in your bed
Until I see the ring!
Nerissa. Nor I in yours
Till I again see mine!
Bassanio. Sweet Portia,
If you did know to whom I gave the ring,
If you did know for whom I gave the ring,
And would conceive for what I gave the ring,
And how unwillingly I left the ring
When naught would be accepted but the ring,
You would abate the strength of your displeasure.[29]

Minna and Tellheim have structurally similar experiences, as do Sie-
gried and Brünnhilde—with tremendous musical-dramatic intensification: The ring, a *Dingsymbol* of a unity that precludes the indifference
of the exchange, is given up, exchanged—an ambivalence that matches
the ambivalence of ir/rational money. The ring is the ambivalent
symbol of the inexchangeability that is complete in itself (why would
self-sufficient lovers such as Siegfried and Brünnhilde in the ring of fire
or Tristan and Isolde in the lovers' grotto have a need for exchange?)
as well as a symbol of exchange (why shouldn't a valuable gold ring

become the object of another's, a third party's, desire?). The ring is an ambivalent symbol of the functional autopoiesis of subsystems and of self-satisfied indifference to the rest of the world, as well as of that passion that militantly sets itself apart from all other worlds. Niklas Luhmann sums up the ambivalence of every erotic passion in the cool-hot title of his love-book: *Love as Passion: The Codification of Intimacy*. This erotic-monetary ambivalence-dilemma is institutionally mediated by marriage, toward the commitment to which the ring dramas (and obviously the ring motif of *Wilhelm Meister's Apprenticeship*) move.

Marriage apparently serves as a guarantee of balance between erotic passion and monetary reason, between irrational inexchangeability and regulated exchange with the outside world. If it accomplishes this feat, then additional functions can be entrusted to it: procreation and child-rearing, the organization of everyday life, administrative functions, the division of labor, social identity, a common reservoir of memories, risk sharing, care of the sick, the creation of bonds between the generations, and so on and so forth. No wonder that, in view of this profusion of functions, there are novels like *Madame Bovary*, *Anna Karenina*, *Effi Briest*, and *Auto-da-Fé*, as well as dramas like Ibsen's and Strindberg's (not to mention Albee's *Who's Afraid of Virginia Woolf*), which, without exception, tell the story of the loss of wedding rings and of the strength of the symbiotic bond. In times of increasing differentiation of subsystems, the functions burdening the institution of marriage, which participates in many subsystems and is supposed to mediate everything while remaining passionately above exchange, increases continually. The ambivalence of exchangeability and inexchangeability, which is the core of all the stories of rings, constitutes the real basis for a connection that is more than etymological between pathos and pathology, passion and the Passion, suffering and ardor.[30] The exchange of equivalents is a delicate affair. For that which is exchanged is not identical at all (otherwise it would not be exchanged), but rather "merely" equivalent. The delicate exchange of goods quickly becomes an "infamous exchange of equivalents"[31]—and how might one more drastically illustrate this infamy than through the exchange, replacement, or substitution of lovers who have pledged themselves to that paradox of symbiotic singularity?

If Shakespeare's and Wagner's protagonists were acquainted with systems theory, Bassanio's cry would be heard—"You would abate the strength of your displeasure." In Shakespeare's drama of the abyss (and similarly in Lessing's comedy), the strength of the displeasure over the broken pledge and the failure of symbiotic mechanisms (the ring that fits on the finger!) is abated not due to systems-theoretical insights into the ways in which communication functions in specific areas, but rather as a result of skillful, feminine dramaturgy: Portia had slipped into the judge's robe, and thus it only appeared that the ring had been given away. The purity of the refusal to exchange is threatened, however, as is the purity of the codes of autopoietic subsystems for once and for all. Shakespeare has found a drastic expression for the interdependencies of love, religion, justice, and money. That Shylock's daughter Jessica loves the Christian Lorenzo and therefore converts to his faith is not without consequences for the economic system and its monetary code.

> *Jessica*. [To Shylock's Christian servant, Launcelot Gobbo.]
> I shall be saved by my husband. He hath made me a Christian.
> *Launcelot*. Truly the more to blame he! We were Christians enow before, e'en as many as could well live one by another. This making of Christians will raise the price of hogs. If we grow all to be pork-eaters, we shall not shortly have a rasher on the coals for money. (3.5.17–23)[32]

Purity/impurity—the ring/the pig. Naturally, the interdiction against the mixing of codes has further validity, in precise accordance with the not terribly original insight that everything is interdependent, and the slightly more subtle insight regarding, for example, specific ways in which the developments of religious systems irritate the system of the economy: Declarations of love, even if the wealth of the bride does not detract from her erotic allure, must be couched in the language of love and not in that of money; notarized marriage contracts are different, of course—they are couched in the language of law; and in the price-lists for pork it will not be stated that the cost of a pound of meat, due to increased demand occasioned by a mass religious conversion, has increased accordingly. But literature observes both: the "impure" interdependencies or irritations between the subsystems that constitute each other's environment, and the striving for purity (of love, of justice—Kohlhaas!—,[33] of thinking, of reason, of power) that is, accordingly, all the more intensely inspired.

In the words of Dietrich Schwanitz's more precise analysis of the codes of Shakespeare's epochal piece:

> The encoding of love is pushed close to money's aura in the fairy-tale scheme of choosing between little boxes, where it always has been in folklore; virgins and treasures guarded by dragons were always metaphorically tied together, and Portia is, by virtue of the halo of radiance, her golden hair, her wealth, and the Golden Fleece, unmistakably associated with gold and money. Against the background of the differentiation between the boxes of gold, silver, and lead, money and the code of love must themselves be all the more differentiated. And this occurs through the inscriptions on the boxes, which, in the case of gold and silver, falsely

attribute the metal's value to the choice (differentiated by alter and ego): "Whoever chooses me receives what many want" (alter), says the gold box, and "Whoever chooses me receives what he deserves" (ego), says the silver. The inscription on the right choice, the lead box, attributes to it, in contrast, the reverse: "Whoever chooses me must give and risk all that he owns." This forbids explicit desire, appropriation, and acquisition; and thereby every move toward claiming possession or justifying this claim on the basis of one's own merit; and love is aligned, instead, with devotion, risk, and uncertainty.[34]

Money functions in Shakespeare's prototypical drama of modernity precisely as the medium of a painful and pain-inducing second encoding. It is always co-present—even when there is something more important going on. For this drama, like Lessing's and Wagner's texts, is "actually" about anything but money: humiliation, power, and revenge (*The Merchant of Venice*), the truth of religious revelation (*Nathan the Wise*), love (*Minna von Barnhelm*), and redemption (*The Ring of the Nibelungs*)—hot problems full of passion that are not quite in tune with the cool code of money. For money is the medium of a speechless semantic poverty that can itself render one speechless or, on the other hand, provoke passionately eloquent protest. The insight widely documented in literature, that money reaches into almost all subsystems and areas of life and is thus more than "merely" the medium of the economic code, inspired the ingenious construction of Samuel Butler's 1872 novel *Erewhon, or, Over the Range*. The title of the book is an anagram for "No where" and marks the text as an inverse utopia.

The protagonists, who are driven into the land beyond the mountains, are amazed, more than by anything else, by the fact that a double currency rules: one hard, cold, and effective, and the other melodic, aesthetic, and ineffective, issued by "musical banks."

> And yet anyone could see that the money given out at these [musical] banks was not that with which people bought their bread, meat, and clothing. It was like it at first glance, and was stamped with designs of great beauty; it was not, again, a spurious coinage, made with the intention that it should be mistaken for the money in actual use; it was more like a toy money, or the counters used for certain games at cards. . . . Of course everyone knew that their commercial value was *nil*, but all those who wished to be considered respectable thought it incumbent upon them to retain a few coins in their possession. . . . Perhaps, however, the strangest thing of all was that these very people would at times make fun in small ways of the whole system.[35]

Because, in its strict functionality, it disregards erotic, religious, ideological, and aesthetic aspects, "normal" money is the effect of an abstraction and differentiation. But this difference reappears in *Erewhon* in the medium of money itself—a classic reentry. That which is excluded (the aesthetic-religious) becomes the included excluded of money. Money takes care of the very dimensions it erodes.

The early Romantic Friedrich Schlegel ironically accentuated the difference between the coldly functional code of money or the dazzling code of gold on the one hand and the difficult shallows/depths of aesthetically and metaphysically demanding linguistic communication on the other. In his famous essay on incomprehensibility he says: "I have often secretly admired, one might even say worshiped, the objectivity of gold. . . . Wherever there is even a modicum of education and enlightenment, silver, gold is understood, and through gold, everything else. When at last every artist has these materials in good enough quality, he may indeed write his works in bas-relief, with golden letters on silver tablets. Who would reject such beautiful writing with the crass objection that it is enigmatic?"[36] Golden words are golden words. And the current saying, "Talk is silver, silence is gold" {"Reden ist silber, schweigen ist Gold"[37]} takes on, if one takes it not as a two-bit piece of pseudoprofound wisdom but as a diagnosis of the supremacy of money's speechless communication over the medium of language, a completely different tone. Gold and money are silent—yet nonetheless they communicate much more efficiently than speech. Speech has, at best, the second-rank value of silver, but of course one can prattle in leaden tones as well—a motif found throughout Canetti's novel *Auto-da-Fé*.

Musical money that fulfills the subjective yearning for beauty with respect to the pecuniary as well, works written in golden bas-relief and thus *eo ipso* "objective"—the early German Romantics and the English antiutopians have, along with many other writers, one and the same intuition: it is simply false to mistake money for filthy mammon that opposes everything spiritual, reasonable, and transcendental. To quote Samuel Butler once again: "People oppose money to culture, and imply that if a man has spent his time in making money he will not be cultivated—fallacy of fallacies! . . . It has been said that the love of money is the root of all evil. The want of money is so quite as truly."[38] Whoever, in any event, looks for the interrelationships between money and art merely with respect to the question of having/not having money misses the fact that money, as a medium with varying materialities and suggestions for its coverage, has had a voice, at the very least, in the state of entire epochs of art.

Ralf Schiebler kindled a considerable fascination with analogy in this respect. But "to think in analogies (says Goethe) is to refrain from reproach." This is true with respect to "modern art and the gold standard"—thus the title of Schiebler's essay. He shows "that those times in which the currency has a high percentage of gold are times of pronounced realism in art." And vice versa.

> The [contemporary] press calls the members of the New Artists' Association, Munich {*Neue Künstlervereinigung München*}—Kandinsky, Jawlensky, Münter, Werefkin and others—"frauds." Their works raise the suspicion that there is "nothing behind them." The Reich's bank notes that were declared the official currency of Germany in 1909 met with comparable mistrust. The paper money had to be imposed on the citizens of the state "with mild violence." For they doubted that the monetary sign corresponded to "something concrete." The currency is being "watered down" like objects in a watercolor.

Thus the realism of academic painting in the nineteenth century corresponds to the gold standard that was still in place at the time, and Dadaism to inflation: everything is art. That Churchill exploited the gold standard in 1925 and then returned to it, that Germany, with the German mark, renewed the vigor of the German currency, and France, in 1928, took control of the franc and stabilized it, contributes to a "stabilization of the picture." And this "occurred in 1925, in popular and luxury editions: New Objectivity {*Neue Sachlichkeit*} and Art Deco." In summary, "That so little attention has been given the correlations between the history of money and the history of art may be due to the fact that the best hiding places are those that are out in the open for all to see."[39]

The medium of money, seemingly so very earthly, establishes not "merely" the aesthetic conditions but also contributes to transcendent and transcendental functions, or—according to the more emphatic thesis—to the extent that money gains acceptance, it sets the forms of rationality familiar to us, as well as transcendental subjectivity, free. The intellectual "hypostasizes as an absolute his intellect, which was only formed through contact with . . . abstract exchange relations, and which can become intellect solely by reflecting on its own conditions."[40] Western rationality and subjectivity are epiphenomena of money. Money creates not only equivalences between dissimilar things but also functional correspondences between abstractions and things, thought abstraction and real abstraction {*Denk- und Realabstraktion*} (Sohn-Rethel), or meaning and being. Money is the ontosemiological major medium of modernity.

10

WHAT COUNTS? MONEY AND VALIDITY

Desine ergo philosophis pecunia interdicere:
nemo sapientiam paupertate damnavit.

{Stop forbidding philosophers money:
no one has condemned wisdom to poverty.}

Seneca, *De vita beata*

"Money makes the world go 'round—Geld regiert die Welt"[1]—the insights of hit songs and common sense do not have a good reputation in the discipline of philosophy. The reverse is also true. Theories of transcendental deduction, discussions of the completeness of the Table of Categories, or insights such as Heidegger's, left out of the second encoding—"The nearing of nearness is the true and sole dimension of the mirror-play of the world"[2]—contribute only modestly to the convergence of philosophy and common sense. In any event, in the world of philosophy conventions and seminars, untouched by such common sense or by a philosophy *à deux sous*, one can be a Kantian, a Hegelian, or a Fichtean and get away with it. In figuring travel costs (even to philosophy conventions), at the checkout counter in the grocery store, at the gas station, in the office, in a job interview, at the IRS, or even at international peace talks, it is best, however, to forget about Kant, Fichte, Hegel (a half-exception!), and Heidegger. For they express truly distinct theories of validity (of judgments, propositions, perceptions, principles) which have lost their footing due to the fact that they take absolutely no notice of the uniquely concrete-abstract, profane-sacred, empirical-transcendent, profane-fetishistic medium that forms and categorizes intersubjective claims to validity: the medium money.

179

The discrepancy between the political, intercultural, juridical, worldly, libidinal, systematic, and altogether nothing less than: intersubjective meaning of money on the one hand and academic philosophy's strained disinterest in filthy lucre and anything monetary on the other is so grotesque that the Thracian maid's giggle would swell to Homeric laughter at the chasm. Or, to turn it around: if one were to look for a functional definition of philosophical outsidedness, the surest measure would be the attention given the validity-logical, intersubjective, and epistemological implications of money (as produced by, among others, Novalis, Gottfried Keller, Marx, Nietzsche, Simmel, and Lukács). Undoubtedly the most decisive analyst and theoretician of the connection between money and validity, Alfred Sohn-Rethel stands in the tradition of these thinking outsiders who, as outsiders, were able to see and thematize the blind spot in philosophy's system of observation. Sohn-Rethel[3] provided the theoretical foundation for the intuition common to these outsiders and yet unheard-of in every sense of the word (especially by university philosophy): that, namely, the transcendental subject is established in connection with the forms of commodities and money, or (as expressed in his letter of November 1936 to Adorno) that "the genesis of [transcendental] subjectivity . . . is the inseparable correlate to the development of the money-form of value."[4] That is (or would be, if Sohn-Rethel had developed his thesis with more philosophical professionalism) the greatest systematic advance in a philosophy oriented to the illumination of specialized problems {Sachprobleme} since Kant's Critique of Pure Reason. Despite the dilettantish aspects of his expositions,[5] Sohn-Rethel was able to expose, through argument as well as empirically, the thoroughly impure implications and the pecunia-olet-genealogy of ostensibly pure reason. His work marks the paradigm shift from the critique of pure to the critique of impure reason—which has, precisely because it is impure through and through, validity, explanatory force, and an overwhelming number of possibilities for creating connections.

A feud, on the other hand, rules the relationship between academic philosophy and money—since the time of Socrates at the latest. At the latest—this means: as early as possible, or since the beginnings of thinking about claims of validity as requiring assent and not long after the invention of the very medium of money, in which intersubjective obligations crystalize in a strange speechlessness. The feud surely has its foundation in the fact that philosophy owes its existence to money. And not, for example, because—much to the horror of Socrates— sophists were paid for their thinking and argumentation. On the contrary, without the medium of money, that elementary achievement of abstraction, philosophy would not be possible; it simply would not exist (according to George Thomson's book *The First Philosophers*, which provides important historical background for Sohn-Rethel's analyses). The "functional parity between monetarism and abstraction" or the "direct connection between monetarism and intellectuality" is the constitutive blind spot of systematic philosophy. To quote Blumenberg once more, and pointedly, philosophy wants what he, the booklover, despite his casually formulated insight into money theory, would hardly express: traditional philosophy will not and hardly can acknowledge that the "money economy and the domination of understanding {*Verstandesherrschaft*} . . . [are] two sides of one and the same distance from reality."[6]

Sohn-Rethel was not the first to be struck by the fact that the current explanations of rationality, transcendental subjectivity, and intersubjective validity are simply not plausible, indeed that they construct the very plane on which they pretend to solve the reason-problem, thereby altering its sober (that is, genealogical and functional) analysis. As early as 1800, a young manager in the booming salt industry attempted a translation of Fichte's *Foundations of Transcendental Philosophy* {*Wissenschaftslehre*} into a theory of commodities and money. Novalis noted with divination: "The *Foundations of Transcendental Philosophy* or pure philosophy is the schema of relations between the sciences generally. It arises from a sudden idea rather than really noteworthy, individual things—general things, for which each thing can be substituted (see concept of money). . . . Forms of construction or relations become—generally valid propositions. . . . This phenomenon arises from the treatment of these things as commodities."[7] For Gottfried Keller, the insight that the categories of identity as well as of difference, and with them the "schema of relations between the sciences generally," are first constituted by the exchange of equivalents mediated by money is condensed to a dictum, and yet presented in the form of a question: " 'Really? Then that is the explanation and the secret of your whole question of identity, the gold made into coins?' "[8]

That admirer of Keller's, Nietzsche (whom the neo-Marxist Sohn-Rethel quoted strikingly often), essentially converts this great philosophical-literary hypothesis and certificate of mortgage[9] into small change when he sarcastically destroys, in one move, the Kantian tradition of epistemology:

"How are synthetic judgments *a priori* possible?" Kant asked himself— and what really is his answer? *"By virtue of a faculty"*[10] but unfortunately not in five words, but so circumstantially, venerably, and with such a display of German profundity and curlicues that people simply failed to note the comical *niaiserie allemande* involved in such an answer. People were actually beside themselves with delight over this new faculty, and the jubilation reached its climax when Kant further discovered a moral faculty in man—for at that time the Germans were still moral and not yet addicted to *Realpolitik.* —The honeymoon of German philosophy arrived. All the young theologians of the Tübingen seminary went into the bushes—all looking for "faculties."[11]

Hegel had already offered a similar rebuke, stylistically similarly pointed (as did Gottlob Ernst Schulze before him, most likely as the first,[12] of the Kantian philosophy and its arrangement of relations between understanding and reason: "He hunts through the soul's sack to see what faculties are still to be found there; and thus by merest chance he lights on Reason. It would make no difference if there had been no Reason there."[13]

"By virtue of a faculty": the concept of a faculty for cognition {*Erkenntnisvermögen*} is obviously ambiguous. One will not stumble onto the monetary implication of this idealistic central term if one disappears "into the bushes" of natural philosophy. For the spirit of the marketplace and the metropolis is the genius loci of a philosophy whose time has come. The agora, where philosophical arguments and their claims to validity are exchanged, is made possible by a two-fold and thoroughly profane condition: That through the exchange of money and commodities at the market, firstly, various things are associated, synthesized, comprehended and subsumed under uniform categories, thus through an abstract turn away from that which is all too concretely practiced and "established" as the basis of legality, and that, secondly, with this synthesis of exchanged commodities, the synthesis of the exchangers, with their intersubjectively compatible claims to validity and categories, is also a given. Ego cannot, obviously, barter with ego, but only with alter.

Those who ignore the urbane ambiguity of a "faculty for cognition" {*"Erkenntnisvermögen"*} will pay a high price for it. Philosophy becomes, in this case, a discourse not of cognition but of systematically false cognition. For this reason, Nietzsche can carry on with his new history of philosophy *in nuce* as the story of a profane awakening:

> A time came when people scratched their heads, and they still scratch them today. One had been dreaming, and first and foremost—old Kant. "By virtue of a faculty"—he had said, or at least meant. But is that—an answer? An explanation? Or is it not rather merely a repetition of the question? . . . [I]t is high time to replace the Kantian question, "How are synthetic judgments *a priori* possible?" by another question, "Why is belief in such judgments *necessary*?" (pp. 18–19, Nietzsche's emphasis).

Nietzsche's first answer to this question, the one in terms of the theory of power, remains well below the level of a second possible answer which he outlines—in monetary terms. For Nietzsche has downright overwhelmingly plausible arguments, when he, following his destruction of Kantian subject-philosophy, suggests, in a second move, a genealogical-monetary counter-direction to the *petitio-principii*-project of a pure reason-critique that is as clear as it is unfinished in its details: "The mind of early man was preoccupied to such an extent with price making, assessment of values, the devising and exchange of equivalents, that, in a certain sense, this may be said to have constituted his thinking."[14] To think up and exchange equivalents; this is the essence of thinking. The literally unheard-of but clear statement of a thinker who is still regarded as a malicious, antirational destroyer of reason. Yet Nietzsche is more Kantian than Kant, the reason-critic, himself. For he has a plausible answer to the central Kantian question: The belief in synthetic judgments is a priori possible and necessary because the exchange of equivalents mediated by money imposes it on the subjects: it synthesizes in every sense of the word.

Novalis, Keller, Nietzsche: Sohn-Rethel's intellectual predecessors[15] have three obvious things in common. They have at their disposal, first of all, the same strange yet (at second, comparative glance) highly plausible intuition; they were not able, secondly, to smuggle this intuition into the institution of the university (this thesis was, if they took notice of it at all, too sociological for philosophers, and too philosophical for sociologists); and, thirdly, they were unable to develop this thesis of a close connection between money and validity into a consistent theory of cognition and of intersubjective validity. The attempts at a theory of money that were worked out and were at least sensitive to the implications for a logic of validity of the medium disappeared behind the thesis of the transcendental subject concealed in the form of commodities. Marx was downright painfully careful to play down the epistemological implications of his theory of the fetishism of commodities, Lukács's allusion to the power of reification for constituting consciousness was sacrificed to his interest in the delicate concept of class-consciousness, and Simmel's philosophy of money remained as exciting a psychology of money as it was one that failed to make its point.

In short, the "soft" thesis that monetarism and abstraction, money economy and the domination of understanding, are two sides of one coin is not new. And the "hard" thesis as well, according to which the transcendental subject is established with the form of commodities and money, has its predecessors—namely Novalis or Gottfried Keller.

The "hard" thesis implies that the *Critique of Pure Reason* could be made plausible (including the analysis of a priori synthetic judgments, transcendental deduction, the Table of Categories and of Judgment, and the theory of formalism) through a point-by-point monetary rewriting into a critique of impure reason. Only then would it be immune to Hegel's reproach that Kant does not actually derive reason and its internal constitution but instead merely "tells it in passing," and to Nietzsche's derision that Kant's reason-critique is about a "*niaiserie allemande*," as laboriously declaimed as it is tautological.

Sohn-Rethel did not actually get involved in this project of precisely translating the Kantian reason-critique into the theory of money and validity. His translation of the Kantian epistemology into the conceptual framework of exchange theory comes out of the blue and thus remains for the most part suggestive. But this does not mean it is of less explanatory value than Kant's pure *petitio principii* ("by virtue of a faculty"):

> One need . . . only [sic!] insert for the identical unit of money, the "unit of self-consciousness," for the synthetic function of money in an exchange society, the "originally synthetic unity of apperception," for its constitutive meaning for capitalist production, "pure understanding," for capital itself, "reason," for the world of commodities, "experience," and for the exchange of commodities according to the laws of capitalist means of production, the "existence of things in accordance with their laws," or "nature," in order to reconstruct Kant's entire epistemology, including its inherent internal contradictions, from the analogy of capitalist reification.[16]

"Only": the bold "only" immediately and justifiably becomes, in the ensuing phrases, a "daring hypothesis." Daring it certainly is. And not, moreover, actually carried out. Nonetheless, no one else declaimed both theses, the "soft" and the "hard," with such differentiation, and moved them forward as decisively as did Sohn-Rethel. Despite its explanatory power—surpassing by far competing theories— the monetary theory of validity[17] is quite obviously dissident. For it offends all rational phantasies of the self-sufficiency of transcendental subjectivity and especially of empirical subjects. At the same time, the testimonial force of this thesis can be made empirically plausible and tested—most drastically in a negative way during the collapse of monetary systems. With them collapse, namely—as a glance at times of high inflation shows (for example in Germany in the 1920s or in Russia after 1989)—reliable structures of intersubjectivity, unquestioned, commonly accepted assumptions of validity, and, often enough, even self-conscious subjects.

Self-consciousness: not for nothing is this a concept of psychology and the theory of consciousness. Elias Canetti, in his grandiose study *Crowd and Power* {*Masse und Macht*}, vividly analyzes the humiliation of self-consciousness which accompanies the presumption that money imprints accepted structures of subjectivity and intersubjectivity:

> One may say that, apart from wars and revolutions, there is nothing in our modern civilizations which compares in importance to {periods of inflation}. The upheavals caused by inflations are so profound that people prefer to hush them up and conceal them. They may also hesitate to attribute to money—the value of which is, after all, artificially fixed by man—an efficacy in forming crowds which is out of all proportion to its practical function, and which seems both contrary to reason and infinitely shaming.[18]

The suspicion that filthy lucre could, far exceeding its essential destiny as a medium for managing the economy, form the categories of consciousness as well as those of intersubjective obligation is, in fact, preposterous and humiliating.

Because this thesis has something "infinitely shaming" for the narcissism of reason about it, it has its place in the history of assaults on the narcissism of the human species that accompanied the theories of Copernicus, Darwin, and Freud. This does not mean the thesis is false. Criticism of Sohn-Rethel's "soft" thesis is not based on the presumption that it is unsound, or even merely on the daring of his central thesis, but on the fact that it is so evident as to border on banality. If it were not for academic philosophy's persistently adversarial image in which Freud's pronouncement that "neuroses exhibit on the one hand striking and far-reaching points of agreement with those great institutions, art, religion and philosophy. But on the other hand they seem like distortions of them"[19] is fulfilled over and over again, the memory of the monetary genesis of abstract thinking would hardly be worth it. What is certainly worthwhile, however, is the discussion of Sohn-Rethel's "hard" thesis that the transcendental subject is concealed in the form of the commodity. This thesis is, according to the subtle judgment of Adorno, who, as the first to take notice of it, hinted in the *Minima Moralia* that it is as little free of "paranoid characteristics" as any theory so pointed as to be worthy of discussion. In contrast to competing theories, however, it has an awareness of the fact that its "idée fixe" concerns, if not the idée fixe that it thematizes, the idée fixe of the commodities market—equivalence.

> There is no theory that does not, due to its essence as a tightly structured construct, carry within it a moment of reification: develop

paranoid characteristics. It is these that secure its effectiveness. The concept of the idée fixe does not concern merely aberrations, it is part of theory itself, the total claim of a particular, which arises as soon as a single aspect is held fast in isolation. Thoughts that suppress their opposite cannot escape it. Nor can theories of the highest dignity escape offering themselves in tangible interpretations. It is as if they were secretly obeying a commandment of the society of commodities.[20]

In order to stimulate discussion about Sohn-Rethel's "idée fixe" (as he himself called it),[21] the main points of a translation of Kant's critique of reason in terms of money theory and the attempt to make it genealogically plausible, at least with respect to its points of connection, will be indicated. Acts of exchange and purchase are, without a doubt, *synthetic judgments;* indeed they are the very model of nontrivial judgments: they necessarily add (in the countless cases of exchange and purchase) to the statements of judgment (x and y both cost z) something (the predicate "equivalent" to be precise) that is not already included in their terms. And the equality of value of the exchanged or purchased goods and services can never be detected visually. Whether these judgments of equivalence are also a priori (thus independent of experience) is—why should it be otherwise?—the truly decisive question.

It is still a matter of controversy, as is well known, whether there are a priori synthetic judgments. Kant regarded the laws of geometry and arithmetic, but also natural laws such as the principle of inertia or of causation, as a priori synthetic judgments. For they represent universally valid and necessary statements about the nature of material reality (and are therefore synthetic) that do not require prior verification through experience (and are therefore a priori—this latter claim is especially controversial, and for good reason). If one accepts this as the basis for a priori synthetic judgments, it is at least as plausibly fulfilled in the judgments of equivalence that are implicit in acts of exchange and purchase as in the Kantian examples. These acts of judgment are a priori in that they must be independent of experience. No experience could confirm the predicate "equivalent" in the judgment "x and y are equivalent." The synthetic judgments of equivalence in exchange and purchase are, however, also a priori in that the exchange qua "real abstraction" (i.e., the equation of materially unlike things) requires a "thought abstraction"[22] and vice versa: both occur *uno actu* and are generally presupposed in the act of exchange that equates the exchanged goods. To revise Hegel's formula once more: there is an identity of identity and difference between real and thought abstractions. For the exchange does not just equate the exchanged goods but the real and thought abstractions as well. It achieves social and cognitive synthesis. For it binds the psychological, cultural, religious, and so on vastly differently disposed traders to the same categories of abstraction.

In the exchange mediated by money *both roots of cognition* (sensibility and understanding) are always already interrelated. Through sensibility objects are *given* to us; through understanding they are *thought*, according to Kant (B 29).[23] That "thoughts without content are empty; intuitions without concepts are blind" (B 75) is made obvious by the act of exchange. Those who perceive the commodities to be exchanged (purchased) as mere things, without the understanding's having formulated this exchange-abstract perception in terms of equivalences, is blind. Those who do not conceive equivalents as equivalents between dissimilar things (and this only works if a perception establishes the thought), experience an empty "thought without content" (e.g., a tautology such as A = A). But that means: it is obvious that money-mediated exchange first achieves an (intersubjectively binding!—see below) *association of the manifold* (A 112) in concepts of unity. To put a price on everything means: consciously perceive, structure, judge, and define disparate objects according to one uniform point of view. In the first and second editions of the *Critique of Pure Reason*, Kant offered differently accentuated versions with respect to this theme of the "association of the manifold," which ensures that self-conscious subjects are not ruined by a flood of incompatible, individual bits of sensory data. The second version, "the *I think* must be *capable* of accompanying all my presentations" (B 131), makes the self-conscious unity of the transcendental apperception responsible for this achievement. And as a result this involves, to quote Dieter Henrich's precise reconstruction of Kant's transcendental deduction, the extremely far-reaching "presupposition . . . that one sees, in the notion of the ego {*im Ich-Gedanken*} a consciousness which demonstrates the highest degree of certainty and which is, so to speak, a priori superior to everything."[24] How are a priori synthetic judgments possible? "Vermöge eines Vermögens. . . ."

The first version is in this respect more complex and nonetheless, if you will, more realistic: that is, it is not so strictly intent as the second version on a self-consciously theoretical-idealistic *petitio principii*. It is not necessary to rewrite Kant's original text in monetary terms, but merely to quote it, in order to gain hints, at the very least, that Kant himself takes pre-subjective preconditions for the association of the manifold in concepts of unity into consideration: "There is a {natural} law whereby presentations that have often followed or accompanied one another will finally associate" (A 100), as it says. Habitualized acts of exchange and purchase together with their implied abstractions can certainly be characterized (despite the concrete divergence) as structurally related ideas that have often followed or accompanied each other and have thus finally "become associated" with each other. In any event, the first version of Kant's reason-critique explicitly takes into consideration that there must be a condition of possibility for the association of the manifold "in the object" as well.

> As regards the empirical rule of *association*, on the other hand, we must indeed assume it throughout when we say that everything in a sequence of events is subject to rules to the point that nothing ever happens without being preceded by something that it always follows. This rule, taken as a law of nature—on what, I ask, does it rest? And how is even this association possible? The basis for the possibility of the manifold's association, insofar as {it}[25] lies in the object, is called the manifold's *affinity*. I ask, therefore, how do you make comprehensible to yourselves the thoroughgoing affinity of appearances (whereby they are, and *must* be, subject to constant laws)? (A 113).

How are we able to make the affinity of appearances comprehensible to ourselves? The wording of the passage cited above is, in one important respect, not uniform. In the academic edition, in contrast to most editions of Kant's work, the phrase reads "insofar as it [*er*] (the basis for the possibility of the manifold's association) lies in the object." This "basis"—still the basis (*causa et fundamentum*) for nothing less than the "manifold's association" can only lie in the disparate and unstructured world of things, however, if it itself already presents pre-subjective "real-abstract" syntheses. And precisely this occurs in the abstraction of exchange that associates and unites manifold elements in a tangible and yet at the same time highly abstract way, under unified points of view such as equivalence, identity (of value), compatibility. The second wording reads "insofar as it [*es*] lies in the object"—it: "the law of nature." The question is, therefore, on what the law for its part "rests" that enables it to account for an "empirical rule of association" that makes it plausible "that nothing ever happens without being preceded by something that it always follows." The unceasing succession of acts of payment and purchase cannot be described more precisely, and it insures that the most widely varying things are brought under a "thoroughgoing affinity of appearances."

> As the final elements of such an economic system, payments have particular characteristics. They are, like actions, temporary events occurring at points in time. As soon as they begin they are already in the process of stopping. A system established on the basis of payments as the final elements that cannot be further broken down must always, above all, be

on the lookout for new payments. It would otherwise simply cease to exist from one moment to another.[26]

Money is the *"transcendental affinity* of which the *empirical* affinity is the mere consequence" (A 113f.).

The monetary translation of Kantian intuitions causes problems, on the other hand, with respect to the full derivation of the Table of Categories.[27] The categories of quantity (unity, plurality, allness[28]) and of quality (reality, negation, limitation) obviously spring from the paradigm of exchange and money—but they spring it as well. And it would be forcing the issue to trace the categories of relation (causality, among others) or of modality back to the internal structures of the thought abstraction qua exchange abstraction. They have, nonetheless, in the abstractions and syntheses that gain ground with the exchange of equivalents mediated by money, their necessary if not sufficient condition. The niveaus of abstraction established with the exchange of money unleashes its own logic as well as categories specific to the endeavor and springing from its genesis.

Highly plausible, on the other hand, is Sohn-Rethel's monetaristic use of the Kantian theory of *schematism.* Kant defined the schema as "something that is third, something that must be homogeneous with the category, on the one hand, and with the appearance, on the other hand, and that thus makes possible the application of the category to the appearance. This mediating presentation must be pure (i.e., without anything empirical), and yet must be both *intellectual,* on the one hand, and *sensible,* on the other hand. Such a presentation is the *transcendental schema*" (B 177). The schemata advanced by Kant are, nevertheless, strangely unspecific: the number (still quite clear) functions as the schema of quantity, "the permanence of the real in time" as the schema of substance, the real as such as the schema of the cause, the simultaneity of determinations as the schema of interaction, and "the harmony of the synthesis of different presentations with the conditions of time as such" as the schema of possibility (B 183), and so on. The schemata named by Kant hardly fulfill what is demanded of them: "to be homogeneous with" the category and with the appearance. In contrast, money undoubtedly fulfills the demands of the schemata: it is "intellectual, on the one hand, and sensible, on the other hand"; it is homogeneous with the categories (of quantity, quality, relation, modality) as well as with appearances (goods and services); indeed it is the very medium of the production of homogeneity—of equivalence. Is it a coincidence that Kant's critique is especially convincing precisely where it does not avoid monetary comparisons: at that point, no less, at which the traditional ontological proof of God is under discussion? "A hundred actual thalers," to quote Kant's analogy with respect to the problem of the actual existence of God, "do not contain the least more than a hundred possible thalers. For, the possible thalers signify the concept and the actual thalers signify the object and the positing thereof in itself; hence if the object contained more than the concept, then my concept would not express the entire object and thus would also not be the concept commensurate with this object. In the state of my assets, however, there is more in the case of a hundred actual thalers than in the case of the mere concept of them" (B 627). Being is not a real predicate; money is not a real value. Money is, rather, the medium of a second encoding which, to the extent of its development, inherits the metaphysical second encoding of the world (through a world behind the world).

The existence of God, according to Kant, is no longer rationally compelling. It is much more a matter of individual belief. Intersubjectively binding, on the other hand, is the medium of money. It cannot (in contrast to God) be denied, even, or especially, in liberal contexts. Those who translate Kant's theory (following Sohn-Rethel) into monetary terms avoid the difficulties of that theory of transcendental subjectivity (and of radical constructivism!) which Hegel so clearly exposed—that is, the inability to arrive at plausible theories of intersubjective validity: "But the knowing subject does not with Kant really arrive at reason, for it remains still the individual self-consciousness as such, which is opposed to the universal."[29] Not "only" is the transcendental subject hidden in the money-form of exchange, intersubjective validity is as well. As a medium of social synthesis, money establishes structural couplings—in Kantian terms, "affinities"—in the world of objects *and* between self-conscious subjects. The improbability that the structures of (self-)consciousness of the ego are at all compatible with those of another decreases through an (in fact a priori intersubjectively valid) exchange mediated by money.

Money produces validity, indeed: money is validity, above and beyond the boundaries of individuality.[30] And vice versa: trade in money only makes sense if subjects know that they have individual faculties/fortunes {*Vermögen*}. Exchange can only occur if the mine/yours boundaries are established between subjects who know what they are/have. "Exchange will have been, above all, a side effect of the institutionalization of property," formulates Luhmann for this reason.[31] It would be more plausible to grasp both—exchange and the institutionalization of (private) property—in keeping with Tacitus's model, as effects of *one* formation:[32] "Gold and silver are withheld from them; is it by the favour or the wrath of Heaven? . . . Certain it is, they do not enjoy the possession and use of those metals with our sensibility. There are, indeed, silver vessels to be seen amongst them, but they were presents to their chiefs or ambassadors; the Germans regard them in no better light than common earthenware."[33]

Real abstraction and thought abstraction are two sides of one coin. Only with money-mediated exchange and the correlated differentiation of private property (singularity and selfhood) is there a form of rationality that can be regarded as specifically Western, and with it something such as the rudiments of transcendental subjectivity. Those who argue thus avoid not only the "*niaiserie allemande*" of a *petitio principii* of reason, but also the highly problematic linking of the mental with the fundamental that Richard Rorty has characterized as the primary error of new philosophy. He thereby avoids, in addition, the specifically Kantian "confusion of predication with synthesis"[34] and the facile newer (even neurophysiologically falsifiable) carrying over of consciousness into communication theory (consciousness is something different from communication). Predicates are governed by their own logic—precisely that logic which was first made possible by that niveau of abstraction that accompanied the real-abstract synthesis of the exchange.

Ontosemiology will not be blinded by any ostensible mirror of nature nor by any theory of communicative competence. A monetary ontosemiology, as outlined here, explicitly links up with the paradigm of exchange and thus with early critical theory's consciousness, which Habermas has forsaken in favor of a paradigm of communication as cheerful as it is implausible.[35] Ontosemiology does not analyze reified, "real," or fundamental correlations between being and meaning, but rather their institutional, cultural, and medial connections. It does not pose questions (as does a theory that can hardly be called critical anymore) about the possibilities, anticipated against all the evidence, of communication free of domination, but about the constitutive effects of the uniquely speechless money-code on consciousness. Thus it attempts an answer to the intricate question of why the consciousness of ego is structured in such a way as to be categorically compatible with the consciousness of alter. Money is certainly not fundamental—but it is a quasi-transcendental, intersubjectively binding, and historically fluctuating a priori all the same. Precisely "a material-immaterial thing full of metaphysical caprice" (Marx) and mental effects.

Different forms of exchange and trade are not "only" accompanied by different mentalities, but by different conceptions of subjects and intersubjective structures of consciousness as well (which allow great latitude for different psychologies, customs, lifestyles, semantic systems, logical systems unique to particular disciplines, and so on). The monetaristic dissolution of the Kantian apriorities allows those structures of reason that are not entangled in the awful aporias of the Kantian tradition, in fact only putatively humanistic, to be historicized. One of the strengths of Sohn-Rethel's intuitions is not least of all that it can dispense with recognizing only Kantian subjects as human beings. Human beings simply have not described themselves at all times in all places as self-conscious, transcendental subjects. They have done so, on the contrary, only there, where, and to the extent to which "rational" means that forms of the money economy fixated on equivalence have gained acceptance. It is, historically, difficult to overlook what has nonetheless repeatedly been repressed: the strong correlation between ego-consciousness, the rationality of exchange, money-mediated exchange of equivalents, and reified intersubjectivity. Transcendental subjectivity and rationality capable of abstraction are epiphenomena of trade in money.

Yet this correlation, too, is subject (why should it be different for a theory of the "critical liquidation of the apriority"?[36]) to major transformations. Those who do not want to squander the high plausibility of Sohn-Rethel's sociogenetic epistemology ought not to underestimate its historicization of the Kantian concept of the apriority. With Sohn-Rethel and his ideas and beyond, the outline (though certainly problematic because decidedly insufficiently complex) of a four-phase model can be drawn out, which plausibly correlates the structures of (self-)consciousness to structures of exchange, money, and validity.

Firstly, the pre-monetary simple exchange of goods, strictly differentiated from robbery, tribal self-sufficiency and even potlatch, establishes, with its implicit "mine-not-yours"-logic, rudimentary forms of abstraction, subjectivity, and ego-consciousness. There is tremendous evidence of pre-monetary ways of thinking in terms of equivalence.[37] "A man ought to be a friend to his friend and repay gift with gift. People should meet smiles with smiles and lies with treachery." Marcel Mauss prefaced his famous *The Gift* {*Essay sur le don*} of 1923 with these verses as a motto.[38] Cultures that do not yet know money are well-acquainted with basal forms of thinking in terms of equivalence. They are eloquently expressed in sayings such as "*do ut des*," "an eye for an eye, a tooth for a tooth," in the Maori saying quoted by Mauss, "Give as much as you receive and all is for the best,"[39] or in the *lex talionis* (punishment should correspond in degree and kind to the crime). The specific differences between this thinking in terms of equivalence and the money-mediated exchange of equivalents is readily apparent. Whether "*do ut des*" or "an eye for an eye," indifferent, "cold," abstract equivalence is not to be found in these forms of relation and exchange, but rather in (for better or worse) "hot," personal, and, from the perspective of money economy, "unreasonable" relationships of reciprocity. With this in mind, Mauss points out "that the spirit of gift-exchange is characteristic of societies which had left the phase of 'total prestation' (between clan and clan, family and family) but have not yet reached the stage of pure individual contract, the money market, sale proper, fixed price, and weighed and coined money."[40]

Secondly, it was the "invention" of coined money around 700 B.C.E. that first formed rationality, intersubjectively binding categories (such as, among others, identity, difference, quantity, quality, modality), and self-conscious transcendental subjects—that formed heads and tails, head and number. With the invention of coins, society was able to shift away from the hot principle of retaliation to the sober-cold medium of money. Max Schmidt[41] described the transition from the communal economy, tinged with the affective and the personal, to the abstract community of commerce, resting on the medium of money and running on competition and private property, thus: "Principles of external trade slowly trickle into the core of society and supplant there the principles of the communal economic internal trade."[42] That this means not only a rearrangement of economic forms, but also unleashes far-reaching mental effects is rendered plausible in the analysis of the same process in Sahlin's ethnological terminology: general reciprocity becomes rarer and rarer, complemented by the concern over the self and—to complete Sohn-Rethel's argument—the differentiation between self-concern and self-consciousness becomes more and more pronounced.[43]

It is clear that the exceedingly strong accentuation of the threshold of the epoch beginning in 700 B.C.E. is not exclusively the whim of Sohn-Rethel but was already essentially interdisciplinary common property. Yet even the monstrous outsiders of thinking—or precisely those—have made this threshold the center of their attention. Heidegger, following Nietzsche, sees the transition from pre-Socratic wisdom to Socratism as the beginning of the obliviousness of being. The ontological difference between being and that which is can be precisely translated into terms of commodity and money theory. To be oblivious to being describes, accordingly, the age that reifies being by making everything that is into a predicable, exchangeable, indifferent commodity. As it says in one of Heraclitus's key fragments (neglected by Heidegger), which testifies to the high consciousness of the repudiation of the history of being: "Everything is exchange of fire and fire the exchange of everything, precisely as wares are exchanged for money and money for wares."[44] That age in which (according to the profound words of Hegel) to the "consciousness . . . Being {Sein} means what is its own {Seinen}"[45] must be regarded as oblivious to being.

Bachofen, too, understood the upheaval of the epoch around 700 B.C.E. as one that accomplished a tremendous leap in abstraction. Though his monumental study *Mother Right* {Das Mutterrecht} may be, in its details, as controversial as anything—that motherhood rests on the certainty of the senses while fatherhood rests on claims of validity which are "logical" is difficult to dispute (see the discussions of the scene of the Mothers in *Faust II* in chapter 6). To recognize the connection between procreation and birth and to maintain it in the face of "gynecocratic" evidence involves pitting abstraction and rationality against the certainty of the senses. In the eloquent words of Bachofen: "An entirely new attitude makes itself felt. The mother's connection with the child is based on a material relationship, it is accessible to sense perception and remains always a natural truth. But the father as begetter presents an entirely different aspect. Standing in no visible relation to the child, he can never, even in the marital relation, cast off a certain fictive character."[46]

Feminine symbols in situations of sacrifice are found with striking frequency on early coins.[47] The social synthesis achieved via the abstraction of money displaced and prevailed over the stage of tribal synthesis that had been gynecocratically organized in symbolic-emblematical terms as well. To express it pointedly in the logic of symbols: the decorative shells that clearly evoke feminine associations are replaced by the phallic obol, the sacrificial staff, from which functional money, useful as a medium of exchange, arises.[48] Walter Benjamin, in his early essay "Socrates," offers a formulation pregnant with meaning: an "erection of knowledge" replaces pre-Socratic profundity.[49] Whether obliviousness to being, patriarchy, or the abstraction of money: the existentially historical, ethnological, and sociogenetic captions all exhibit a forceful accentuation of a new form of rationality. It is abstract in the literal sense. Only the monetary abstraction, however, develops its own binary code and its own medium that achieves transubjective and universal validity: money.

Psychic, religious, and otherwise fundamental revolts against the domination of this cold-rational medium have been notorious from the beginning. "Abolished are money and property!" it says paradigmatically in a work of 1843 by Büchner's friend August Becker,[50] at a time when many—from the old Chamisso to the young Marx—establish and for the most part repudiate the triumphant advance of the "money system" (Becker). Phenomena such as corruption, nepotism, and favoritism can still be conceived of as attempts to smuggle the principles of the "*do ut des*"-economy and its quasi-familial warmth into the cold economy of money. Precisely then does it become clear, however, that one can qualify this, from the perspective of the developing money economy, as pre-rational and not self-interested/self-conscious, but also as not in the public interest, thus clannish (mafiose, Mediterranean, Catholic, "southern").

Not least among the difficulties of the German unification of 1990 was the fact that the two countries to be reunited differed in that they knew "the right money" (the Federal Republic's) or the money that was precisely not-right (that of the German Democratic Republic). Many citizens of the GDR were used to conducting important transactions with individual stories rather than with payments (as in: if you repair my friend's Trabant,[51] he will help me build a cottage, and I will give your daughter violin lessons). No wonder the people of the GDR perceive(d) the West German economic world as "cold," and the people of the FRG the former Easterners as oddly overemotional and pre-rational. Thorsten Becker's novella of 1985, with the hot title *Die Bürgschaft*, clearly outlines the opposition FRG versus GDR as equivalent to count versus recount in its very first sentence: "There is perhaps still one place in Germany where the West Germans tell stories. This is the autobahn to the GDR. In my personal opinion the GDR ought to raise the transit toll as soon as possible on these grounds." To raise the transit toll is at the very least to suspect that the code of money could be more successful than that of storytelling.

Thirdly, in the years around 1600 C.E., a far-reaching restructuring of the monetary sphere occurred and was attentively registered by literature (in works such as adaptations of *Fortunatus*, *The Merchant of Venice*, and *Timon of Athens*). Not for nothing have theoreticians as diverse as Benjamin, Adorno, Foucault, and Deleuze devoted such strikingly intense interest (primarily concerning language or code history) to the Baroque period. Around 1600, a far-reaching decoupling of signifier and signified and of "les mots et les choses" gains ground. It is for good reason that Hofmannsthal places Lord Chandos's letter in this epoch in which Don Quixote makes a fool of himself for believing in a fixed reference between the alphabet and reality, and the cleverer Hamlet, when asked what he is reading, does not offer topic or title but answers, simply, "words, words, words."

The simple but far-reaching discovery that language is not materially covered was surely only possible due to the gradual erosion of the realistic semantics of Holy Communion which began in the sixteenth century: the general belief that bread and wine are more than "mere" symbols dissolves. The function of the ontosemiological major medium is taken over by the medium (which at that time still appeared to be "realistically-substantially" covered) of money. Money's "language of commodities" (Marx[52]) and its unique, functional and digital code (pays/does not pay) easily gain wide acceptance. In the age of the worldwide spread of trade, the universalized exchange of equivalents, and the thorough monetization of almost all functional systems, a sphere of banking quickly develops that facilitates something like a monetary meta-communication: it is no longer the case that only commodities can be exchanged, but money itself can be bought and sold, thus insuring a widespread decoupling of space and time. Money, as the medium that is indifferent to the temporal, spatial and personal dimensions of acts of exchange, unleashes the experiences of allegorization and de-materialization {*Derealisierung*[53]} that are to become the signature of the Baroque period. Bread and wine can certainly still be physically consumed; but words decay like moldy mushrooms in the mouth, and money shouldn't even cross one's lips— it has no intrinsic value.

De-substantialization, semantic crisis, (slowly developing) functionalism, (the beginnings of) the differentiation of functional subsystems with their own codes (for example, Galileo's specific scientific language versus the traditional religious semantic of universality), the strong emphasis on subjectivity, the newly structured experience of time (one can monetize time, that is, buy and sell promissory notes; see chapter 7)[54]—these are a few of the key words that characterize the age which, thoroughly imbued with a sense of crisis as it shifts from religious to monetary ontosemiology, allows a new framework for reason to be prescribed. This shift seems to have succeeded in breaking through: "For in this sign all now can find salvation." The medium of money is primarily responsible for the specifically modern move toward rationalization and mobilization. It advances to the ontosemiological major medium and achieves functionally the social synthesis which the substantial ontosemiology, after the age of religious civil war, is obviously no longer capable of guaranteeing. Thus the modern age begins with the acme of money: heads and/or tails, head and/or number.

Fourthly, where there is success, risk, too, increases. Precisely because the ontosemiological medium of money "wins the prize" (over sword and pen, over God and might), and because money does not function "merely" as a medium of control over economic processes but also participates, for example, in the oversight of the religious dimensions of meaning whose erosion it also ensures, the consequences of crises in the medium money are enormous. Modernity is forced to experience this on a grand scale (after preceding events such as the collapse of Law's reforms or the French assignats[55]). With the collapse of the medium of money—as, among other things, the great periods of inflation of the twentieth century have shown—collective reason, "Kantian" subjects, and reliable intersubjective relationships largely collapse.

Additionally, around 1900 a new ontosemiological major medium emerges that begins to encroach upon money and erode the monetary medium just as money had dispersed, for its part, the religious ontosemiology: the new audio-visual media. They overwrite not only the classical form of metal and paper money by turning electronic money into the form in which the sums that really count are handled. They also establish a "second currency" in societies, particularly for those groups among whom the majority have achieved a high standard of living: celebrity. If money is for many no longer alarmingly scarce, the scarcity of time and fame counts all the more. Electronic media allow relatively many (of those, that is, who have nearly everything) relatively regular access to the limited market of celebrity. Many private broadcasters stand ready to defend this, their mark: they systematically confound the border between public and private, or the transcendental and the immanent, which the media of Holy Communion and money still clearly differentiated. They organize social synthesis not just in a different way than did the old mass media of Communion and money; they allow (and have since the end of the legitimate public monopoly of media systems) social synthesis to erode altogether—enough material and problems for a study titled "The Poetics of the Media," which will follow this book and conclude the series of ontosemiological analyses.

De-substantialization or the obvious medialization of money, the discovery of the lack of cover for (not just) money, de-materialization, constructivism, nihilism, social erosion, wavering forms of consciousness: these are the key words that characterize the fate of the self-conscious subject in the age of immaterial money and electronic media. After cultic sacraments, money was the first technical mass medium that preserved, in spite of its tremendous, inherent power of abstraction, tangible dimensions. Money unleashed transcendental subjects and functionally and reliably regulated relationships of intersubjectivity on a grand scale. The fundamental monetary connection between traders is that of inclusion by exclusion—or, in the words of Sohn-Rethel, which are very close to Luhmann's systems theory: the functional association through nonparticipation of ego and alter. " 'Society'

is . . . a connection between human beings with respect to their existence, and certainly on the level on which a piece of bread that one
person eats cannot satisfy another"[56] . . . and one person's money (in
contrast to knowledge or discourse) is, by definition, not someone
else's. As Sohn-Rethel once put it in a letter to Adorno: "Yes!—
precisely the negation of the contents of society is the genetically
constituted product of society—the human being imagines himself
mere ego precisely to the extent of his association, and mere subject
precisely to the extent of his objectification."[57] Things are no longer so
dialectically ordered in the postmodern age of the media. Traditional
subjects metamorphose and erode in it, along with money. As it says in
Bodo Morshäuser's story *Berliner Simulation*, "Sometimes, when I visit
this bar, I think about the fact that I don't know anyone who doesn't
have any debts, strictly speaking, and I wonder where all the money is.
Sometimes I see an economist here. I told her that once, and she said
I was right, that 'strictly speaking there isn't money any more' [only
information], and she wasn't drunk."[58]

11

MONEY: SYMBOL, ALLEGORY, FETISH—
MARX WITH BENJAMIN AND GOETHE

Magic Philology—Exorcistic Philosophy

In the correspondence between Adorno and Benjamin, Sohn-Rethel's theory is one of the main themes. Adorno reacted to Sohn-Rethel's intuitions emphatically, which is all the more remarkable given the fact that emphatic agreement was not exactly Adorno's standard reaction to the intellectual achievements of others. His "favorite game" was, on the contrary—according to Benjamin's pointed diagnosis—"digging up the hatchet"[1] *in theoreticis.* The following lines from his letter are therefore surprising: "Alfred, I do not think I am exaggerating when I tell you that your letter occasioned the greatest intellectual shock that I have experienced in philosophy since my first encounter with Benjamin's work—and that occurred in 1923! . . . That I have been counting the days until our meeting ever since goes without saying. This is how Leibniz must have felt when he heard about Newton's discoveries, and vice versa. Please don't think I'm crazy."[2] Adorno reacts with these exclamations to an extensive letter of November 4, 1936, in which Sohn-Rethel develops his central thesis, according to which "the form of cognition {*Erkenntnis*} . . . [is] always determined by the object," "the origin of subjectivity . . . [is] the inseparable correlate of the development of the money-form of value," and "intersubjectivity [is] established with" the money (fetish).[3]

"The most important event of last week was a visit from Alfred Sohn-Rethel, who had just written me a most exciting letter outlining his thesis, and then discussed it with me in detail. He arrives at results oddly similar to my current endeavor from an utterly different angle. My conversation with him was actually highly significant." Thus Adorno writes to Benjamin on November 28, 1936[4]—and so to the one to whom he owed his "greatest intellectual shock" prior to his contact with Sohn-Rethel's intellectual goods. Benjamin was also well acquainted with Sohn-Rethel's theses—he was supposed to write an expert opinion on them for Horkheimer. Benjamin was, to be sure, much more skeptical toward Sohn-Rethel's theoretical approaches than Adorno, who, for good reason, was able to present himself in his correspondence with Benjamin as the better dialectical materialist: "If you," he wrote to Benjamin at the beginning of August 1935, "transpose the dialectical image as 'dream' into consciousness, then not only has the concept been demystified and rendered sociable, but precisely through this it has also forfeited that objective liberating power that could legitimize it materialistically. [Sohn-Rethel's central argument follows:] The fetish character of the commodity is not a fact of consciousness, but it is dialectical in the preeminent sense of producing consciousness."[5]

Benjamin accepted this thesis (which is in fact rather impudent) with reservations. For his perception of a modernity determined by money is, first of all, diametrically opposed to Sohn-Rethel's: it appears to him not as the age of thoroughly formed rationality and strong subjectivity, but as an epoch of impoverished allegorical meaning and of ego of the dimensions of the Baroque—in a word, as an epoch of ghostly incomprehensibility. The fact that Adorno referred to Sohn-Rethel ironically as "So'n Rätsel"[6] in their later correspondence, thus conceding that, even if one accepts his thesis, many questions (and particularly aesthetic ones) remain unanswered, may have made it psychologically easier for Benjamin to accept Adorno's emphasis on Sohn-Rethel.[7] Yet without the backdrop of Sohn-Rethel's thesis, Benjamin's thoughts on the allegorical character of a modern society of commodities would be less plausible as well. To clarify the point, Sohn-Rethel's thesis suggests (thoroughly in keeping with Marxist tradition) the money-fetish as a functional mediator between the abstraction of thought and real abstraction, or, to force a modern transcription of the Parmenidean theorem, for conceiving of thinking and being. Money thus fulfills (in a profane and functional way—not aesthetically and assuredly not in the religious sense!) the literal sense of the concept "symbol": it joins separate spheres. Benjamin, in contrast, accentuates the allegorizing effects of the unfolding economy of commodities and money: it drives being and meaning apart.

The correspondence between Adorno and Benjamin also centers repeatedly on the appropriateness of these diagnoses. After reading Adorno's essay "On the Fetish Character in Music," Benjamin asks his intellectual friend the Gretchen-question—what he thinks of the decline of religiously reconciling sacredness and symbolicity that he discerned in modern music after Wagner. "In music—or similarly in lyric poetry—" thus reads Adorno's essay,

> the society which judged them comic becomes comic. But involved in this laughter is the decay of the sacral spirit of reconciliation. All music today can very easily sound as *Parsifal* did to Nietzsche's ears. It recalls incomprehensible rites [of the Eucharistic community of the Holy Grail] and surviving masks from an earlier time, and is provocative nonsense. The radio, which both wears out[8] music and overexposes it, makes a major contribution to this. Perhaps a better hour may at some time strike.[9]

With his theorem of the quasi-sacral "empathy with the commodity and exchange value," Benjamin links up with Adorno's exciting and stimulating, though not explicit, juxtaposition of (eucharistic Parsifal-) rites, (exchange-)society, and the new media (radio), to ask, then, "Or does the decline of sacred reconciliation connote something positive to you?"[10]

Adorno's answer is clear: yes. "In fact, I see . . . in the 'disintegration [instead of: decline] of sacred reconciliation' something exceedingly positive, and surely this passage of mine has more in common with your work on reproduction[11] than any of my other work. If that is not clear from my text I would regard this as a serious flaw."[12] Adorno's statements and positions are not, as is well known, always so unequivocal. In the same letter to Benjamin, he clear-sightedly characterizes the "weakness of an {his} essay" and other texts of his as well:

> It lies, roughly speaking, in the tendency to bellyache and complain. The lament over the present state of affairs, in this you are right, of course, is as useless as I would say in reverse that the historical philosophical aspect of today hinders its "deliverance." Today, I think the truly possible question concerns the *experimental arrangement* {*Versuchsanordnung*}: what will become of human beings and their aesthetic apperception under the conditions of monopolistic capitalism?[13]

Benjamin consistently questioned the fate of aesthetic apperception under the conditions of monopolistic capitalism (of the money-fetish would surely be the more appropriate formulation, presumably more closely attuned to Adorno's intention). His fundamental diagnosis is relatively clear: despite or indeed precisely because of the fetishistic implications of the developing exchange of commodities and money, modernity has an allegorical deep structure beyond all symbolic-"sacred reconciliation." In modernity being and meaning split apart as unreconcilably and yet yearn to come together as intensely as text and image of Baroque emblem and signified and signifier of allegory. Thus Benjamin can offer the following formulation: "Emblems return as commodities. / Allegory is the armature of modernity."[14] Each of the next two fragments from *Zentralpark*—Benjamin's early Romantic collection of aphorisms written late in his career—sets up a strained relationship between a sociological or historical-philosophical category (commodity or modernity) and an aesthetic category (emblem or allegory). They are thus paradigmatic for the habit of thought of the late Benjamin, who is forcing one of his early motifs. For the habit of thought, namely, that can be characterized, as Benjamin does, as magic philology with a sociological and, more specifically, a historical, philosophically revolutionizing intention.

For Benjamin, the philology that conjures up, from texts, sound and valid diagnoses of the state of the historical-philosophical clock, is magic. The formulation of the "allegory as the armature of modernity" means, then: One can read speed, acceleration, and one's own instantaneous spatial-temporal displacement in the allegorical textures of modernity, as one can in cars or planes. That machinery, however, with which modernity has armed itself and made itself mobile may also be called "the armature of modernity." And this machinery is thoroughly allegorical—and that means above all: estranged from meaning and God. Magic, too, is a philology and philosophy of history which, at the same time, beyond intervening in the armatures that register the state of things, attempts to determine the state of things—as if one could stop a car by pushing the tachometer back to zero.

"On est philologue ou on ne l'est pas," Benjamin writes to Adorno on February 23, 1939, from Paris. With that he takes up the motifs of his previous letter, in which he says of "the genuinely philological demeanor": "Philology is the examination of a text, which, proceeding on the basis of details, magically fixates the reader on the text."[15] Magical fixations on texts are not merely philological-fetishistic spleen at *those* times when these texts—like the contract between Faust and Mephistopheles signed in blood—have perlocutionary power, that is, when they are more than capricious combinations of letters on patient paper, when they are texts of law, contract, or incantation—in short: when they intervene in the texture of the real itself.

In his correspondence with Adorno, Benjamin explicitly points out that there is a close kinship between his essay on Baudelaire and the *Passagen-Werk* on the one hand, and his early works on Baroque tragedy and Goethe's *Elective Affinities* on the other. It is important to him to show "that the critique of the philologist's stance is an old concern for me—and most profoundly identical with my critique of myth. Each time, the critique provokes the philological work itself. To use the language of my essay on *Elective Affinities*, it pushes for a display of material content in which truth-content is historically revealed."[16] Traditional philology and myth have the same habit: they revere texts and stories without taking them seriously in an objective way (see chapter 2). Myth makes it possible to avoid the question of whether the stories it tells are factually true. And the philology that Benjamin critiques, too, is an arrangement that allows, say, Goethe to be revered, so that his texts do not have to be taken seriously, or—to generalize: to avoid crediting poetic texts with the "display of material content in which truth-content is historically revealed."

The actual "philological achievement itself" is only possible after working through the critique of the current stance of the philologist who does not perceive poetic texts as a medium for diagnosing their content. The magic philologist, in contrast, takes texts as armatures, in both senses of the word, seriously. He trusts that poetic texts (such as Goethe's or Baudelaire's) develop the contents of their works in new ways, in ways different from those of the disciplines into which they are organized, and yet, or perhaps for that very reason, they do so appropriately. Thus the magic philologist locates his work (according to Adorno's precise characterization of Benjamin's essay on Baudelaire) "at the intersection of magic and positivism. This passage is enchanted. Only theory might be able to break the spell: your [that is, Benjamin's] own, relentless, good speculative theory," writes Adorno to Benjamin on October 11, 1938, taking up the double project, firstly, of opening up material content via texts and making it compatible with theory, and, secondly, of reading, in this way, the armature of modernity and intervening in it to display the "truth-content" of texts as historical constellations, and to exorcize philosophically the enchantment of modernity. If Benjamin's Gretchen-question for Adorno concerned his thoughts on the decline of sacred reconciliation, Adorno's Gretchen-question for Benjamin is how seriously he, the singular dialectical materialist, takes theology, magic, and exorcism.

Symbol, Fetish, Allegory

The framework of modernity that the magic philologist Benjamin wants to decode is an allegorical one. And the code of this framework is that of the "language of commodities" (Marx). Benjamin's designation of the commodity as the revenant of the allegory in the modern world of signs-for-realities that actually count is at first glance highly improbable. Especially from a Marxist perspective, into which the "late" Benjamin attempts to enter. Not for nothing did Marx characterize commodity and money as fetishistic rather than allegorical. And the fetish is something like a supersymbol—and not, for example (like allegory), something that undercuts the symbol's promise of reconciliation. Strictly from the perspective of the history of ideas, it is striking that the concept of the symbol, traditionally nearly without exception highly regarded, is addressed by many cultural critics and semiologists (such as Cassirer and Jaspers, Peirce and Mead, Habermas and Schwemmer), but never by neo-Marxist theory. It favors the concepts of allegory and fetish.

Benjamin's designation *allegory* is at first glance very conventional —and close to Goethe's. "The allegory as the sign that is sharply differentiated from its meaning has its place in art as the opponent of the beautiful appearance {*schönen Scheins*}, in which signifier and signified flow into one another. If this friability of the allegory is lost, it loses its authority as well."[17] The realm of beautiful appearance is the realm of the symbol. For the symbol participates meaningfully in what it means—and this victory over semiological binarism is of course only possible in appearance. Because the symbol is a part of that to which it refers, it allows the emergence of the beautiful appearance that there is no break between signified and signifier, between being and meaning, between soma and sema, but rather a meaningful passageway—precisely that of the symbol, the rite of passage into spheres of higher wisdom than the world of mere things makes possible. The symbol (Greek *symbolon*) thus brings together, as much in appearance as with beauty, that which (from the perspective of the symbol) only appeared to be separated and broken.

Because this condition—even if under the auspices of the extremely profane—is fulfilled, the sensible-transcendent commodity-thing is (at the very least!) symbolically structured. The commodity as thing participates in the sphere of meaning and of values; it is, as an abstraction of commodity, a signifier and, as the thing indicated by the expression of value, a signified as well. It can express its kind: the commodity is as dense, as condensed as a symbol. And this signifying expression occurs in such a tangible sense that the commodity constantly oversteps the border between the symbol and the *fetish*. An important semantic surplus value clings to the old pun that the commodity alone is the True.[18] That is, even the symbol's promise to reconcile the break, the split, between signified and signifier, to unite them in a symbolic, but also precisely only symbolic, (as of yet) unrealized unity, is not enough for the fetish. If the symbol promises to achieve an ontosemiological unity of signifier and signified on the part of signs, the fetish promises this on the part of that which is {des Seienden}. Thus the fetish is a supersymbol, to a certain extent an overcharged symbol. A thing, in other words, capable of bringing about the supernatural, a signifying thing that not only partakes of the sphere of the signified, but is capable of forming and enchanting it. In the precise words of Marx: a sensible-transcendent thing, a thing that is capable, paradoxically enough, of conditioning the presumably unconditional, the absolute. A theological subtlety, a metaphysical anomaly.

Not for no reason does the fetish appear in sexual and religious double form.[19] The commodity- and money-fetish, together with this doubling, completes the Holy Trinity: whoever has money can say, in unison with the inscription on the dollar bill and coin, "In God we trust." It is every bit as potent and pious as it is spiritually solvent. In a revealing travelogue from West Africa, V. S. Naipaul reports that he consulted a "féticheur," who (like the taxi driver who takes him to the place where the absolute has become tangible), to his disappointment, is only truly interested in one fetish: his client's money.[20] Freud and Lacan have characterized the fetish as a supplemental phallus: "The fetish is a substitute for the woman's (the mother's) phallus that the little boy once believed in and—for reasons familiar to us—does not want to give up."[21] The fetish is not only capable of bearing witness, it can also procreate. It can even engender and bear witness to meaning: "the signification of the phallus."[22] The religious fetish (and half-ironically the mascot) acquires quasi-godly potency. It is capable of affecting that which it is denied mere things to affect. Yet the fetish is no more a mere thing than the phallus or the commodity. It has such great semantic surplus value that it causes the collapse of the jagged line of demarcation between physical nature and significance.

When Benjamin, obviously with a high degree of awareness, abandons this Marxist line of argument and aligns the commodity not with the symbol, nor money with the fetish, but the commodity with the allegory, he is forced to take refuge in the specific understanding of the allegory as expressed in his book on the Baroque. Accordingly, the allegory is the historical-philosophical signature of the early modern period, precisely because it does not, in contrast to the symbol and the fetish, attest to the possibility of the fluid transition, nor even the magic fetishistic identification, between signified and signifier. For this epoch, after the religious civil wars of the seventeenth century, is experienced as the epoch of the "depths which separate visual being from meaning."[23] In the famous words of Benjamin's book on tragic drama:

> Whereas in the symbol destruction is idealized and the transfigured face of nature is fleetingly revealed in the light of redemption, in allegory the observer is confronted with the *facies hippocratica* of history as a petrified, primordial landscape. Everything about history that, from the very beginning, has been untimely, sorrowful, unsuccessful, is expressed in a face—or rather in a death's head. And although such a thing lacks all "symbolic" freedom of expression, all classical proportion, all humanity—nevertheless, this is the form in which man's subjection to nature is most obvious and it significantly gives rise not only to the enigmatic question of the nature of human existence as such, but also of the biographical historicity of the individual. This is the heart of the allegorical way of seeing, of the baroque, secular explanation of history as the Passion of the world; its importance resides solely in the stations of its decline. The greater the significance, the greater the subjection to death, because death digs most deeply the jagged line of demarcation between physical nature and significance.[24]

Grave, depths, jagged line of demarcation, digging: easy passages between being and meaning are denied the allegory. Baroque allegory forcefully articulates the revolutionary theological experience of early modernity, the realization that revealed religions are obviously not obvious[25] and that symbolic images of the world have reached the end of their plausibility. The developing economy of commodity and money reacts to this experience. Cross, dove, flag, Holy Communion: the fundamental rhetorical move of symbolic or (as in the central case of the Eucharist[26]) fetishistic semantics was to open up fluid (revelatory-)passageways from the realm of transcendent significance and infinite meaning to the realm of the signified and finite existence. Commodity and money: that is the attempt, after the collapse of this movement, to turn it around and to start the Babylonian project once again, and on a large scale. "The alphabet is really now superfluous / For in this sign all now can find salvation." The new language of unity, after the Babylonian confusion of language, is the internationally valid code of money. Languages, and the languages of the creation in particular—according to a widespread theological motif—are of divine origin. The language of money, however, is purely earthly: God does not face problems of scarcity that can be headed off monetarily, and God is not dependent on the money-code.

With their ostentatious unification of head and number, image and writing, numbers and alphabet, the tangible and the conceptual, coins and paper money push their way out of the realm of the profane into the theological. This motif resounds clearly—as early as Shakespeare. In *Timon of Athens* money is called the visible deity:

> Thou visible god,
> That solder'st close impossibilities
> And makest them kiss![27]

To solder impossibilities and to unite the most disparate spheres in a kiss—that is the achievement of the symbol. To force this soldering, this kiss, and to procure for things the dignity of the appearance of the absolute—that is the dubious achievement of the fetish. Marx quotes these words of Shakespeare's in his *The German Ideology*,[28] and Derrida quotes this quote yet again and comments upon it:

> The quotation will also make apparent . . . a theologizing fetishization, the one that always links ideology irreducibly to religion (to the idol or the fetish) as its principal figure, a species of "invisible god" to which adoration, prayer, and invocation are addressed ("Thou visible God"). Religion . . . was never one ideology among others for Marx. What, Marx seems to say, the genius of a great poet—and the spirit of a great father [that is, Hamlet's father]—will have uttered in a poetic flash, with one blow going faster and farther than our little bourgeois colleagues in economic theory [Max Stirner is meant in the context of the Marx-quotation commented on by Derrida], is the becoming-god of gold, which is at once ghost and idol, a god apprehended by the senses.[29]

The monetary advance from the profane into the religious realm is only possible at the price of fetishistic overstimulation of symbolic promise. Symbols arise from their divine origin, fetishes are the creation of human beings.

Benjamin's diagnosis, then, is that even the remnants of symbolic experiences ultimately collapse through the monetary overstimulation of symbolic promises. Behind the fetishistic excitement and fervor of the universally mobilizing economy of commodities, the cold, allegorical Golgotha of the world spirit can be glimpsed. When money succeeds in pushing into regions other than the profane, fundamental-semantic erosions that occasioned the inversion of God and money may be revealed. These erosions include, however, both spheres—that of the world of things as well as that of meanings. "That power of mortal indifference that is money"[30] misspeaks when it promises symbolic transfigurations of things into values, of being into meaning. The limited medium of money inflates to some extent the (commodities-) things and the (traditional) meanings in the same way. In Benjamin's words: "The devaluation of the world of things through allegory is outdone within the world of things itself through the commodity."[31] There is nothing the commodity-fetish is less interested in than the thing to which it attaches, only to free itself again as quickly as possible. The commodity- and money-fetish drives the extensive devaluation of the world of things. In Hegel's words: it revokes the "tenderness for things"; and in Heidegger's (and in opposition to Heidegger— Heidegger was of course unwilling and unable to translate his whispering diagnoses into sociological categories): the commodity-fetish creates first of all the ontological difference and arouses indifference in the face of that which is and in the face of the miracle that being is at all rather than is not/nothing. What matters about a wooden shoe is never indicated by its price, though possibly by a painting of van Gogh's, whose price on the art market looks, from this perspective, like money's revenge against art, which seemed to be indifferent to monetary indifference.

New French simulation theory's interest in Benjamin's not so esoteric reflections is not difficult to understand (see chapter 4). Benjamin's later work registers an illuminating change in the tradition of neo-Marxist theory: it shifts from the critique of reification {*Verdinglichung*} to the critique of de-materialization {*Entdinglichung*}.[32] That under the conditions of capitalist society "a definite social relation between men, that assumes . . . the fantastic form of a relation between things"[33] and thus confronts "living labour-power as products and working conditions . . . which are personified"—this chiasma constitutes, according to Marx, the "religion of everyday life"[34] in capitalistic modernity. That the fundamental structures of transcendental subjectivity, too, are reified, that is, imprinted by the commodities- and money-thing—that was the neo-Marxist radicalization of Marx's diagnosis of reification by Lukács[35] and Sohn-Rethel. Benjamin was certainly the first in the circle of neo-Marxists to acknowledge this *ordoinversus* argument (things advance to subjects, subjects are reified) and to stand it on its head: commodities- and money-things can only have powers of reification because they de-materialize things.

In his letter to Benjamin of August 2, 1935, Adorno recognizes the "glowing core of theology" in Benjamin's argumentation—that the commodity-fetish inherits religious symbolism, including its fetishistic religious practices, and for that very reason drains it dry:

> We have the promise of immortality in commodities and not for people, and—to develop the relationship to the book on the baroque, which you rightly establish—the fetish is a treacherously final image for the nineteenth century, comparable only to the death's head. It seems to me that this is where the decisive epistemological character of Kafka lies, especially in Odradek, as the commodity that survives to no purpose: surrealism may come to an end in this fairy tale, just as the *Trauerspiel*

does in *Hamlet*. . . . A restoration of theology, or rather a radicalization of the dialectic down to the glowing core of theology, would concurrently have to mean a most extreme intensification of the sociodialectical, even economic, motif. The motif would also have to be dealt with historically. The commodity character *specific* to the nineteenth century, i.e. industrial commodity production, would have to be worked out materially and much more clearly because, of course, commodity character and alienation have existed ever since the beginning of capitalism, i.e. the age of manufacturing and specifically the age of the baroque—just as, on the other hand, the "unity" of the modern age has lain precisely in its commodity character ever since that time.[36]

To draw it out as Adorno does and to take it one step further: the unity of modernity since about 1600 lies "in the commodity character" and in the universalization of the abstraction of exchange mediated by money, with its (inter)subjectivity-formation effects; the specific mark of the nineteenth century is its going overboard via "industrial production of commodities" with its reifying effects; and the historical sign of the twentieth century, as it comes to an end, is the tendency toward immaterialization and de-materialization.

Goethe's Allegorical Late Work

In his critique of the allegorical devaluation of the world of things in modernity and in his discovery of the allegorical structure of the commodity, Benjamin can hardly cite Marx, but he can, most assuredly, cite the late work of Goethe. Thus it is hardly surprising that the correspondence between Adorno and Benjamin regarding the *Passagen-Werk* repeatedly touches upon central passages of Goethe's work. Goethe's late work is the text that makes the magic philologist Benjamin's historical-philosophical diagnosis of modernity possible. For it marks, with the highest authority, the end of an art of uninterrupted and symbolic narration and dramatic presentation.

Adorno recognized this and summed it up with acuity. In his letter to Benjamin of September 6, 1936, he says, "If I'm not terribly mistaken, the first sentence of *Elective Affinities*, with the hesitant introduction of the names, which you have also analyzed, has its origin in Goethe's awareness—a result of his unerring historical-philosophical sense—of the impossibility of narration."[37] The classic narrator attests to a continuum between signified and signifier. His speech is symbolic; the stream of his narration will hold together what threatens to break apart and will unite what is already shattered. That this powerful insistence on symbolical uniting—no one in Goethe's

novel represents this as clearly as the Hermes-allegory, Mittler[38]—
fails, Goethe's prose about the "well-to-do baron in the prime of his
life" makes clear.[39] For this reason, too, Adorno can write, pointedly, to
Benjamin: " 'Elective Affinities' [meaning Benjamin's essay on Goethe]
and the baroque book are better Marxism than the wine tax and the
deduction of phantasmagoria from the writers of feuilletons [that is,
Benjamin's studies on Baudelaire]."[40]

Adorno and Benjamin could have cited a passage from Goethe's
Wilhelm Meister's Journeyman Years as well in their discussions about
the "religion of everyday life" in modernity, the erosion of the symbolic
orientation to the world in narration, and the state of allegory. It
correlates with and confronts in a remarkably allegorical way two
fetishistic requisites: the mysterious little box and an antiquarian cross.
The events preceding this scene are easy to recall. Wilhelm's son
Felix—*nomen est omen*—has made a fortunate discovery. In a cave
(reminiscent of the Plutonian cave that Fortunatus visited—see chapter
6) he comes across a crevice in which he finds a "large box" that has a
smaller one inside. The latter, itself twice enclosed, cannot be opened;
the key to the heavily decorated lock is missing. Wilhelm and Felix
meet an antiquarian to whom they present their precious secret, with
the question,

> whether it should be opened. The old man did not think so.
>
> "To be sure, I suppose it could be done without undue harm. However,
> since you came by it through such a curious chance, you ought to try
> your luck on it. If you were born fortunate, and if this casket has any
> significance, then the key to it must turn up sometime, and precisely
> where you least expect it."
>
> "There probably are such cases," Wilhelm replied.

And now a breathtaking story follows, a parallel to the story of
the little box that very clearly combines motifs of treasure and wealth
with the symbolism of birth-(cave) and phallus-(key). That that which
belongs together (such as box and key, vulva and phallus, or—cross
and the body of Christ) does not always meet or join, the antiquarian
knows, too. He can even report on an especially profound allegorical
case of an allegedly merely symbolic resynthesis.

> "I have experienced several [such cases] myself," answered the old
> man, "and here you see the most remarkable example before you: this
> ivory crucifix. For thirty years I owned the body with head and feet all
> in one piece, and because of its wonderful artistry kept the object in a
> most precious little box. About ten years ago I obtained the cross which
> belonged to it, along with the inscription, and I let myself be seduced
> into having arms attached by the most skillful carver of our times. But

this good man lagged so far behind his predecessor! Still, I left it as it was, more for the sake of edifying reflections than out of admiration for the craftsmanship."

"But now imagine my delight! Not long ago I obtained the original arms, as you see them here refitted in the most exquisite union. Delighted by such a fortunate set of coincidences, I cannot but see in this the fate of the Christian religion, which, often enough dismembered and dispersed, must in the end always come together again around the Cross."[41]

This story stands before the abyss. It tells almost too clearly of allegorical dismemberment: The ivory body of Christ is missing not only "the cross which belonged to it, along with the inscription," it is also broken itself. For it is missing the arms and hands that can offer blessings and break bread, but without which Jesus could not be nailed to the cross. Hands, to which such careful attentiveness is dedicated in Goethe's work, especially where they are amputated or fail in the service of their craft for other reasons: from *Goetz from Berlichingen with the Iron Hand* and Werther's hand, shot through with the bullet, to the "cold devil's fist," the erotic beat of the *Roman Elegies*, and the significant motif of the failing handwriting in the "Diary"-poem and in *Elective Affinities* (and in the context of this scene from the *Journeyman Years*, too, it says explicitly: "All living, all activity, all art must be preceded by technical skill"). The allegorically incomplete, however, ought not to be. Thus the antiquarian has "arms attached by the most skillful carver of our times," a forced, symbolic completion that clearly has the character of a supplement. The body completed in this way, however, never hangs under the inscription on the cross; inscription and requisite cannot meet in emblematic significance and, united, arise from the dead. The crossless Corpus Christi, on the contrary, in keeping with the leitmotif of the novel's little box allegory, was "kept . . . in a most precious little box," thus entombed in its cross- and salvationless dismemberment.

The missing parts gradually return to the antiquarian's ivory arm-, hand- and crossless crucifix. First the replaced parts, then the cross and finally, after a lapse of more than ten years, the "original arms." They are, as if Goethe's late prose wanted to fulfill the literal sense of the word symbol, "refitted in the most exquisite union," thus mortifying allegorically the previously dismembered, now happily arisen or symbolically reintegrated "body with head and feet all in one piece," including the refitted "original arms," and for this very reason make it possible to nail it to the cross once again. That which, therefore, "must in the end always come together again around the Cross" is the allegorical insight that in the conceptual pair "collect" and "disperse," the second word is, and has, the last word. "Those who live long . . . see many things collected and many others dispersed."

The protagonists of the *Journeyman Years* have a cross to bear like the angel of Benjamin's historical-philosophical theses, who "would like to tarry, awaken the dead, and repair the broken"—but cannot. For "a storm is blowing in from paradise that has been caught in his wings and is so strong that the angel cannot close them anymore. This storm drives him relentlessly into the future, on which he turns his back, while the rubble before him grows into the heavens. That which we call progress, is *this* storm."[42] In view of this "storm driving relentlessly into the future" that is called progress, all attempts to get around modernity and current times together with its major media of money and AV-media are at best touching. In the worse, more usual, case, however, they are inciting: that is to say, they radicalize the current potential for catastrophe through antimodern impulses. Goethe's and Benjamin's allegorical diagnostics of history deserve all our attention for this very reason, because both know that only one option is available: to endure modernity.

As if this bit of wisdom from the *Journeyman Years* were not clear enough, an economic seal closes the crucial scene that marks the crossroads of a novel whose cross it is to bear allegorical times: "The young joint owner appeared, and Wilhelm declared his intention of delivering the casket to their care. A huge book was fetched, and the entrusted article was entered." Wilhelm and Felix now have (like Michael Kohlhaas) a piece of paper with something written on it, instead of a real value in their hands, or more precisely: a "receipt . . . which would be valid regardless of who should present it, but would be honored only when the bearer gave an agreed-upon sign"—in short, an assignat. The "Reflections in the Spirit of the Wanderers" relieves interpreters of this scene of their work. "As little as the steam engines can be throttled can anything similar be done in the moral realm. The liveliness of commerce, the continual rustle of paper money, the increase in debts to pay off other debts—all these are frightful elements that the young man of the present confronts."[43]

One could revolt romantically against Goethe's cool diagnosis that one cannot damp a steam engine nor take away money's validity—and thereby hardly avoid confirming their validity. Thus in Achim von Arnim's story of 1826 "Wunder über Wunder," clearly conceived as a reply to the first version of the *Journeyman Years*, "Montan & Co." determine "that money has assumed the position that had otherwise been claimed by honor, faith, and a thousand other trifling trivialities":[44] "It was impossible that all the rationality of the principle of monarchy could stand up to the anarchic rush of the people's sovereign demagogue which is called *money*, to the metaphysical constitution of those chaotic demons which are called *mortgages*, to the paper constitution of the *draft*."[45]

The series of substitutions—little box motif, story of the cross, receipt, honorarium, paper money—leads directly to the allegorical realm of *Faust II*. That this work (despite the fact that Goethe himself repeatedly spoke in favor of symbolism over allegory!) is allegorical through and through, it itself declares, as does Heinz Schlaffer (as an exception to Germanists' usual repression of this kind of labeling), vividly and compellingly.[46] "After all, we're allegories, / and you therefore ought to know us," {"Denn wir sind Allegorien / Und so solltest du uns kennen"} (5531f.), says the Young Charioteer, in the Masquerade scene, about the figures he leads in (5331f.). Which figures? Those who see an analogy between themselves and "commodities": "What is sold and those who sell it / well are worth your crowding closer" {"Würdig sind sie zu umdrängen, / Krämerinnen wie die Ware"} (5114f.). Those who, like the Herald, in the tradition of allegorical interpretation, ". . . would like to do my duty / and expound these figures' meaning" {"die Bedeutung der Gestalten / . . . amtsgemäß entfalten (möchte)"} (5506f.) must, and can, too, indicate, why "these wretches . . . {are} allegories" {"die Lumpe . . . allegorisch sind"} (10329): because the figures have assumed the form of the commodity and this has, for the first time, turned them into rational subjects. Even the resurrection of the ghost of Helen in the drama of Goethe's old age has its price. She who had most assuredly turned the heads of her contemporaries prior to the invention of the medium of money, now resurrected in modern times, finds herself reviled by Phorkyas/Mephistopheles as "Wares gained in war, sold secondhand in market places!" {"Erobert-marktverkauft-vertauschte Ware du!"} (8783).

"The commodity has replaced the allegorical mode of intuition,"[47] says Benjamin in a fragment from his *Zentralpark*. A note in the *Passagen-Werk* completes this thought: "The form of the commodity as society's embodiment of the allegorical mode of intuition first occurs in Baudelaire."[48] Baudelaire was not the first: the nexus of allegory, exchangeable commodity and (paper) money was worthy of explicit reflections and theorems by Goethe as well. "*Verba valent sicut nummi*" {Words are as valuable as money}. But there are different sorts of money: gold, silver, and copper coins, or paper money. The coins are real to a degree; the paper money is only convention."[49] Thus writes Goethe under the entry "Symbolism" in his writings on the natural sciences. In his ingenious study with the short, deflationary title

"Faust, Geld," Werner Hamacher comments that Goethe "attributes that authority of convention traditionally associated with allegory to paper money."[50]

In fact, Goethe names the reason for the end of the symbol with allegorical clarity: The degree of abstraction in modern, functionally differentiated, commodity and (paper) money economies no longer permits symbolical unity. For "that which is a concern of the allegorical intention has become separated from life's context: it reaches its end and yet is conserved. Allegory clings to the ruins. It offers an image of fossilized disquiet."[51] Thus the expectation evaporates that the modern trade in money, with its incalculable theological connotations, can participate in the maintenance of religious functions. For religion is per se symbolically or perhaps fetishistically organized, while trade in money (despite the churchly architecture of banks, inscriptions like "In God we trust," and all the other religious associations) can only proceed allegorically, releasing "fossilized disquiet" but never promising redemption. "Lost materiality: that is the elevation of the commodity to the status of the allegory."[52]

Only through intoxication (or in the transfiguring misunderstanding of the moment of Faust's death) can it still be forgotten that allegorical money relations make the talk of "fossilized disquiet" literally come true and have us, like Faust, reeling from desire to gratification and languishing, in gratification, from desire. For this reason, too, it is plausible to characterize modernity, as do Goethe and Benjamin, as both the time of (economic) rationality and the epoch of systematic drugging with the soberest of all drugs: the money-drug. Walter Benjamin emphasized this double aspect when he read the allegorist Baudelaire and Goethe together. Baudelaire

> artificially came to the aid of the historical hallucination of equality, which had taken root along with the commodity economy. . . . The commodity economy arms the phantasmagoria of sameness which, as the attribute of intoxication, at the same time authenticates itself as the central trope of illusion. "With this libation in your body, you will soon come to see Helen in every woman." The price makes the commodity equal to all of those that can be bought for the same price. The commodity does not only and not also establish itself . . . in the buyers, but above all in its price. It is precisely in this regard, however, that the flaneur attunes himself to the commodity; he imitates it completely; in the absence of demand for him, namely a market price, he makes himself at home in venality itself.[53]

The inventor of paper money, Mephistopheles, is just such a flaneur. In *Faust II* he saunters through the millennia, and the most distant open country. His ubiquity is that of money. Compared to this floating-functional force, Faust's initial striving for something substantial seems absurd. In one of the *Maxims and Reflections* it says: "Everything ideal, as soon as it is claimed by the real, consumes this and itself in the end. As credit (paper money) consumes silver and itself."[54] Against the allegorical devaluation of the sphere of things and the sphere of meaning, against the allegorizing power of paper money, "the poet's coin / that promises plenty for everyone" {"die Münze der Poeten, / Die Fülle jedermann verheißt"[55]} is powerless. It is, of course, just as uncovered as paper money. The metaphor of the "poet's coin" may be golden words. Still it is and remains "merely" a metaphor, put down on paper. The "poet's coin" has no face value. The alphabet is, when it makes a poetic appearance in order to balance out deficits of meaning of monetary provenience, for the first time, truly superfluous. Goethe deleted the turn of phrase "the poet's coin" in the published version of *Faust*.

12

Schlemihl's Shadow—
Nietzsche's Shadow

The Amazing Treasure in the Secret Shrine

In Adelbert Chamisso's unfinished dramatization of the Fortunatus story,[1] there is a passage that is as profound as it is superficial. Andolocia, who, together with his brother Ampedo has inherited his father's magic sack that continually produces money, is drawn out of the monetary sphere of the profane and the secondary. He sets out, as is fitting for one who has more than enough of everything, on a search for oneness, pure and simple, for the primary in every sense, for the amazing treasure in the secret shrine in which transcendent meaning lies hidden, waiting to reveal itself as truly present.

> From far away, from inside the secret shrine,
> A treasure so amazing beckons.
> Knowing alone whom it means,
> And the place where it is hidden.
> And we strive, and we mean,
> Striving, meaning incessantly,
> Roving through the world of life,
> Without thought of its dangers.
> We long for oneness,
> We long incessantly,
> Always, too, it is willing to appear,
> Oh! always disappearing.

Fernher, aus geheimem Schreine,
Winkt ein Schatz so wunderbar.
Weiß allein selbst wen er meine,
Und den Ort, wo er bewahrt.
Und wir streben, und wir meinen,
Streben, meinen immerdar,
Schweifen durch des Lebens Weite,
Und verachten die Gefahr.
Wir begehren nur das e i n e,
Wir begehren immerdar,
Immerdar auch wills erscheinen,
Ach! verschwinden immerdar.[2]

This Romantic text reads as an early test of George Steiner's fundamental aesthetic of real presences. The distant, secret shrine, with its amazing treasure that brooks no intervention by an interpreter because it alone knows whom it means and where it is hidden, sets free a desire that is destined to be frustrated: the desire for that oneness that leaves the many distractions behind, for the real-present center that effaces the periphery, for the primary and original that degrades everything secondary to mere painfulness. This desire for oneness, real presence, and the primary is destined to be frustrated because it is inhabited by a systematic paradox—or, to use Goethe's formulation—an obvious secret. "Always, too, it is willing to appear, / Oh! always disappearing." The secret of oneness is obvious: it is as present as it is absent, it is only present as something absent, its presence is one with its absence.

As a secret, it is revealed, and because it is revealed, it is not a secret. For this very reason, one can secret away a great deal into it. Since the shining yet enshrined, hidden treasury of meaning is "always *willing* to appear" but is of course not always (except, possibly, in Christian cultural contexts, each Sunday morning after the transubstantiation, when the thing is holy and no longer profane) really present, since the meaning it offers can obviously only occur as a withdrawal of meaning (in a profound way, too, the Host, transubstantiated into the truly present body of the Son of God, is not unceasingly worshiped, but consumed), since its appearance is to be as unceasing as its disappearance (both processes occur "always"), supplementary and thus necessarily secondary verses like Chamisso's are not only possible, they are unavoidable, especially if one intends to compose/condense meaning. In the beginning was the secondary, for at the origin the one and the primary are always already split. For this reason unceasing talk that attempts to fill the gaps, fissures, and abysses is necessary. The model of the tabernacle with its absent-present, sealed-revealed sense of the real is more profound than the theology that is allied to it and whose intention it is to repress the deconstructive depths of this model (promising a sense of the real and in the process continually compromising itself).

That real-present meaning, despite this different insight, is a tempting and enticing hallucination is evident in Chamisso's drama as it progresses. In the very next scene Andolocia appears, after a successful crossing, at his destination: at the court of the English king. This crossing, however, as he is quickly forced to note, may have transported him to the other side (of a distinction—for example between island and mainland), but not thereby into transcendent spheres. On the other side of the water, namely, it is not the other pure and simple that shines, but the other of that which he had left behind. In England, Fortunatus's son (and, characteristically, the Romantic drama, in contrast to the early modern model, deals with Fortunatus's sons and thus in this respect as well with the "secondary," or, to be precise, with two secondary sons), searching for primary meaning and for the meaning of the primary, participates in a tournament to win Agrippina, the king's daughter. Beautiful and clever women have of course always been (together with fetishes) the epitome of the primary and primarily-sensually experienced meaning. The tournament, however, does not simply take place; it must be ceremoniously called into being in the name of the king, by his chancellor, and thus proclaimed before it actually takes place. This proclamation occurs in such an overly ornate way that the "correspondence between world and word"[3] that the chancellor's words are intended to establish is, from the moment of their inception, overstrained and deconstructed.

The chancellor, who says of himself "the king speaks to you through my mouth," promises, in fully formed terza rima—thus in secondary words that are precisely as perfect in form as they are threatened with meaninglessness—"the interpretation of the games that are now ending." This secondary interpretation of fleeting tournament games which precedes that which they interpret[4] shows profundity and an unmistakable appreciation for art, but it is not easy to understand. And why should words that revolve around the relationship between "world and word," between being and meaning, be easy to understand? They are of course entangled a priori in the paradox that the ontosemiological relationship between "world and word," being and meaning, cannot be expressed by an authority not belonging, itself, to the semantic sphere. How "les mots et les choses" stand in relation to each other, only the fluctuating signs, and not the things, can say. The things could (mystics, from the beginning and on through to Wittgenstein have believed this), if need be, show or reveal it. Such a revelation, however, obviously cannot be translated into the intersubjectively and interculturally binding language of theory: religious revelation is the other of theoretical evidence.

The chancellor's secondary words of interpretation in Chamisso's proto-Romantic drama are also indebted to this original insight into the ontosemiological supremacy of insecure signs over the (allegedly) stable (in fact, however, temporally feeble) things.

> The spoken word seems quickly to float away,
>> A similar fate awaits the song,
>> And even to deprive accomplished deeds of their life.
> The breath will leave the fleeting sounds,
>> The moment, continually sinking
>> to the depths of antiquity, leaves no trace behind.
> Yet awaits, not lost, what one day would call
>> Time into existence out of the place of nothingness,
>> Whether, as seed of the future, it sleeps as yet.
> The spoken word penetrates the ear's gate.
>> It lives its life in the bosom of the shrine,
>> And deeds are words that have blossomed in the light.

> Es scheint gesprochnes Wort rasch zu verschweben,
>> Das Lied ein gleiches Schicksal zu erfassen,
>> Und selbst vollbrachte Taten zu entleben.
> Es will die Luft den flüchtigen Schall verlassen,
>> Nicht das Moment, das zu der Vorzeit Tiefe
>> Sich ewig senket, Spuren hinterlassen.
> Doch unverloren harret, was einst riefe
>> Die Zeit zum Dasein aus des Nichtseins Orte,
>> Ob Zukunftkeim es lautlos annoch schliefe.
> Gesprochnes Wort dringt durch des Ohres Pforte.
>> Es lebt sein Leben in des Busens Schreine,
>> Und Taten sind ans Licht erblühte Worte.

That is beautifully said, but difficult to understand and interpret. The king's fool is the first to recognize that there is a paradox surrounding "the interpretation of the games that are now ending." It is his job, of course, not, as is usual, to place paradoxes under taboo, but to observe and express them. The fool has the last laugh when he definitively translates the chancellor's administrative terza-rima-profundity into that clear text that cannot be had without losses of meaning and of sense: "Listen, Papa, I did not understand him any better than you, but he speaks so well, your chancellor, and it seems to me that he said, with many words, what would have been clear without the many words."[5]

The joke of this fool's speech is unmistakable even for the contemporaries of the Romantic Chamisso, who had to do without the pleasure of reading George Steiner's polemic against everything secondary.[6] The chancellor's words, namely, just like those of the fool, belong to the primary register as well as to the secondary, explanatory, derivative, superfluous, and merely verbose. They count, rightly so, as primary literature to which secondary literature (like this text) turns and often enough appropriates for its own purposes.[7] And they are, moreover, utterly explicit primary words of proclamation that fully intend to call events into existence. Yet these words of proclamation are also words of commentary. And as such, they are of an exaggerated, superfluous, artificial beauty that rests on and is threatened by the fact that they merely amass "words, words, words." The fool's critical words about the superfluous words of the chancellor do not reduce the amount of commentary. It is not just we philologists who pile words upon words. What else are we supposed to do—especially since we know that we cannot not communicate? Demands for silence, beyond a few kairological moments, cannot be carried out without terrible paradoxes and totalitarian implications.

The text of the Romantic drama illustrates the paradoxes of allegedly primary words as well. After the chancellor, the fool, and the king have had their say, plenty of unclear, clarifying, and additionally obfuscatory words have been said. The tournament that follows provides clarity. It reduces overly complex words for wooing a beautiful woman in the most tangible way. Someone has to be first. Andolocia wins the hand of Agrippina; he fancies himself within the aureate circle of the shrine of meaning sensibly experienced; and he sacrifices (in a dense scene that weaves the symbolism of the little box with the Danae motif: "Andolocia pulls out the sack and throws gold on her lap," the stage directions read) to this primary shrine the essence of the secondary: gold from his lucky purse. Yet it is obvious that Agrippina wants more; the single pieces of gold interest this beauty less than the "source" that produces gold in abundance. Thus she gives Andolocia a sleeping potion, steals the lucky sack from him, and replaces it with a fake. This starts that game of cat and mouse between Agrippina and Andolocia, between love and money, between the primary and the secondary, whose praises Chamisso's famous song of the cats sing. "Always, too, it is willing to appear, / Oh! always disappearing."

Primary Language—Secondary Money

Not for no reason did the Fortunatus theme, established in the sixteenth century in the centers of the modern money trade (Hans Sachs

based a dialogue on the material in 1553; Thomas Dekker's *The Pleas-*
ant Comedie of Old Fortunatus appeared in London in 1600[8] and was
translated into German as early as 1620, where it obviously received
a lot of attention; in 1615 the *Kasseler Fortunat* appeared; and in 1643
Johannes Gibertius and the Dutchman Bernard Fonteyn published
their versions)—not for no reason, that is to say, did the Fortunatus theme, after this early development, experience a second boom
in Romanticism.[9] It represents, of course, the initial conditions for
modernity, with its accelerating pace and its major medium. That these
initial conditions are monetarily formed, moreover—Romantic prose
writers leave no room for doubt. There is hardly another epoch in
which they are less interested than the Middle Ages.[10] To be sure, they
are fascinated by its autumn and end. The great Romantic prose texts
take place with remarkable regularity in the Fuggers' Augsburg and
in fifteenth- and sixteenth-century Nuremberg. The protagonist of
Novalis's bildungsroman, Heinrich von Ofterdingen, travels to Augsburg (without concern for the actual dates of his historical model) in
the company of merchants; Chamisso's Fortunatus sets out from there
to find out how money holds the world together; Wackenroder's art-
loving friar pours out his heartfelt sorrow over such a prosaic new age
in Dürer's time; and not just for Dürer's sake, but also in order to be
a contemporary witness to the initiation of modernity, does Tieck's
vagabond hero Franz Sternbald intend to end his wandering at his
point of departure: in Nuremberg. And Arnim's novel *Kronenwächter*
has its protagonist Berthold, of all things, convert Barbarossa's palace
into a textile factory in the southern Germany of 1500.

At its thematic center (accentuated by the Romantics), the Fortunatus theme, which is (at the very least co-)present in these and many
other texts from around 1800, deals with a double conflict: the conflict,
namely, between primary and secondary discourses on the one hand,
and, on the other, the conflict between discourses and the speechless
modern guiding medium of money. Language at all versus money, or
linguistically manifest meaning versus speechless functioning: such are
the alternatives at which Chamisso, too, points the material. Money
is the material that formed, fundamentally, the initial conditions for
modernity. And money is the essence, indeed the (if the word is not an
oxymoron in these contexts) incarnation of the secondary. It cannot
be primary for the simple reason that neither gods nor human beings
were originally dependent on this diabolical medium. God may have
taken a tremendous theological risk when he created the world, yet no
single myth of creation tells of a necessity for divine venture capital
in order to erect the cosmic system. The medium of the creation was

of course language and not speechless money. Even creatures with a mastery of language, whom God, through speaking, created in his image, did without money for millennia—and created high cultures at that. Even after the invention of money, social systems such as religion and art were able to present themselves for hundreds and thousands of years as if they could succeed in organizing themselves without the medium of money. Money first advanced to an obviously unavoidable major medium in modernity. Indeed, the strangely mute historical-philosophical signature of the modern age—as Friedrich Schlegel, Adelbert von Chamisso, and, later, Adam Müller, among the Romantics, have most clearly recognized—is money.

When the Romantic age took up the Fortunatus theme, by then already 300 years old, modernity could become self-reflexive for the first time. For it had learned, in the wake of the French Revolution, that history (even if with incalculable and unintended consequences) can be made, or that (to use Hegel's classic words) "the human being turns himself on his head, that is, his thought, and erects reality according to this."[11] Money is the speechless guiding medium of this modern world turned on its head: the secondary (at least chronologically) advances to the (functionally) primary. That which is apparently fully superfluous and without any intrinsic value whatsoever, the very medium of money itself, becomes the essence of that which cannot be renounced.

The archrational medium of money—under whose sign modernity, no longer primarily recounting but secondarily counting, begins its triumphant advance—nonetheless has its inescapably paradoxical, irrational, and uncanny aspects. To name just a few: money is superfluous *and* (in modernity) indispensable; it is (historically) secondary *and* (functionally) primary; it is the medium of an artificial scarcity which, as an artificial scarcity, establishes regulated access to limited goods *and* yet it knows no boundaries; it is highly significant *and* of an alarming semantic poverty; it has divine *and* diabolical aspects; it is of timeless functionality, void of memory, *and* nonetheless makes sovereign interaction with time possible: one can take credit on the future here and now, and one can store the unexpended past with interest. Secondary money has even the temporal order at its disposal, which certainly seemed to be an irreversibly primary, in every sense original, that is to say, divine, fact.

The Romantic interest in money as the speechless major medium of modernity is also a condition of money's temporal virtuosity. The openly reactionary tendencies of some Romantics are paradoxically indebted to the most advanced possibilities of modern times at their inception: that is, of the idea, not least of all monetarily induced, of a suspension of the traditionally unquestioned impossibility of turning back the flow of time. One can trade and trade back in timeless, infinite circles. Or, in historical-philosophical terms, one can of course spin out and reverse the major modern idea of a humanity monetarily standing on its head, and making its reality and its history. If the species that chooses, in money, a divine-satanic medium that enables it to grasp itself as the subject of history, succeeds in making history, then it must also be possible to rescind history.[12] In the magnificently clear words of Friedrich Schlegel's lecture of 1801, held in Jena, on transcendental philosophy: "All states are founded on money, but money arose by coincidence; it could therefore be taken away again, and the foundation of the states would be removed. All contemporary states would collapse in a heap,"[13] thus revealing the historically contingent basis of modern rationality. Under the sign of the speechless major medium of money, modernity begins its victory march.

Language Inflation

Among the losers in this victory march is (the idea of primary) language. It is, to use Goethe's wonderful word, "superfluous": the alphabet succumbs, in modernity, to the supremacy of the numerical (see chapter 1). An antimodern fraction has mobilized against this fiscal subversion of the primary medium, against this monetary-functional desiccation of substantial language. Criticism of the power of cold, satanic, functionalistic, reifying money: this is clearly the common denominator in the critique of modernity from the right and the left. It has, to be sure, very different measures. The specifically liberal, leftist critique of modernity uses the medium of money to criticize the contrast between poor and rich (without distinguishing adequately between the critique of the medium of money and of social inequality), and advocates expansion of the linguistic sphere, a countermove intended to check the power of "big money." Thus it places its bet on participation and having a say. Everyone, that is, should be permitted to have a little bit of a say. A theory of universal communicative competence is then, in fact, the left's option, one that is as congenial as it is harmless, for the integration of a theory, no longer critical, that has taken leave of the paradigm of exchange.

The right or reactionary critique of modernity, in contrast, hardly objects to social inequality, though all the more to money as medium (paradigmatically clear is the downright muddled treatise *L'Argent*, published in 1913 in Péguys, that polemicizes against professors of the Sorbonne and money with the same passion). It thus intends to keep the decisive ruling words as limited and exclusive as possible. Carl Schmitt has noted this option most clearly:

> German romantics possess an odd trait: everlasting conversation. . . . Catholic political philosophers such as de Maistre, Bonald, and Donoso Cortés—who are called romantics in Germany because they were conservative or reactionary and idealized the conditions of the Middle Ages— would have considered everlasting conversation a product of a gruesomely comic fantasy. . . . Everyone formulated a big either/or, the rigor of which sounded more like dictatorship than everlasting conversation.[14]

If language that has lost its potency is to achieve value again (according to the equally antimodern as antidemocratic suggestion that George Steiner shares with some converted Romantics and antimodernists such as Stefan George), then it must, like everything valuable, be limited.[15] How, then, are speaking and writing to have value, if everyone is freely permitted to put in their two cents worth, if everyone can read and write, if anyone is permitted to have their uninhibited say and even to vote, if everyone, even those who can only babble, can speak on tape and video, if every thirty year old finds a publisher who is not above a bribe for publishing yet another autobiography? In short: the mere number is an outrage. Universal freedom of speech and the right to vote have devalued the medium of language through inflation. Gossip and idle talk must be put to a stop, in order, once again, to perceive decisiveness and to speak the decisive word. In this the critics of journalism such as Kierkegaard and Karl Kraus (who, to ward off palaver, published 30,000 pages) agree with decisionists such as Carl Schmitt and Heidegger, whose oeuvre pits over seventy volumes against the gossip of "man."

George Steiner's aesthetic theology[16] stands in this antidemocratic and antimodern tradition. In a German field of gravity, Steiner's rejection of the secondary is accentuated in another way, which its author surely did not intend. The intricate difficulty involved in correctly translating the deceptively simple title of Steiner's treatise illustrates this. *Real Presences*, in the plural, is the title of the book that appeared in London in 1989. This was published in German as *Von realer Gegenwart {Of Real Presence}* a year later. The aesthetic plural had become, so to speak, the Catholic singular. Steiner's reflection exhibits, however, through this concession of the plural, remnants of liberality: that which is overwhelming, aureate, sacred, and entirely incommensurate can be, if not in incomprehensibly numerous, at least in several works, incarnate: real presences. The authors of sacred works, however, must be called Dante or Shakespeare, Mozart or Goethe—God did not call his artists by the name of Mallarmé.

To be sure, George Steiner leaves no doubt about the theological implications of his exorcism of everything secondary: "Unendingness is Satanic chaos. It follows that heresy can be defined as 'un-ending re-reading' and reevaluation. . . . Secondary discourse is schismatic" (pp. 44–45).[17] *What* the theology that one has to defend to the last letter against the schismatic talk of "man" looks like, then, is almost irrelevant. The main point: the one God together with the one primary meaning as expressed in a few exclusive aesthetic incarnations in opposition to all secondary polytheistic liberalisms and deconstructions. The precision of the religious metaphors, a small selection of quotes that looks like a potpourri of journalistic superficialities, is obviously not important to Steiner. Literary scholarship (according to Steiner) is the "power-house[18] of secondary discourses" (p. 34), and Steiner condemns "The Byzantine dominion of secondary and parasitic discourse over immediacy" (p. 38) for six more pages. Was it not Byzantium itself that developed an impressive liturgy and iconic art of real presence;[19] was it not supposed to be called "Alexandrian"? That two pages later "the lamps of [Talmudic] explication . . . burn . . . before the Tabernacle" (p. 40), then, is no longer surprising. Puzzling, to be sure, is the following passage that rambles from Byzantium via Alexandria, Jerusalem, and Rome to—Weimar: "It is less, perhaps, Byzantium and Alexandria which typify our condition than it is the Weimar of the 1920s" (p. 48). The Weimar Republic was terrorized, according to Steiner's bold metaphor, by the "paper Leviathan of secondary talk" (p. 48), not by brawling troops shouting "Heil" in unison who believed, dry-eyed, that meaning is really present in an incomparable and primary, in every sense of the word, Führer. At that time Goebbels, among many others (such as Carl Schmitt and Heidegger), polemicized most effectively against the parliamentary chatter-shack, journalism, and talk in general. One of his very first official deeds was to forbid the establishment of new magazines (and this ban was kept in place until 1935).

George Steiner's habit of quoting does not exactly bespeak reverence for primary texts from the Weimar of the age of Goethe. That Goethe has asked "How can I be when there is another?" (p. 137) strikes this philologist who, though not entering the field of battle from the powerhouse of literary scholarship, comes nonetheless with a certain reverence for primary texts from a reliable library, as improbable. Yet he has (in contrast to the author of the treatise, his translator, the reader, and the author of the afterword Botho Strauß) Goethe verses running through his head that go like this: "Can one live if others live?" {"Lebt *man* denn, wenn andre leben?"[20]} Goethe answered this question (mark it well: whether *one* lives when others live), in any event, in the affirmative. Botho Strauß, who once wrote such clever, stylistically sure texts such as *Kalldewey Farce* or *Devotion {Die Widmung}*, and who provided George Steiner's text with an emphatic afterword, proclaimed, then, indeed, in his "Anschwellender Bocksgesang," culture and religious war to be unavoidable, and pleaded that it not be put off any longer.[21] His neo-nationalist pathos punishes him immediately: Botho Strauß never penned such bad German as in the blissfully Germanic "Anschwellender Bocksgesang."

Enough destructive criticism! That Steiner's polemic against the inflation of the secondary, to which it also contributes, hits upon some irritating phenomena is undisputed. It is striking, nonetheless, that he hardly considers the common tricks for managing this profusion. There are, namely, some measures for dealing pragmatically with the flood of talk and print.[22] To ignore it, or, as they say in Vienna, not even to ignore it, is the most common practice for reducing the complexity of the world of publications. If this does not get one anywhere, there are always the many Reich-Ranickis[23] with their highly regarded art of the attack which, on the battlefield of the "aesthetic brawl," creates lucid, if not exactly new and stimulating, relationships. In academic contexts one could consider doing away with the requirement to publish the dissertation. And Heinz Schlaffer offers a romantically ironic, yet solid suggestion: those who contribute to the endless production of books should come under a sanction of speechlessness. All publicists would receive a premium for abstaining—let's say 2,000 German marks per month. Those who nonetheless publish will have 200 marks per page deducted from their professor's, editor's, journalist's, commentator's, or whatever, salary. There would be, in other words, something like a premium for holding one's tongue. Thus anyone who contributed to the endemic logorrhea with twenty manuscript pages would pay for the pleasure with the loss of their monthly salary. And those who ruin everyone's fun by publishing a book 300 pages strong would have to believe that this dubious fame is worth a modest yearly salary. Bet we would quickly find a new clarity?

Schlemihl's Shadow

Suggestions of this kind may be sought in vain in George Steiner's work. His treatise is openly uninterested in ironic pragmatism in the treatment of the secondary. This secondary advertisement for the primary is strictly concerned with the fundamental task: driving out the superfluous and superfluity. With this it falls behind the state of the discussion that had been reached by the end of the age of Goethe, or the beginning of the new age of communication. And this state of the discussion was reached precisely through the insight that what matters, in modern times, is no longer the conflict between allegedly primary and secondary discourses, but rather the conflict between the communication media, language, and money. The medium money overshadows, in modern times, the traditional medium of language.

Among the little noticed points of Chamisso's story is the fact that, of all things, it is the figure of the "gray man," in whom no less than the devil is camouflaged, who resists the modern transition from a metaphysical to a monetary second encoding. He cares nothing for money. He certainly, however, has a fierce interest in the shadows of Plato's cave. The devil buys shadows because his desire is directed at the Platonic world behind the world—and (like the desire of Goethe's Mephistopheles—see chapter 6) men. Heinrich Detering[24] (linking up with suggestions of Gert Mattenklott's) has pointed out the motifs of subliminal homosexuality in Chamisso's powerful story. The gray man is quite openly after Schlemihl's love and affection; he follows him; he wants to "cover" him with the shadow he had purchased. And, in a secluded corner of a park, he makes Schlemihl, who "felt like a bird under the spell of a snake," an obviously indecent "proposition," explicitly so named:

> "The gentleman will please pardon my importunity if I make so bold as to impose my uninvited presence; I have a request. Please be so kind as to forgive me—"
>
> "But for heaven's sake, my good man!" I burst out in terror, "What can I possibly do for a man who—"
>
> We both fell silent, and both of us, it seemed to me, turned red at the very same instant.[25]

The gray man offers essentially unlimited sums for Schlemihl's shadow. Detering's study does not address the connection between the homosexual latencies of the gray man and Schlemihl on the one hand, and the homosexually procreating money, sovereignly developed by Goethe in *Faust II* (see chapter 6), on the other. Schlemihl's sack is always potent. He always has an unlimited stash of money on him. The gray man who kneels before Schlemihl is, however, not interested in such lowly things alone. On the contrary, he has a striking interest in higher things. That the devil is the last metaphysician (and a metaphysician a reluctant devil?) is clear in that he, the poor devil, even in post-metaphysical times, clings to the protometaphysical call "to find the key to all mysteries." "He elaborated his views on life and matters of worldly consequence, and soon came to the subject of metaphysics, challenging himself to find the key to all mysteries."[26]

Peter Schlemihl is only immune to satanic temptations because he is immune to metaphysics and is not involved in the quest for the primary word. "You know, my friend, that though I once fancied myself a student of ideas, I have long acknowledged a lack of aptitude for philosophical speculation, and abandoned the field." The devil, on the other hand, has a most resolute interest in a closed system and a "solid, self-sustaining argument supported by its own inner necessity." And he insists on primary identity; indeed he has an identity-fetish. He does not want any old exchangeable soul, but this particular, individual one—and the young man's body no less. He who makes a pact with the devil must sign his own name, in his own blood. God, on the other hand—in this the metaphysicians' interpretations agree—has the liveliest interest in that which transcends identity. The self's other interests him—indeed, that an I can become an Other, that Jacob can become Israel, and Saul, Paul, is the essence of his divine mercy.

Throughout the entire text, Schlemihl's shadow never achieves "a fixed meaning. . . . It marks the center of a narrative game that circles around an empty space that has to be filled in; it bears witness, doubly, to a *différence*, a delayed significance in Derrida's sense, for the character as well as for the reader."[27] Schlemihl, who learns to honor the shadow and money, has completed a psycho-dynamic training program that has taught him to survive the modern age. The modern age that compels us to grasp that shadows are not reflections of light from metaphysical worlds behind the world, but effects of thoroughly earthly second encodings. Money is the essence of post-metaphysical shadows.[28]

Nietzsche's Shadow: The Light-Dark Preface

One hundred and sixty years after Peter Schlemihl got his shadow back, the Romantic theme of the shadow, together with the rehabilitation of the secondary, is making a philosophical comeback.

> *The Shadow.* As it is so long since I heard your voice, I would like to give you an opportunity of speaking.
> *The Wanderer.* Someone said something:—where? and who? It almost seems as though it were I myself speaking, though in an even weaker voice than mine.
> *The Shadow (after a pause).* Are you not glad to have an opportunity of speaking?
> *The Wanderer.* By God and all the things I do not believe in, it is my shadow speaking; I hear it but I do not believe it.

The Shadow. Let us accept it and think no more about it: in an hour it will all be over. (p. 301)[29]

Thus begins the *second* part of the *second* volume of Nietzsche's "Book for free spirits" that appeared in 1886 under the title *Human, All Too Human {Menschliches, Allzumenschliches}*.[30] This doubly second position of a dialogue split into two parts, which open and close the second volume of a book with a double title, obviously has highly constructive implications. The aphorisms framed by the dialogue between the Wanderer and his Shadow are about ungrounded versus appropriate ways of handling everything secondary.

The strange dialogue aims at eliminating or bracketing everything presumably primary, principle, original, and fundamental. Not for no reason does it begin with the Shadow speaking. A shadow is the sheer essence of the secondary and derivative—or es*sense* and precisely not an in*carnation*. There would be no flesh- and bloodless shadow if it were not preceded by something primary that throws/sub-jugates/makes a sub-ject of it and constitutes, accordingly, the condition of its existence. Despite its secondary status, however, the Shadow (Nietzsche's) has the first word. And this first word of the secondary Shadow is one that certainly does not claim to be the condition of existence of the primary, but it nonetheless offers the same, "an opportunity"—the opportunity to (mis)take itself, on the strength of the secondary, for the primary. The precise purpose of this opportunity (to listen—for what?—or to speak—of what?) remains otherwise unsaid. The Shadow thrown by the Wanderer has not heard his creator speak for a long time, and so the "opportunity" hinted at might be the opportunity for speaking, which, independent of what is said, will find an open ear and a response. *What* is said in this speech doesn't count; what matters is *that* it does take place at all, rather than not.

This talk is a "foreword" (p. 872)—a foreword in a double sense. It precedes (firstly) as speech, as a discussion between the Wanderer and his Shadow, the written notes that follow and would not exist without this foreword—they capture "how we talked together." The Wanderer takes up this phrase of his Shadow's (the phrase thus occurs twice) and emphasizes in so doing the "how," in order, then, to differentiate it from the "what" of the talk that is supposed to congeal in writing: "*How* we talked together? Heaven defend me from long-spun-out literary conversations! If Plato had taken less pleasure in spinning-out his readers would take more pleasure in Plato. A conversation that gives delight in reality is, if transformed into writing and read, a painting with nothing but false perspectives: everything is too long or too short. —But shall I perhaps be permitted to tell *what* it was we were in accord over?" (Nietzsche's emphasis, p. 302).

"Everything is too long or too short": what (not only in view of the Platonic transcription of Socratic dialogues) is true of the relation between living speech and writing that attempts to capture speech is obviously also true of the relation between the Wanderer and the Shadow. Indeed, it is true of the relation between everything allegedly primary and secondary. Those who wish to fashion this relationship (for example between body and shadow, speaking and writing, being and meaning, physics and metaphysics, commodities and money, the state of things and thoughts, and so on) in the Platonic-Aristotelian tradition as a relationship of adequacy, those who, in other words, allow the two correlates of one relation to correspond to each other and obligingly weave, write, spin them together, fall prey to a Platonic "pleasure in spinning-out"—and spin.[31] Against all overwhelming "first" attempts to force adequacy in the interest of stability of meaning, the dark foreword stages disproportion as the regulatory antiprinciple of significance. ("Meaning" {"*Sinn*"} is—according to Heidegger's lovely thought—"clearly delineated conceptually as that from which and on the grounds of which Being in general can become manifest as such and can come into truth."[32] The concept of "significance" is not supposed to denote a unified meaning of being or a transcendental signified, but to grasp semanticity altogether as an effect of the temporal conception of being.[33]) Accordingly, this foreword is also a foreword in a second respect. It humorously illuminates and reveals the structures that always underlie speaking. In this foreword, Nietzsche stages the fundamental semiological question of why significance exists at all, and does not not exist. And the doubled, dark suggestion of an answer is this: because differences and disproportions are irreducible, and because time provides for endless differences. Significance occurs in the removal (as the deconstruction) of a solid basis of meaning. The deconstruction of meaning is the Shadow, without which the construction of significance would not be.

The foreword to *The Wanderer and His Shadow* has no actual, clear theme. It exposes no "what" of the talk. Thus, obviously, the opportunity (to talk) that the Shadow offers the Wanderer is pure opportunity (without thematic stipulations), a pure offering of the possibility of assertion and judgment. The author of this offering, which the one addressed accepts ("Let us accept it"), cannot be personally identified. "Someone said something:—where? and who?" The conversation between the Wanderer and his Shadow thus begins with the question of discourse analysis par excellence—the question of the place (topos) and the subject of the speech that is occurring. Whether the Wanderer is "[him]self speaking, though in an even weaker voice than mine," or whether the Shadow actually speaks, remains undecided— as undecided as the question of what it would mean if the question "who said something" could be unambiguously answered and thus the subject of the speech given. For it would still remain unclear whether this subject had reason to conceive of itself as master or as the subject of the speech: subject—sub-ject. A shadow satisfies the literal meaning of the concept "subject." It, the one thrown to the ground and now lying there, is a sub-jectum, a hypokeimenon.[34] Nietzsche's Shadow fulfills the literal meaning of the word "subject" and is nonetheless a free spirit. Whether an auditory hallucination of a listening-to-himself-talk[35] or the free speech of his/an Other: the Shadow speaks, opens up, offers opportunity. With all this confusion and ambiguity, how should this opportunity be authenticated? "By God and all the things I do not believe in, it is my shadow speaking; I hear it, but I do not believe it."

This ear is open to a consideration that is, if not unheard-of, at least rarely proclaimed (for example in Meister Eckhart, Angelus Silesius, and Hegel)—to the consideration, that is, according to which the secondary has functional primacy over the primary, the justified over the justification, the derived over its origin, the creature over its creator. In the words of the closing dialogue that follows 350 reflections and very explicitly alludes to the most famous sentences of Hegel's:

> The Shadow. If the reward were a perfect knowledge of man I might even agree to be your slave.
> The Wanderer. But do you know, do I know, whether you would not then change unawares from slave to master? (p. 394)

What Nietzsche's Wanderer hears, accepts, and offers, is, measured against traditional habits of thought, unbelievable. If he, "by God and all the things [he] do[es] not believe in," hears and accepts the speech of his shadow, but does not authenticate it, the paradox of this (non-)authentication is not wantonly provoked but unavoidable. For those who say that that which they say is also truly meant how it was said; those who, in other words, explicitly authenticate their speech and thus insist that it be believed, will be forced to authenticate their statement of authenticity all over again and will thus achieve the opposite of what they intend with their discursive strategies: they undermine the credibility of their speech in the very attempt to establish it. Those who look for fixed foundations tumble into the abyss.

The Wanderer does not become entangled in this paradox. For indeed he does not believe in the essence of the original, beginning, fixed, principal, and primary—he does not believe in the fixed foundation of metaphysics and physics, in God and "all things." But he also does not believe in the Shadow's speech, which he certainly, sensibly, hears. The Shadow is also completely uninterested in the authentication of his speech, in the listener's acceptance of his words obtained through the force of Socratic argument. His discourse prefers—is it not the discourse of a shadow, after all—to be dark.

> *The Shadow.* It is well we are both indulgent if our understanding for once comes to a stop: thus we shall converse together without recriminations and not press one another too hard if we fail to understand something the other has said. If we know not what to reply, it will be enough to say something: it is under this reasonable condition that I agree to converse with anyone. (p. 301)

This openness to the dark side sets enlightened, lucid insights free. "For there to be . . . clarity of speech . . . shadow is as needful as light" (p. 301). Those who cannot bear shadows must turn off the light. Those who abhor dark speech will have to do without illuminations (and especially profane illuminations). Not without reason does this dark discourse, one that allows and accepts "expressions {that} are somewhat shadowy" (p. 302) and dares an "obscure word," take place in the dusk's limited span of time, bringing the "longest day" (p. 394)—the dialogue takes place on a Sunday, on the longest day of summer and thus of the year—to an end. "In an hour it will all be over" (p. 301), says the Shadow to the Wanderer right at the beginning of the conversation. And near the end of the foreword the Wanderer warns the Shadow: "There are a couple of hundred questions pressing upon my soul [and not a single question about the only fixed, unified foundation], and the time you have in which to answer them is perhaps only brief." In the time between high noon, at which point the sun stands so directly overhead that no shadow is thrown, and the evening, when "the sun [sinks]" (p. 395) and extinguishes, with the light, the shadow,[36] the Wanderer and his Shadow turn the shadows of the history of philosophy and theory, but also of everyday hermeneutics, into the "what" of their dialogue.

Divine Fullness, or One's Own Shadow

" '*In the beginning.*'—To glorify the origin—that is the metaphysical aftershoot that breaks out when we meditate on history and makes us believe that what stands at the beginning of all things is also what is most valuable and essential" (p. 302). The very third note of *The Wanderer and His Shadow* is about this metaphysical "aftershoot" to which, despite his very precise reading of Nietzsche, Heidegger, too, fell prey in a fateful way. The following reflections try relentlessly to think against the pull of such a fetishism of the origin and the beginning. This is no easy task. For Platonism itself, as the original form of systematic thought—according to Nietzsche's too little regarded thesis—began with a reversal of the thinking about the beginning. He regards Plato as the artist of thinking, who cannot bear reality and to whom the "shadow-like remainder" of the real seems more valuable than the real itself.

The question of the logically and chronologically primary and truly real is the genuinely Platonic question. Nietzsche brings it to a head:

> An artist cannot bear reality, he looks away, back: his earnest opinion is that the value of a thing, that *shadow-like* [emphasis J. H.] remainder, is to be gained from colors, shape, sound, thought; he believes that the more delicate, attenuated, scarce a thing, a human being becomes, *the more its value increases: the less* [emphasis Nietzsche] real, the more valuable. This is Platonism: but with yet more audacity in the turning of it around:—he measured the degree of reality in inverse proportion to its value and said: the more "idea," the more being. He turned the concept of "reality" around and said: "What you all take for reality is erroneous, and the closer we get to the 'idea,' the closer we get to 'reality.'"—Is this understood? This *was the greatest rechristening:* and because it was adopted by Christianity, we fail to see this astounding feat. Artist that he was, Plato fundamentally *preferred appearance* to being![37]

Incipit metaphysica: with this reversal of being and appearance, the domination of the shadowy world-behind-the-world (= metaphysics) over the world (*physis*) begins. Because he does not remain true to the world, deserting it in favor of "shadow-like" ideas which he then proclaims to be the True and that which is, Plato is Nietzsche's primary opponent. To fight Platonism and its Christian popularization, however, is no easy task. Plato himself, who of course elevated the value of the "shadow-like remainder" so relentlessly, denounced the shadow in his most famous text (the metaphor of the cave in *The Republic*, 6.1). For Plato, the shadow is the essence of the secondary, the derivative, the farthest removed from the idea's true being. "Draw a distinction": the act of founding systematic philosophy is the declassing of the shadow and the differentiation between the primary and the secondary. It is expressly done in order then to allocate to philosophy (and later to the Christian religion) the task of rescinding the *chorismos* between the secondary and the primary and to lead the things back to the idea (or, from a Christian perspective: the earthly to heaven, time to eternity, and so on).

Nietzsche, who had begun to turn Platonism upside down—meaning: to reverse Plato's reversal of being and appearance—certainly cannot escape, in one respect, the pull of Platonism. Plato's critics intend, from the very beginning of systematic philosophy, to restore being, displaced from first to second rank, to predominance over the shadow (of metaphysics). But that means: the metaphysics-critic Nietzsche must give up his second anti-Platonic motif, namely the deconstruction of the Platonic distinction between the primary and the secondary. He devalues, like his antipode Plato, the shadow, and celebrates "high noon" as the shadowless clearing for the truth of being.

An aphorism of *Human, All Too Human* praises high noon, and thus the hour at which no shadows are thrown.

> *At noon.*—He who has been granted an active and storm- filled morning of life is overcome at the noontide of life by a strange longing for repose that can last for months or years. It grows still around him, voices recede into the distance; the sun shines down on him from high overhead. Upon a concealed woodland meadow he sees great Pan sleeping; all things of nature have fallen asleep with him, an expression of eternity on their face—that is how it seems to him. He wants nothing, he is troubled by nothing, his heart stands still, only his eyes are alive—it is death with open eyes. (p. 387)

Zarathustra, too, the lonely one, wants to flee everything secondary and all shadows. "About the hour of noontide, however, when the sun stood exactly over Zarathustra's head" {*Thus Spake Zarathustra*} (p. 336), and he therefore throws no shadow, the world is quiet and thus "perfect." "O happiness! O happiness! Wilt thou perhaps sing, O my soul? Thou liest in the grass. But this is the secret, solemn hour, when no shepherd playeth his pipe. Take care! Hot noontide sleepeth on the fields. Do not sing! Hush! The world is perfect" (p. 338). The world is perfect when it has no double, when it is free of everything secondary, when it is not disturbed by the shadow of a world-behind-the-world, when no voice startles the pure experience of pure being.

The ambivalence is clear: in the dialogue between the Wanderer and the Shadow, Nietzsche values the shadow highly in opposition to the Platonic tradition; in the aphorism of high noon (and in many other passages of his work), on the other hand, he devalues the shadow and other doubles. There is a tradition of such ambivalence in the history of this motif. The shadow is of course the double, pure and simple. And as double it is profoundly doubled in its significance.[38] A shadow can have deadly associations: one can be a mere shadow of one's former self, and ultimately visit the underworld in the form of a shade. The first part of *Human, All Too Human* ends with a "Descent into Hades" that Nietzsche ventured in order "to be able to talk with the dead," who seem more alive to him than the living, who "sometimes appear to me as shades." The shades of the dead are more alive than the living, who are already shades in this life. If Nietzsche associates shades with life rather than with death, in this, too, he links up with a long tradition in the history of the motif. A shadow, after all, offers protection from a sun that scorches everything living. There is a reason why the shadow belongs to the unalterable inventory of the locus-*amoenus*-scenery that erotically competes with Hades. Nor does this conclude the series of ambivalences. A shadow can give, to a certain extent, a reliable picture of that which throws it. A monopolistic shadow, however, as the captives from Plato's cave must learn after they are set free, can be responsible for confusions between simulacrum and reality. A shadow can also be absent and present. Even the conditions of its absence are two-fold: shadows disappear when there is no light. Yet shadows also disappear at the hour of Pan, high noon, when an overabundance of light drives out all doubles and all consciousness or contemplation {*Besinnung*}.

Nietzsche's thinking occupies the space of this ambivalence. It begins to overcome (Platonic) metaphysics and yet remains captive to its ground rules. Heidegger's Nietzsche reconstruction emphasizes this— and enshadows it at the same time. The first volume of Heidegger's Nietzsche book closes with the words

> while reading Nietzsche we will experience first and foremost how decisively Being is already overshadowed by beings and by the predominance of the so-called actual. The overshadowing of Being by beings derives from Being itself—as Being's abandonment of beings, in the sense of the refusal of the truth of Being. Yet by descrying this shadow *as* a shadow we already stand in another light, without finding the fire from which its radiance comes. Thus the shadow is itself already something else. It is not gloom.

> Many wanderers tell of it,
> And the deer stray in crevices,
> And the horde sweeps over heights;
> But in holy shadow,
> On the green slope dwells
> The shepherd and looks to the summit.
>   Hölderlin, "To Mother Earth"[39]

A classic three-step:

Firstly, being is forgotten in the history of being to the extent that it is overshadowed by that which is. Oblivious to being, "one" becomes interested, the farther from the beginning the more recklessly, in that which is, rather than in being and time themselves. The author of *Being and Time* had another illuminating formulation (borrowed from none other than Georg Lukács) for this overshadowing or this materialistic "predominance of the so-called real" at his disposal: "there is a danger of 'reifying consciousness.' "[40] A formulation that comes close to conceiving of the predominance of secondary entities over primary being in a sociologically enlightened fashion: That which is, and can produce and condition existence to the extent that being is forgotten, is nothing but a thing that has become a commodity. Heidegger later completely obliterated the question of whether oblivion can also be spelled out in terms of money and commodity theory.

Secondly, "The overshadowing of being by that which is" is not only a mistaken form of comprehending being, it is also a possibility that "[comes] from being itself." For without the ontological difference between being and that which is (always already temporalized by virtue of its temporal state), being would not be what it is and what "there is": being. That which is, is therefore the necessary shadow of being; it differentiates itself and is set apart or below. Oblivion of being is accordingly an authentic possibility for being itself.

Thirdly, when we see this "shadow *as* shadow," we are standing "in another light" than in the light of enlightened, reified thinking. This "other light" allows no inferences about the consuming "fire, from which this illumination springs." But it reveals nonetheless that the shadow that it brings and that brings it with it is irreducible, because it is not derivative but original. Original in the sense that through it, it is illuminated and revealed that there is a split at the very "origin" {"*Ursprung*"}, that shadow and light belong together equally originally. "The shadow is thus an other and not a darkening."

The Shadow of Money— Nietzsche's Platonic Chrematophobia

"Only at times can our kind bear the full impact of gods" {"Nur zu Zeiten erträgt göttliche Fülle der Mensch"}. Thus it says in Hölderlin's elegy "Bread und Wine" (l. 114). Hölderlin changed this line decisively in the latest version. It now reads: "Only at times can our kind bear its own shadow" (l. 118).[41] After the end of metaphysics and ontotheology, the human being is alone with his own shadow. He can no longer metaphysically attribute shadows to a world-behind-the-world. Moreover, he no longer has reason to suspect, behind shadows, true being. Nietzsche (like Hölderlin before him) tried over and over again "to interpret [post-metaphysical times] positively." Post-metaphysical times are times of liberation from the shadows of the world-behind-the-world, liberation from all teachings of two worlds. The psychological mega-training program that Nietzsche outlined was, to be sure, no unmitigated success: "*Death.*—The certain prospect of death could introduce into every life a precious, sweet-smelling drop of levity—and yet you marvelous apothecary souls have made of it an ill-tasting drop of poison through which all life is made repulsive!" (p. 390).

For the failure of a "gay science" {"fröhliche Wissenschaft"} in the literal, lighthearted (and precisely for that reason meaningful!) life of post-metaphysical times, Nietzsche holds *the* shadow, heir to the shadow of metaphysics, primarily responsible: the shadow of money. "Danae and the god with gold" heads an aphorism from *Morgenröte*. It says, in lapidary style: "What one used to do 'for God's sake' is now done for money's sake, or for the sake of that which provides the greatest feeling of power and good conscience *now*" (*Werke*, vol. 1, p. 1151). Nietzsche recognized as clearly as none save Goethe and Chamisso, Marx and Max Weber, the epistemological and cryptotheological implications contained in the turning of metaphysics into meta- and mega-fiscalism. But he refrained from decisively thinking this realization through to its conclusion, which would mean grasping money as the medium of liberation from metaphysical fixations. His critique of money is not particularly original. Nietzsche is, rather, as chrematophobic as Socrates and Plato.

Nietzsche rejects, as usual, "that truly international homeless hermit, money" (*Werke*, vol. 3, p. 283). And in aphorism 63 of *Human, All Too Human*, he criticizes (with remarkable parallels to Marx in terminology) the "moral fancy-dress" to which strong individuals can degenerate under the pressure to conform to social norms: "In those ages when the fancy-dress worn by the different classes is considered as firmly fixed as the classes themselves are, moralists are tempted to regard *moral* fancy-dress too as absolute and to depict it as such. Thus Molière is comprehensible as a contemporary of the society of Louis XIV; in our society, which is characterized by transitional forms and halfway stages, he would seem, though still a man of genius, a pedant" (p. 326). The concept of "fancy-dress" {"Charaktermaske"}[42] is a neologism of Jean Paul's that Marx and Eichendorff take up and which achieves a certain popularity when Alfred Meißner[43] uses it as the title for his cycle of novellas of 1861. Jean Paul is in any event mentioned in aphorism 99 of *Human, All Too Human*, where he is characterized as a "fatality in a dressing gown" (p. 335). Jean Paul is a fatality in Nietzsche's eyes for the sole reason that he makes Platonic idealism presentable once again.

As a critic of the "great world of money" (p. 314), Nietzsche wants to impart a "philosophy of cheerful rejection of changing places and absence of envy" (p. 297). The price for this effort, which is as friendly as it is conventional (especially in the context of Nietzsche's other reflections), is high. As a critic of the post-metaphysical shadow, namely the thoroughgoing monetary second encoding of the world, Nietzsche, otherwise the decided anti-Platonist, opts for the primary. The very wording of his great characterization of Platonism comes close to turning his philosophical-historical diagnosis into a monetary one. "The more delicate, attenuated, scarce a thing, a human being becomes, *the more its value increases: the less* real, the more valuable": the modern age steps forth under this sign. Nietzsche's algorithm proclaims implicitly, though certainly not explicitly, the most delicate, most attenuated, most scarce—money—to be the medium of the universal second encoding and the functional equivalent of the Platonic idea.

If metaphysics, however, is replaced by economy, and God by money, a hermeneutic opens up that proceeds on this side of Platonism and Christianity and beyond. It allows no more teachings of two worlds. Money ensures, more effectively than any philosophy, that being and time are experienced as limited resources to whom it pays to be loyal. Money is, as all fundamentalists know, the essence of the innerworldly. Nietzsche, on the other hand, did not seize the chance to grasp money as the shadowy medium, liberated in a purely innerworldly way from metaphysical fixations on God and from transcendent signifieds, allowing the "shadow to be seen *as* shadow." It would have been easy to lay hold of it as such. For the most popular novella of money and shadow ever—Chamisso's *Schlemihl*, of course—after having unfolded a story that God knows leaves room for a critique of money, ends explicitly with the phrase, now quoted for the second time: "But you, my friend, if you wish to live among your fellow men, learn to honor your shadow, and then, money."[44] Nietzsche refused this veneration. He recognized the deep structures of the post-metaphysical era, but he tried to get around them. Thus we find in Nietzsche both anti-Platonism as well as the Platonic reaction against everything secondary, inferior, derivative, low.[45] This made it possible for fundamentalists of the primary to link up with his thinking (as with Heidegger's). And that distinguishes his shadow-metaphysics from Celan's threshold- and shadow-poetry that does not fear a second speaker—"Speak, You Also" {"Sprich auch du"}:

Speak, you also,
speak as the last,
have your say.

Speak—
But keep yes and no unsplit,
And give your say this meaning:
give it the shade.

Give it shade enough,
give it as much
as you know has been dealt out between
midnight and midday and midnight.

Look around:
look how it all leaps alive—
where death is! Alive!
He speaks truly who speaks the shade.

But now shrinks the place where you stand:
Where now, stripped by shade, will you go?
Upward. Grope your way up.
Thinner you grow, less knowable, finer.
Finer: a thread by which
it wants to be lowered, the star:
to float further down, down below
where it sees itself glitter: on sand dunes
of wandering words.

Sprich auch du,
sprich als letzter,
sag deinen Spruch.

Sprich—
Doch scheide das Nein nicht vom Ja.
Gib deinem Schatten auch den Sinn:
gib ihm den Schatten.

Gib ihm Schatten genug,
gib ihm so viel,
als du um dich verteilt weißt zwischen
Mittnacht und Mittag und Mittnacht.

Blicke umher:
sieh, wie's lebendig wird rings—
Beim Tode! Lebendig!
Wahr spricht, wer Schatten spricht.

Nun aber schrumpft der Ort, wo du stehst:
Wohin jetzt, Schattenentblößer, wohin?
Steige. Taste empor.
Dünner wirst du, unkenntlicher, feiner!

Feiner: ein Faden,
an dem er herabwill, der Stern:
um unten zu schwimmern, unten,
wo er sich schimmen sieht: in der Dünung
wandernder Worte.[46]

13

"THE SOURCE OF THE CENTER," OR:
THE GIFT OF MONEY, THE GIFT OF POESIE

> Who rings? The ringing of bells, the surging
> and swelling of bells supra urbem, above the
> whole city, in its airs overfilled with sound.
> Bells, bells, they swing and sway, they wag
> and weave. . . . Ringing from the height and
> ringing from the depths. . . . Who is ringing
> the bells?
>
> Thomas Mann, *The Holy Sinner*

"There is": it was easy to turn a deaf ear to the unfathomability of this simple phrase before Nietzsche, Heidegger, and Derrida renounced the old project of looking at the truth and began to practice philosophizing with the ear.[1] "*Es gibt,*" "*il y a,*" "there is/are": fundamental philosophical gestures are effects of grammars that cannot be overheard and that generate fundamental texts.[2] "*Es gibt*"/"it gives"/"there is": Being and things and time, texts and meaning and signs, rain and wind and sun, the animate, the inanimate, the dead, women and men, telephones and events, money and shortage and infinitely more; it gives and does not stop giving (and taking). Who gives, who takes? Whoever gives, takes. It gives/there is the giving, there is the taking. "O star and blossom, spirit and garb, / Love, sorrow, time, eternity!" {"O Stern und Blume, Geist und Kleid, / Lieb, Leid, und Zeit und Ewigkeit"}.[3]

It gives/there is diversity in such overwhelming abundance that the question of what originally binds the infinitely many creatures, things, actions, elements, affairs, and events together (and separates them) is hardly to be avoided. Toward the end of the eighteenth century, following the prolonged erosion of the traditional ontotheological attempts (the Lord giveth, the Lord taketh away, praised be the name of the Lord) to answer the question of what, deep within it, binds the universe together (and drives it apart), the question was phrased in a fundamentally new way. The many new answers have been locked, since then, in a never-ending conflict of interpretation. Some of the new attempts to

241

answer it that got their start in Romanticism before and around 1800 enjoyed the prospect of a degree of academic standing. Transcendental subjectivity as the basis for constituting the association of the manifold, consciousness of the self as the source of synthesis or, depending on the theory's design, exchange, money, communication, the constitutions, the world formulae, the institutions, the decisions, or power can look back on more or less successful careers as the wild card in universal achievements of mediation. These great entities are credited with (or denied) being serious candidates for answering the Faustian question of what, deep within it, binds the (modern) universe together.

It gives/there are, since the Romantic movement, moreover, increasing numbers of texts which observe the repeated, newer attempts to answer the Faustian question of who or what it is that gives ("*it gives*") the diverse giving, without bringing new candidates for answering it into the obviously serious play of questions. They are struck by the fact that all attempts to answer the question have two things in common: they differ, and they arrive (how could it be otherwise?) in the form of (spoken, written, sung, babbled, shouted) texts. Questions and answers are texts, and texts consist of different combinations of letters. Ever since then, the *niveau* on which the question of what, deep within it, binds the universe together, finds its answer, could not be easier and more difficult, more superficial and more profound. The answers to the question of the (pen)ultimate things may not fall below the *niveau* of "a truly transcendental buffoonery"[4] if they intend to be "timely" according to early Romanticism. Nearly all Romantic texts are, because they respect this *niveau*, text-texts or, according to Friedrich Schlegel's epochal appellation, "transcendental poetry" or "poetry of poetry."[5] At the center of E. T. A. Hoffmann's "The Golden Pot," in the innermost tunnel of the mines that Heinrich von Ofterdingen visits, at the narrative source of Tieck's *Phantasus*, in the genealogical depths of Brentano's *Godwi*, and in essentially all Romantic texts about the origin, texts effervesce, "it gives" texts, there are texts to read, to live, texts take pre-understanding, texts arise and fade away.

It gives/there is a Romantic fable that can be read as if it were explicitly written in order to illustrate these remarks. Its title is *Adelberts Fabel*; Adelbert von Chamisso wrote it in 1806 while looking back, thus from a close vantage point, on early Romanticism's ironic treatments of questions of origins; it appeared then a year later in a volume edited by Wilhelm Neumann and Karl August Varnhagen titled *Erzählungen und Spiele*.[6] A paradigmatic Romantic text about texts at the "source of the center"; such a transparent, fabulous, autopoetic story about storytelling that its explicit interpretation can hardly be distinguished from its retelling. "Adelbert sensed, when he awoke, that he must have been asleep for a long time." The very first sentence (paraphrased from *Heinrich von Ofterdingen*) conjures up an awakening from dogmatic slumber and in addition a careful noting (even if a fleeting one) of this awakening. A memory of his half-forgotten intention "to go on a tiresome journey out into the world in order to see it" follows, yet it is delayed for years by a continually repeated alternation between falling asleep and fleeting awakenings, always accompanied by the same commentary: "It is truly strange." With each awakening the walls of ice around Adelbert have closed in on him a little more. One day, however, as the "walls of ice surrounding him" seem hardly to be surmounted anymore, "a noble feminine figure in glorious form" stands before him. She says her mysterious, "unearthly" name and . . . gives the frozen Adelbert a lock of her hair as well as a ring. Yet not only does she give (in a feminine rewriting of the gift of the neutral "it gives"/"there is"), she takes at the same time: "Then she cut a lock from his head and took it with her, and threw a lock of her own hair at him . . . ; then she was taken away from him by a harsh power, and a veil of silence was thrown over her." When Adelbert, after a renewed alternation of slumber and awakening and after futile efforts to decipher the message, observes the ring more precisely, he notices "by the light of the North Star" the "engraved sign on the ring": "Do I want? So be it! I want!" So be it; I want: Adelbert has arrived there, where it is, there, where "it gives"/"there is" is. Adelbert comprehends that "it gives" him, and, with a start, he apprehends, repeatedly, this— "strange"—gift. The "there is" (his being there/his existence[7]) must be united, in the act of a second symbolical (feminine) gift of birth, with the gift of significance. The newborn Romantic Fichtean, no longer merely marveling "it is truly strange," magnified by this outer impetus to a self-reading, self-conscious ego, traverses (as does his author later) the entire world, eventually standing before the gate of a "subterranean hall without light" which he courageously walks down. "The way before him became brighter and brighter, more resonant; but to arrive at the source of the center which he was approaching, he had to climb and climb down into immeasurable depths."

It gives/there are unfathomable turns (of phrase) in Romantic narratives. They tend to occur most frequently when things head down into "immeasurable depths." The "source of the center" constitutes one such turn. Where it promises the transcendental-Romantic investigator of caves the discovery of one last fundamental layer, it immediately breaks this promise. For the center cannot be the true center if it itself requires a source from which it springs forth. The center, however, has its source in an "immeasurable depth" that can hardly be reasonably differentiated from a significant surface. "In a vast, subterranean storey were countless weavers' looms" and weaving women, over whose shoulders Adelbert watches as they compose, condense the most diverse strands into one weaving, into a texture. "The weaving they wove was—his own life." To weave, to provide texture, to compose: that which binds being and existence and significance together are incomprehensibly numerous texts, fables, fabulous texts, that weave the most diverse threads into one pattern. The student of Fichte, grown self-conscious and explicitly desirous, must grasp by now that he can, if need be, constitute himself, but he cannot give himself to himself. If he is the center, this center itself has yet another source that precedes him and that he cannot overtake. And in a fabulous— in every sense of the word—way, the text now completes the turn from the center to the source. The text ends fabulously, if not terribly originally, as if it wanted to illustrate the dangers of fundamentalism to which Romantic texts are exposed when they get involved in that wise game of transcendental buffoonery that knows that a source underlies every center, and every source, a woven text, in such a way that each one is destroyed in the other. Adelbert, namely, looks up after his walk into the depths and his viewing of the weaving, and he sees, "in the middle of the room, an old man sitting on a sublime throne in exalted majesty; he wore his name on his forehead, and this name is (though expressed differently in a thousand tongues): ANA KH." A Romantic narrative about the quest for the "source of the center" could hardly undercut itself more scandalously. The fact that the misery of the nonfulfillment and non-correspondence of meaning and being has the last word, that this last word can be expressed in a thousand different ways, that this patrilineal closing figure is preceded by an "it gives"/"there is" and a "she gives/she is," that this vision is a dream which is followed by a renewed awakening, and, finally, that the text signals its fable-like quality in its very title, undercuts, to be sure, this self-undercutting in many ways.

It gives/there is also a peril, a divergence, a discrepancy, a fissure that precludes understanding of this "source of the center" as the original source that dispenses and covers every single narrative moment in the great and fabulous narratives of the attainment of the "source of the center." Romantic narratives are narratives of the irrevocable fissure of the origin that sets narratives in motion to begin with. If one wanted to express this narrative gesture in a formula, the following might be appropriate: Romanticism consciously converts metaphysics to metaphor on a grand scale. The truths of metaphysics have become fables as far as it is concerned. That means: the epochal event "Romanticism" makes it clear that metaphysics was metaphor that had not been seen through. This means, however, the reverse as well: metaphysics is unavoidably like metaphor. Metaphysics dared to take the leap from the unlimited numbers of things to the one absolute, to the "source of the center"; the Romantic post-metaphysics looks for the absolute everywhere and finds only things that owe their existence to the discrepancy between source and center; thus it tells (fabulously and metaphorically) of the fissures, gaps, and breaks that have always already turned up when a digression (from plurality to unity, from being to meaning, from things to the absolute, among other things) is supposed to take place. Center and source cannot be and become one. Therefore the metaphorical narratives that cannot bridge this gap do not end. It does not stop not writing itself. Metaphysics can be overcome; Romantic narrative, however, even after overcoming metaphysics, does not stop stopping. For the deconstruction of fixed answers cannot destroy the questions that continually set texts in motion.

It gives/there are, after Romanticism, narrative texts which—if a pun may be permitted in such an earnest context—determine that the *niveau* of Romantic insight (according to which the unfathomability of the foundation and the breaks in the origin constitute the conditions for the possibility of storytelling) is remarkably high, but that the world, society, the modern controlling media, and everyday figures of communication never take place on this *niveau*. Post-Romantic, realistic storytelling is determined by the thematization of this discrepancy in *niveau*. In order to grasp, *ex negativo*, how Romantic storytelling proceeds, it may be productive to analyze one of the most successful post-Romantic avoidances of fabulous storytelling and compare it to the strategies of Romantic transcendental buffoonery. There is a text from the pen of the realistic storyteller Adalbert Stifter, with the eponymous hero *Abdias*. Its author partly revoked the name that was given him in order to adopt a new one conforming to Romanticism. Albert Stifter renamed himself Adalbert Stifter. His tale, first published in 1843, however, is programmatically distinct from *Adelberts Fabel*. Its very beginning, magnificently laconic, leaves no room for doubt:

> There are people on whom such a series of misfortunes falls out of the blue that they finally stand and let the hail-storm roll over them, just as there are others whom good fortune visits with such extraordinary wilfulness that it seems as though the laws of Nature had been reversed in a given case so that things should turn out solely for their good.

In this way the ancients arrived at the concept of fate, we at the milder one of destiny.

But there is indeed, too, something terrifying in the indifferent innocence with which the laws of Nature operate, so that it seems to us as though an invisible arm were reaching out of the clouds and enacting the incomprehensible before our eyes. For a blessing comes with the same smiling face today and tomorrow the terrible happens. And when both are over, Nature is dispassionate as before. . . .

For the ancients this was fate, frightful, final, inflexible cause of events, farther than which one cannot see and beyond which nothing more exists, so that even the gods themselves are subject to it: for us it is destiny, therefore something sent by a higher power which we should accept. The strong submit to it humbly, the weak rebel against it complainingly, and the base are dully amazed when the monstrous occurs, or go mad and commit crimes.

But in fact perhaps there is neither fate as the final irrationality of existence nor is its individual occurrence visited upon us; rather, a serene chain of flowers hangs through the infinity of the universe and transmits its shimmer into men's hearts—the chain of cause and effect—and into man's brain was cast the most beautiful of these flowers, reason, the eye of the soul, in order to attach the chain to it and by means of it to count {its} way down flower by flower, link by link, until {it}[8] comes finally to that hand in which the end rests. And if some day we have counted correctly and if we can comprehend what we have counted: then chance will not exist for us anymore but consequence, not misfortune but only guilt; for the gaps which now exist are the cause of the unexpected, and misuse creates unhappiness. Certainly the human race is already able to count from one millennium to another, but only individual petals of the great chain of flowers have as yet been discovered, events still flow past us like a sacred mystery, suffering still enters and leaves the human heart at will— is this suffering perhaps itself a flower in that chain? Who can fathom that? . . . Let us not ponder the nature of these things further but simply tell of a man who exemplifies much of this and of whom it is uncertain which is stranger, his destiny or his heart. . . .

It is the Jew Abdias whose story I want to tell.[9]

Those who, in the mid-nineteenth century, no longer brood on the discrepancies between center and source, on the unfathomability of the foundation or on the unavoidability of metaphor, but wish, instead, simply and unpretentiously, to tell a story, must realistically account for the functional inversions which do not refute the Romantic project of transcendental poetry but simply undercut it. The wonderful beginning of Stifter's narrative of Abdias does account for this. It links up with the *aurea catena Homeri*—with the image of a golden chain that binds heaven and earth. The locus classicus of this topos is the eighth book of the *Iliad*, in which Zeus calls the gods to assemble on Mount Olympus with the following words:

> Come, gods, and try, so all of you may know.
> Let down a golden rope from heaven, take hold,
> all of you gods and all you goddesses.
> But you can't drag down Zeus, high counsellor,
> from heaven to earth even if many pull.
> But if I wished and were inclined to pull,
> I could drag up the very earth and sea,
> and tie the cord around Olympus' peak,
> and everything would dangle in mid-air,
> I'm so much stronger than the gods or men.[10]

This powerfully effective metaphor[11] for the superior force of the most powerful god has been recast early (perhaps as early as Neoplatonism). Out of the cord in the triumphant macho-speech of the highest god emerges the gentle tie of a cosmological connection exhibiting, instead of insurmountable hierarchy-chasms, a continuous transition between the heavenly being(s) and the earthly. A similar Plotinian-pantheistic transformation of the image can be found in Goethe, who remembers, in *Poetry and Truth*, his early reading of Welling's *Opus mago-cabbalisticum*, "which, like all writings of the kind, could trace its genealogy back in a straight line to the Neo-Platonic school." Goethe also read a work with the title *Aurea Catena Homeri*—it was most likely written by Anton Joseph Kirchwege and appeared anonymously in 1723: "I was especially drawn to the *Aurea Catena Homeri*, which represents nature in a beautiful, though perhaps fantastic, synthesis."[12]

Stifter's story obviously links up with this mild transformation of the wild Homeric image. Yet the "serene chain of flowers [which] hangs through the infinity of the universe—the chain of cause and effect" seems, as an image for the association that has Abdias's life at its disposal, appropriate only to a limited extent. Stifter's prose simply and unpretentiously establishes, when it takes up the old question about the chain which holds everything that exists together, four changes of perspective.

Firstly, the metaphysical question about the God of gods or the absolute center and the source in which the various things are interwoven into a unity is replaced by the postal question of sender, addressee, and the channels for messages and transmissions. The ultimate substantiation that was "for the ancients fate, frightful, final, inflexible cause of events" and that has become unfathomability fluid and textualized through the Romantic art of narration seems to "us" post-Romantics as "destiny, therefore something *sent*." The leading question is not which power synthesized the many at the origin, but whether "that which is sent" reaches its destination and can be correctly deciphered.

Secondly, the metaphysical break, the digression and the metaphor, and ontotheological and transcendental deduction are replaced by the regulatory idea of the reasonable "counting his way down" the chain of links between cause and effect. It destroys the metaphysical remnants through the concept of transmission, of fate and of destiny.

> But in fact perhaps there is neither fate as the final irrationality of existence nor is its individual occurrence visited upon us; rather, a serene chain of flowers hangs through the infinity of the universe and transmits its shimmer into men's hearts—the chain of cause and effect—and into man's brain was cast the most beautiful of these flowers, reason, the eye of the soul, in order to attach the chain to it and by means of it to count his way down flower by flower, link by link.

The universe is seam- and fissureless; it is hypercomplex, but not actually mysterious. The physics of transmissions and of chains of cause and effect leave no room for metaphysics, which would simply have to belong to other orders, and would be *totaliter aliter.*

Thirdly, for those who count their way down the chain of links between cause and effect, storytelling is a stopgap measure. Counting versus recounting, counting instead of recounting:[13] thus the maxim of the fully enlightened earth. "Reason, [as] the eye of the soul," is no longer the other of that which it analyzes and turns into the object of reflection; it is, rather, only one among many elements of *one* natural continuity. If it "counts" this continuum "down, . . . link by link until {it} comes finally to that hand in which the end rests," then the riddle of the world is solved by correct counting. "And if some day we have counted correctly and if we can comprehend what we have counted: then chance will not exist for us anymore but consequence, not misfortune but only guilt; for the gaps which now exist are the cause of the unexpected, and misuse creates unhappiness." Until, however, things have gone this far, storytelling supplements counting. Storytelling belongs to the "still" of the chronological order. "{E}vents still flow past us like a sacred mystery, suffering still enters and leaves the human heart at will—is this suffering perhaps itself a flower in that chain? Who can fathom that?" Storytelling no longer metaphorically bridges the breaks between the categories of metaphysics. Storytelling bridges, instead, the gaps that persist in the modern project of the seamless countdown. Stories are reduced in post-Romantic times: from self-assured transcendental poetry come narrative confessions of gaps.

Fourthly, those who participate in this project of modernity— counting instead of recounting, digitalization instead of analogization

—stumble, in a moment of truly profane illumination in which enlightenment and serenity blend into complete unity, upon a substitute that is as scandalous as it is functional. "{I}t seems to us as though an invisible arm were reaching out of the clouds and enacting the incomprehensible before our eyes." The invisible arm from the cloud of tragedy that directs the destiny of mortals: that is the material out of which Romantic narratives of breaks at the origin are, no, were, made. The simple and unpretentious story of the Jew Abdias that follows these introductory thoughts which are "still" reflective leaves no doubt that the invisible arm from the cloud of tragedy has been released from metaphysical contexts and metamorphosed into the invisible hand of the national economy.[14] Abdias, who is still counting the blows of fate and already counting his money, is forced to learn that no *totaliter aliter* has become transparent through his fate: Ab-dias[15] can no longer find Romantic rhyme or reason in that which is sent to him. His life becomes an enactment of a specifically modern Job story. The invisible hand hath given, the invisible hand hath taken away; who wants to praise it together with the profane insights it inspires?

Abdias reacts to the blows fate has dealt him with sublime speechlessness. This speechlessness is hardly to be distinguished from the speechlessness of the modern medium of control. Money is speechless, money is not amenable to argument, money's semantic poverty is nothing less than sensational, money has no stories to tell. But money can be counted, money functions, money, utterly devoid of pathos, is what, deep within it, binds the modern universe together (and pulls it apart). In a word: in a world in which substantiality is disappearing and the multitude of signs increasing, demonic money advances to the "only thing"—at least according to a standard formula in Stifter's Viennese feuilleton.[16] The irritating thing about money (from the perspective of the Romantic observer) is that it is, despite its speechlessness, a highly functional medium of communication. It establishes unity, it makes the most different things compatible, it synthesizes variety in a remarkably unpretentious way. It is there/it gives, it takes, it counts.

Romantic narratives did not so attentively observe the specifically modern, speechless medium of control—money—in vain. Money and the intersubjective power of authority uniquely its own are the genuine material of Romantic narratives. The Romantic rediscovery of the *Fortunatus* material by Chamisso, Tieck, and Uhland, as well as the insistent money motifs in countless realistic texts, continually reestablish that: "It is truly strange." It is truly strange that the poorest basic text and code (pays/does not pay) can establish itself in modernity as the most successful functionally. Romantic texts have no reason to revise their thesis of the break in their origin-texts once they have discovered that the medium of money truly is the determinant medium of communication in the current age—definitely, however, to be astonished at how undemanding the post-Romantic, functional equivalent of the great metaphysical entities can be, and at how superfluous communication that proceeds aesthetically can become in the age of the speechless media of control. The dialectical suspicion that that which is superfluous can be a necessary superfluity remains. In the words of Odo Marquand, aesthetics becomes the "official" fundamental philosophy in the post-metaphysical age. Monetary modernity can be grasped as the epoch which conjures up, in the form of the omnipresent commodity-, commercial-, and media-aesthetic, the beauty of that which is produced and driven it out of that which is not produced. The *Aurea Catena Homeri*, or the serene chain of flowers which hangs through the infinity of the universe, has been replaced by "the golden One." "It gives/there is" what is to be seen in the TV- or PC-monitor.

14

DECONSTRUCTION OF MONEY

The Babylonian Tower of Debts

Money and language are two objects of inquiry that are as profound and abstract as their use is general. They stand in closer relationship to each other than one would suspect. The theory of the one explains the theory of the other; thus they seem to flow from a common source. The wealth of all human knowledge rests on the exchange of words; and it was a theologian of penetrating wit who described theology . . . as a grammar of the language of the Holy Scripture. All goods of civil or social life, on the other hand, can be related to money as their general standard of measure, for which even Solomon is supposed to have recognized it after just a few translations. One should thus not be surprised that oratory carried as much weight in the activities of the state in ancient times as finance does in the prudence and prosperity of ours. In the current century it would appear as useful to Julius Caesar to become an extraordinary mint-master as it seemed to him laudable in his day to be a fine grammarian.[1]

So it says in the "Vermischte Anmerkungen über die Wortfügung in der französischen Sprache," which the dark thinker and learned salesman Johann Georg Hamann composed in 1761. To reflect on the "common source of origin" of language and money may seem absurd. In terms of evolutionary history, language of course arose eons earlier than money. Currently accepted views on the history of culture and religion, too, purport this to be the case. In the beginning of all being was the spoken, divine word. Being itself is secondary to the language of God. The God of the monotheistic religions of the written word created the world through the power of speech, and the human being in his image: as one who speaks. Not, however, as one who exchanges, whose validity is tied to the medium of money.

Thus language is an element in the Jewish, Christian, and Islamic God's creation through and through; money, not at all. Indeed, language is more than a high-ranking element in the work of creation— it is the element of creation itself, the precarious presupposition of God('s creation). Capital, on the other hand, was not necessary when God created the world. And money has no business in paradise either. In the unlimited abundance of life in paradise, money would be entirely superfluous. Money only has value there (and thus everywhere except for paradise) where it, as the medium of artificial scarcity, regulates access to limited goods.

Hamann's talk of a "common source" from which language and money "flow" must not refer, then, to chronology but rather to the logical relations of their establishment. And they must be aimed at the communicative, im-parting language of the (post-Babylonian) human being, and not at the language of God.[2] Only in a world of want, or in a wanting world, do human language and money share reasons for existing. Language, like money,[3] establishes intersubjectivity; both make the cherished (ex-)change and the fostered im-parting possible. They put forward claims of validity, they impose laws (the *nomos* and the economy), they represent or simulate "world"; and it is incumbent upon them to see that their achievements of representation or simulation are plausibly covered in order to be universally valid media. Language and money share a presupposition as well as a threat: both only make sense in a wicked world of want and unending problems. If there were no discord and misunderstandings, language would be superfluous; if there were no scarcity and no conflicts over limited resources, money would serve no purpose. Yet not only their conditions of existence, the questions that language and money raise "flow" from the same "source": language is—at least since the building of the Tower of Babel—as labile as this tower. It is always under the suspicion that its claims are not covered and that it is built on ground no more solid than that of the Tower of Babel; there is always the potential that money, however, will be questioned on the grounds that it is no more covered than language. The lie is the counterfeit money of language; counterfeit money is money's lie; but both the lie and counterfeit money represent genuine possibilities of language as well as of money. Both, that is, language as well as money, live on credit, are dependent on good faith, make debts, and rely on guarantees that can hardly be plausibly redeemed.

Language and money face these threats in structurally comparable ways: they increase their value through systematic scarcity. It is not intrinsically necessary for money and language to be scarce. With its grammar of a large but finite number of rules, countless different discourses can be constructed, as is well known. And an infinitely large number can be printed or written on a banknote or check. Death, of course, limits the time for talk or exchange for any given individual. Language and money, however, are not in and of themselves limited. Yet in order to function correctly, they must be artificially limited.[4] Even in societies that take pride in their liberality, not just anyone can say anything anytime anywhere without penalty. Those who would like to make use of the simple right to speak publicly and give lectures at a university must submit to a remarkably intensive rite of initiation at the end of which those who succeed receive their *venia legendi* (*nomen est omen*). Those who pronounce justice must be appointed judges, otherwise their judgments have no validity. Those who perform marriages must be public officials, otherwise the marriage is not official. And whoever announces the Federal Bank's new discount rate must be one of the directors authorized to do so.

This is why Foucault was able to represent the "order of discourse" as discourse's institutionally arranged or ordered limits.[5] It is not endless conversation but decisive judgments that establish the authority of language, of speaking, and of the speaker. Control of language, like that of money, is motivated by an obvious but uncommonly effective phantasm: that one can say what is right and fair, what the case is and what the case really is. This corresponds to the economic phantasm that there is a just, right, and fair price. Both phantasmata are based on the enchanting notion that there is equivalence and adequacy. If this is so, statements that adequately represent the facts of the case would be true; prices that were equal to the value of the wares would be just. And because truth, like wealth, is rare, scarce, and valuable, language, which expresses truth, and money, which represents valuable "things" by means of prices, must be kept in short supply. The logical presupposition and the regulating idea of this notion is a one-to-one correspondence between money and goods or between language and being.

As is well known, however, there is no such thing. It is there just as little as there is "there is." There is no "there is" (being, time, rain, equivalence, truth, and so on).[6] There is, in any event, the necessity of questioning such "there is"-expressions all the more resolutely, as they assume an even balance, an equivalence, a relationship of correspondence between "give and take," debit and credit, creator and created, being and sign. Hegel has already considered the unfathomability of idioms that use the words "take and give": those who take their own life give themselves death and experience (or, more precisely, no longer experience) "the double meaning implicit in what it did, viz. when it took hold of life and possessed it; but in doing so it really laid hold of death."[7] Just how problematic, how destructive, how deconstructive things stand with respect to "give and take" first becomes apparent, for good reason, in the *Phenomenology of the Spirit* as the "science of the experience of consciousness," where it relies on economic metaphors—and must recognize that metaphors are unavoidable in the economy of thinking: " 'True' and 'false' belong among those determinate notions which are held to be inert and wholly separate essences, one here and one there, each standing fixed and isolated from the other, with which it has nothing in common. Against this view it must be maintained that truth is not a minted coin that can be given and pocketed readymade. Nor *is* there such a thing as the false, any more than there *is* something evil."[8]

The Pentecostal Spirit of Money

There is no true and no false.[9] "Can you say the truth?"—thus the playful children's question that not only children answer with "yes." The demand, "Then say it!" puts the one who happily answered "yes" in an embarrassing position. Those who hear quotation marks in the question, "Can you say 'the truth'?" are well prepared, and they answer the foolish question with a cheerful "the truth." Yet the clever answer has its price. One becomes indifferent toward the truth. One can say or pronounce "the truth" just as well, or poorly, as any other word—including the word "lie." There is no truth, it cannot be pronounced or said as such, but only as a series of letters. For it is (if it is at all, is there, at hand, and not simply functioning) an attribute of sentences. And there is no true and no false—at least not in the way that there are things that exist. On the other hand, there is money (coins, notes, checks, drafts, and so forth) in precisely the same way that there are things that exist. At the same time, however, money is more than this or that specific thing; it is the universal equivalent for any arbitrary thing. It has validity as such. Of course, this is a necessarily precarious validity. Money must, as a "documented promise of value with universal validity,"[10] be valid. Money is, in this sense, a deed of debt—the world owes the money the redemption of the promised value that it represents.[11]

This is its character: that is, a promise to be, the promise that it can be exchanged for something that really has value (in and of itself, not just for something else); concrete money shares this with verbal promises. The promise, however, is particularly problematic. Its basic structure is that A promises B something that it cannot give here and now. "I promise (on the telephone and far away from you) to come tomorrow. I promise you I'll really remember to bring the book that I promised I'd bring next time I see you but keep forgetting," and so on. Promises occur when sentences cannot be covered by reality here and now. Promises are the taking of verbal credit, and it is always a matter of doubt whether they can be paid back and covered in the future.

The lovers in Gotthelf's novel of 1842–43, *Wealth and Welfare* {*Geld und Geist*[12]}, experience this dilemma, too. Andrew {Resli}, born in Bern to farming folk as God-fearing as they are well-off, falls in love with Mary Anne {Anne Mareili}, whose family is just as well-situated but is godless and greedy. The possession-hungry father of the bride, with his unreasonable demands for money, stands in the way of the marriage. The young lovers cannot, therefore, marry right away, but they can promise to marry each other. And so they secretly become engaged. " 'Hear me,' said Andrew, 'if you will engage yourself to me, and be constant, I shall be very much surprised if anything prevents our marriage, but all depends upon yourself; if you are not steadfast, all is over. If you resolve to be so, give me your hand, and say, 'Yes, in God's name.' "[13] Mary Anne repeats the formula—in God's name. Yet having the eternal God as a witness is not enough. True to its title, which binds money and the godly Pentecostal spirit with an "and" rather than separating them with an "or," Andrew surrenders a "marriage pledge"[14] to his fiancée which, as a reminder of temporality, represents an obvious symbolical analogy to the witness of the eternal God: a "handsome heavy watch and chain."

Mary Anne, however, declines the watch. Not because it is too strong a reminder of the finiteness of even a love which should last forever, but because the watch as a pledge of their secret engagement cannot be kept secret in her family. Exchanged chains or rings would also make an open secret of the two lovers' exclusive one. For this reason the lovers exchange—at the suggestion of the bride—not a traditional symbol of engagement, but the meta-symbol of money, which, all abstraction uniquely its own notwithstanding, is nonetheless more tangible than the name of God. " 'I should not dare to take either ring or chain,' said the young girl, 'but give me a piece of money . . . and I will give you one.' " A peculiar engagement scene, it initiates an entire series of supplementary moves. An engagement is a supplement to a marriage that is not yet possible. Thus an exchange of a "marriage pledge" is central. It incarnates the promise whose fulfillment must be postponed. This "marriage pledge" must itself be pledged, however—with a coin that is the pledge of the pledge.

The lovers are obviously aware of the potential awkwardness of this substitution—or they experience it, at the very least, subconsciously. For they do not exchange simple coins that can be exchanged for anything. They exchange, instead, two rare coins, removed from the universal movement of exchange and thus unique. Individualized money, however, is a contradiction in itself: "They pulled out their money, inspected it, and Andrew chose a loyal and honorable twenty from Bern with an upright man of Switzerland on it, but Mary Anne chose a new coin. They would not use these coins, they said, but they could be mistaken for a five-franc piece, and so no one would suspect what they meant if they saw the money."[15] Money, in fact, does not mean anything (specific). Money is, on the contrary, the "most annihilating signifier"[16]—cold, indifferent metal, which, in the words of Mephistopheles, can be turned into anything. The coins which Andrew and his fiancée exchange are, on the other hand, highly significant—at the price of never being available to function as money again. The secret of the affianced can be declared and yet remain a secret.

The standard formula of love, "no one but him," explicitly attempted by Mary Anne, is simply not compatible with the medium of money, which establishes universal equivalence—and equivalence means, of course, indifference (see chapter 9). The indifference of money was experienced (and still is) as potentially awkward, and often as the manifestation of scandal. Adam Müller, the conservative Romantic, pointed out long ago, in his *Versuche einer neuen Theorie des Geldes* (1816), that classic money, on which not just any old words but the noble, lordly, valuable, great words "In God we trust" or "Liberté, Egalité, Fraternité" are to be read, is minted from precious or, as they say in German, "noble metals" for good reason. Noble materials and golden words are supposed to allow us to forget that money is the essence of non-exclusivity. Money will lower itself to anyone and anything. Its noble material and noble symbols are therefore supposed to ennoble (objectively and interpersonally) the relationships that they systematically establish. And Andrew and Mary Anne, too, have chosen significant coins as a pledge of their love: "a loyal and honorable twenty from Bern with an upright man of Switzerland on it."

That hardly, however, dispenses with the most awkward thing about money. With the twenty from Bern, embossed with an "upright man of Switzerland," Andrew unquestionably pledges an image of himself, the essence of the character that is his alone—and no one else's—to his betrothed, who wants "no one but him" in marriage. Yet even if this coin is relatively rare, it exists, by definition, in huge quantities; it is precisely as valid as all the other coins of its kind and can be, moreover, easily converted into other coins. That there is a substitute for Andrew, too, or, more precisely, that Andrew himself is a poor substitute for an (even) richer, more valuable son-in-law—this is the conclusion Mary Anne's father cannot escape. The substitute, the supplement, the pledge, the secondary threatens ultimate triumph in Gotthelf's novel. The text sets out to defend the original and, in every sense of the word, primary spirit (of God) against the world of the secondary whose essence is money. Its basic argumentative metaphor is obvious: as long as money is piously used in the right way, as long as it yields to the "spirit," as long as it remains secondary, no objections can be raised; when it becomes autonomous, however, when it forgets that it is mere supplement, when it assumes the place of the primary, it becomes satanic.

The informative dilemma of Gotthelf's upright novel resides in the fact that he repeatedly shows the unavoidability of that which he would like to eradicate through preaching: with money, the spirit of the secondary has definitively triumphed over the primary spirit. An unlikely turn of phrase on the very first page of the novel indicates as much. "In the Canton of Berne," so it begins,

> are many fine properties, many substantial farmhouses, where dwell many a worthy pair well reputed for their God-fearing ways and good household management, as also for an amount of wealth, garnered up in barns and granaries, chests and troughs, which this frivolous new-newfangled generation, turning everything into money because it wants so much money, has no conception of. Over and above these stores, however, in such a house as we are speaking of there is always a round sum kept for the casual wants of the good folk themselves, or their neighbours, the like of which you might look for in vain, from one year's end to the other, in the mansions of many of the gentry. Very often this sum has no fixed place. Like a familiar spirit, by no means a bad one, it flits about the house, now here, now there, sometimes in the cellar, sometimes in the barn, sometimes in the parlour, sometimes in the great carved chest, and sometimes in each and all these at once, and half-a-dozen more. For should a piece of land bordering on the farm chance to come into the market, it gets bought, and has to be paid for in ready money, neither father nor grandfather having ever been known to be in debt, but paying for whatever they bought on the spot, and, of course, with their own money . . . without either bond or interest—merely upon the faith of a

heavenly reckoning by and bye, the other world being still believed in as it ought.

Money, too, is a spirit—if only a "familiar spirit." But it has the advantage of being able to materialize spirit. Money converts the beyond into the earthly, it literally makes spirit. Without writing and figures, there can be no money. An economy cannot function for long on the basis of loyalty and faith, a handshake and one's word. Even Andrew and Mary Anne pledge more than simply their word. They pledge coins; they pledge that which, like "a familiar spirit, by no means a bad one," hangs around the house. These two ways of using money are aporiae: those who use a particular coin as a marriage pledge deny it its function as a means of exchange. And those who keep a lot of money like "a familiar spirit, by no means a bad one, . . . now here, now there, sometimes in the cellar, sometimes in the barn, sometimes in the parlour, sometimes in the great carved chest," and refuse to let it leave the house (except to buy "a piece of land bordering on the farm"), fulfill, so to speak, the literal meaning of the word "economy" but not the spirit of money: it puts money under the law of the house.[17] Yet the spirit moves where it will. And money, too, is a "spirit," a "familiar spirit," a good "house spirit," even if it does get restless when not permitted to leave the house because its owner has failed to recognize that it is exogamous and cannot be bound to the sphere of the home. This constitutes its uncanniness.[18] Money, in fact, creates the relationships, alliances, and syntheses that Christian theology regards as the genuine achievement of the "Pentecostal spirit." There is a reason why the language of money is international.[19] It is the profane inspiration of the post-Babylonian confusion of languages. The language of money makes a secular medium of permanence out of the kairological exception of the miracle of the Pentecost.

Simulation of the Economy—
Economy of the Simulation

Gotthelf's novel circles relentlessly around the close affinities of money and spirit. It notes with astonishment that money is the Pentecostal spirit come true: it allows everyone to understand everyone else. The pious Adam Müller perceives this as money's contribution:

> Among things it is the precious metals, among the personal capacities of the human being it is the word, through which each achieves that alliance in its own sphere, which the human being always strives to establish among all of his personal and material affairs: precious metals are the most

natural bond among things, the word is the most natural bond among all personal capacities. The word and the precious metal are thus the two great forms in which money appears; the two sensible manifestations of the economic state.[20]

The precious metals from which coins are minted establish "the most natural bond among things"; words establish alliances among people— if precious metal and great words embossed on coins enter into a pact, then states, and in them values such as persons, have lasting permanence. Money and language unite, bind, synthesize—but not just lovers such as Andrew and Mary Anne. Adam Müller's comparison of language and money therefore absolutely demands a distinction between the two media. Relationships established linguistically are easier to break off than economic ones. One can refuse to speak with others intimately. Money, on the other hand, establishes relationships even, or precisely, with competitors, strangers, even enemies.

According to Max Weber's great and laconic insight, the market and money affect "originally an association of those who are not comrades, thus enemies."[21] The fact that, as he immediately continues, "the intensive expansion of exchange relationships . . . runs parallel to a relative peacefulness,"[22] is of course a euphemism which the adjective "relative" is intended to relativize right away. If money, that is, establishes social relationships between non-comrades and enemies for the very first time, it also creates problems that it may be able to solve relatively peacefully on occasion. Often, however, it cannot. Without money there would be far fewer (cultural, religious, personal, and so on) contacts that contain within them and unleash the potential for conflict, even if money can solve such conflicts more peacefully than thievery, robbery, and war. Nevertheless, Goethe's words, pregnant with meaning and according to which "war, trade and piracy together are / a trinity not to be severed," remain valid.

What God hath joined together, let no man sunder. Gotthelf's novel reads like an epic illustration of this biblical saying. What money hath joined together, people often enough want to separate. For the syntheses that money establishes are often enough full of unreasonable expectations: money is rational and irrational, money is canny (= economic) and uncanny, money is concrete and abstract, money is real and irreal, money merely simulates real values and money is regarded at the same time as the actual value, money is satanic and godly, money is lifeless-cold and ghostly alive, money is sheer means and becomes purely an end; in short: money is the essence of the secondary that threatens to raise itself to the primary—money threatens (godly) spirit. Revolts against the (un-)spirit of the secondary are, these days—since postmodernism—on the agenda. Fundamentalists of every stripe: from the mullah and the writer grown pious to the professor in Genf and Cambridge, the call demanding the overcoming of everything secondary resounds like thunder. If it were to be heard, it would cost us a great deal.

15

Ruin/Ruins

That the first word of the national anthem of the German Democratic Republic is straight out of the lexicon of the central articles of the Christian faith cannot be missed: "Resurrected out of ruins" {"Auferstanden aus Ruinen"}. Theologizing politics is by no means the exclusive right of militantly conservative politics. The lines from the hymn composed by Johannes R. Becher which follow this word signaling religion leave no room for doubt that the task of universally historic redemption should not be entrusted to a historically exhausted God but rather to those human beings who take an active role in managing their fate, "trusting to {their} own strength." Thus the miraculous achievement of building up the nation of workers and farmers, a nation that liked to describe itself as the "first socialist state on German soil," corresponds to the theological miracle of the resurrection.

> Resurrected out of ruins
> Turned toward the future,
> Let us serve you for the good,
> Germany, united Fatherland.
> Old sorrow shall be overcome,
> And we shall overcome it together,
> For we must be successful,
> So that as never before, the sun
> Will shine on Germany,
> Will shine on Germany.

Happiness and peace are granted
Germany, our Fatherland.
The whole world yearns for peace,
Reach out to all peoples.
When we unite as brothers,
We shall defeat the foe of the folk!
Let the light of peace shine,
So that never again a mother shall
Cry for her son,
Cry for her son.

Let us plow, let us build,
Learn and create as never before,
And trusting to our own strength,
Rise up as a free people.
German youth, the strongest striving
Of our people united in you,
You will be Germany's new life.
So that as never before, the sun
Will shine on Germany,
Will shine on Germany.

Auferstanden aus Ruinen
Und der Zukunft zugewandt,
Laß uns dir zum Guten dienen,
Deutschland, einig Vaterland.
Alte Not gilt es zu zwingen,
Und wir zwingen sie vereint,
Denn es muß uns doch gelingen,
Daß die Sonne schön wie nie
Über Deutschland scheint,
Über Deutschland scheint.

Glück und Frieden sei beschieden
Deutschland, unserm Vaterland.
Alle Welt sehnt sich nach Frieden,
Reicht den Völkern eure Hand.
Wenn wir brüderlich uns einen,
Schlagen wir des Volkes Feind!
Laßt das Licht des Friedens scheinen,
Daß nie eine Mutter mehr
Ihren Sohn beweint,
Ihren Sohn beweint.

Laßt uns pflügen, laßt uns bauen,
Lernt und schafft, wie nie zuvor,
Und der eignen Kraft vertrauend,
Steigt ein frei Geschlecht empor.

Deutsche Jugend, bestes Streben
Unsres Volks in dir vereint,
Wirst du Deutschlands neues Leben.
Und die Sonne schön wie nie
Über Deutschland scheint,
Über Deutschland scheint.[1]

This text, stylistically not exactly elegant and semantically not particularly original, was no longer sung publically in the GDR as of the
early 1970s. The national anthem sounded forth thereafter (not least
of all due to the downright suggestive adoption of the melody from
the hit "Good bye, Johnny") only in its instrumental version—if not
without ceremony, at least without words of praise. "Resurrected out
of ruins": even those in power no longer wanted to hear those words.
For all that, one could still find, now and then, on the decaying walls of
houses of the late GDR, graffiti warning of the end, which took up and
alluded to the leading words of the hymn in inverted form: "Creating
ruins without weapons" {"Ruinen schaffen ohne Waffen"}. The state,
always "serving the good," that had intended to resurrect a society out
of the ruins of the Second World War, no longer captive to the ruinous
logic of capitalism, had dealt itself both: many ruins of construction
and reconstruction, and its own ruin.

This is a remarkable achievement, because it came to pass without
an all-out war or a civil war. Usually, that is to say, *ruin* and *ruins* should
(are supposed to) be mutually exclusive.[2] Only all-out war, that is, a
war no longer bounded, unites them. In un- or pre-warlike fashion,
one is willing to risk (symbolical) ruin in order to prevent ruins (and
thus the destruction of property). Or vice versa, one risks ruins to
prevent the ruin of the state, one's honor, one's own identity, and so
on. Ruin and ruins thus stand in a relationship of exclusive inclusion or
inclusive exclusion. They are closely related, and yet there is tension
in the relationship between them. Ruins find a symbolical Other in
ruin; ruin finds in ruins its real Other. To secure property: that is the
function of ruin. To secure the survival of symbolic orders: that is the
function of ruins, which for good reason often become the fetishized
locations of symbols that create identity. One swears to remain true
to symbols, flags, confessions, and values at ruins which may not be
permitted to be ruined, and for which one is therefore prepared to risk
real ruins as well.

Ruin and ruins belong together etymologically and in the history of
conceptions. Indeed, "ruin" and "ruins" form *one* analogously different
word-pair. It originates in the Latin *ruina/ruinae*, a word which, in the
singular, denotes collapse and defeat, devastation, and downfall; in the

plural, however, the collapsed remains and ruins are the remaining effects of a defeat. The older of the German pair, according to the dictionaries, is the feminine borrowing from French or Latin (ruins). The *Grimms Wörterbuch* (Leipzig, 1893) offers the following: *"RUINE {ruins}, f.(eminine), from the French ruine, often abbreviated as ruin in the seventeenth century; the term ruin has evolved to describe the concept of defeat, or decline, while ruine denotes wreckage, decaying remains, yet this distinction has entered the language gradually."*[3] Thus ruin has recently joined the old ruins, about which the *Grimms' Wörterbuch* remarks: *"RUIN, m., from the French ruine with a change in gender, probably due to its abbreviated form that was common, though in the feminine, in the seventeenth century. . . . ruin is usually used in the sense of decline, collapse, decay, and primarily in the figurative sense."*

"Ruins" is feminine; "ruin" is masculine. One can lay one's hands on ruins; ruin is strangely abstract and yet is experienced as a very concrete (psychic, mental, judicial, symbolic) incident. A ruined firm no longer exists; a ruined fortress, or one that is in ruins, persists nevertheless. The term ruins is primary and in this sense real; ruin is secondary and thus symbolic. Ruins are the basic foundations that remain, even if the superstructure collapses. Ruin takes place in the symbolical realm, ruins are something real. "Ruin" has no plural form (in English and French, as in the German, "the ruin" or "la ruine," when used in the plural, does not denote multiple ruin at all, but the many ruins); but there are ruins in the plural.

A peculiar closeness and distance thus define the relationship between ruin and ruins. It is especially peculiar that ruin leaves everything as it was—and yet changes everything. The ruined firm, the ruined bank, the ruined state, or the family ruined by divorce come through without real ruins. The entrepreneur, the banker, or former spouses may suffer psychically from "burn out" (as it is now fashionable to say in German as well) after the ruin of the institutions that controlled them. But this word, too, like the word "ruin," is used "in the figurative sense," as is indicated by yet another turn to the *Grimms' Wörterbuch*. In fact, after ruin, everything still exists, externally intact: the factory buildings, the banking equipment, the real estate, the employees, the family members, and so on. But the post-ruinous settling of accounts is completely different. Everything that comprised the firm, the bank, the family, or the state is still there. And yet these entities have ceased to exist. Ruin means, for them, "done for."

Thus "ruin" is the conceptual counterpart to "constitution," and "ruins" the Other of the "creation." A constitution, too (in the epistemological sense or in the sense of constitutional law), symbolically creates a unity (association) out of that which was already available as such (dissociated). The regions, the citizens, and the cities that have a constitution given them (have given a constitution) and have thus become *one* polity must of course already exist before a constitution can take effect, just as the diversity of objects must be present so that a transcendental subject can constitute them into its/a synthesis of apperception. "Ruins" on the other hand, is the conceptual counterpart to "creation." What is created or made is materially destroyed beyond the point of recognition when ruins arise. Those who are burned out are, in current German slang, "finished."[4] Those who are finished nonetheless continue to live. The ruined institution, however, is done away with. Though unchanged in its material existence, it simply stops existing.

Paradoxes of this kind, in which something is still there (in real terms) and yet (symbolically) no longer exists (or vice versa: in its last days Hitler's German Reich collapsed in the State Chancery, which was surrounded by ruins), have fascinated (modern) literature since its inception. A few examples can illustrate this.

Firstly, Walter Benjamin's interest in Baroque literature is not least of all tied up with his interest in the opposition between permanence and the lapsing of time, between significance and *physis*. In the publisher's preface to the complete works of Jacob Ayrer (1544–1605), author of musical comedy and Shrovetide farce, in which the marketing interest in the new medium of the printed book is obvious and which Benjamin quotes extensively in his book on tragedy, this opposition is emphasized: buildings deteriorate with time; intellectual works, insofar as they can be mass-produced, escape the "justice of the material" (Simmel).

> Considering that pyramids, pillars, and statues of all kinds of material become damaged by time, or destroyed by violence, or simply decay . . . that whole cities have sunk, disappeared, and are covered with water, whereas writings and books are immune from such destruction, for any that disappear or are destroyed in one country or place are easily found again in countless other places, so that in human experience there is nothing more enduring and immortal than books.[5]

Secondly, Kleist's texts are fascinated by ruin and ruins from beginning to end—and especially by the dialectic of the destruction that preserves and the preservation that destroys inscribed in the conceptual pair:

> Stand, stand now firm; firm as the arch must stand,
> Because each stone longs but to crash to earth.

Steh, stehe fest, wie das Gewölbe steht,
Weil seiner Blöcke jeder stürzen will!

Thus the paradigmatic lines from *Penthesilea* (ll. 1349f.)[6] The dramatic formulation mirrors a profane illumination which Kleist experienced as he intended to solve his ruinous life-crisis in November of 1800. "There exists a teacher who is excellent, when we understand him; it is *Nature*. I won't try to prove it to you," writes Kleist in a letter of November of 1800 to his bride,

> through a lot of talk, but will demonstrate it through examples, which may be most effective anyway, especially for women. On the evening before the most important day of my life, I went on a walk in Würzburg. I shuddered at the thought that I might have to take leave of everything dear to me. I went, lost in thought, through the arched gate and, brooding, back into the city. Why, I thought, doesn't the arch collapse, since it has *no* support? It stands, I answered, *because all of the stones want to fall in at the same time.* (*Sämtliche Werke*, 2, 593)

Those who are not "lost in thought" in this way risk, with the ruin of their bodies, "the ruin of a soul" (*Penthesilea*, l. 2789; p. 258).[7]

Thirdly, Goethe had unique experiences with ruins in his commercial hometown of Frankfurt as well as in Italy. In his letter from Frankfurt of August 16, 1797, to Schiller, he describes the real-estate market with irritation and fascination: "The establishment [a large, valuable old house in the best location] went to pieces during a bombardment under strange circumstances, but even as a pile of rubble it is still twice as valuable as what the present owners paid to my family eleven years ago."[8] It remained for the addressee of these lines to transpose this insight into the standard terms of the educated: "The old will pass, and times will suffer change— / From out the ruins new life blossoms forth" {Das Alte stürzt, es ändert sich die Zeit, / Und neues Leben blüht aus den Ruinen}.[9]

The charm of this and many other texts derives from the possibility of conceiving ruin as an apotropaism against ruins. The refusal to acknowledge this complementarity and an insistence on totality without regard for losses may be among the most reliable semantic indications of totalitarian literature. Those who do not recognize and acknowledge that a totality can only exist when, as a self-identical, plural, or singular totality, it makes room for its other (in and of itself), think, write, and act in a totalitarian fashion. To name just a few paradigms: Hegel showed in the relationship between master and slave, Marx in the relationship between capital and work, Kant in the relationship between consciousness of objects and consciousness of the self, de Saussure in the relationship between signifier and signified, Lacan in the relationship between desirer and desired, and Luhmann in the relationship between government and opposition, that whoever excludes the self's other also excludes itself and unwillingly prepares its own end.[10]

To translate this insight into political terms: The greatest weakness of totalitarian regimes such as that of the GDR, with their extremely pronounced standard semantic, is their very homogeneity and uniformity. Nothing damaged the GDR more than its megalomaniacal secret service {*Staatssicherheitsdienst* or *Stasi*} whose bureaucratic passion (which tied up and blocked tremendous resources) it was to establish the state resurrected out of ruins as an unruinable permanence. One could hardly think less dialectically than did the leading minds of a state that took such pride in its dialectical thinkers. A basic insight of political dialectics is the recognition and acknowledgment that opposition, as long as it is not, itself, committed to a ruinous totalitarianism, strengthens, as a general rule, the very structure against which it directs its protest. Those who refuse to see such deconstructive processes risk destruction. (N.B. From a purely semantic point of view, it is notable that the German reception of deconstruction resulted in a great deal more hysteria than the earlier, friendly reception of Heidegger's incomparably more violent presumption of a "destruction" of metaphysics.) Not for nothing did Hitler's architect Albert Speed think about "ruins-worthiness" even as he drew up the plans for his structures: they were supposed to bear witness, beyond the millennium, to the idea that the thousand-year Reich would not suffer ruin. In contrast, a willingness to risk symbolic ruin in the interest of avoiding ruins is an indication of liberal literature.

Prior to the high point of totalitarian literature of the twentieth century, Thomas Mann's middle-class novel of success courted and shaped the clever dialectic of ruin and ruins once more. *The Decline of a Family* is its subtitle. Its title consists—*nomen est omen*—of a family name which itself suggests collapse, decline, and ruin: *Buddenbrooks*. "Ruin," "to ruin," and "bankruptcy" are the recurring words of this novel, which, as is well known, did not ruin its author but made him rich and famous. His theme is unmistakable: money. And money is the (antitotalitarian) medium in which the dialectic of (abstract) ruin and (real) ruins is first unfolded in a way that can be calculated.[11] Money makes double-entry bookkeeping with respect to the conceptual pair "ruin/ruins" possible. That his wife's need for luxury is ruining him is the constant complaint of Tony Buddenbrook's husband Grünlich.

Tony, for her part, complains about this complaint when the banker Kesselmeyer comes looking for her husband for an important reason: " 'Namely,' Tony continued, 'Grünlich claims that I am ruining him!' At this point Kellesmeyer looked at her . . . and then he looked at Mr. Grünlich . . . and then he broke into laughter such as had never been heard! 'You ruin him . . . ?' he exclaimed. 'You . . . ruin . . . you . . . you are ruining him? . . . Oh God! Oh God!' "[12]

Kesselmeyer has every reason to break into, if not Homeric, at least a pleasant fiscal laughter. For Grünlich's firm can hardly be ruined by the small additional expense of one more maid which Tony has demanded of her spouse. The banker has come to visit unbidden, due to sums of a different order of magnitude. Grünlich's firm is so laughably in the red that only a substantial financial injection from his father-in-law can prevent total bankruptcy. The consul Johann Buddenbrook makes this clear in a conversation with his daughter: "Grünlich going bankrupt . . . ? . . . In this moment, for the first time, Tony became aware of everything that is meant by the word 'bankruptcy,' everything vague and fearful that she had sensed as a small child at the mention of the word . . . 'bankruptcy' . . . that was something more horrible than death, that was tumult, collapse, ruin, humiliation, disgrace, desperation and misery. . . . 'He's going bankrupt!' she repeated."

Ruin is more horrible than death. Death marks the end of a body that disintegrates and turns into ruins. Bankruptcy and ruin, however, mean the end of the name of a firm or a renowned and respected family. In order to "regain respect" Grünlich requests, indeed begs Kesselmeyer for an increase in his line of credit. But Kesselmeyer has lost faith in his debtor. Only the heavenly Father or the earthly father-in-law can save him now. The theological connotations of the scene cannot be escaped. The father is expressly characterized as "he, the sacrosanct one" (p. 236), with the power to deliver or destroy. And he, the heavenly one, after a scene that culminates in Grünlich's scandalous pauper's oath ("I only married you for your money"[13]), expressly bids him, "Get a hold of yourself. *Pray*."

Grünlich, however, was not to be redeemed from ruin, even before. He faced almost certain ruin before he asked for Tony's hand. Thomas Mann carefully composed and escalated the scene in which this becomes crassly obvious. At first Grünlich threatens his father-in-law that he will take his own life, thereby making a ruins of himself, if he refuses to protect him and his family from ruin and disgrace. "Father . . . I beg of you, think of what you are doing! . . . Isn't this about more than me alone? Oh, I, . . . *I* may be ruined anyway. But your daughter, my wife, she whom I love so much, whom I struggled so hard to win . . . and our child, our honest, innocent child . . . she, too, in misery! No, father, I could not bear it! I would kill myself! Indeed, with this my very own hand I would kill myself . . . believe me! And may heaven forgive you for it!" (p. 230).

This ruinous threat, however, is of no avail, because Tony has already revealed to her father that she does not love Grünlich and that the reputation of the Buddenbrook firm means far more to her than Grünlich's. The father was thoroughly prepared to bail out Grünlich's firm if his daughter had asked him to—fully cognizant of and alluding to the fact that the reputation of the Buddenbrook firm could also be damaged by such a step. "The word 'firm' had hit home. It was most likely more effective than even her aversion to Mr. Grünlich. 'Don't do it, Papa!' she said, totally beside herself. 'Do you want to go bankrupt, too?'" (p. 223). If words "hit home" and prevent disaster, then they also prevent real things from being destroyed through violence. A melancholy scene, symbolic to the letter, prepared the way for the confession with which Tony dissociates herself from her spouse and pledges herself to the descent of the paternal firm. After the paternal clarification of the ruinous condition of the spousal firm, "[Tony] sobbed into her cambric handkerchief, which carried the monogram AG in needlepoint. She still cried like a baby: utterly without embarrassment and affectation" (p. 219). The monogram AG on the luxurious handkerchief, which had done its small part in the ruin of Grünlich's firm, stands for "Antonie Grünlich," of course. It is also the well-known abbreviation for a joint-stock company {*Aktiengesellschaft*}.

Tony cries "utterly without embarrassment and affectation" into her cambric AG-handkerchief. When the reputation is not yet ruined, one can cry without embarrassment in the most intimate private circle, if necessary. "Only after the reputation is ruined, can one live in public without embarrassment."[14] After the divorce from Grünlich, with her second marriage to Permaneder, Tony becomes tied to someone who has made this popular expression his maxim for life. Joseph Viktor von Scheffel was the first to rhyme these two words (*ruiniert* and *ungeniert*), indeed, to make synonyms of them, in his popular song, "König Krok" (this rhymes with "Buddenbrook"), which says, "Everything must get unembarrassed" ("Alles muß ungeniert werden"). Not surprisingly, these lines quickly found their way into the songbooks of the dueling clubs which, as is well known, live and die most strikingly by the connection between human ruins and horror at the ruin of symbols. This bowdlerization, "ruinieren-verungenieren" became known beyond the dueling clubs through David Kalish's farce *Berlin, wie es weint und lacht* (1858).

Grünlich, in any event, is to go on living after the ruin of his firm and his reputation, his threats to the contrary notwithstanding— if indeed with a little embarrassment. Tony's second husband lives, in contrast, utterly unembarrassed from the start. The unembarrassed life is a life beyond, or this side of, a strict order of the symbolic. That it is simply a regulative idea, or even more likely an idée fixe, which proclaims that that which the books show must correspond to the Book of the World, and the business's books to the business's transactions, even Consul Johann Buddenbrook is forced to learn—if a little too late. When it becomes clear to Kesselmeyer that the consul is not going to bail out his son-in-law, he speaks clearly and without embarrassment: "How did it actually get started, this ferreting out of the little daughter and the eighty thousand marks? Oh-ho! That can be arranged! With a little quickness and ingenuity that can be arranged! One presents the redeeming father with right good-looking books, charming, clean books in which everything looks its best . . . except that they don't completely agree with raw reality. . . . For in raw reality drafts have already been drawn on three fourths of the dowry" (p. 232). Dowry[15] (on paper)—poison ("in raw reality"): Thomas Mann's first major novel tells the story of various "drafts drawn" {"Wechselschulden"} on the real and the symbolic. They can lead to symbolic ruin, but also into scorched landscapes of ruins. The author of *Buddenbrooks* (as later the author of *The Magic Mountain*) is already pleading that death not be permitted to dominate over life.

One does not have to read Thomas Mann's first major novel in order to know that the books are not always in agreement with the transactions of a business. How could they be? Books are not always in agreement with each other.[16] The real and the symbolic systematically exist in a precarious, and often enough ruinous, relationship to each other. For ruin and ruins are the different expressions of extreme lack of agreement between the symbolic and the real. Thus Walter Benjamin could define the allegory, and with it the figurative potential of poetry that knows it is separated by a jagged line of demarcation from that which it represents, as the intellectual counterpart of ruins. "Allegories are, in the realm of thoughts, what ruins are in the realm of things."[17] It is impossible for either realm to come together unbroken, just as it is impossible for being and meaning to do so. The gap that separates them and constitutes, in this very separation, their complementarity, is much too deep. It is an abyss.

Ruins arise primarily when this abyss is supposed to be filled in, or when "raw reality" is supposed to conform to ideas, confessions, and symbols at any price—as the collapse of the various grand political concepts of the twentieth century shows. As a general rule, modernity and postmodernity are described as the age of decreasing immediacy, increasing arbitrariness and the growing domination of the secondary in which all "referential orders" have gradually come to an end. As a description of some few less clever and unfortunately failed cultural options, this may be true. On the other hand, it would be utterly absurd to tie the historical mega-processes of the last two centuries to this slogan (the end of referential orders). For no other epoch has mobilized so obsessively and with such technical sovereignty as the twentieth for the project of a total, reliable, and pure referentiality, for fundamentalist programs, and for the glorious correspondence between the symbolic and the real.

In this century, what remains of the regulating idea of entertaining war has come to an end. All-out war for the sake of a total correspondence between a "pure" idée fixe on the one hand and a purifying (socially or "ethnically cleansed") empire on the other revokes the enlightened relationship of mutual exclusivity between ruin and ruins, developed in modernity under the sign of the medium of money. The total mobilization of the twentieth century takes place in the name of a seamless correspondence between the real and the symbolic. Racist, fascist, religious, quasi-religious, and social fundamentalisms of all kinds have begun their victory march in this century. They are leaving landscapes of ruins behind them, and they will leave more. The protocivil, apotropaic relationship between ruin and ruins ultimately threatens to turn into a relationship of identity in the totalitarian twentieth century. Precisely then, however, when one takes such totalitarian deep structures as a point of departure (and the fanatical forcing of a correspondence between the symbolic and the real is the basic totalitarian impulse pure and simple), utmost differentiation in the analysis of particular historical events is indicated. In this way the fundamental difference between the collapse of Nazism and so-called real socialism {Realsozialismus} is not difficult to recognize: The collaborating state socialism let go with an acknowledgment of its ruin and, in contrast to Nazism, dispensed with all-out war, scorched earth, and the prototypical fascist battle cry "Viva la muerta" (which comes close to Castro's ruinous slogan "Socialism or Death").

Traditional analytical models are hardly adequate for getting at the exclusion-inclusion relationships between ruin and ruins. Those who want to observe and describe what we experience as ruinous in all its complexity will have to (as Nietzsche first recognized) take leave of two well-intentioned but ruinous analytical models that have regularly accompanied modernity's project of general mobilization, independent of its respective envisioned (political, social, religious, philosophical) options; namely, models that proceed morally and/or historically. For such analyses contribute, precisely to the extent that they are publicly discussed and intent on the consent of all those of good will, to the escalation of conflicts and thus to ruinous processes.[18]

The basic structure of these paradoxes is easy to illustrate with many examples. The first: "Let us serve you for the good," as it says right at the beginning of the national anthem of the GDR. That those who would serve the Good (and who wouldn't?[19]) are also obliged, unified and united, to "defeat the foe of the folk!" is made paradigmatically clear by the next lines. Nearly everyone counts him- or herself among those working for the Good and draws from this the legitimation, indeed the duty, to fight evil. Those who have pledged themselves to this good moral are hardly in a position to take an interest in the illuminating reentry of the distinction between good and evil, much less in the question of whether the very distinction itself is a good or evil one. For the amoral answer would be difficult to avoid, according to which the distinction between good and evil itself often enough produces "evil" effects and is therefore not a good distinction. To make the point clear: there are good reasons for a-morality in public debates—morality ("obviously"—or not?).

The literature of the GDR, like the state itself, was pledged to the project of the ethically "Good" to a striking degree. The self-legitimation of the GDR was not a function of an electoral system or economic effectiveness, but of moral and historical arguments. Not coincidentally does its self-image crystallize in the formula of the "better Germany." And it was, for example with respect to the antifascist past of the leading politicians of the GDR (who at least did not allow career-oriented former Nazis such as Globke to assume positions of leadership), not inappropriate.

The dialectic of such a historical-moral orientation quickly became clear—and was successfully repressed. "Those who find no delight in such a doctrine, do not deserve to be called human" {"Wen solche Lehren nicht erfreun, verdient es nicht, ein Mensch zu sein"}, as it says in Mozart's *The Magic Flute*. But what can or should one do with people who . . . find no delight in such a doctrine, and refuse to participate in the good project? One of the worst works in prose by Stephan Hermlin, *Die Kommandeuse*, brought this dialectic to life, most likely inadvertently: one must of course fight them and thus, according to the degree of their moral failing, put them to death, send them to Bautzen, exile or expatriate them. All, of course, in the name of a "good" politics, meaning morally oriented. That June 17, 1953, was possibly something other than the fascists' revenge against the better Germany, resurrected out of ruins, as Hermlin's novella in all good conscience attempts to show, escapes a literary establishment that works with the moral schema of good and evil. For it reaches the razor-sharp conclusion that the impulse to think, to analyze, and to write beyond good and evil can only be evil, because the allegedly protofascist Nietzsche was the first to suggest it.

The second example: Taking possession of the "cultural heritage" (along with the pathetic "it is ours") was an additional refrain of the GDR, which perceived itself as the legitimate heir of all of Germany's "good" previous history. This self-labeling remained deaf to the observation that German culture, from the standpoint of literary history, was not just distinguished by positive moments but by (in comparison to European literature) the suppression of two great movements that were adept at problematizing the good-evil distinction.[20] The dark side of Romanticism and the literature of decadence are the empty pages in the book of the literature of the German language; it knows no de Sade, Byron, Baudelaire, d'Annunzio, Huysmans, or Wilde (though it does have E. T. A. Hoffmann and Richard Wagner, two half-exceptions). Instead, the rhetoric of the Good dominates in the history of German literature and in its institutionalized reception within the school and university—from Goethe's "Noble let man be, / Helpful and good" {"Edel sei der Mensch, / Hilfreich und gut!"}[21] and the horrible, horribly insensitive word "Reparation" {"Wiedergutmachung," literally, to make it good again} to Mielke's last speech before parliament, which may well have been meant with absolute sincerity, goodness, and honesty: "I do love you all." This proto-German shortage of symbolic evil has not ushered in a shortage of real evil.

In the culture (politics) of the GDR, moral and historical arguments alike are giving way. Historical arguments, however, as a general rule, are counterproductive (to put it mildly) in public debate. The conflicts in the countries of the former Yugoslavia,[22] supposedly legitimized through historical arguments, drastically illustrate this. Ritualized reenactments of the battle of Amselfeld of more than 600 years ago and the battle against the Turks on the outskirts of Vienna disguise the fact that the participants in the civil war of the last half-century were neighbors who, paradoxically, describe themselves, even today, in structurally similar ways: We Croats belong to Middle Europe because we were and are Catholic; enemy territory begins at the edge of Croatia, because Byzantium, with the schism of 1500 years ago . . . and so on. Or: We Serbs belong to Middle Europe because we, the truly orthodox Christians, defended the entirety of Christendom from the Islamic Turks with great sacrifice. Or: We Muslims belong, like the Turks as well, to the European Union and NATO, because we represent the border of the pre-enlightened culture beyond Europe. The paradox is obvious: the rearmament of historical consciousness makes the functional and clear observation of elementary commonalities impossible.

It was Heinrich Heine who, as a young student in Göttingen, was a contemporary of the development of historical consciousness and who immediately recognized the militant effects of such a consciousness of history: "Once, in a beer cellar in Göttingen, a young Medieval-German asserted that one had to take revenge against the French for Conrad of Staufen, whom they had beheaded in Naples. You probably forgot that long ago. But we have not forgotten. See, some day when we feel like picking a fight with you, we won't be without sound reasons. In any event, I advise you to be on the look-out."[23] In fact, it all comes down to this, especially in view of the presumed self-evidence of the phrase "be on the look-out," which one believes may not and cannot be refused acquiescence. This refusal to accept that which appears to be irresistible (most bluntly expressed in the works of Brecht and Heiner Müller) is the strength of the literature of the GDR. Its weakness was its failure to question the moral and historical consciousness for which it opted.

Literature is (like money) the medium that is disposed to be "on the look-out" for ruinous analytical models. For literature defines itself (like money) precisely as the medium that decouples the real and the symbolic—what it tells, invents, and puts together in rhymes is free of the duty to be correct (just as money has validity for the sole reason that it knows how to be free-floating). Realistic literature is the preferred option of all totalitarian cultural politics for good reason (just as fixed prices are the promise of all totalitarian economies): reliable correspondence between *res* and *intellectus*, "world" and "book," or "(the state of) things" and "signs" is, in the world of the "spirit," what fixed equivalence and fixed prices are in the world of the economy. Totalitarianism presses for a ruinous correspondence between the real and the symbolic. This correspondence is staged in ruins.

To this extent, ruins present themselves as fetish-places. They can also be places of remembrance of the advantages of ruin. After the ruin of the ancien régime, Constantin François de Volney wrote his long essay of 1791, *The Ruins, or, Meditation on the Revolutions of Empires; and The Law of Nature*, which appeared in 1794 in German translation with a preface by Georg Forster. In the invocation which introduces this text and makes it clear that the invocation to the ruins is modernity's counterpart to the classical invocation of the muses, it says: "Hail solitary ruins, holy sepulchres and silent walls! you I invoke; to you I address my prayer. While your aspect averts, with secret terror, the vulgar regard, it excites in my heart the charm of delicious sentiments—sublime contemplations. What useful lessons, what affecting and profound reflections you suggest to him who knows how to consult you!"[24]

16

THE MEDIAL BLOOD OF THE ECONOMY—
KLAUS HEINRICH OR DRACULA

Three capital novels that appeared around 1900 concern ruins and ruin: *In the Land of Cockaigne {Im Schlaraffenland}* by Heinrich Mann (1900), *Royal Highness {Königliche Hoheit}* by Thomas Mann (1909), and *Dracula* by Bram Stoker (1897). These three novels, despite differences in style and content, have in common that they place the constellation of Host, money, and the new media at the center of their literary concern. A comparative analysis of these texts is particularly worthwhile because authors of such widely varying dispositions arrive at such affinitive arrangements of themes and motives.

The young, only moderately talented but socially highly ambitious *literatus* Andreas Zumsee renamed himself Andreas zum See {Andreas of the Lake}—whether inspired by a reading of Gottfried Keller's story *The Misused Love Letters* (see chapter 5) is not divulged in Heinrich Mann's novel. Zumsee enjoys the protection and financial support of the wife of the wealthy banker Türkheimer, who is impressed by him because he presents himself not as a talented poet but as a pious Catholic. When he receives his beloved, he is wearing a monk's cowl, and he adheres, in keeping with this religious camouflage, to the economic principles of frugality, which contrast so ostentatiously with the religious orientation. "In Berlin, West-End, nothing could strike them as more unheard-of than an orthodox, practising Catholic."[1]

Heinrich Mann's further arrangement of his arsenal of motifs is exaggerated to a degree reminiscent of trashy literature. With the help of Mrs. Türkheimer, Zumsee speculates on the steep increase in the price of stock in a bank with the name of "Texas Bloody Bank" of all things. It is not left up to the reader to conclude that the proletarians, pale and tubercular-anemic due to poverty, are in a bad way, or that the speculative increase of money is perverse in a society that has shifted from the "sacramental" (the word appears in the novel often: e.g., at pp. 205, 300) circulation of blood to the circulation of money. This interpretation is delivered at no extra cost: "So your banknote has had little ones" (p. 198), says the solicitous lover to her disciple. That it was important to Heinrich Mann to link up with the *Fortunatus* theme (pp. 298, 303) and to bring in the motif of the "Masquerade" (p. 303) is also made exceedingly clear. He need only mention these words.

If Heinrich Mann's early novel deserves attention, despite its cheap pretension, it is because of his doubled contextualization of the motif of money: the monetary motifs have a rendezvous not only with theological themes, but also with the those of the media. The novel *In the Land of Cockaigne* takes up motifs from Balzac's epochal novel *Illusions perdues* (in three volumes from 1837–44). Zumsee/zum See becomes a journalist—like his predecessor in the Paris of 1821–22, Lucien Chardon, who adopts the noble name de Rubempré. In the newest medium of the time, the daily newspaper, which was already putting the stream of news from the telegraph to good use, Balzac's protagonist observes the economic circulation of blood: namely money and its bloody sacrifices. Heinrich Mann's novel about the pseudopious poet, who first attempts the stock exchange then besieges the editor's office in an attempt to wangle some money for his hack writing, also treats the conflictual interplay between public opinion, precise (bourse-mis-)information, and the code of money.

Thomas Mann's *Royal Highness* is characterized by a very similar but incomparably more subtly organized arrangement of motifs. The true protagonist is not his royal Highness nor the clever and remarkably emancipated daughter of an American industrialist rich enough to finance the German city. The true hero of this novel is the economy. Klaus Heinrich and Imma Spoelmann get closer, for good reason, when they study the same books—not books that tell of Lancelot and Guinevere or other great love stories that make a reader hot. Klaus Heinrich and Imma read, instead, specialized literature in the field of political economy: "They were works of a sober and school-bookish appearance, with glazed paper backs, ugly leather sides, and coarse paper, and the contents were divided up minutely into sections, main divisions, sub-divisions, and paragraphs. Their titles were not stimulating. They were manuals and hand-books of economy, abstracts and outlines of State finance, systematic treatises on political economy" (pp. 300–301).[2]

The title and themes of these books may appear to be sober. Reading them is exciting nonetheless. In sovereign persiflage of Dante's well-known words about the reading lovers Paolo and Francesca— "They read no further that day"—the prince and the wealthy beauty, too, read no further, after having gotten so hot from the stimulation and excitement over the circulation of money-blood. Klaus Heinrich

> read about the State expenditure and what it always consisted of, about the receipts and whence they flowed in when things were going well; he ploughed through the whole subject of taxation in all its branches; he buried himself in the doctrine of the budget, of the balance, of the surplus, and particularly of the deficit; he lingered longest over, and went deepest into, the public debt and its varieties, into loans, and relation between interest and capital and liquidation, and from time to time he raised his head from the book and dreamed with a smile about what he had read, as if it had been the gayest poetry. (p. 301)

The prince blesses the millionaire's daughter with the fruits of his reading as well. He recites no love poetry but rather theories of political economy. They make Imma (whose name in palindromic reversal reads "Ami") so hot that she gives herself over, first to the books then to their reader, as if to confirm and at the same time satirize the theories of the stimulating effects of media consumption avant la lettre: "Imma and Klaus Heinrich sat down at the gilt table with their books, and plunged heads together into the Science of Economics"; "The cheeks of both were burning when Klaus Heinrich had said all he knew—even on Miss Spoelmann's usually pearl-white cheeks there was a shade of red to be seen. . . . But as they went so deeply into things, they did not get far in one afternoon, so made a mark in the book at which to start next time" (pp. 305, 304–5).

Blood rushes to the heads of the readers. And due to the alliance between petty nobility and the nobility of great possession, productivity, national trade, and money circulation in the small state climb. It can float, and becomes solvent again. It flourishes—like the allegorical rosebush that no longer withers away, once the country in which its growth is said to be full of significance experiences an enormous influx of money. The rosebush, which previously gave off a "smell of *decay*" (p. 35), blossoms bloodred again. The emphasis on the word "decay" {"Moder"} is Thomas Mann's. One more letter, and the word "Moder" becomes "modern." Indeed, this novel is about the successful monetary modernization of a decaying {*modernd*} small land. Accordingly, it modernizes the traditional corporate metaphor (for more on this, see the excursus to chapter 6). The novel repeatedly alludes to the *Leviathan* (p. 138 and elsewhere) as the essence of the general body of the state which integrates countless individual bodies. But the Leviathan of the novel is no longer the sovereign celebrated by Thomas Hobbes, thus no longer, as the minister of finance quotes with precision, "the King [who] can do no wrong" (p. 18). For "the sovereign is beyond the reach of reproaches. But here we have to do with a default . . . in both senses of the word!"

This default in both senses of the word can only be made good by the super rich American industrialist. Thus the name "Leviathan" refers not to the king but to the "railway-king" (p. 138) in Thomas Mann's sovereign novel about the provincial German "sovereign" (p. 9 and elsewhere), whose trespass and debts do not allow him to appear very sovereign. This sovereignty overshadowed by debts finds its incarnation in the crippled hand of Klaus Heinrich. His "organ inferiority,"[3] however, does not lead Klaus Heinrich, as it did Wilhelm II, who was likewise marked by a deformed hand, to pound the table in overcompensation and an attempt to play the strong man. Thomas Mann's prince makes a public virtue of his personal debility. He gives his hand in marriage, despite his slightly incestuous attraction to his sister, to a middle-class woman. Thus he supplies his family with fresh, exogamous blood, and his state with fresh American money. And for this reason public enterprise flourishes, like the rosebush that is no longer in decay. It has access to wealth that the American money-"Leviathan" contains within it. Not for no reason did Imma's father get off at the Spa Hotel—as elsewhere, *nomen est omen*. There Dr. Watercloose—he, too, has a liquid name—will get him on his feet again, just as his daughter will the prince with the weak hand, and the prince the public enterprise of his country.

The press has also been taken care of. Journalists from two "New York newspapers" accompany the multimillionaire and show the ceremonious princely household what public relations is all about. And then, as things are shifted from decay {*Moder*}) to modernity {*Moderne*}, everything begins to revive and flow: blood rushes to the lovers' cheeks, freshly planted fields ensure new blossoms on new rosebushes, the impoverished public enterprise is roused and turns from the hand that almost exclusively takes (to be precise: collects taxes) into a helping hand. In short, the inflow of money insures that in Thomas Mann's land of economic miracles, things are going uphill fast.[4] The body of the state is quickened—in its veins flows young, enterprising blood, or money.

The effective metaphor of (the circulation of) money as (the circulation of) blood of economies is indeed to be found in Hobbes's *Leviathan* (1651), thus at a remarkably early point in time. The discovery of blood circulation was still new at the time. The physician and friend of Hobbes's, William Harvey, who had published his sensational knowledge of the circulatory system in his *Exercitatio anatomica de motu cordis et sanguinis* of 1628, is responsible for the discovery. Hobbes immediately recoined this discovery in his smithy for constitutional and economic metaphors:

> Mony (of what matter soever coyned by the Soveraign of a Common-wealth,) is a sufficient measure of the value of all things else, between the Subjects of that Common-wealth. By the means of which measures, all commodities, Moveable, and Immoveable, are made to accompany a man, to all places of his resort, within and without the place of his ordinary residence; and the same passeth from Man to Man, within the Common-wealth; and goes round about, Nourishing (as it passeth) every part thereof; In so much as this Concoction, is as it were the Sanguification of the Common-wealth: For naturall Bloud is in like manner made of the fruits of the Earth; and circulating, nourisheth by the way, every Member of the Body of Man. . . . And in this also the Artificiall Man [that is, the body of the state] maintains his resemblance with the Naturall; whose Veins receiving the Bloud from the severall Parts of the Body, carry it to the Heart; where being made Vitall, the Heart by the Arteries sends it out again, to enliven, and enable for motion all the Members of the same.[5]

The money = blood metaphor quickly gained acceptance, in economic literature in any event. Thus it is to be read in John Law's work: "Money is to the state what blood is to the human body. One cannot live without the latter; one cannot trade without the other."[6] Yet not just economists, writers, too, have taken note and made use of this coinage. "Money is the second blood of the human being," notes Goethe in his diary.[7] The figure of Plutus in the Masquerade scen in *Faust II* uses the money = blood metaphor and artistically ties it in with the little box/-key-phallus motif:

> It's time to free our treasures from their fetters!
> I take the Herald's staff and smite the locks.
> The chest flies open. Look! See how, bloodred,
> in brazen pots, gold surges up.

> Nun ist es Zeit, die Schätze zu entfesseln!
> Die Schlösser treff ich mit des Herolds Rute.
> Es tut sich auf! schaut her! in ehrnen Kesseln
> Entwickelt sich's und wallt von goldnem Blute
> (5709–12).

Achim von Arnim's novel *Die Kronenwächter*, too, employs the turn of phrase, money as the blood of the body of state: "Money is," as Maximilian lectures, "the blood of the state. The sight of a farthing makes me think about how much art, action, happiness, and wisdom can be encouraged or hindered by such a little piece!"[8]

These and other literary references to the political-economic central metaphor of the circulation of money are noteworthy because they counterbalance the powerful religious tradition of the talk of "blood money." In Amos 5:11 of Luther's translation it says: "Forasmuch therefore as your treading *is* upon the poor, and ye take from him burdens of wheat: ye have built houses of hewn stone, but ye shall not dwell in them; ye have planted pleasant vineyards, but ye shall not drink wine of them. For I know your manifold transgressions and your mighty sins: they afflict the just, they take {blood money}, and they turn aside the poor in the gate from their right."[9] Those who understand money as the life-giving blood of the state affirm a concept which, at least implicitly, indicates extreme depravity. Matthew, namely, speaks of "blood money" in reference to the thirty pieces of silver for which Judas betrayed Jesus. In Luther's translation: "And the chief priests took the silver pieces, and said, It is not lawful for to put them into the treasury, because it is {blood money}."[10] The modern metaphor of money as the circulation of blood of the body of state thus had to assert itself against the long tradition of the repudiation of "blood money." An illuminating recasting: from the "blood money" extorted and leeched from the poor and the just comes money as the blood of the state that quickens both the body of the state and individuals, animating them to productive work "for the whole."

Not everyone has participated in this prototypical modern reorientation. Societies that shift from the substantial major media of bread and wine or body and blood, respectively, of the Redeemer, to the functional major medium of money or indeed the simulative major media, must be prepared for dogged resistance. Around 1900, and thus after a century of economic mobilization and the apparently irreversible shift to a monetary ontosemiology, this resistance found a characteristic incarnation. Its name is Dracula. The figure of the countly vampire quickly became prominent. Even a *literatus* as serious as Thomas Mann knew of him. While working on *Royal Highness* he wrote, in a letter of June 1904, to his bride Katja Pringsheimer, "You know that I have not been able to grow, in a personal and human way, like other young people, and that a talent can have the effect of a vampire: blood-sucking, absorbing."[11] As all the interpreters of and handbooks on Thomas Mann emphasize, he wrote, in *Royal Highness*, the novel of a cool, great, and rigorous good fortune, the coolness of which in any event has less to do with courtly manners than with the medium of money. Bram Stoker, in his *Dracula*, has written the novel of the unhappy one who cannot bear this coolness, and leads a bloodthirsty partisan campaign against modernity.

Dracula can't leave warm blood alone. He has enough cold money; it holds no charm for him. Thus he, the original noble, becomes the prototype of the fanatical denier of modernity. He repudiates everything secondary. His obsession is primary in every way: earth and blood. Not for nothing does the ship that brings his boxes of earth to London and thus to the center of capital-intensive modernity carry the pre-Christian as well as premodern name of "Demeter."[12] Dracula, the one who disdains everything secondary, has no mirror image. For he intends to live without the second encoding that Communion, money and the media provide for covering the surface. Money leaves him especially cold. But money does not leave him in peace. It has pushed him as far as Transylvania, as Harker realizes while searching for the secret of the castle in which he is imprisoned. "The only thing I found was a great heap of gold in one corner—gold of all kinds, Roman, and British, and Austrian, and Hungarian, and Greek and Turkish money, covered with a film of dust, as though it had lain long in the ground. None of it that I noticed was less than three hundred years old" (p. 66). Even behind vast forests, Dracula is not able to secure himself against the monetary and secondary. It had arrived in Transylvania long ago. The old aristocrat, in contrast to his British adversary, cannot do a thing with it. It gathers dust.

The fact that he cares nothing for gold and money does not help the count at all. For he cannot escape the new medium. It is so omnipresent, overwhelming, and penetrating that it still runs through the veins of the one who disdains it the most. As if Sohn-Rethel's powerful word had literally become flesh, the money abstraction resides inside Dracula: no blood flows through Dracula's veins—money flows there instead, thus the very thing he so vehemently disdains. That becomes clear when Harker tries to fight the Un-Dead with a "lethal weapon": "I did not myself know," notes Dr. Seward in his diary,

> whether our lethal weapon would avail us anything. Harker evidently meant to try the matter, for he had ready his great Kukri knife, and made a fierce and sudden cut at him. The blow was a powerful one; only the diabolical quickness of the Count's leap back saved him. A second less and the trenchant blade had shorne through his heart. As it was, the point just cut the cloth of his coat, making a wide gap whence a bundle of bank-notes

and a stream of gold fell out. The expression of the Count's face was so hellish, that for a moment I feared for Harker, though I saw him throw the terrible knife aloft again for another stroke. Instinctively I moved forward with a protective impulse, holding the crucifix and wafer in my left hand. I felt a mighty power fly along my arm; and it was without surprise that I saw the monster cower back before a similar movement made spontaneously by each one of us. . . . The next instant, with a sinuous dive he swept under Harker's arm, ere his blow could fall, and, grasping a handful of the money from the floor, dashed across the room, threw himself at the window. Amid the crash and glitter of the falling glass, he tumbled into the flagged area below. Through the sound of the shivering glass I could hear the "ting" of the gold, as some of the sovereigns fell on the flagging. (pp. 393–94)

Dracula's body, struck by the blow, does not spill blood, but banknotes and coins. Anyone who springs through a glass window risks bloody injuries—Dracula loses not drops of blood but merely "some sovereigns."

This is a key scene of the novel. "{L}ethal weapons" like knife and sword are useless against Dracula. He is overpowered, however, by the alliance of Host and money. Dracula's pursuers note with interest that he, the one who would suck warm blood in order to put an end to the monetary-metallic coldness of his body, scoops up a handful of the lost money. " 'Why take that money?' " asks Professor Van Helsing. " 'You follow quick. You are hunters of wild beast, and understand it so. For me, I make sure that nothing here may be of use to him, if so that he return.' As he spoke he put the money remaining into his pocket" (p. 395). The clever professor is determined to drive Dracula into a crisis of liquidation. " 'We can know now,' " such is his answer to the question he had posed to himself, " 'what was in the Count's mind when he seize that money, though Jonathan's so fierce knife put him in the danger that even he dread. He meant escape' " (p. 403)—in the very center of the capital. In London, one needs money, as even Dracula knows.

Luckily, Dracula's adversaries have no problems of solvency. Mina's diary makes no idealistic illusion about what will be necessary for success in the fight against Dracula. As a diligent secretary who, with all due respect for Professor Van Helsing, cannot accept that the latter's education in history was the most important thing in the fight against the power of darkness, Mina writes with monetary clarity: "And, too, it made me think of the wonderful power of money! What can it not do when it is properly applied; and what might it do when basely used. I felt so thankful that Lord Godalming is rich" (457). Indeed, this is the gist of it. Lord Godalming (what a name) is rich—he is an all-powerful money-god. In a banking city like London Dracula has a difficult time fulfilling his mission "to invade a new land" (439). Yet neither do Dracula's opponents have it easy. They need access not only to money but to ample Hosts and crucifixes as well—and to typewriters, telegraphs, and phonographs. They need access to the oldest and the most modern media (technology).

Friedrich Kittler, in a brilliant essay, analyzed Bram Stoker's novel as the apotheosis of media technology and secretaries who can take dictation in shorthand faster than they can read. "With paper money and typing paper . . . the destruction of the count begins. Shippers and lawyers who have been bribed betray to his hunters all of the hitherto unknown places which guarantee the homesick six feet of Transylvanian earth even in foreign lands."[13] And with the "inclusion of women in the know," the destruction of the earthbound count ends. Dracula is foiled by women who simply transcribe in shorthand and archive everything, and use, in the process, the newest media technology such as the phonograph and typewriter. In women who, in view of the alternatives "type-writer or vampirism,"[14] opt for the latter, he has his most loyal followers. Women are, as Bram Stoker, like Offenbach, obviously suspects, particularly susceptible to the temptation to renounce everything secondary and consecrate themselves chthonically to the earth of Demeter and to blood.

In order to withstand the temptation of the primary which emanates from Transylvania, all three ontosemiological major media must enter into a transhistorical alliance. Dracula's enemies mobilize: they use Hosts, money, and media technology at once. Dracula's project is foiled by this sacred ontosemiological trinity. Heinrich Mann, Thomas Mann, and Bram Stoker were not the last to arrange (if in very different ways) possible constellations of these ontosemiological major media. To name just two newer examples, one finds in novels by Harry Mulisch and Cees Nooteboom, *Die Entdeckung des Himmels*[15] and *Rituals {Rituelen}*,[16] respectively, constellations of motifs that correspond to the *Dracula* novel. In this newest literature it is especially difficult to overlook the fact that it observes the medial reshaping of money as attentively as older literature registered the monetary bedazzling of the religious ontosemiology.[17] There is much to suggest that the Western project of developing a binding ontosemiology in the so-called New Media is reaching both a precarious conclusion and its destruction at the same time. God, money, and subjects that refer being to meaning and vice versa will be subsumed in information.

As it says in Joel Kurtzmann's book *The Death of Money:*

This new money [= electronic] is like a shadow. Its cool-gray shape can be seen but not touched. It has no tactile dimension, no heft or weight. No other money matters. . . . Money is now an image. Simultaneously, it can be displayed on millions of computer screens on millions of desks around the world. . . . In this new environment, millions of computers are linked in a vast twenty-four-hour, global-trading and information exchange of unimaginable complexity. This immense network has in some ways begun to resemble the network of neurons grouped together inside the brain. Millions of "smart" terminals of one kind or another are all interacting in a syncopated electronic dance, producing an overall rhythm of market ups and downs not unlike the rhythms pulsing through the brain. Money, in its new electrical form, jumps from computer to computer the way nerve impulses jump across synapses. But in the case of money, each time an electron makes its leap, units of buying power—big and small—are exchanged. Goods, wealth, dreams, and power change hands. (pp. 16–17)

Whether the old medium of poetry, which owes its existence to the traditional cultural technique of combining roughly twenty-five letters in different ways, is thematically up to such medial displacements remains uncertain. Because a book with the title *The Poetics of Money* should not, however, close with unpoetic reflections on computer money which is turning into a mega-brain, some lines by Paul Celan will have the last word. They attempt to understand the drumbeat from which our "two cents" falls. Celan's poem "Ich trink Wein" {"I Drink Wine"}, like other lines by Celan, despite prevailing opinion, is easy to understand, if one simply clarifies a few things that are truly not difficult. Hölderin "toiled" {*zackern*}, according to a remark in one of his letters, "over the king's caesura" {"an der Königszäsur"} as he translated Pindar into German. And "two cents" {"Deut"} is not only an element of the word for interpretation {*Deutung*}, it is also the name of a Dutch coin of little value. The striking thing about these lines of Celan's is that they thematize binaries throughout. The first line speaks of "wine from two glasses"; a caesura separates one line into two parts; "I" and "he" denote the two figures of a comparison; a tuning fork consists of two single tines that are supposed to harmonize, like being and meaning. If God strikes the tuning fork, then there must be, in addition to him, at least one second, theologically relevant entity which will attune us to new and unheard-of correlations between being and meaning.

I DRINK WINE from two glasses
and toil
over the king's caesura
like he did
over Pindar,

God strikes the tuning fork
as one of the insignificant
righteous

From the starting drum falls
our two cents.

ICH TRINK WEIN aus zwei Gläsern
und zackere an
der Königszäsur
wie Jener
am Pindar,

Gott gibt die Stimmgabel ab
als einer der kleinen
Gerechten

aus der Lostrommel fällt
unser Deut.[18]

NOTES

[Unless otherwise noted, all quotations from Goethe's *Faust* are taken from Stuart Atkins's translation. The first exception is the line Hörisch uses in the title of this chapter, "For in this sign all now can find salvation," which I have had to modify in order to capture particular details under analysis—in this case the doubled use of the word "now" (*nun*): "Das Alphabet ist nun erst überzählig, / In diesem Zeichen wird nun jeder selig" (6081–82). I also depart from Atkins in my rendering of line 6085, "Astonished as I am, I have to let it count" ("so sehr mich's wundert, muß ich's gelten lassen") in order to preserve a pun of the author's. Trans.]

1. [(*Schein-*)*Geld* is the author's term that I have rendered "(phantom/paper) money" here. This is a play on the German word *Schein*, which means "appearance" but also "banknote." Trans.]

2. Cf. Hans Christoph Binswanger, *Money and Magic*. Footnotes here and elsewhere refer to the sources through keywords alone; bibliographical information is provided in the Bibliography.

3. [The German term *decken* has a wide range of meaning, and so I have rendered it here as both "to secure" and "to cover." Cf. the author's discussion of *decken* below. Trans.]

4. Cf. Heinz Schlaffer, "Goethes Versuch, die Neuzeit zu hintergehen."

5. Cf. on this thought of Goethe's, Jochen Hörisch, *Gott, Geld und Glück.*

6. Notes were individually signed until well into the nineteenth century.

7. [In German, "heads or tails" is literally "head or number." Trans.]

8. *Kopf oder Zahl* is also the (German) title of a 1980 French feature film by Robert Enrico.

9. Cf. Günter Schmölders's *Psychologie des Geldes*, a classic study that does not address, however, precisely the same issues.

10. Verena Lobsien called my attention to John Donne's last sermon of February 25, 1630, in which he uses the word "contignation" (in German, "Deckung") and which, in turn, the Oxford English Dictionary (1933 edition) uses as evidence for the claim that this meaning of "contignation" had in the meantime become obsolete: "The joining or framing together of beams or boards; the condition or manner of being joined together." In Donne's sermon he says: "Buildings stand by the benefit of their *foundations* that susteine and *support* them, and of their *butteresses* that comprehend and *embrace* them, and of their *contignations* that knit and *unite* them: The *foundations* suffer them not to *sinke*, the *butteresses* suffer them not to *swerve*, and the contignation and knitting suffers them to *cleave*" (*The Sermons of John Donne*, p. 230).

11. Just as Police Sergeant Studer in Friedrich Glauser's detective novel *Matto regiert* knows, "One can get the details from Dr. Laduner, who wants to be covered, covered by the authorities. And the District Police Chief made another joke on the word 'covered' that was rather foul and smelled like the barn" ("Alles Nähere werde man von Dr. Laduner erfahren, der gedeckt sein wolle, gedeckt von der Behörde. Und über das Wort 'gedeckt' hatte der kantonale Polizeidirektor noch einen Witz gemacht, der ziemlich faul war und nach Kuhstall roch"), p. 9. Glauser's novel then uncovers who covered whom, how, and why, in the mysterious murder case in a psychiatric clinic.

12. To use Tarski's simple yet well-known example illustrating what it means to understand the circumstances under which an assertion is true or false, respectively: Proposition p ("it is raining here and now") is true if and only if p ("if it is raining here and now").

13. [Though it stretches its meaning in English, I will use "cover" for *decken* from now on, with just a few exceptions. The use of this same word in different contexts is, as the context above indicates, appropriate in German, and it is important to the author's argument. Trans.]

14. A striking portrayal of how dubious it is can be found in Elias Canetti's autobiography, *The Torch in My Ear*. The young Canetti is setting out for a long awaited hike in the mountains, when, at the last minute, his mother forbids him to go, remarking that "she had no money for such luxuries." At that, Canetti grabs a pad of paper and "covered page after page with gigantic capital letters: MONEY, MONEY, AND MONEY AGAIN. . . . Since my handwriting was huge, such as it had never been, every page was soon filled; the torn-off pages lay scattered around me on the large table in the dining room. There were more and more of them, then they dropped to the floor. The rug . . . was covered with them, I couldn't stop writing" (pp. 137–38). Cf. Dietmar Widdig's commentary, "Tägliche Sprengungen," p. 898: "In this scene Canetti stages his own private inflation." The point of the passage, however, is that money and literary broadsheets are similarly inflationary and uncovered.

15. Heads can be, as even a brief look at numismatic collections reveals, of widely different origin: the head of a god, a king, a president, an artist or even of a productive scientist.

16. So reads Thomas Hobbes's famous formulation: *Leviathan* (chapter 19ff.).

17. [The author is referring to the "economic valence" of the German term for money, *Geld*, which is etymologically related to the German term *Geltung*, validity or value, but also authority, prestige, importance, respect, recognition. Trans.]

18. For an examination of the etymology of *Geld* and *Geltung* do not consult the entries "Geld" and "Gelten, Geltung" in the *Historisches Wörterbuch der Philosophie*, whose author/s clearly show/s no interest in this connection, but rather the Grimms' dictionary.

19. [There is a *Kirchensteuer* or church tax in Germany that is required of members (membership itself being optional) and administered by the state. Trans.]

20. Epigram 56. [Trans. from *Goethe's Roman Elegies and Venetian Epigrams*, pp. 110–11.]

21. Hans Kästner, *Fortunatus*, pp. 239ff.

22. *Fortunatus*, p. 409.

23. Even the president of the German bishops' conference has declined to take up the medieval topoi of the ecclesiastical critique of money again; cf. Karl Lehmann's contribution to the collection of essays edited by Helmut Hesse and Otmar Issing titled *Geld und Moral*. On social-democratic attempts to make the market and morality more sensitive to each other, cf. Siegfried Blasche et al., *Markt und Moral*.

24. Cf. Anna Mühlherr, *"Melusine" und "Fortunatus"*; Mühlherr demonstrates the ways in which traditional imagery and emblematic narrative patterns are questioned in *Fortunatus* (thus at the very beginning of the genre of the novel!).

25. Ibid., p. 580.

26. Many of these references are from Hans Tucher's "Reisebuch," thus from a factual account or "historia." It first appeared in Augsburg in 1482 (published by Schönsperger). Further editions quickly followed (Nuremberg, Zenninger, 1482; Augsburg, Schönsperger, 1482; Nuremberg, Zenninger, 1483; Strasbourg, Knoblochtzer, 1484; Augsburg, Sorg, 1486). Hans Tucher was a wealthy patrician of Nuremberg, as of 1476 a member of Nuremberg's City Council and in 1480 its mayor. In 1479 he set out on a pilgrimage with Sebald Rieter, Jr., that took him to Venice, Jerusalem, Cairo, Alexandria, and the Sinai. Cf. Barbara Weinmann, *Studien zur Gebrauchssituation früher deutscher Druckprosa*, p. 151.

27. Cf. the essay of 1990 that paved the way for this book: Hörisch, "Poesie des Geldes."

28. Cf. above all Marc Shell, *The Economy of Literature* and *Art and Money*, and John Vernon, *Money and Fiction*, as well as Bertram Schefold, ed., *Die Darstellung der Wirtschaft und der Wirtschaftswissenschaften in der Belletristik*. Henriette Hoffmann's dissertation "Eine Untersuchung ueber Kapital, Industrie und Maschine von Goethe bis Immermann," completed in 1942 under the direction of Josef Nadler in Vienna, is an exception in German scholarship. It was not published.

29. ["Geisteswissenschaftler," Trans.]

30. Even in a volume on "Arbeits- und Darstellungsformen von Literaturwissenschaft" under the promising title of *Geist, Geld und Wissenschaft* (edited by Peter J. Brenner) one finds much that is informative on the forms for organizing the spirit (e.g., on editions, reviews, and bibliographies), but hardly a thing on the connection between money and spirit. "Geld" (money) is not worthy of inclusion in Elisabeth Frenzel's standard work of reference *Motive der Weltliteratur* (though "Goldgier" [lust for gold] is); in Daemmrich's *Themen und Motive* there is half a page on "Geld," yet three on "Nichts" (nothing).

31. Hegel, *Wastebook*, in *Werke*, vol. 2, p. 548.

32. ["Was die Welt im Innersten zusammenhält," *Faust*, pp. 382–83. Trans.]

33. [Atkins's translation reads "wishing to reward the bard." I have changed this line to its present reading in order to reflect the sense of the German "zum Lohne" as discussed by J. H. Trans.]

34. *Hamburger Ausgabe*, vol. 7, p. 126. [Translation from *Wilhelm Meister's Apprenticeship*, Goethe, vol. 9, p. 71. Trans.]

35. Ibid., p. 74.

36. For more on the theme of money in *Wilhelm Meister,* see Hörisch, *Gott, Geld, und Glück.*

37. For information on Goethe's financial resources, cf. the study by Volker Bohn, "J. W. von Goethe."

38. Letter of January 1, 1821, Weimarer Ausgabe IV/34, p. 62.

39. Andreas Steffens brought this letter to my attention in a New Year's letter of 1993; in chapter 7 of his dissertation "Literarischer Monetarismus" (Mannheim), Enrik Lauer points out several similar passages in Goethe's work.

40. This letter was not considered worthy of inclusion in the Hamburg edition of Goethe's correspondence.

41. [In this play on the classical formulation "The Good, The True, The Beautiful," there is also a German pun that is lost in translation: "the Pure" is one meaning of the German *Baren,* but it also refers to "cash." Trans.]

42. Robert Gernhardt, "Der Kunstler und das Geld," in *Weiche Ziele,* p. 92f. On the livelihood of German writers, cf. the essay collection edited by Karl Corino, *Genie und Geld—Vom Auskommen deutscher Schriftsteller.*

43. [The title could be translated as: *Bread and Wine—The Poetics of Communion.* Trans.]

44. Karl Otto Hondrich, "Wann ist eine Gesellschaft liberal," p. 1081.

45. [Poetry, fiction, or literature. Trans.]

46. [To write, compose; the stem *dicht,* with which the author plays in this passage, means dense, compact, tight, thick, close-woven, concise, and *verdichten* means to condense, compress, solidify, concentrate. English definitions are from *Cassell's German-English English-German Dictionary.* Trans.]

47. This study shares the uncertainty regarding the deep structural displacements of fundamental syntax and semantics that regulate the relations between things/circumstances and signs in Foucault's epochal study of 1966, *Les mots et les choses.* Foucault, however, applies his question at too deep a level; he reconstructs to a certain extent a semantic *structura structurans* and does not analyze, as his later works would suggest he should, the institutions, rites, and authorized algorithms that establish such relations and assure them intersubjective acceptance. Foucault investigates discourses on money, but not on money's code. This study also shares an interest in the correlation of the "logic of things" and the "logic of signs," or in a "kind of grammar of the symbolic functions as such" with Cassirer's *Philosophy of Symbolic Forms* (vol. 1, pp. 85f.). Money is nonetheless anathema to Cassirer. In his analysis of the "configurations *towards* being" (p. 107) provided by myth, art, language, and science, he does not mention it once, even in passing.

48. Cf. Walter Benjamin, "The Storyteller," *Illuminations,* p. 101: "What draws the reader to the novel is the hope of warming his shivering life with a death he reads about."

49. Cf. Hans Blumenberg, *Die Lesbarkeit der Welt.*

50. With the admittedly pronounced difference that Christianity and Islam, but not Judaism, mandate proselytizing.

51. Thus reads the edict of the Second Council of Lyon of 1274; cf. Blumenberg, pp. 49ff.

52. [Lessing is playing with the German words for revelation and evident: *Offenbarung* and *offenbar,* respectively. "Offenbar" might best be translated as "obvious," but I have used "evident" and "revealingly" in this passage, because they more accurately reinforce the point the author illustrates. See also chapter 11. Trans.]

53. [*DaSein* is a play on the words *Dasein* or "existence," and *da* and *sein*, "there" and "to be," respectively. Trans.]

54. Two new studies arrive at similar conclusions, though they start with different questions. In a chapter of the uncommonly well-documented study *Corpus Christi: The Eucharist in Late Medieval Culture*, titled "Uses and Abuses," Miri Rubin establishes, though in passing, the extent to which the Holy Sacrament was in danger of being economized in the late Middle Ages (pp. 334ff.). And Louis Marin writes, in his clever study *Portrait of the King*, about the relationship between Host and coins in Louis XIV's France: "Such would be the mystery of medal-money. It would show as thing, marked in its very matter become engraved form, what it signifies as representation, by giving something to be seen and told. In the manner of Eucharistic symbols—but better than them, since it shows whereas they hide—medal-money is the real presence of the power of state, the presence of the absolute monarch . . . just as the sacramental Host also is, at the moment of consecration, a 'narrative' reiteration of the historical sacrifice of Jesus Christ" (p. 128). Thanks to Jacques Derrida for bringing Marin's book to my attention.

55. Cf. Wolfram Weimer on the history of money, pp. 11, 109: "In 1581 the General Assembly of the Calvinist [!] Church (in the Netherlands) decreed that neither bankers nor their employees were to be permitted to participate in Holy Communion."

56. Cf. the study *Moral und Geld* by Heinrich Brinkmann, who traces the shift from "medieval" transcendence to "modern" immanence in the orientation to money instructively, despite occasional odd turns of phrase such as "eschatology, which Jesus introduced into Christianity" (p. 471).

57. ["Hinterlist" means deceit or treachery. Trans.]

58. Niklaus Manuel, *Der Ablaßkrämer,* v. 259–63. [The English translation offered here is very approximate. Trans.]

59. *The Poems of Schiller,* p. 119.

60. Cited in *Aubrey's Brief Lives,* p. 46.

61. Stephen Greenblatt, *Marvelous Possessions,* p. 71.

62. In a letter to Dietrich von dem Werder of January 20, 1651, no less a luminary than Georg Philipp Harsdörffer explicitly compared coins and Communion wafers. Cf. Dieter Merzbacher's edition of the text and commentary in "Der Abendmalhstreit," including the remark that the discussion between Harsdörffer and Werder over Communion "in the connection between the transfer of money and the doctrine of Communion fits clearly and historically accurately into Hörisch's line of argumentation" (p. 359 n. 28).

Chapter 2

1. ["Wozu Dichter in dürftiger Zeit?" is the well-known original from Hölderlin's "Brod und Wein." Trans. by Michael Hamburger in *Friedrich Hölderlin: Poems and Fragments.* Trans.]

2. The 1970s and 1980s brought a regular boom in the writing of literary history. Cf. Jürgen Fohrmann, "Über das Schreiben von Literaturgeschichte," and ("on stylistic and other deficiencies of a certain type of text"—the type literary history) R. Moritz, "Wie schreibt man eine Literaturgeschichte? Zu stilistischen und anderen Defiziten einer Textsorte." Also to be mentioned, among others, is the multi-volume *Sozialgeschichte der deutschen Literatur, Kindlers Literaturgeschichte der Gegenwart: Autoren, Werke, Themen, Tendenzen in der BRD seit 1945* (1987); the series edited by

H. A. Glaser, *Deutsche Literatur*; W. Kohlschmidt's (ed.) *Reallexikon der deutschen Literaturgeschichte;* the three- volume *Geschichte der deutschen Literatur von den Anfängen bis zum Beginn der Neuzeit* overseen by J. Heinzle; the volume titled *Literaturgeschichte kurzgefaßt* by Eva-Maria Kubisch; V. Zmegac's *Kleine Geschichte der deutschen Literatur;* W. Grabert's *Geschichte der deutschen Literatur;* the six-volume series *Die Deutsche Literatur—Ein Abriß in Text und Darstellung* by O. Best; and H. Haerhütter's *Deutsche Literaturgeschichte.* Not one of these is arranged by motif, or historically by subject matter and/or problem.

3. Cf. on this subject, Peter Fuchs, "Vom schweigenden Aufflug ins Abstrakte."

4. [The Ingeborg Bachmann competition is an annual event that takes place in Klagenfurt, Austria. Poets read their works and critics offer their immediate reactions. It is televised. Trans.]

5. Klaus Modick, *Weg war weg*, pp. 245f.

6. Cf., in addition, the interview with the husband of the author of *Not without My Daughter* in *Spiegel* 30 (1991): 162–65.

7. Cf. Jean-François Lyotard, *The Differend: Phrases in Dispute.*

8. Cf. Richard Münch, *Dialektik der Kommunikationsgesellschaft.*

9. Cf. among others, Theodor W. Adorno, *Aesthetic Theory* passim, especially p. 74; Falk Wagner, *Geld oder Gott*, p. 78; and Jochen Hörisch, *Die Wut des Verstehens*, pp. 80ff.

10. This excommunication usually occurs with the remark that it was self-imposed.

11. ["Verstehende Soziologie" is rendered here as "interpretative sociology," as it is in *Max Weber: Selections in Translation*, p. 10. Trans.]

12. Jacques Lacan's, Jacques Derrida's, and Jean-François Lyotard's discourse theories are exceptions, as is Adorno's *Aesthetic Theory*, p. 74: "For communication is the adaptation of spirit to utility, with the result that spirit is made one commodity among the rest; and what today is called meaning participates in this disaster." Just how far Habermas has distanced himself from this central impulse of critical theory is clear if one contrasts Adorno's statement with the phenomenologically fully untenable expression of Habermas's, who understands "art as the genuine embodiment of communicative reason" (*The Philosophical Discourse of Modernity*, p. 48).

13. Niklas Luhmann, *Social Systems*, pp. 59ff., esp. p. 62: "Meaning always refers to meaning and never reaches out of itself for something else. . . . Thus meaning is an unnegatable category devoid of difference."

14. Paul Watzlawick, Janet Helmick Beavin, and Don D. Jackson, *The Pragmatics of Human Communication*, p. 49. Cf. on the other hand, Margot Berghaus's insightful thoughts about the possibility of turning on the television in order to avoid communication, "Nicht-Kommunikation durch Fernsehen." The statement that one cannot not communicate is only valid for the interaction between those who are in each others' presence. Perhaps the old media of letter and telephone have been so successful, in part, because they allow non-communication: one does not have to send or open a letter, one does not have to answer the telephone. Stanley Kubrick's cult film *Clockwork Orange* shows, in a drastic way, what it means to be forced to communicate.

15. Luhmann, "Das Kunstwerk und die Selbstreproduktion der Kunst," p. 624; cf. Dietrich Schwanitz, *Systemtheorie und Literatur.*

16. Luhmann, "Das Kunstwerk," p. 660.

17. [Short for "Staatssicherheitsdienst," the secret police of the former German Democratic Republic. Trans.]

18. Cf. Ulrich Beck, *Risk Society.*

19. Cf. on this point, Hans Ulrich Gumbrecht and Karl Ludwig Pfeiffer (eds.), *Paradoxen, Dissonanzen, Zusammenbrüche.* [Many of these essays are available in translation in their *Materialities of Communication.* Trans.]

20. The phrase originates with none other than Friedrich Schleiermacher; cf. in this regard, Hörisch, *Die Wut des Verstehens,* chapter 6.

21. This distinction between symbolic and diabolical communication follows Luhmann.

22. [I have added "Original" to the translation. Trans.]

23. Cf. in this regard, among others, Ernst Robert Curtius, *European Literature and the Latin Middle Ages,* chapter 15, and Herbert Anton, "Lügende Dichter und die Kunst des Rhapsoden."

24. Friedrich Dürrenmatt offer a forceful allegory of this possibility in his novella *The Assignment, or, On the Observing of the Observer of the Observers.*

25. Cf. Arthur Henkel, "Die 'verteufelt humane' Iphigenie."

26. It is striking that the word "Willkür" (caprice, arbitrariness, discretion), discredited in other systems of discourse, has had positive associations within the system of literary analysis since the age of Romanticism at the latest. In this context, cf. Paul Feyerabend, *Against Method.*

27. Dietrich Schwanitz, *Systemtheorie und Literatur,* p. 38.

28. In Andreas Thalmayr, ed., *Das Wasserzeichen der Poesie,* p. 154.

29. Cf. Paul Ricoeur, *Le conflit des interprétations* (esp. pp. 64–79).

30. Benjamin, *The Origin of German Tragic Drama,* p. 182. For Benjamin, this is firmly established fact: "It is nevertheless certain that. . . ."

31. Cf. Heinz Schlaffer, *Poesie und Wissen.*

32. Philosophical texts tend to establish new ultimate authorities in which to ground themselves—for example, omniscient subjects or irrefutable claims of the validity of communication. Texts by philosophers such as Nietzsche, Adorno, or Derrida, who forgo this inclination, are often characterized as recklessly overstepping the boundaries between philosophy and poetics.

33. Cf. among others, Lutz Braun, *Geschichte der Philosophiegeschichte;* Michael S. Batts, *A History of Histories of German Literature 1835–1914;* and Klaus Weimar, *Geschichte der deutschen Literaturwissenschaft.*

34. Even comparative literature, which sees itself as "progressive," is often aimed at finding uniformity rather than differences. Albrecht Schöne demonstrated this programmatically at the International Congress of Germanists (*Internationaler Germanistenkongreß*) in the summer of 1990: "The efforts to expand German literary scholarship by the 'expansion of the concept of the text,' by an 'openness toward social history' and by rectifying the 'theoretical deficit' have reduced the energy for the comparatist's endeavor. But, in the long run, Germanics will only become a truly important discipline, one that is significant to more than its own practitioners, if it is more open to the variety of perspectives that it has acquired since it has become an international discipline. For each person who concerns him- or herself with German language and literature, and is not a native speaker, is a potential native comparatist. And in an age in which physical distances, at least, are becoming less and less of an obstacle, it would be desirable to work together to remove those distances of the mind and spirit that keep us farther apart from one another more than we, in truth, are." Schöne's example ("Auf Biegen und Brechen" {On Bending and Breaking}, pp. 125f.) proves, despite its intent, nothing less than the high degree of strangeness in the perception of that which is supposedly the same: a tree that bends but doesn't break. Devoting

literary scholarship to internationalization—who wouldn't agree? Current literature sees with striking frequency, however, in the economic, public, medial, and scholarly tendencies toward internationalization, grounds for conflicts and problems, not their solution.

35. Cf. Benjamin, "Goethes Wahlverwandtschaften," in *Gesammelte Schriften*, I/1, pp. 126ff.

36. *The Origin of German Tragic Drama*, p. 182; cf. the parallel considerations at the very beginning of the essay on Goethe's Elective Affinities ("Goethe's Wahlver-wandtschaften").

37. Ibid., pp. 172f.

38. The plan aimed at putting together a picture atlas that was intended to represent the survival, through many epochs, of "pathos formulae," or figures depicting the overcoming of feelings of fear, in European art (and to some extent also art outside of Europe). Cf. in this regard, Ernst H. Gombrich, *Aby Warburg*, pp. 283ff.

39. It is striking that in the literary scholarship of the last three decades, which has exalted in methodological innovation, the concept of the history of problems has been completely unable to gain acceptance—in utter contrast to studies of subject matter, motif, and symbol. Cf. Elisabeth Frenzel, *Stoff-, Motiv- und Symbolforschung*, and Manfred Beller, "Stoff-, Motiv- und Themengeschichte," among many others.

40. Robert Musil, *The Man without Qualities*, p. 442.

CHAPTER 3

1. Locus classicus of the poetic critique of money are surely verses 295ff. from Sophocles' *Antigone*, which Marx liked to quote: "No current custom among men as bad / as silver currency. . . ." Cited in *Capital I*, p. 132.

2. Heidegger grows pensive, while interpreting Heraclitus's words on "Logos," on the ambiguity of the word "lesen" [to read and to gather or glean, Trans.]; even he valued the gathering of grain and grapes for wine more highly than the reading of books. Cf. Heidegger, "Logos (Heraclitus, Fragment B 50)."

3. Erasmus, *Collected Works of Erasmus: Poems*, pp. 217–19.

4. Cf. Hans-Jürgen Horn's entry on "Gold" in the *Reallexikon der Antike und Christentum*, column 907 (see citations there as well).

5. The founding of the society occurred in 1633 in response to the founding of the fashionable and financial "Fruchtbringende Gesellschaft" {"Fruitful Society"} in Weimar in 1617.

6. Cited by Ralf Borchers, ed., *Arm und reich*, p. 190.

7. P. 397.

8. Cited by Borchers, p. 15.

9. Ibid., p. 107.

10. A classic illustration of the critique of money's power to destroy morality and (which is more interesting!) of the assumption that each of these critiques shares, is Thomas More's *Utopia* of 1516, in which he says: "Who does not know that fraud, theft, rapine, quarrels, disorders, brawls, seditions, murders, treasons, poisonings . . . die out with the destruction of money?" (p. 149).

11. Sebastian Brunt, *Ship of Fools*, pp. 271f (emphasis J. H.).

12. Brecht, of all people, recognized this and, contrary to the mainstream, re-peatedly sang paradoxical songs in praise of money. Cf., for example, the "Song of the Stimulating Impact of Cash" {"Lied des belebenden Wirkung des Geldes"}: "That's the fate of all that's noble and splendid / People quickly write if off as trash / Since with

empty stomach and unmended / Footwear nobody's equipped to cut a dash." {"So ist's auch mit allem Guten und Großen. / Es verkrümmert rasch in dieser Welt / Denn mit leerem Magen und mit bloßen / Füßen ist man nicht auf Größe eingestellt. / Man will nicht das Gute, sondern Geld."} Similarly, the poem "Vom Geld" {"Of Money"}, in which is said, among other things: "Money is good! Take care of money! / Human beings catch each other with traps. / Evil is great in the world. / Therefore you should win money / For their love of money is greater. . . . Money is truth. Money is heroism. . . . Without money your only companion will be the unreasoning animal." {"Das Geld ist gut! Auf das Geld gib acht! / Die Menschen fangen einander mit Schlingen. / Groß ist die Bösheit der Welt. / Darum sollst du dir Geld erringen / Denn größer ist ihre Liebe zum Geld. . . . Geld ist Wahrheit. Geld ist Heldentum. . . . Ohne Geld bleibt bei dir nur das unvernünftige Tier."}

13. Vol. 1, cols. 1551–68. Cf. Carsten Zelle (who rediscovered this informative text), "Moneten, Moral und Motivation."

14. Peter Sloterdijk, *Thinker on Stage*, p. 18 (without reference to Krüger, of course).

15. Cited by Zelle, "Moneten, moral und Motivation," pp. 256f.

16. Cited by Borchers, p. 24.

17. This is surely a Germanization of Publilius Syrus's dictum, "Pecunia una regimen est rerum omnium."

18. M. Claudius, *Asmus omnia*, vol. 1, p. 170. [Trans. Herbert Rowland, *Matthias Claudius*, pp. 105–6.]

19. Lion Feuchtwanger, *Gesammelte Werke*, vol. 14, p. 242. ["The Ballad of Mr. B. W. Smith," in *Pep: J. L. Wetcheek's American Song Book*, pp. 58–59.] See also Christoph Weiß, "Lion Feuchtwanger und sein Roman 'Erfolg.' "

20. *Asmus omnia*, p. 57.

21. [A line from Schiller's "Die Worte des Glaubens": "Und wäre er in ketten geboren!" Trans.]

22. This is quite different in English and French, which offer a range of, in some cases, subversive rhymes with "man" and "homme," respectively; compare, for example, Jacques Offenbach's play with the words "l'homme de la pomme" for Paris.

23. Cf. Freud's lovely thesis that "a good joke" comes about "when what children expect proves correct and the similarity between the words is shown to be really accompanied by another, important similarity in their sense." *Jokes and Their Relation to the Unconscious*, p. 147 n. 5.

24. Cf. Hörisch, *Der Mensch*. Cf. also Paul Celan's verses from the poem ". . . Plashes the Fountain": "We shall sing the nursery rhyme, that one, / do you hear, that one / with the hu, with the man, with the human being, the / one / with the scrub and with / the pair of eyes that lay ready there as / tear-upon- / tear" (*Paul Celan: Selected Poems*, p. 73). (". . . rauscht der Brunne": "Wir werden das Kinderlied singen, das, / hörst du, das / mit den Men, mit den Schen, mit den Menschen, ja das / mit dem Gestrüpp und mit / dem Augenpaar, das dort bereitlag als / Träne-und- / Träne," *Gedichte*, vol. 1, p. 237.)

25. Cf. Luhmann, *Die Wirtschaft der Gesellschaft*.

26. *Wilhelm Meister's Apprenticeship*, pp. 116, 121 (emphasis J. H.).

27. Act 2, scene 1; Hamburger Ausgabe, vol. 4, pp. 41f. [Trans. from *Goethe's Plays*, p. 52.]

28. [It is tempting to say "those who cannot make heads or tails of . . . ." Trans.]

29. Cf. Hörisch, *Brot und Wein*, pp. 138ff.

30. Cf. with respect to this, Hörisch, "Poetische Überproduktion."

31. Hamlet's melancholy reflection on the discrepancy between the wisdom found in books and what takes place between heaven and earth is philosophically grounded by George Berkeley: "We know many things w[hi]ch we want words to express". And vice versa: we know many words (being, modality, and so on) for which we have no things. Cf. Hans Blumenberg, *Hölenausgänge*, pp. 150f., and Luhmann, *Die Wissenschaft der Gesellschaft*, pp. 526f.

32. Cf. in, among others, Kluge's *Etymologisches Wörterbuch* and the Grimms' dictionary: "Geld" (money)—but not "Geltung"! (validity, value, worth, or authority).

33. Cf. Luhmann, *Die Wirtschaft der Gesellschaft*, pp. 46, 54, 70, 197.

34. Cf. Eberhard Moths, "Die Preise schweigen."

35. Cf. with respect to this problem, the instructive thoughts of Hans Christoph Binswanger, *Geld und Natur*. Even politicians like Otto Schily, who states that "Nature declines, money thrives" (*Flora, Fauna und Finanzen*, p. 44) assume that the decline of nature can be checked by an increase in money—to be more concrete: through the monetization of the limited resource, the environment. Direct political attempts at taxation—in extreme cases an ecodictatorship or a war against ecologically destructive countries: which? one's own?—would be even more disastrous for the ecosystem than "business as usual."

36. According to none other than Luhmann, *Die Wirtschaft*, p. 248.

37. A standard poetic accusation against money, cf. the wonderful anthology by Manfred Frank, *Das kalte Herz*, and the collection of popular sayings about money in Volkmar Muthesius's study.

38. Luhmann, "The Economy as a Social System," in *The Differentiation of Society*, p. 207. This indifference is a favorite theme of modern novels; compare the investigations by P. Zima.

39. [This is the title of a song by Brecht. Cf. chapter 3 note 12 and chapter 9. Trans.]

40. In view of the history of communications, a distinction between fiction (as a possibility of language/writing) and simulation (as a possibility of the new media of film, radio, and TV) must be made. Cf. Friedrich Kittler, "Fiktion und Simulation," and Hörisch, *Die Wirklichkeit der Medien*.

41. Heidegger, "The Age of the World View," p. 13.

42. [The German term is "das sich vor-stellende Subjekt." Trans.]

43. This is the subtitle of Kracauer's *Theory of Film* (1960); cf. above all, pp. 300ff. Also cf. Hörisch, "Non plus ultra."

44. Ibid., p. 302 (emphasis J. H.). Cf. on this subject, Hörisch, "Optionen der Gegenwartsliteratur."

45. Cf. Hans-Georg Pott's instructive study of this problem, *Literarische Bildung*.

46. Cf. the final chapter of Hans Blumenberg's *Lesbarkeit* ("Der genetische Code und seine Leser").

47. In *Experienta* 26 (1970): 810–16 (cited by Blumenberg, *Lesbarkeit*, p. 379).

CHAPTER 4

1. Cf. the study by Harald Weinrich, "Münze und Wort," which has become a classic.

2. The central methodological suggestion of *Anti-Oedipus*, not to ask the question "What does that mean?" but instead, "How does that function?" has its legal basis in the functional primacy of monetary over literary communication. Not without reason does this book carry the subtitle *Capitalism and Schizophrenia*.

3. Cf. Luhmann, *Die Wirtschaft der Gesellschaft.*

4. ["Sie sollen den Schein des Geldes, sie sollen den Wert des Geldscheines decken helfen" plays with the double meaning of "Schein" as appearance and banknote. Trans.]

5. It is noteworthy that the misuse of money for purposes varying from the luxurious to the depraved (inhaling cocaine through a tube made of—expensive!—dollar bills) is a literary constant.

6. Uwe Timm, *Headhunter,* p. 277.

7. Ibid., p. 230.

8. Ibid., p. 231.

9. Cf. the following with the detailed and ingenious exposition by Manfred Escherig, "Bei der Betrachtung einer Dollarnote."

10. The number 13 is traditionally regarded as a disruption of the true order symbolized by the number 12 (= 3 x 4; e.g., 12 months, 12 tribes of Israel, 12 tasks of Hercules, 12 gates of heavenly Jerusalem, 12 apostles—plus a non-apostle, Jesus Christ). Among the Babylonians it was viewed as the embodiment of the disruption of perfection; the cabala has 13 evil spirits; chapter 13 of Revelations deals with the Anti-Christ. Thirteen hardly plays a role at all, with the exception of its place on the dollar bill, in the symbolism of Free Masonry, most likely because of its tendency to divide. Cf. Lennhoff-Posner's *Internationales Freimaurerlexikon,* cols. 1733–40.

11. Lawrence Ferlinghetti, "Oral messages," in *A Coney Island of the Mind,* pp. 49f. and 63. The literal sense of the last sentence presents a problem: the phrase "In God We Trust" is there for all to see on the dollar bill.

12. In other words, the Federal Bank of Germany prognosticated more precisely than, for example, the CIA or the BND (Federal Intelligence Service of Germany). There are, of course, various literary and essayistic statements that predict a collapse of the nations of the Warsaw Pact. The most amazing is surely that of James P. O'Donnell, who, in 1979, in *Reader's Digest* of all places, wrote: "The year was 1989. The wall fell. Everywhere along its entire horrible length of 165 kilometers, Berliners from East and West streamed in to tear it down" (cited by Melvin Lasky, *Wortmeldung zu einer Revolution,* p. 12 n.). [Lasky notes that this article appeared in a few international editions of *Reader's Digest.* Because this edition was unavailable to me, I have retranslated the passage from the German. Trans.]

13. Cf. with the following the excellent essay by Albrecht Betz, "Geld und Geist."

14. Ibid., p. 72.

15. [The fairy tale is very well known in Germany. A poor girl whose parents have died, leaving her with nothing but the shirt on her back and a crust of bread, goes out into the world. She meets an old man who is poor and hungry, and she gives him her bread; then she meets a child who is cold, and gives him her cap. Eventually she gives all of her clothes to three more, freezing children. As she stands there naked, the stars begin to fall from the heavens, and they turn into coins. Trans.]

16. Betz, "Geld und Geist," p. 74.

17. Cf., among many others, the classic studies by Ernst Curtius, *On the Religious Character of Greek Coins;* Bernhard Laum, *Heiliges Geld,* as well as his *Viehgeld und Viehkapital;* and the investigation by Horst Kurnitzky, *Triebstruktur des Geldes.*

18. Cf. Klaus Heinrich, *Arbeiten mit Ödipus,* pp. 194ff.

19. Cf. among others, Ernst Samhaber's *Das Geld—Eine Kulturgeschichte,* Erich Achterberg's "Was ist Geld?" and René Sédillot's *Muscheln, Münzen und Papier.*

20. On the iconology and imperialistic intentions of credit cards, whose names,

"American Express," "Eurocard," Mastercard," or "Visa" imply more, cf. the essay by Theodor T. Heinze, "Verdammte Wirklichkeit."

21. The series *Que sais-je* has just dedicated an instructive volume to it; cf. Didier Martres and Guy Sabatier, *La Monnaie électronique*.

22. Wolfram Weimer, "In Zukunft zählt die Zahlungselektronik—Zur Geschichte und Gegenwart des Papiergeldes," in *Frankfurter Allgemeine Zeitung*, June 16, 1990, p. 13.

23. Obviously he meant "to create their daily supply of money themselves." That the "daily need for money" in a consumer metropolis such as Munich is, for the most part, also "self-created," is the deeper wisdom of the commissioner's sentence. Cited from *Frankfurter Allgemeine Zeitung Magazin* of September 27, 1991, p. 6.

24. France, as is well known (together with other countries), was able to disturb the currency system established at the Bretton Woods Conference by trading its holdings in dollars for gold—at the fixed rate of exchange, suggestive of substantial coverage, that had been set in 1944.

25. The word "inflation" entered the vocabulary of economics late. "*Inflatio* is a concept from Classical Latin; it is found in the works of Cicero and Pliny. It is derived from the verb *flare*, which essentially means 'to blow'; *inflatio* means nothing less than 'swelling.' With the (American) Civil War it (the word inflation) finally entered the vocabulary of economics. The concept 'inflation' was used for the first time, in the sense in which it is understood today, in a short piece by an author by the name of Alexander Del Mar, titled . . . *A Warning to the People; the Paper-Bubble*" (R. Sédillot, *Muscheln*, p. 214).

26. Cf. the amusing investigation by Holger Bonus, *Wertpapiere, Geld und Gold— Über das Unwirkliche in der Ökonomie*.

27. This work—originally a series of articles for the *Allgemeine Zeitung*—was written by Heine for the express purpose of covering a draft. In a letter of January 25, 1832, to his publisher Cotta, he says, "The purpose of these lines is to advise you of yesterday's draft of 300 Gulden, to the order of Mr. S. Haber, Sr., for a month starting today. Please cash it and put it on my bill. I promise to balance this last very soon with the submission of manuscripts."

28. Heine, *French Affairs*, in *The Works of Heinrich Heine*, vol. 7, p. 229.

29. Ibid., pp. 230–31.

30. Ibid., p. 233.

31. Zola, *The Money*, pp. 296f.

32. Alexandre Dumas, *The Count of Monte Christo*, vol. 2, p. 76. So-called belles lettres carefully registered the new technology of the telegraph. The optic telegraph lines between Paris and Lille, installed in 1794 at the behest of Napoleon, continued in the form of a star to Mainz, Amsterdam, Venice, and Trieste, and its effects on politics, the military, and life in general is laid out in Grabbe's drama *Napoleon oder die Hundert Tage*. Ludwig Börne, Victor Hugo, and (as illustrated above) Dumas were fascinated by this technology. Several of Fontane's novels show a lively interest in the electronic telegraph developed by Siemens starting in 1847 (the Russian network was installed in 1853, and the first underwater cable in 1857, between Cagliari and Malta). Cf. Frank Haase's and Jean Maurel's contributions to the volume *Armaturen der Sinne* as well as the preface by the editors, Hörisch and Michael Wetzel.

33. *Understanding Media*, p. 139. Of all the critiques of Marx, McLuhan's is the most comprehensive: "Marx and his followers . . . reckoned without understanding the dynamics of the new media of communication. Marx based his analysis most untimely

on the machine, just as the telegraph and other implosive forms began to reverse the mechanical dynamic" (ibid., p. 38).

34. Cf. Bernhard Vief, "Digitales Geld."

35. Cf. Hörisch, *Brot und Wein* (chapter 1, "Das Abendmahl, das Geld und die neuen Medien").

36. Vief, "Digitales Geld," p. 117. The increasing percentage of the GNP represented by trade in "immaterial" valuables can be intra-economically inferred from this development. What are the largest automobile manufacturers in comparison with the insurance industry and banks, that have, as is well known, nothing tangible to sell?

37. The birth of the stock exchange resulted from the spirit of chaos (of voices, wishes, desires, powers, and so forth) and the insight into its inevitability; the birth of research into chaos out of the spirit of the stock exchange. Cf. on the subject the wonderful passage from Volker Erbe's chaos-novel *Die Spur des Schwimmers*, p. 91: "In the research on chaos there is a particularly intimate relationship to numbers, even economic ones. Ironically, it was none other than Mandelbrot who fed his first subversive programs with cotton prices. . . . In truth, he was supposed to give a lecture on the distribution of income. Then he saw a graph on the blackboard of the professor who had invited him to speak that was exactly the same as the one he wanted to present. 'How did my diagram get onto your blackboard before I have even held my talk? Ha ha.' It turned out that the diagram had absolutely nothing to do with the distribution of incomes. It depicted the changes in the price of cotton over a period of eight years. . . . And Mandelbrot . . . promptly finds out. . . ." (Please read further yourself!)

38. Wulf R. Halbach, "Simulated Breakdowns," p. 341.

39. Johann Georg Zimmermann, *Memoire*, p. 87.

40. John Vernon, *Money and Fiction*, pp. 18f.

41. Jean-Joseph Goux, *The Coiners of Language*, pp. 92–93. Cf. with Vernon's and Goux's treatises the detailed review by Thomas DiPiero, "Buying into Fiction," pp. 2–14.

42. Goux, "Banking on Signs," p. 20.

43. Cf. Sédillot's remarks on the French franc, *Muscheln, Münzen und Papier*, pp. 217ff.

44. Reprinted in the variants and commentary on Hugo von Hofmannsthal's *Sämtliche Werke—Gedichte 2*, p. 228. Thanks to Uwe Steiner for bringing this to my attention.

45. Hugo von Hofmannsthal, *Gesammelte Werke—Gedichte, Dramen I, 1891–1898*, pp. 94f.

46. Of course one could publish novels and lyric poetry on CDs. But it does not seem likely that this will provide the materiality for the belles lettres of the future (reference works and so-called specialized literature are a different story). The prognosis is much more likely that the future of (bellestristic) books lies in their status as anachronisms—even with respect to their outer form. Messages belong, in the future, in books; information in electronic repositories.

CHAPTER 5

[The original German title of this chapter is "Der Beziehungswahn des Geldes." Trans.]

1. Nestroy, " 'Nur keck!,' " pp. 49f.

2. *Delusions, Confusions*, p. 47.

3. This is supposed to change soon—despite the strong objections of most banks; a corresponding law novella is in the making.

4. Alfred Sohn-Rethel has repeatedly tried to show this—cf. his correspondence of 1936–69 with Adorno. Cf. especially the details on the "derivation of subjectivity from money" (p. 49), which Sohn-Rethel advances convincingly, especially under "increasingly desperate material conditions" (p. 50) or under a "very great shortage of money" (p. 28).

5. [The German word "Schuld" means debt as well as guilt, or sin. Though not as obvious, "debt" also conveys both meanings and should be understood in both senses. Similarly, when sin and debt are discussed in tandem, the author is most likely playing with the German term "Schuld." Trans.]

6. Gustave Flaubert, p. 269.

7. ["Schuldige Gläubige" become "Gläubiger und Schuldner," says the author, playing not only with the double meaning of "Schuld" (see note 5 to this chapter) but also with "Gläubiger," meaning, as the context indicates, both "believer" and "creditor." Trans.]

8. Freytag, Debit and Credit, p. 564.

9. Simmel, Philosophy of Money, London, p. 431.

10. Kretschmer, Der sensitive Beziehungswahn, p. 151.

11. [The entire cycle has been translated under this title by M. D. Hottinger (Freeport, N.Y., 1970). This translation was not available to me, and translations from this work are Michael Bullock's, who renders "Seldwyla" as "Seldville." Trans.]

12. [Von Strahlheim means "of the radiant home"; von Nordstern, "of the north star"; vom Meere, "of the sea." Trans.]

13. Cf. Jacques Lacan: "The different kinds of mania need, in fact, no interpretation at all, because they express splendidly, in their very themes, those instinctive and social complexes which psychoanalysis draws out of neurotics with the greatest of difficulty." [This is a translation of a passage from "Das Problem des Stils und die psychiatrische Auffassung paranoischer Erlebnisformen" of 1933, in S. Dalí, "Unabhängigkeitserklärungen der Phantasie," Gesammelte Schriften, p. 356, and thus a translation of a translation. Neither Lacan's original French nor an English translation was available to me. Trans.]

14. On the homosexual aspects of paranoia, cf. Freud, "A Case of Paranoia Running Counter to the Psycho-analytic Theory of the Disease."

15. Cf. the comments of Gerhard Kaiser on the "Motif of the manwife, of the hermaphrodite in his unfruitfulness" (Gottfried Keller, p. 363). Kaiser overlooks, to be sure, the economic- paranoiac motifs of the novella.

16. Note the businessman's talent for developing an economy of the aesthetic of love.

17. Lacan has analyzed the basic narcissistic crisis in Écrits, pp. 800ff.

18. Cf. among others, Dieter Wellershof, "Frauenfeind und Dr. Krebs—Über Namen."

19. As early as 1697, Gottlieb Wegner characterized the phrase "Priests leave books and children behind" as a folkloristic expression; Gottlieb Wegner, Liberis et libris sacerdotum oratio. I am grateful to Günter Rohe for calling this to my attention.

20. Sloterdijk, Critique of Cynical Reason, p. 541.

21. [The German for waiter, "Kellner," is close to Keller. Trans.]

22. [I have added the following words, which were omitted from the translation: "not knowing it was an old and genuinely German word." Trans.]

23. Cf. on this subject, the works of Alfred Sohn-Rethel.

24. Cf. the quite different analyses by Robert Kurz, *Der Kollaps der Modernisierung*, and Niels Werber, "Von Feinden und Barbaren."

25. Aby Warburg, *Heidnisch-antike Weissagung*, p. 504.

CHAPTER 6

1. Cf. Heinz Schlaffer, "Knabenliebe."

2. The psychoanalytic theory of money accentuates this side and has virtually ignored the phallic—cf. the documentation edited by Ernest Bornemann, *The Psychoanalysis of Money*.

3. ["A term vulgarly used for a wealthy spendthrift," Freud, "Character and Anal Erotism," p. 174 n. Trans.]

4. Freud, "Character and Anal Erotism," p. 174. [Freud's translator notes that Freud used the English "refuse" in his original paper. Trans.] Cited by Bornemann, *The Psychoanalysis of Money*, p. 77.

5. Cf. Michael von Engelhardt, *Der plutonische Faust*; also Hans Blumenberg, *Höhlenausgänge*—an incomplete study, only superficially touching upon money motifs in connection with caves.

6. Cf. Engelhardt, *Der plutonische Faust*. The following attempt refers to this work with gratitude, though specific references are not given.

7. In addition to Engelhardt's study, Heinz Schlaffer's *Faust II*, Werner Hamacher's "Faust, Geld," and Hans Christoph Binswanger's *Money and Magic* also deserve mention.

8. [The author is playing with the German words "bezeugen" and "zeugen" which mean "to testify" but also "to beget." To be "begotten" is to testify to the potency of the father. He proceeds to play with the word "scheinen": to seem, to shine. Trans.]

9. Albrecht Schöne, *Götterzeichen, Liebeszauber, Satanskult*, p. 111.

10. *Faust* citations with verse numbers refer, from now on, to Schöne's edition. [This pertains to the German text; English translations remain Stuart Atkins's. Trans.]

11. According to Schöne's commentary, p. 331.

12. [That is, the version of 1808, in which the words "ungeheuren Loch" or "gaping whole" and "rechter Propf" or "fitting cock" (4138, 4142) are omitted. Trans.]

13. Heinrich Mann, *In the Land of Cockaigne*, p. 198. Cf. chapter 16.

14. Cf. Schöne, *Götterzeichen, Liebeszauber, Satanskult*, pp. 154ff.

15. [I have substituted "tail" for Atkins's "coattails" in this line. Trans.]

16. Cf. Horst Kurnitzky, *Triebstruktur des Geldes*.

17. Pp. 189ff.

18. Cf. Hörisch, *Gott, Geld und Glück*, p. 73.

19. A travesty of Matthew 25:32ff.: "And before him shall be gathered all nations; and he shall separate them one from another, as a shepherd divideth *his* sheep from the goats" [emphasis J. H.].

20. *Faust I (Paralipomena)*, ed. Schöne, p. 553. [Translations from Schöne's *Paralipomena* are my own. Trans.]

21. *Paralipomena*, 50, p. 554.

22. On the metaphor of the "economic miracle," cf. the comparative study on economic success stories from different countries by Alain Peyrefitte, *Du "miracle" en économie*.

23. Cf. with the following the instructive study by Jacques Le Goff, *Wucherzins*,

which also offers further evidence and examples of the intensity of the discussion of interest, usury, and procreation in the High and Late Middle Ages.

24. This prohibition, recognized today in "Islamic banking systems" in Saudi Arabia, Pakistan, and Iran, is circumvented to a certain extent by simple tricks of nomenclature. The banks do not charge "interest" on loans but rather a processing fee, or something along those lines.

25. *Summa Theologiae*, Secunda Secundae, Question 78, Article 1, p. 235, cited by LeGoff, *Wucherzins*, p. 28.

26. *Nicomachean Ethics*, V, 8, 1132 b 31.

27. *Politik*, I.10, 1258 b. Otmar Issing purports, with respect to the "contra naturam" argument, that "In fact, no other conclusion of Aristoteles' has had such immediate as well as long-term effects" ("Aristoteles," p. 117).

28. Cited by LeGoff, p. 28.

29. Making theology conform to the economy with respect to the interest question was usually attempted with the help of the parable of the talents (Matthew 25: 13–30). In order to use it, however, one must ignore its allegorical aspect and take it literally. It is revealing that the reversal of the classic critique of interest also appeals to "nature" in its argument and evokes perverse associations: money may not fall into "sterile hands" (François Quesnay), it may not "go on strike" (Silvio Gesell), but must (like blood) circulate fruitfully. It may and even should propagate itself—but only "heterosexually," that is, in contact with work and natural wealth, not just in contact with itself.

30. My thanks to Masaki Nakamasa for these remarks.

31. On the critique of interest, cf. also *The Inferno*, XVII.

32. Ezra Pound, Canto XLV.

33. Cf. Rolf Engert's interpretation, which addresses the perverse implications, though not the functional aspects, of Shakespeare's analysis of money: *Silvio Gesell*.

34. Cf. the repudiation of money in *Timon of Athens*. On the historically extraordinarily effective distinction between friends and brothers, from whom one may not accept interest, and the "others" (non-brothers, non-friends—e.g., Jews), from whom one may exact interest and who for their part may demand it as well, cf. the classic study by Benjamin Nelssons, *The Idea of Usury*. It demonstrates forcefully that modernity converts economically to the idea of the universalized Other. Alter is for ego, at least in an economic sense, always a stranger at the start. When it comes to money, friendship ends, *homo homini lupus est*.

35. Pp. 943f.

36. And to that in Schiller's *The Maid of Orleans*: "*Du Chatel*. There isn't any / More money, Sire, left in your treasury. *Charles*. Then get some" (I, 475).

37. [In the German, "Jupiter" replaces "Luna fein" rather than just "Luna." "Fein" means "fine" and contributes more to meter than to meaning. It is not rendered into English in Atkins's translation. Trans.]

38. Cf. on this point, the study by Maximilian Beck, *Der Geiz als Wurzel der faustisch-dynamischen Kultur.*

39. *Poetry and Truth*, Goethe's *Collected Works*, vol. 3, p. 77. Cf. Jutta Prasse, "Kästchen."

40. Cf. on this, C. Kerényi, *Eleusis: Archetypal Image of Mother and Daughter*, p. 106.

41. Cf. the relationships between this letter and the symbolism of the little box in the *Wanderjahre*. Arthur Henkel, *Entsagung*, p. 89.

42. ["Big Jimmy" refers to money; cf. the passages from *Fellow Culprits* in chapter 3. Trans.]

Excursus

1. Cf. on this in general, Sigrid Schade, Monica Wagner, and Sigrid Weigel, eds., *Allegorien und Geschlechterdifferenz.*

2. *The Republic of Plato*, 556 e.

3. See the metaphor of the body in Ephesians 1:23 and Colossians 1:18 as well.

4. Cf. Otto G. Oexle, "Tria genera hominum."

5. According to Jacob Taubes, publisher of the volume *Der Fürst dieser Welt.*

6. Cf. on this, the excellent article "Organ" in the dictionary, *Geschichtliche Grundbegriffe* that, to be sure, consistently ignores the question of the sex of corporations, even in Paul's passage quoted here, and does not cite the Romantic speculation (above all Novalis's) on the subject either. Similarly the article "Körperschaft," in the *Historiches Wörterbuch der Philosophie.*

7. [The German for "subsidiary" is "Tochtergesellschaft," literally, "daughter company." Trans.]

8. P. 62.

9. [Kießling was a general in the German Army who was erroneously suspected of being homosexual and dismissed from the service on those grounds. Trans.]

10. *Der Spiegel*, no. 35, August 28, 1989, p. 62.

11. Klaus Theweleit has collected a wealth of such material in his *Male Fantasies;* see also Jacques Derrida, *The Post Card.*

12. ["Unter den Talaren / Muff von tausend Jahren," literally, "Under the gowns / the mustiness of a thousand years" was a slogan of the student protests of the 1960s, referring to the failure of the university to adapt to new circumstances. Trans.]

13. [Literally, "Father of the Doctorate." This is the German term for dissertation director. Trans.]

14. On the following, see Curtius, *European Literature and the Latin Middle Ages.* For more detail see Otto Weinrich's afterword to Aristophanes' *Sämtliche Komödien* (Zürich, 1968), and Werner Dobras's *Plaudereien vor dem Bücherschrank.* My thanks to Reinhard Häußler for this valuable classical reference.

15. *The Poems of Hesiod*, p 27. Similarly, Pindar, *Nemean Odes*, III, 1.

16. Cited by Heinz Weis, *Iocosa*, p. 22 (the source is not noted).

17. *Anthologia Palatina IX*, 192, 1–2.

18. Sueton, *Vita Vergilii*, 22.

19. Ovid, *Tristia III*, 14, 13f.

20. *Elective Affinities*, pp. 239f.

21. [This is one of the novellas from *The People of Seldwyla.* It might be translated as "The Smith of his Fortune." Trans.]

22. *Die tageszeitung*, June 30, 1987.

Chapter 7

[The translation I am using for the epigraph from *Peter Schlemihl* says "beating the clock" instead of "overcoming time." In the context of the author's discussion, it is important to capture what the latter rendering conveys. Trans.]

1. [A-13 designates a salary level—and a high one—for employees of the German government. One might say "six-figure income." Trans.]

2. [*Laib* (loaf) is a homophone of the German word for body, *Leib*. Trans.]

3. Bloy, *Auslegung der Gemeinplätze*, p. 38; cf. p. 346, with its lapidary "Der liebe Gott ist Geld" ("God is money"). Bloy's entire, unique "Exégèses" are intended to be, and must be, understood in the spirit of the title: they interpret the texture of freedom of religion in such a way that its unacceptability should jump out at the reader.

4. Cf. Weber, "Protestant Asceticism and the Spirit of Capitalism," in *Selections in Translation*, p. 141. [The original is titled "Asketischer Protestantismus und kapitalistischer Geist," in *Soziologie, Weltgeschichtliche Analysen, Politik*. Trans.]

5. *The Writings of Benjamin Franklin*, vol. 2, p. 370. Quoted by Max Weber in *The Protestant Ethic and the Spirit of Capitalism*, p. 50 (*Die protestantische Ethik*).

6. "The Way to Wealth," *The Writings of Benjamin Franklin*, vol. 3, pp. 417–18. Quoted by Needleman, *Money and the Meaning of Life*, p. 142; emphasis Franklin's.

7. *Doctor Faustus*, pp. 229–30.

8. Of course, everything has its price: this perspective is more insightful philosophically, but poetically it is clearly less interesting.

9. Hugo von Hofmannsthal, *Der Rosenkavalier, Gesammelte Werke— Dramen*, vol. 5, p. 43. [Trans. from Hofmannsthal, *Selected Plays and Libretti*, p. 428.]

10. [I deviate from the translation here: "Pater" has been rendered as "parson," but "priest" is more accurate, as is reflected in the ensuing remarks. Trans.]

11. [The "Prater" is an amusement park on the outskirts of Vienna. Trans.]

12. *The Cavalier of the Rose*, p. 437. On the motif of time, cf. among others, P. A. Stenberg, *Der Rosenkavalier.*

13. This is a common motif; the scent of Madeleine, which carries Marcel into the past in Proust's *Recherche du temps perdu*, has become the classic example.

14. Hegel, *Phenomenology of Spirit*, p. 359.

15. This according to Augustine's classic analysis in the *Confessions*, book 11.

16. Hegel, *Vorlesungen über die Philosophie der Religion II, Werke*, vol. 17, p. 320.

17. Hofmannsthal, "Terzinen—über Vergänglichkeit," in *Gedichte, Dramen I*, p. 21. [Trans. by Michael Hamburger in Hofmannsthal, *Poems and Verse Plays*, p. 29.]

18. An allegorical prop, the handkerchief that Sophie drops, has, of course, the last, silent, temporal word. On the double meaning of the concept "Ewigkeit" (eternity), cf. Michael Theunissen, *Negative Theologie der Zeit*, p. 310: "The first, non-aeonian eternity is found beyond time; it creates its opposite as an eternity that is nothing but the Other of time. The second, aeonian eternity appears in contrast, although it exceeds time, in time; in it time is—as Hegel would say—the Other of itself."

19. Cf. the classic study by Emil Staiger, *Die Zeit als Einbildungskraft des Dichters*. It loses its potential right in the introduction when it pronounces that the sense of "literary history" resides not in the accentuation of the historical changes in experience, but in its "contribution . . . to general anthropology" (p. 9). This is precisely what literature does not do; it observes, on the contrary, how all phantasmata of an ahistorical "general anthropology" break down in view of the changes in human conceptions.

20. The changes and dislocations in the conception of time have most recently become a fashionable topic (without a doubt justifiably so!) once again. To mention only two instructive volumes of essays: Martin Bergelt and Hortensia Völckers, eds., *Zeit-Räume—Raumzeiten—Zeitträume*, and Georg C. Tholen and Michael O. Scholl, eds., *Zeit-Zeichen.*

21. Cited here on the basis of the photograph of the gravestone in Ilse Schnack, *R. M. Rilke—Leben und Werk im Bild*, p. 251. [Trans. from *The Selected Poetry of Rainer Maria Rilke*, p. 279.]

22. Celan's poem "Psalm" obviously links up with Rilke's epitaph. Many of Celan's interpreters overlook the enthusiastic moments of his lyric that are intended to glorify and praise the "no man's rose"—as the groundless, meaningful, and beautiful gift of earthly existence so gruesomely rejected, especially in the twentieth century.

23. Michael Theunissen, *Negative Theologie der Zeit*, pp. 45ff.

24. Cf. Derrida, *Given Time: I. Counterfeit Money*. [In German "there is" is rendered by "es gibt," the verb being "geben," "to give," so that this statement reads in the original as "it 'gives' no time" rather than "there 'is' no time"—hence the remark on the "gift without giver." See chapter 13. Trans.]

25. *The Cavalier of the Rose*, p. 482.

26. This and the following citations are from Rilke's *The Notebooks of Malte Laurids Brigge* (p. 148).

27. [The German for "dizziness" and for "swindle" are the same: "Schwindel." Trans.]

28. Cf. on this topic Georg Braungart, "Die Fremdheit der Sprache am Beginn der Moderne."

29. In his book *Momo*, which is certainly not just a children's book, Michael Ende takes up this motif and fills it out tremendously.

30. Cf. Dirk Baecker, *Womit handeln Banken?* p. 17.

31. [The German term for "promissory note" is "Zahlungsversprechen," quite literally, a "promise to pay." Trans.]

32. ["Shift to the long bank" is an expression meaning "to delay." Trans.]

33. Cf. Luhmann, *Die Wirtschaft der Gesellschaft*, p. 145: "Banks have the essential privilege of being able to sell their own debts at a profit." Also Baecker, *Womit handeln Banken?* p. 60: "The banks are always seen as large creditors and rarely as large debtors. Actually, however, the greatest risk the bank faces resides in its passive business, that is, in the possibility that at any moment the bank's many depositors may demand cash for its promissory notes."

34. Heidegger quotes Nietzsche's translation of this passage ("The Anaximander Fragment," p. 13). [The passage here is thus an English translation of Nietzsche's translation.]

35. [As noted in chapter 5, *Schuldner* and *Gläubiger*, debtor and creditor, also mean sinner and believer, respectively. Trans.]

36. This last is one of Thomas Mann's favorite themes, as a glance at the figure of Naphta in *The Magic Mountain* or at Adrian Leverkuhn's diabolical purchase of time in *Doctor Faustus* shows.

37. Georg Franck, "Aufmerksamkeit, Zeit, Raum," in *Zeit-Räume*, p. 80.

38. Benjamin, *Das Passagen-Werk, Gesammelte Schriften*, V/1, p. 120. On modernity as the age of acceleration and mobilization, cf. the most recent Anthony Giddens, *The Consequences of Modernity*.

CHAPTER 8

1. Cf. Freud, "Negation," in the *Standard Edition*, 19:235–40, and Lacan, *Écrits*, pp. 369–400.

2. Cf. the articles "Negation" and "Negation der Negation" in the *Historisches Wörterbuch der Philosophie*, vol. 6, pp. 667f. and 686ff, respecitively.

3. Heidegger, *The Essence of Reasons (Vom Wesen des Grundes)*, pp. 126, 127 (Heidegger's emphasis).

4. Arnold Gehlen, *Man: His Nature and Place in the World*, p. 13. Cf. also the explanations of "man's chronic state of need" (p. 49). Gehlen's anthropology makes no secret of the fact that it is less an anthropology than a doctrine by and for institutions, for whom it suggests a "Menschenfassung" ("universal theory of man") (Walter Seitter).

5. Even gaps in research usually only occur to those who want to apply for a stipend or fellowship.

6. *Negative Anthropologie*, p. 295.

7. *Lyceum*—Fragment 80: "I'm disappointed in not finding in Kant's family tree of basic concepts the category 'almost', a category that has surely accomplished, and spoiled, as much in the world and in literature as any other. In the mind of natural skeptics it colors all other concepts and intuitions." [Translation from Friedrich Schlegel, *Philosophical Fragments*, p. 10.]

8. Without shortages there would be no logic of existence and no existent logic, as the very beginning of Hegel's *Logic* demonstrates.

9. Luhmann, *Die Wirtschaft der Gesellschaft*, pp. 46f.

10. Sohn-Rethel, *Soziologische Theorie der Erkenntnis*, p. 39.

11. [From the *Sonnets to Orpheus*, I, 7. The title is Stephen Mitchell's translation. See p. 235 in *The Selected Poetry of Rainer Maria Rilke*. Trans.]

12. The reference to Herbert Marcuse's "Über den affirmativen Charakter der Kunst" is obligatory here.

13. [*Überfluß* is the original term; I have used "excess" most often, and on occasion "abundance" or "superfluity." Trans.]

14. Georges Bataille, *The Accursed Share*, I, p. 21.

15. Cf. on this topic, Heinz Schlaffer, *Faust II*.

16. Thus the stage directions prior to verse 5178.

17. [Translation by Michael Hamburger, in Goethe, *Selected Poems*, p. 267.]

18. Quoted in Nestroy, *Komödien in drei Bänden*, vol. I, p. xx (preface).

19. Cf. W. Hogrebe, *Prädikation und Genesis*, p. 127.

20. Nestroy, *Komödien in drei Bänden*, p. 204 (I/5).

21. Ibid., p. 241 (III/7). Knieriem's not-so-curt commentary on Peppi's lack of discernment in matters of astronomy simply cannot go unquoted: "She doesn't believe in comets, she'll roll her eyes.—I figured it out a long time ago. The astrological fire of the sun's circle reaches Orion's golden number from the constellation of the solar system to the universe of the parallel axes by way of the fixed-star quadrants to the ellipse of the eclipse; as a result the next comet must crash into the earth through the diagonals of approximation of the perpendicular circles. This calculation is as clear as shoe polish. Of course, not everyone has science under their belt like I do; but even the less educated can observe enough things every day that clearly prove that the world will not exist much longer. In short, one sees, above as well as below, that we are headed straight for the end."

CHAPTER 9

1. *Werke*, vol. 1, p. 527.

2. Cf. on the history of the topos, Aleida Assmann, "Pflug, Schwert, Feder," and Lutz Köpnick, *Nothungs Modernität*, pp. 50ff. and chapter 3 ("Zur Ästhetik des Schwertes in der Literatur des neunzehnten Jahrhunderts"); though they do not mention Chamisso's lines.

3. François Lyotard, *The Differend*, p. 178 (par. 253); cf. par. 263: "The only insurmountable obstacle that the hegemony of the economic genre comes up against is

the heterogeneity of phrase regimens and of genres of discourse. This is because there is not 'language' and 'Being,' but occurrences" (p. 181).

4. *Tagebuch 1953–55*, January 1, 1954, p. 176; Thomas Mann returns to this coarse remark once again (p. 186).

5. *Der Gute Gerhart*.

6. Sonja Zöller, *Kaiser, Kaufmann und die Macht des Geldes*.

7. Cf. Irmgard Gephart, *Geben und Nehmen*.

8. On the role of the ministry of state in the epic of the Middle Ages, cf. Gert Kaiser, *Textauslegung und gesellschaftliche Selbstdeutung*.

9. *Geld-Abenteuer—Extravagante Geschichten aus dem europäischen Wirtschaftsleben*.

10. Hegel, *Vorlesungen über die Aesthetik III, Werke* 14, p. 393.

11. *Werke*, vol. 1, p. 762.

12. Cf. on this subject, the introductory considerations of this book (chapter 2) and Adorno's *Aesthetic Theory*, p. 42: "Collective labor is conceivable in art; the extinguishing of its immanent subjectivity is not. Any change in this would depend on the total social consciousness having reached a level where it no longer conflicts with the most progressive consciousness, which today is exclusively that of the individual."

13. *Gesammelte Werke*, vol. 2, p. 65. [*Bertolt Brecht: Poems & Songs from the Plays*, no. 103.]

14. A recent exception is Christiaan Hart-Nibbrig's study, *Übergänge* (chapter 3: "Tausch und Täuschung: Geld, literarisch").

15. This is the formulation Kenneth Burke uses in his study *A Grammar of Motives*; cf. p. 111: "Money is . . . a 'technical substitute for God,' in that 'God' represented the unitary substance in which all human diversity of motives was grounded." This stands in contrast to older literature—to which of course newer literature is indebted; cf., for example, Wilhelm Weber, *Geld, Glaube, Gesellschaft*. Burke calls attention to alliances, and to joint ventures, but definitely not to competition between religion and the economy.

16. ["Gläubiger" is the German term, and it means, as mentioned above, both "creditor" and "true believer." Trans.]

17. ["Lobpreis" or the "singing, extolling or glorification of God" is a compound word whose root "Preis" means "price" as well as "praise." Trans.]

18. [The German word "Messe" means "mass" as well as "fair" or "market." Trans.]

19. Cf. on the mediating function of money, the chapter titled "Geld als Medium" in N. Bolz's *Theorie der neuen Medien*.

20. Cf. for more detail on this point, Hörisch, *Brot und Wein*, pp. 138ff.

21. Cf. on this, Hörisch's "Die Tugend und der Weltlauf in Lessings bürgerlichen Trauerspielen," in *Die andere Goethezeit*.

22. According to George Thomson's extensive and painstakingly developed thesis in *Die ersten Philosophen*.

23. Kant, "Metaphysical Foundations of Morals," p. 182 in *The Philosophy of Kant*.

24. Adorno, *Minima Moralia*, pp. 79–80.

25. Cf. Theo Stemmler, *Stemmlers kleine Stil-Lehre*, p. 196.

26. Cf. Luhmann, *Love as Passion*, pp. 20f.

27. Richard Wagner, *Götterdämmerung*, Prelude.

28. Cf. on this point, Hörisch, *Gott, Geld und Glück*, pp. 83f.

29. Shakespeare, *The Merchant of Venice*, 5.1.179–214.

30. [In German, "leiden" and "Leidenschaft," respectively. Trans.]

31. Adorno, "On the Classicism of Goethe's *Iphigenie,*" *Notes to Literature,* vol. 2, p. 165.

32. Shakespeare as essentially the inventor of the famous "pork cycle" of the science of business administration: increased demand for pork makes its price climb—therefore more farmers raise pigs; the price for pork falls as a result of the surplus which quickly accumulates—the farmers raise fewer pigs. . . . Shakespeare's model is more complex than this ABC's of business management. It does not concern merely internal regulatory systems, but irritations between subsystems as well (such as religion and the economy).

33. [This is a reference to Heinrich Kleist's *Michael Kohlhaas.* Trans.]

34. Schwanitz, *Systemtheorie und Literatur,* p. 243.

35. Samuel Butler, *Erewhon,* p. 241. [Cited from the appendix to the 1981 reprinting of the 1872 edition showing changes made in the 1901 edition; p. 136 of 1901 edition. Trans]

36. "Über die Unverständlichkeit," *Kritische Ausgabe,* II, p. 365.

37. In *Büchmanns geflügelte Worte* this saying is traced back to Psalm 12:6: "The words of the Lord *are* pure words: *as* silver tried in a furnace of earth, purified seven times" (emphasis in original). This obviously has, however, a different meaning than the current epigrammatic truth. In G. W. Freytag's collection of 1838–43, *Arabum Proverbia,* it says "Narratio argenta, silentium vero aureum est" (vol. III/1, p. 92, no. 548—according to *Büchmanns geflügelte Worte*). This corresponds more closely to the German saying, with its melancholy that is easy to miss—"narratio" means, of course, "story": the monetary communication is more important (weightier) than the narrative.

38. Butler, *Erewhon,* pp. 169 and 247.

39. Ralf Schiebler, *Frankfurter Allgemeine Zeitung,* April 29, 1995.

40. Adorno, *Minima Moralia,* p. 132.

CHAPTER 10

1. [Money rules the world. Trans.]

2. Heidegger, "The Thing," in *Poetry, Language, Thought,*" p. 181.

3. The following links up with my earlier works on Sohn-Rethel's social genetic epistemology, which reconstructs Sohn-Rethel's argument in more detail. Cf. Hörisch, "Identitätszwang und Tauschabstraktion," "Die Krise des Bewußtseins," "Die beiden Seiten einer Münze."

4. Adorno and Sohn-Rethel, *Briefwechsel,* p. 24.

5. Cf. Enrik Lauer's critique of Sohn-Rethel, *Literarischer Monetarismus.*

6. Blumenberg, *Höhlenausgänge,* p. 76.

7. Novalis, *Schriften,* vol. 3, pp. 378f. Cf. on this note, Hörisch, "Herrscherwort, Geld und geltende Sätze."

8. *Green Henry,* p. 585. Cf. Hörisch, "Gott, Geld und Glück," pp. 120ff.

9. [The German "Hypothesen- und Hypothekenschein" plays with the similarity of the words for hypothesis and mortgage (*Hypothek*) as well as with the word "Schein," which can mean banknote but also appearance. Cf. chapter 1. Trans.]

10. [*Vermöge eines Vermögens.* Walter Kaufmann, Nietzsche's translator, notes that *Vermöge eines Vermögens* means "by virtue of some virtue, or by means of a means." *Vermögen* indeed means capacity or faculty, but also fortune, wealth, property; hence the author's ensuing comments. Trans.]

11. Nietzsche, *Beyond Good and Evil,* p. 18.

12. In his powerful philosophical-historical work, *Aenesidemus oder über die Fundamente der von Herr Professor Reinhold in Jena gelieferten Elementarphilosophie* (1792), Schulze criticizes Reinhold for assuming, because of the existence of ideas (*Vorstellungen*), that there exists a "capacity" for ideas (*Vorstellungs-"Vermögen"*), pp. 97ff.—a critique that had a profound influence on Herbart and on Schulze's young student, Schopenhauer. Manfred Frank called this passage and its historical significance to my attention.

13. Hegel, *Lectures on the History of Philosophy*, vol. 3, p. 443.

14. Nietzsche, *The Genealogy of Morals*, p. 202.

15. The lists of those who have had an intuition, however diffuse, about the connection between the abstraction of thought and of exchange can of course be lengthened. It would include, to name just a few, G. W. Leibniz, who characterized money as "notes of exchange of understanding"; Thomas Hobbes, who understood non-dictatorial words as "the money of fools"; John Locke, who was directly involved in currency and national banking issues; Jean-Jacques Rousseau, who repeatedly (in *Emile* and in *The Government of Poland*, among others) analyzed and criticized money as the medium of social synthesis (cf. Christiaan Hart-Nibbrig, *Übergänge*, pp. 88ff.); and Paul Valéry, who has his Monsieur Teste identify money as the objective spirit of society.

16. Sohn-Rethel, *Warenform und Denkform*, pp. 35f.

17. Rudolf-Wolfgang Müller offered, in his *Geld und Geist*, similar theories (though inadequately demonstrated) in connection with Sohn-Rethel.

18. Canetti, *Crowds and Power*, p. 183; cf. p. 90: "A man identifies himself with the unit of his money; doubt cast on it offends him. . . . He feels slighted and humiliated by the lowering of the value of his monetary unit and, if this process is accelerated and inflation occurs, it is *men* who are depreciated until they find themselves in formations which can only be equated with flight-crowds." Canetti even establishes a connection between the German experience of inflation and the industrial mass murder of the Jews: "In its treatment of Jews National Socialism repeated the process of inflation with great precision. First they were attacked as wicked and dangerous, as enemies; then they were more and more depreciated; . . . and finally they were treated literally as vermin. . . . The world is still horrified and shaken by the fact that the Germans could go so far. . . . It might not have been possible to get them to do so if, a few years before, they had not been through an inflation" (p. 188).

19. Freud, *Totem und Taboo*, p. 73 in vol. 13 of the *Standard Edition*.

20. Adorno, *Minima Moralia*, *Gesammelte Schriften*, vol. 4, p. 294. Cf. also the continuation of Adorno's remarks: "Thinkers who avoid paranoid characteristics—such a one was Georg Simmel . . . remain without effect or are quickly forgotten." [These remarks are from the appendix, which was not included in the published translation of the work, hence the translation is my own. Trans.]

21. "I remained an outsider all my life with my idée fixe," as he says in the preface to *Intellectual and Manual Labour*, p. xiii.

22. Sohn-Rethel, *Intellectual and Manual Labour*, pp. 20ff.

23. The page numbers in parentheses refer here and henceforth to the first (A) and second (B) versions, respectively, of the *Critique of Pure Reason*.

24. Dieter Henrich, *The Unity of Reason*, p. 198.

25. [Kant's translator renders "es"—the grammatically neuter form of "it"—as "this basis" (*der Grund*). "Der Grund" is grammatically masculine, which would require

the pronoun "er" instead of "es"; indeed, in the academic edition of Kant's work, "er" appears. This is important in the author's ensuing remarks. Trans.]

26. Luhmann, *Die Wirtschaft der Gesellschaft*, p. 17.

27. Cf. on this topic, Lauer, *Literarischer Monetarismus*, pp. 111ff.

28. [*Einheit, Vielheit, Allheit*. For Werner S. Pluhar's glossary that accompanies his translation of Kant's *Critique of Pure Reason*, upon which I rely heavily in this and other passages, I am most grateful. Most of the rest of the terms used in this paragraph are cognates: *Realität, Negation, Limitation; Relation, Kausalität; Modalität; Schematismus*. Where this is not the case, I will continue to note the German in parentheses. Trans.]

29. Hegel, *Lectures on the History of Philosophy*, vol. 3, p. 443.

30. The new mythology postulated by Manfred Frank and others is functionally superfluous in this respect. "We must come to terms with the unity of our . . . world, . . . because we cannot reach back to a previously existing and secured universal independent of the subject." Thus reads the grounds for the mythological-communicative postulate (*Die Unhintergehbarkeit von Individualität*, p. 120). In the ontosemiological major media, however, this universality is always already present.

31. Luhmann, *Wirtschaft*, p. 190.

32. Cf. on this, Gunnar Heinsohn, *Privateigentum*.

33. Tacitus, "Germania," in *Tacitus: Historical Works*, vol. 2, p. 31.

34. *Philosophy and the Mirror of Nature*, p. 148.

35. Cf. Jürgen Habermas, *The Theory of Communicative Action*, vol. 1, pp. 366ff. In parrying the arguments of Lukács and Sohn-Rethel, Habermas entangles himself in a remarkable formulation: "The abstraction of exchange is only [!] the historical form in which identifying thought develops its world-historical influence and determines the forms of intercourse of capitalist society"—it is otherwise obviously not an issue deserving attention. The genesis of the "identifying thought" that lends the abstraction of exchange its form (a strange reversal of Adorno's thesis) is not of interest to Habermas (p. 378).

36. Sohn-Rethel, "Zur kritischen Liquidierung des Apriorismus."

37. Often enough negatively—as for example in the *Iliad* (6236): "The swapping of Glauko's gold armor for Diomedes' bronze armor is often interpreted as a sign of confusion visited upon Glauko by the gods" (Hans-Jürgen Horn, "Gold," in the *Reallexikon für Antike und Christentum*, col. 896, where there are additional insightful references to the "aura" of money in antiquity as well).

38. *The Gift*, p. xiv.

39. Ibid., p. 69.

40. Ibid., p. 45.

41. *The Primitive Races of Mankind*.

42. Berhard Strecker, *Geben und Nehmen*, p. 4.

43. Marcus Sahlins, *Stone Age Economics*.

44. Wilhelm Capelle, *Die Vorsokratiker*, p. 143.

45. Hegel, *Phenomenology of Spirit*, p. 145.

46. Bachofen, *Mother Right*, p. 109, in *Myth, Religion, and Mother Right*.

47. Cf. Kurnitzky, *Triebstruktur des Geldes*, chapter 6.

48. Cf. Heinrich, *Arbeiten mit Ödipus*, pp. 193ff.

49. "Socrates," in *Walter Benjamin: Selected Writings*, vol. 1, p. 53.

50. Cited by Jan-Christoph Hauschild, *Büchner*, p. 319.

51. [Car manufactured in the German Democratic Republic. Trans.]

52. Marx, *Capital I*, p. 52.

53. [*Realisieren*, from which the term *Derealisierung* is coined, means not only to materialize, but also to purchase with cash. Trans.]

54. Cf. on this subject the characteristic analyses of Ernst Bockelmann.

55. Cf. on this, among others, Sédillot, *Muscheln*, pp. 185ff.

56. Sohn-Rethel, *Soziologische Theorie der Erkenntnis*, p. 39.

57. Sohn-Rethel to Adorno, August 15, 1937; Adorno and Sohn-Rethel, *Briefwechsel*, p. 71.

58. *Berliner Simulation*, pp. 93f.

CHAPTER 11

1. Benjamin to Adorno on June 19, 1936; Adorno and Benjamin, *Briefwechsel*, p. 336.

2. Adorno and Sohn-Rethel, *Briefwechsel*, p. 32.

3. Ibid., pp. 23f.; the final citation is from the letter of August 15, 1937, p. 71.

4. Adorno and Benjamin, *Briefwechsel*, p. 213.

5. Adorno to Benjamin on August 2, 1935; *The Correspondence of Walter Benjamin*, p. 495.

6. [Pronounced very similarly to the name, Sohn-Rethel, "So 'n Rätsel" translates as "such an enigma." Trans.]

7. Adorno and Benjamin, *Briefwechsel*, p. 307. Benjamin adopted this play on his name (p. 309).

8. ["Abschleifen" means, indeed, to wear out in the sense of overexpose, but also to polish. Trans.]

9. *The Essential Frankfurt School Reader*, pp. 297–98.

10. Benjamin, *The Correspondence of Walter Benjamin*, p. 591. Letter of December 9, 1938.

11. [Adorno is alluding to Benjamin's essay "The Work of Art in the Age of Mechanical Reproduction." Trans.]

12. Adorno and Benjamin, *Briefwechsel*, p. 398.

13. Ibid.

14. *Gesammelte Schriften*, I/2, p. 681.

15. *Correspondence*, p. 587.

16. Ibid., p. 588.

17. *Passagen-Werk, Gesammelte Schriften*, V, p. 473.

18. [The author refers to an old pun in German: "die Ware" (commodity) [is] "das Wahre" (the True). Trans.]

19. The word "fetish" can be traced back to the Portuguese "feitico," which in turn can be traced back to the Latin "facere" (to make) or "facticius" (artificially produced). The term "fétichisme" was coined by Charles de Brosse in 1760 as a designation for the cult and "belief of the negroes of Africa." Cf. the insightful text by Liliane Weissberg, "Gedanken zur 'Weiblichkeit.' "

20. Cf. V. S. Naipaul, "The Crocodiles of Yamoussoukro," in *Finding the Center*, pp. 131ff.

21. Freud, "Fetishism," *Standard Edition*, vol. 21, pp. 152–53.

22. Lacan, *Écrits: A Selection*, pp. 281ff. [The German words for "bearing witness," "procreating," and "engendering" are closely related and overlap semantically: "bezeugen," "zeugen," "erzeugen," respectively. The author is playing with this in this passage. Also see note 8 to chapter 6. Trans.]

23. *The Origin of German Tragic Drama*, p. 165.

24. Ibid., p. 166.

25. [In German, revealed religions are "*Offenbar*ungsreligionen"—thus the author plays with the term in the ensuing commentary on its "obviously" not being "obvious" ("offenbar nicht offenbar"), my emphasis. See chapter 1. Trans.]

26. With respect to Kant's reproach that the Catholic conception of bread and wine is "fetishistic," see Hörisch, *Brot und Wein*, chapter 8.

27. Act 4, scene 3.

28. *The German Ideology*, p. 102.

29. Derrida, *Specters of Marx*, p. 42.

30. Ibid., p. 45

31. Benjamin, *Zentralpark*, in *Gesammelte Schriften*, I/2, p. 660.

32. In his *Phänomenologie der Entgeisterung*, Robert Menasse inverts Hegel's novel of the world spirit in an ingenious way. Sohn-Rethel's arguments assume a pivotal position in it. To my joy, my early presentation on Sohn-Rethel has found its way into this witty novel of the spirit (cf. pp. 27ff. and Hörisch, "Identitätszwang und Tauschabstraktion," pp. 50ff.)

33. Marx, *Capital I*, p. 72.

34. Marx, *Capital III*, p. 815.

35. Cf. Lukács, "Reification and the Consciousness of the Proletariat," in his *History and Class Consciousness*.

36. *The Correspondence of Walter Benjamin*, p. 498.

37. Adorno and Benjamin, *Briefwechsel*, p. 192. A strange sentence, at first glance. For one can hardly speak of the "hesitant introduction of the names" in describing the famous first sentence of *Elective Affinities*: "Edward—as we shall call a well-to-do baron in the prime of his life—[Edward] had been . . ." (p. 93). The careful reader will take issue with Adorno's argument: the immediate doubled naming of the names is as forceful as the lordly narrative attitude—"as we shall call." It reacts powerfully to the erosion of symbolic images of the world. [I have inserted the repeated "Edward," omitted by Judith Ryan, translator of *Elective Affinities*. Trans.]

38. [The name of this character, "Mittler," means "mediator." Trans.]

39. Cf. on this point, Hörisch, "Goethes bestes Buch," in *Die andere Goethezeit*.

40. Adorno to Benjamin, November 10, 1938, *Briefwechsel, 1928–1940*, p. 370.

41. Goethe, *The Journeyman Years*, p. 197.

42. *Gesammelte Schriften*, I/2, p. 697.

43. *The Journeyman Years*, p. 298.

44. "Wunder über Wunder," p. 648.

45. Ibid., p. 654; cf. G. Neumann's notes in the commentary of his edition of *Wanderjahre*, pp. 907f.

46. Heinz Schlaffer, *Faust II*.

47. Benjamin, *Gesammelte Schriften*, I/2, p. 686.

48. *Gesammelte Schriften*, V, p. 422.

49. *Scientific Studies*, trans. Douglas Miller, p. 24.

50. "Faust, Geld," p. 174.

51. Benjamin, *Zentralpark*, *Gesammelte Schriften*, I/2, p. 666.

52. Benjamin, *Passagen-Werk*, *Gesammelte Schriften*, V, p. 274.

53. Benjamin to Adorno, February 23, 1939; *The Correspondence of Walter Benjamin*, p. 598.

54. Cited by Hamacher, "Faust, Geld," p. 175. For further relevant Goethe quotes see Lauer, *Literarischer Monetarismus*.

55. Thus reads a variant of Goethe's text, the Herald's answer to the Young Charioteer (*Faust*, ed. A. Schöne, p. 607; cf. Hamacher, p. 157).

CHAPTER 12

1. The drama fragment was written between August 22 and October 22, 1806, during the Battle of the Weser; it was published posthumously for the first time, albeit without the poems "Gesang auf dem Schiffe" and "Katzennatur," in 1895.

2. Adelbert von Chamisso, *Fortunati Glückseckel and Wunschhütlein*, *Werke*, vol. 1, p. 612. This poem was published under the title "Nach der Abfahrt" in the "Jahrbüchlein deutscher Gedichte auf 1815."

3. George Steiner, *Real Presences*, p. 119 and elsewhere.

4. Cf. Thomas Mann, who has his Joseph figure reveal the "mystery of dreaming": "the interpretation is earlier than the dream, and when we dream, the dream proceeds from the interpretation" (*Joseph the Provider*, p. 59).

5. Chamisso, *Fortunati Glückseckel*, pp. 616f.

6. Cf. Steiner, *Real Presences*.

7. Cf. Hörisch, *Die Wut des Verstehens*.

8. Cf. on this, the instructive work by Klaus Reichert, *Fortuna oder die Beständigkeit des Wechsels*, which highlights the moody-womanly aspects of the money motif in Dekker's piece.

9. The material of the Fortunatus chapbook of 1509 was adapted not only by Chamisso but also by August Wilhelm Schlegel (1801), Ludwig Uhland (1814, unfinished), Ludwig Tieck (1817, with its roughly 500 pages the lengthiest text of his *Phantasus*), and by Viennese literati such as Matthäus von Collin (1814), Matthäus Stegmayer (1810), Ferdinand Raimund (1823), and Lembert (1829), among others. Cf. the article "Fortunatus" in Frenzel's *Stoffe der Weltliteratur.*

10. Cf. for a current view on this point, Ernst Behler, "Die italienische Renaissance in der Literaturtheorie der Brüder Schlegel," and Peter Rau, "Die Vorbereitung der romantischen Interpretation der Renaissance bei Karl Philipp Moritz."

11. Hegel, *Vorlesungen über die Philosophie der Geschichte*, *Werke* 12, p. 529.

12. The theological charm of psychoanalysis lies in the fact that it promises for individual lives what progressive philosophies of history promise for the entire human race—the removal of traumatizing primal scenes or the nightmare of misspent history that burdens the living—and that means nothing less than changing the past, checking the presumably irreversible flow of time. Rescinding history means, to the Romantics, checking the recently initiated conversion which has, ever since 1789, taken hold in a modern way, from the decisive major media of (religious, poetic, political) language to the speechless guiding medium of money, and restoring to interpretive and signifying language its ancestral, divine, though monetarily devalued, rights.

13. *Kritische Friedrich-Schlegel-Ausgabe*, vol. 12, p. 47.

14. Carl Schmitt, *Political Theology*, pp. 53–54.

15. Gerd Bergfleth published an anthology with a neoconservative bent as early as 1984, under the title *Zur Kritik der palavernden Aufklärung*. It escapes him, as it does all other militantly conservative critics of modernity, that there can hardly be simpler suggestions for coming to terms with the modern problems of complexity than dictates and dictatorship.

16. For another critique of George Steiner's aesthetic fundamentalism, cf. Manfred Frank's " 'Zerschwatzte Dichtung' vor 'Realer Gegenwart,' " in *Conditio moderna*, and

Hans-Robert Jauss's "Über religiöse und ästhetische Erfahrung—zur Debatte um Hans Belting und George Steiner," in *Wege des Verstehens*.

17. Page numbers refer to *Real Presences*.

18. [The German translation of Steiner's work renders "power-house" as "Mekka." According to Hörisch, Steiner read and approved the translation. Thus Hörisch comments, in the original text, upon "Mekka," of all things, as the "essence of secondary dissociations." Trans.]

19. Cf. Hans Belting, *Likeness and Presence*.

20. Goethe, *Westöstlicher Divan*, Hamburger Ausgabe, vol. 2, p. 43 (Buch des Unmuts!). [*West-Eastern Divan*, p. 79 (Book of Displeasure!). Trans.]

21. Cf. Botho Strauß, "Anschwellender Bocksgesang," p. 257: "Between the powers of convention and those of continuous progress, clearing away, and annihilation, there will be war. . . . Since history has not stopped reflecting its inclination to tragedy, no one can foresee whether our non-violence is not simply delaying the war, forcing it on our children." Cf. also the reactions to this "Bocksgesang," reprinted in the same volume.

22. Cf. Hörisch, "Poetische Überproduktion."

23. [Reich-Ranicki is a German literary critic and television personality who hosts a show in which contemporary literature is discussed. His judgments have tremendous consequences for the market success or failure of the books he discusses. Trans.]

24. *Das offenbare Geheimnis.*

25. *Peter Schlemihl*, p. 6. [Chamisso's translator renders the simile "wie ein Vogel, den eine Schlange gebannt" figuratively, and so the English "like a bird under the spell of a snake" is my own translation. Trans.]

26. Ibid., p. 63. [The German original, translated as the "key to all mysteries," is "das Wort, das aller Rätsel Lösung sei," literally, "the *word* that solves all riddles." Thus the author's ensuing reference to Peter Schlemihl's lack of interest in the quest for the "primary word." Trans.]

27. Rolf Günter Renner, "Schrift der Natur," p. 654.

28. " 'Black shadows' forbidden in Leipzig," reads the *Frankfurter Allgemeine Zeitung* headline from September 2, 1994: the District Court of Leipzig had forbidden an enterprise that was flourishing; its angle was to have defaulting debtors trailed by men in black with top hats or derbies, under contract to their creditors, until they broke down and found a way to pay up—at any price.

29. The page numbers in parentheses refer to Nietzsche, *Human, All Too Human*, trans. R. J. Hollingdale.

30. The book with the preface (signed "Nizza, Spring 1886") combines two earlier publications: the book *Menschliches, Allzumenschliches—Ein Buch für freie Geister* [*Human, All Too Human: A Book for Free Spirits*] and its sequel *Der Wanderer und sein Schatten—Ein Buch für freie Geister* [*The Wanderer and His Shadow: A Book for Free Spirits*], of 1880.

31. [In German, this has two meanings: to spin, but also to be crazy. Trans.]

32. Heidegger, *Nietzsche*, I, p. 18.

33. On the difference between meaning and significance (*Sinn, Bedeutung*) cf. Hörisch, *Brot und Wein*, pp. 275ff., and "Das Sein der Zeichen und die Zeichen des Seins," in his *Die andere Goethezeit*.

34. Cf. Heidegger, "Metaphysics as History of Being," in *The End of Philosophy*, p. 26.

35. Derrida, *Speech and Phenomena*.

36. To be philologically precise: the interval in which the conversation takes place is designated by the phrase "In an hour it will all be over" (301). "Hour" may be meant, however—in view of the time that the 350 reflections would take up—not chronologically but metaphorically.

37. *Aus dem Nachlaß der Achtzigerjahre, Werke in drei Bänden* III, p. 880.

38. C. G. Jung's somewhat simplistic analysis of shadows takes advantage of this situation. Cf. also Edmund Husserl's use of the concept "Abschattung" (to shade or cast a shadow).

39. *Nietzsche*, III, pp. 137–38.

40. *Being and Time*, p. 487. Heidegger puts the phrase in quotation marks; he does not, however, explicitly mention Lukács's treatise, *History of Class Consciousness*, of 1923. The formulation "reification of consciousness" occurs in section 10 of *Being and Time* as well. Cf. on this, Hörisch, "Die Krise des Bewußtseins und das Bewußtsein der Krise," pp. 11ff.

41. *Elegien und Epigramme*, pp. 251 (l. 114) and 261 (l. 118). [The English translation of l. 114 is from Michael Hamburger's *Friedrich Hölderlin: Poems and Fragments*, p. 249. For l. 118, I have substituted "its own shadow" for "the full impact of gods" to reflect Hölderlin's change. Trans.]

42. Cf. Hörisch, "Charaktermasken und ders., Larven und Charaktermasken," in his *Die andere Goethezeit*, pp. 29–46, 212–21.

43. *Charaktermasken*.

44. [These lines are my translation. Trans.]

45. Cf. Urs Marti, *Der grosse Pöbel und Sklavenaufstand*.

46. Paul Celan, *Gedichte in zwei Bänden*, vol. 1, p. 135 (*Von Schwelle zu Schwelle*). [Translation from *Paul Celan: Selected Poems*, p. 43. Trans.]

CHAPTER 13

1. Cf. Peter Sloterdijk's "Wo sind wir, wenn wir Musik hören?" in *Weltfremdheit*, ed. Sloterdijk, pp. 294ff.

2. [The ensuing sentences play with the German equivalent of "there is/are," namely "es gibt," which translates literally as "it gives." I use the German, its literal translation, and the idiomatic English to introduce this passage, so that the following play on giving and taking makes sense. Elsewhere, I will use both literal and idiomatic renderings for the same reason. See note 24 to chapter 7. Trans.]

3. Clemens Brentano, January 20 (1835), after immense suffering, in *Werke*, vol. 1, pp. 601ff., as refrain. [Trans. by Mabel Cotterell in John F. Fetzer, *Clemens Brentano*.] In the context of this poem, the oft-cited and interpreted lines (Brentano used them, as is well known, in many other texts) quite obviously have the function of indicating the astounding diversity and preparing the question of how unity can be woven out of this scattered diversity: "the word, it weaves itself a body" ["es webet / . . . das Wort sich einen Leib"].

4. Friedrich Schlegel, *Philosophical Fragments*, p. 6 (*Lyceum* Fragment 42).

5. *Philosophical Fragments*, pp. 50–51 (*Athenäum* Fragment 238).

6. The following passages are quoted from Chamisso's *Werke in zwei Bänden*, vol. 2.

7. [In German, "Da-sein," a play on "Dasein," meaning "existence," and "da" and "sein" or "there" and "to be," respectively. Trans.]

8. [The translator uses "his" and "he" where I have substituted "its" and "it." This shifts the antecedent from "man" to "reason," a shift that is both important to the author's discussion and brings the meaning closer to the original text. Trans.]

9. Adalbert Stifter, "Abdias," in *Brigitta; with Abdias, Limestone, and The Forest Path,* pp. 21–22.

10. *Homer's Iliad,* book 8, 18–27.

11. Cf. Ernst Robert Curtius, *European Literature,* pp. 106f., and Arthur O. Lovejoy, *The Great Chain of Being.*

12. Goethe, *Poetry and Truth,* pt. 2, bk. 8, pp. 255–56.

13. Cf. Eva Meyer's comments on "the pulling of the beyond into the here and now," in *Zählen und Erzählen,* pp. 143ff.

14. Heinz-Dieter Kittsteiner, *Naturabsicht und Unsichtbare Hand.*

15. [The first syllable of Abdias's name, "ab," means "down" or "away from" or "through"; the German "dias" may refer to "diaphanous." Trans.]

16. Christian Begemann, *Die Welt der Zeichen.*

CHAPTER 14

1. Johann Georg Hamann, *Sämtliche Werke,* 2, p. 159.

2. Walter Benjamin, "On Language as Such and on the Language of Man," in *Walter Benjamin: Selected Writings. Vol. 1.*

3. It was, long before Hamann, a philosophical fad to compare language and money. This was undertaken by Bacon, Hobbes, and Leibniz—cf., among others, Marcelo Dascal, *Language and Money.*

4. Cf. Luhmann, "Knappheit, Geld und bürgerliche Gesellschaft."

5. Michel Foucault, *L'Ordre du Discours.* [The essay is available in English under the title "The Discourse on Language."]

6. Cf. Jacques Derrida, *Given Time: I. Counterfeit Money.*

7. Hegel, *Phenomenology of Spirit,* p. 220.

8. Ibid., p. 22; Hegel's emphasis. He quotes Lessing with this turn of phrase, *Nathan the Wise,* ll. 352f.: " . . . as if the truth were coins!" [" . . . als ob die Wahrheit Münze wäre!"].

9. As Nietzsche, too, knows: "es giebt keine 'Wahrheit.'" ["There is no 'truth.'" Trans.] *Nachgelassene Fragmente,* in *Kritische Studienausgabe,* vol. 12, p. 114.

10. Thus the classic definition of money in modern finance and money psychology. Schmölders, *Gutes und schlechtes Geld,* p. 21.

11. Cf. J. P. Bethmann, *Der verratene Kapitalismus;* also Peter Krieg, *Die Seele des Geldes,* p. 53: "The sum total of money is thus equal to the sum total of all debt."

12. [The title, literally rendered, would be "Money and Spirit." This is important below. Trans.]

13. Jeremias Gotthelf, *Wealth and Welfare,* pp. 260–61.

14. ["Ehepfand"—which I, in departure from Gotthelf's translator, have rendered literally as "marriage pledge"—is an expression for "child." Trans.]

15. [My translation. These sentences have not been included in the translation *Wealth and Welfare.* Trans.]

16. Lacan, *Écrits,* I, p. 37.

17. Derrida reads this law as follows: "Among its irreducible predicates or semantic values, economy no doubt includes the values of law (*nomos*) and of home (*oikos,* home, property, family, the hearth, the fire indoors). *Nomos* does not only signify the law in general, but also the law of distribution (*nemein*), the law of sharing or partition [*partage*], the law as partition (*moira*), the given or assigned part, participation. Another sort of tautology already implies the economic within the nomic as such. As soon as

there is law, there is partition: as soon as there is *nomy*, there is economy." *Given Time*, p. 6.

18. [The author is playing with the words for home, "Heim," and uncanny, "unheimlich," in this passage, as well as with the complex relationship between the two. Trans.]

19. Cf. on the close connection between language and economy, and particularly on the costs of language, Florian Coulmas, *Language and Economy*.

20. Adam Müller, *Versuche einer neuen Theorie des Geldes*, p. 267.

21. *Wirtschaft und Gesellschaft*, p. 385.

22. Ibid.

CHAPTER 15

1. Quoted from Hermann Kurzke, *Hymnen und Lieder der Deutschen*, pp. 151f. Cf. Kurzke's commentary, ibid., p. 154: "With 'resurrected,' the first word of its national anthem, the founding of the German Democratic Republic identifies itself as an Easter event, after the Good Friday of the war." On another note, the national anthem of the GDR is, in its first four beats (including its syncopation), musically identical to the hit "Good-bye Johnny," sung by Hans Albers in the film *Wasser für Canitoga*. See Theo Stemmler, "Ein Hymnen-Test."

2. Georg Simmel's classic study, "Die Ruine" (ruins) does not go into the concept of "ruin." The following remarks were stimulated by and are indebted to this essay, as well as two treatises by Hartmut Böhme, "Die Ästhetik der Ruinen" and "Ruinen-Landschaften." Cf. also Günter Hartmann, *Die Ruinen im Landschaftsgarten*, and Anne Janowitz, *England's Ruins*.

3. Col. 1475.

4. [The German term here is "geschafft," which is the past participle of the verb "schaffen," to manage. "Schaffen" also means, however, "to create." The author contrasts the term with "abgeschafft," which I have rendered "done away with," in the next sentence. Trans.]

5. Jacob Ayrer, *Dramen I*, p. 4, cited by Benjamin, *The Origin of German Tragic Drama*, p. 141. Uwe Jochum (*Kleine Bibliothekgeschichte*, p. 99) links up with Benjamin in his comments on these sentences: "With that, the [Baroque] paradigm is established: the superfluity of the world, which is consolation for the destruction of particular cultural effects because there is something similar somewhere else, stands in contrast to the book, which alone and uniquely survives all destruction. In its survival, however, the book bears witness to all the destruction it has survived, while ruins are nothing but ruins whose significance is only divulged in books."

6. [Translation from *Heinrich von Kleist: Plays*, p. 209. Trans.]

7. On the contrast between a ruinous desire for death and its symbolic overcoming in Kleist's work, cf. Arthur Henkel's penetrating study "Traum und Gesetz in Kleist's 'Prinz Friedrich von Homburg,'" in his *Der Zeiten Bildersaal*.

8. *Correspondence between Goethe and Schiller*, p. 209. Cf. on this subject, Schlaffer, *Faust II*, pp. 13ff.

9. Schiller, *Wilhelm Tell*, 4.2.2425f. [Trans. by William F. Mainland, p. 104. Trans.]

10. The most subtle delineation of this argument is probably Michael Theunissen's; cf. "Begriff und Realität," in his *Sein und Schein*.

11. In this respect it is not surprising that totalitarian states and ideologies regularly disdain and waste money.

12. *Buddenbrooks—Verfall einer Familie*, p. 206. (Quotations from *Buddenbrooks* will be noted in parentheses.)

13. It is one of the qualities of this novel that it is always conscious of the constitutive force of form and formality. Thomas Buddenbrook feels obliged to make an essentially identical, though incomparably more subtle, confession in a letter to his mother: "I fervently adore Gerda Arnoldson, but I am not in the least inclined to descend deep enough into myself to try to fathom whether and to what extent the large dowry, which was somewhat cynically whispered in my ear at our very first meeting, has contributed to this fervor. I love her, but the thought that I win along with her a substantial influx of capital for our firm increases my good fortune and my pride all the more" (295).

14. ["Ist der Ruf erst ruiniert, lebt es sich auch öffentlich ganz ungeniert." Note that "ruiniert" or "ruined" rhymes with "ungeniert" or "unembarrassed." Trans.] The origin of this very well-known phrase is not identified in either *Büchmanns geflügelten Worten* (33rd edition) or *Mackensen's 10.000 Zitaten, Redensarten, Sprichwörter.*

15. [The German term for dowry is "Mitgift," which breaks down into two words, "mit" or "with" and "Gift," meaning "poison." Trans.]

16. Cf. Blumenberg, *Die Lesbarkeit der Welt.*

17. Benjamin, *The Origin of German Tragic Drama*, p. 178.

18. The following thoughts should not be construed as a plea for amoral action and the doing away with what remains of historical education. Certainly, however, as an analysis of the effects that tend to accompany the public use of moral and historical categories. Hans Magnus Enzensberger, often reproached for allegedly swift and cynical changes in his viewpoint, wrote as early as 1966 in *Kursbuch* 6: "The moral rearmament from the left leaves me cold. I am no idealist. I prefer confessions to arguments. I prefer doubts to sentiments. Revolutionary chatter is odious to me. I have no use for worldviews free of contradiction. In doubtful cases, reality decides."

19. Cf. the debate between Gadamer and Derrida, in Philippe Forget, ed., *Text und Interpretation.*

20. Cf. Hörisch, *Brot und Wein*, pp. 168ff.

21. [Trans. from *Johann Wolfgang von Goethe Selected Poems*, p. 79.]

22. Cf. on this point, Dietrich Geyer, "Gewalt in der postkommunistischen Welt." Geyer demonstrates that in those areas where communist power has given way, historical myths have made their (re-)entry. From Belgrade to Tashkent, historians are right there on the front lines, fighting in the war for territories, memories, and symbols.

23. *Sämtliche Werke*, vol. 3, pp. 64f.

24. C. F. Volney, *The Ruins*, p. 1.

CHAPTER 16

1. *In the Land of Cockaigne*, p. 117. Page numbers will be given in parentheses.

2. References to *Royal Highness* will be indicated in parentheses.

3. Alfred Adler's concept.

4. In *Joseph*, Thomas Mann broadly develops these motifs once again. Joseph runs a New Deal economy in Egypt that would have made Keynes and Roosevelt proud. Economy and money are the main themes in Thomas Mann's art of the novel.

5. Thomas Hobbes, *Leviathan*, pp. 300f. (bk. II, XXIV).

6. Cited by Sédillot, *Muscheln*, p. 181. [Unable to find the original source, I have retranslated this passage into English. Trans.]

7. Cited by Michael von Engelhardt, *Der plutonische Faust*, p. 418.

8. *Die Kronenwächter*, p. 170.

9. [The King James Version says "a bribe" in place of "blood money," which Luther, according to the author, used in this passage. Trans.]

10. [Again, I am using the King James Version but preserving the reference to Luther, and making changes as necessary to reflect the words of Luther under discussion. In this case the English text reads, instead of "blood money," "the price of blood." Trans.]

11. Cited in the afterword of *Königliche Hoheit*, p. 379.

12. *Dracula*, pp. 109, 293. Additional references to Stoker's novel will be indicated in parentheses.

13. Kittler, *Draculas Vermächtnis*, p. 44.

14. Ibid., p. 51.

15. Cf. the theme of the media, pp. 310, 382, 408, and elsewhere; the theme of Communion, pp. 611, 648, and elsewhere; and the theme of money, pp. 10, 176, 222, 227.

16. The many allusions to Communion in this novel (pp. 19, 36, 37, 77–78, 122, 140) are systematically presented in the context of the motif of money. Not for no reason does the first sentence of the novel read as follows: "On the day that Inni Wintrop committed suicide, Philips shares stood at 149.60. The Amsterdam Bank closing rate was 375, and Shipping Union had slipped to 141.50" (p. 1). Sentences like the one about "vindictive, Calvinist modernity" (29; cf. "I shouldn't think he has a very high income, would you?" p. 119) or about "an institution that is based on suffering and death" (p. 63) could also be from Bram Stoker's novel.

17. This will be the theme of one further, concluding ontosemiological investigation.

18. *Zeitgehöft*, p. 46.

BIBLIOGRAPHY

Achterberg, Erich. "Was ist Geld?" In *Geld—Gestern und heute.* 9–25.

Adorno, Theodor W. *Aesthetic Theory.* Ed. Gretel Adorno and Rolf Tiedemann. Trans. Robert Hullot-Kentor. Minneapolis, 1997.

———. *Minima Moralia: Reflections from Damaged Life.* Trans. E. F. N. Jephcott. London, 1974.

———. *Minima Moralia: Reflexionen aus dem beschädigten Leben. Gesammelte Schriften in 20 Bänden.* Frankfurt, 1980.

———. *Notes to Literature.* Vol. 2. Ed. Rolf Tiedemann. Trans. Shierry Weber Nicholsen. New York, 1992.

———. "On the Fetish Character in Music and the Regression of Listening." In *The Essential Frankfurt School Reader.* Ed. Andrew Arato and Eike Gebhardt. Intro. Paul Piccone. New York, 1978. 270–99.

Adorno, Theodor W., and Walter Benjamin. *Briefwechsel 1928–1940.* Ed. H. Lonitz. Frankfurt am Main, 1994.

Adorno, Theodor W., and Alfred Sohn-Rethel. *Briefwechsel 1936–1969.* Ed. Christoph Gödde. Munich, 1991.

Allen, Woody. *Without Feathers.* New York, 1975. Rpt. New York, 1986.

Altenhein, Hans-Richard. Geld und Geldeswert im bürgerlichen Schauspiel des 18. Jahrhunderts. Diss. Cologne, 1952.

———. "Geld und Geldeswert—Über die Selbstdarstellung des Bürgertums in der Literatur des 18. Jahrhunderts." In *Festschrift für Horst Kliemann.* Ed. F. Hodeige. N.P.: 1956. 201–13.

"Der Alltag—Die Sensationen des Gewöhnlichen." *Thema: Das liebe Geld* 67 (March 1995).

Anton, Herbert. "Lügende Dichter und die Kunst des Rhapsoden." In *Neue Hefte für Philosophie* 4. Göttingen, 1973.

Aquinas, Thomas. *Summa Theologiae.* Latin text, English trans., intro., notes, appendices, and glossary Marcus Lefébure O. P. New York, 1975.

321

Aristotle. *The Nicomachean Ethics*. Trans. and intro. David Ross. Oxford, 1980.

———. *The Politics*. Ed. Stephen Everson. Trans. Benjamin Jowett. Revisions Jonathan Barnes. Cambridge, 1988.

Arnim, Achim von. *Die Kronenwächter. Werke in 6 Bänden*. Vol. 2. Ed. R. Burwick et al. Frankfurt am Main, 1992.

———. "Wunder über Wunder." *Sämtliche Erzählungen 1818–1830. Werke in 6 Bänden*. Vol. 4. Ed. R. Moering. Frankfurt am Main, 1992.

Assmann, Aleida. "Pflug, Schwert, Feder—Kulturwerkzeuge als Herrschaftszeichen." In *Schrift*. Ed. H. U. Gumbrecht and K. L. Pfeiffer. Munich, 1993. 219–31.

Aubrey, John. *Aubrey's Brief Lives*. Ed. Oliver Lawson Dick. Ann Arbor, Mich., 1957.

Augustin, Ernst. *Gutes Geld—Roman in drei Anleitungen*. Frankfurt am Main, 1996.

Ayrer, Jacob. *Dramen I*. Stuttgart, 1965.

Bachofen, Johann Jakob. *Mother Right*. In *Myth, Religion, and Mother Right: Selected Writings of J. J. Bachofen*. Trans. Ralph Manheim, preface George Boas, intro. Joseph Campbell. Bollingen Series LXXXIV. New York, 1967. Princeton, 1967.

Bachorski, Hans Jürgen. *Geld und soziale Identiät im "Fortunatus"—Studien zur literarischen Bewältigung frühbürgerlicher Widersprüche*. Göppingen, 1983.

Baecker, Dirk. "Die Beobachtung der Paradoxie des Geldes." In *Paradoxien, Dissonanzen, Zusammenbrüche*, ed. Gumbrecht and Pfeiffer. 174–86.

———. *Womit handeln Banken? Eine Untersuchung zur Risikoverarbeitung in der Wirtschaft*. Frankfurt am Main, 1991.

Bahr, Hans-Dieter. "Schatz-Häuser." *Daidalos—Architektur, Kunst, Kultur*. Berlin, September 15, 1994. 28–35.

Bataille, Georges. *The Accursed Share: An Essay on General Economy. Vol. 1: Consumption*. Trans. Robert Hurley. New York, 1988.

Batts, Michael S. *A History of Histories of German Literature 1835–1914*. Montreal, 1993.

Baudrillard, Jean. *Der symbolische Tausch und der Tod*. Munich, 1982.

Beck, Maximilian. *Der Geiz als Wurzel der faustisch-dynamischen Kultur*. n.p. n.d. Rpt. South Windsor, Conn., ca. 1994.

Beck, Ulrich. *Risk Society: Towards a New Modernity*. Trans. Mark Ritter. Newbury Park, Calif., 1992.

Becker, Thorsten. *Die Bürgschaft—Eine Erzählung*. Zürich, 1985.

Begemann, Christian. *Die Welt der Zeichen—Stifter-Lektüren*. Stuttgart, 1995.

Behler, Ernst. "Die italienische Renaissance in der Literatur der Brüder Schlegel." In *Romantik und Renaissance—Die Rezeption der italienischen Renaissance in der deutschen Romantik*. Ed. S. Vietta. Stuttgart, 1994.

Beller, Manfred. "Stoff-, Motiv- und Themengeschichte." In *Literaturwissenschaft Grundkurs 2*. Ed. H. Brackert and J. Stückrath. Reinbek, 1981.

Belting, Hans. *Likeness and Presence: A History of the Image Before the Era of Art*. Trans. Edmund Jephcott. Chicago, 1994.

Benjamin, Walter. *The Correspondence of Walter Benjamin 1910–1940*. Ed. and annotated Gershom Scholem and Theodor W. Adorno. Trans. Manfred R. Jacobson and Evelyn M. Jacobson. Chicago, 1994.

———. *Gesammelte Schriften*. Ed. R. Tiedemann and H. Schweppenhäuser. Frankfurt am Main, 1974–.

———. "On Language as Such and on the Language of Man." In *Walter Benjamin: Selected Writings. Vol. 1: 1913–1926*. Ed. Marcus Bullock and Michael W. Jennings. 62–74. Originally appeared in English in *Reflections*. New York, 1978. Rpt. Cambridge, Mass., 1996.

———. *The Origin of German Tragic Drama*. Trans. John Osborne. Intro. George Steiner. London, 1985.

———. "Socrates." In *Walter Benjamin: Selected Writings. Vol. 1: 1913–1926*. Ed. Marcus Bullock and Michael W. Jennings. Originally appeared in English in the *Philosophical Forum* 15, Nos. 1–2 (1983–84): 52–74. Cambridge, Mass., 1996.

———. "The Storyteller." In *Illuminations*. Ed. Hannah Arendt. Trans. Harry Zohn. New York, 1977. 83–109.

Bergelt, Martin, and Hortensia Völckers, eds. *Zeit-Räume—Raumzeiten—Zeiträume*. Munich, 1991.

Bergfleth, Gerd, ed. *Zur Kritik der palavernden Aufklärung*. Munich, 1984.

Berghaus, Margot. "Nicht-Kommunikation durch Fernsehen." In *Formen und Möglichkeiten des Sozialen—Eine Gedenkschrift für Janpeter Kob*. Ed. A. Deichsel and B. Thuns. Hamburg, 1988. 29–48.

Bergler, Ernst. "Zur Psychologie des Hazardspielers." *Imago* 22 (1936).

Berkeley, George. *Philosophical Commentaries: The Works of George Berkeley, Bishop of Cloyne*. Vol. 1. Ed. A. A. Luce and T. E. Jessop. London, 1964.

Bethmann, Johann Philipp von. *Der verratene Kapitalismus: Die Ursachen der Krise*. Königstein, 1984.

Betz, Albrecht. "Geld und Geist—Die neuen Banknoten und ihre Gesichter." *Merkur* 502, No. 1 (1991).

Binswanger, Hans Christoph. *Geld und Natur*. Stuttgart, 1991.

———. *Money and Magic: A Critique of the Modern Economy in the Light of Goethe's Faust*. Trans. J. E. Harrison. Chicago, 1994.

Blasche, Siegfried, Wolfgang R. Köhler, and Peter Rohs, eds. *Markt und Moral—Die Diskussion um die Unternehmensethik*. Bern, 1994.

Bloy, Léon. *Auslegung der Gemeinplätze*. Frankfurt am Main, 1995.

Blumenberg, Hans. *Höhlenausgänge*. Frankfurt am Main, 1989.

———. *Die Lesbarkeit der Welt*. Frankfurt am Main, 1981.

Böhme, Hartmut. "Die Ästhetik der Ruinen." In *Der Schein des Schönen*. Ed. D. Kamper and Ch. Wulf. Göttingen, 1989. 287–304.

———. "Ruinen-Landschaften—Naturgeschichte und Ästhetik der Allegorie in den Filmen von Andrej Tarkowskij." *Konkursbuch* 14 (1985): 115–57.

Bohn, Volker. "J. W. von Goethe." In *Genie und Geld—Vom Auskommen deutscher Schriftsteller*. Ed. Karl Corino. Nördlingen, 1987. 140–50.

Bonus, Holger. *Wertpapiere, Geld und Gold—Über das Unwirkliche in der Ökonomie*. Graz, 1990.

Borchers, Ralf, ed. *Arm und reich—Geschichten und Gedichte*. Frankfurt am Main, 1987.

Bornemann, Ernest. *The Psychoanalysis of Money*. New York, 1976.

Brant, Sebastian. *Ship of Fools*. Trans. Edwin Zeydel. New York, 1944.

Braun, Lutz. *Geschichte der Philosophiegeschichte*. Trans. F. Wimmer. Darmstadt, 1990.

Braungart, Georg. "Die Fremdheit der Sprache am Beginn der Moderne: Lebenskult, Ritual, Remythisierung, Mystik." In *Akten des VIII. internationalen Germanistik-Kongresses Tokyo 1990*. Vol. 6. Ed. E. Iwasaki. Munich, 1991. 117–27.

Brecht, Bertolt. *Bertolt Brecht: Poems & Songs from the Plays*. Ed. and mainly trans. John Willett. London, 1990.

———. *Gesammelte Werke in acht Bänden*. Frankfurt am Main, 1967.

Brenner, Peter J., ed. *Geist, Geld und Wissenschaft—Arbeits- und Darstellungsformen von Literaturwissenschaft*. Frankfurt am Main, 1993.

Brentano, Clemens. *Werke*. Vol. 1. Ed. W. Frühwald et al. Munich, 1978.

Brinkmann, Heinrich. *Moral und Geld—Vom Untergang der Moral durch das Geld—Ein geschichtsphilosophischer Versuch.* Pfungstadt, 1994.

Burke, Kenneth. *A Grammar of Motives and a Rhetoric of Motives.* Cleveland, Ohio, 1962.

Butler, Samuel. *Erewhon, or, Over the Range.* Ed. Hans-Peter Breuer and Daniel F. Howard. Newark, Del., 1981.

Canetti, Elias. *Auto-Da-Fé.* Trans. C. V. Wedgewood. New York, 1963.

———. *Crowds and Power.* Trans. Carol Stewart. New York, 1963.

———. *The Torch in My Ear.* Trans. Joachim Neugroschel. New York, 1982.

Capelle, Wilhelm, ed. *Die Vorsokratiker—Die Fragmente und Quellenberichte.* Trans. and intro. Wilhelm Capelle. Stuttgart, 1968.

Cassirer, Ernst. *The Philosophy of Symbolic Forms. Vol. 1: Language.* Trans. Ralph Manheim. New Haven, Conn., 1953.

Celan, Paul. *Gedichte in zwei Bänden.* Frankfurt am Main, 1975.

———. *Paul Celan: Selected Poems.* Trans. Michael Hamburger and Christopher Middleton. Harmondsworth, Middlesex, 1972.

———. *Zeitgehöft—Späte Gedichte aus dem Nachlaß.* Frankfurt am Main, 1976.

Chamisso, Adelbert von. *Peter Schlemihl: The Man Who Sold His Shadow.* Trans. Peter Wortsman. New York, 1993.

———. *. . . und lassen gelten, was ich beobachtet habe—Naturwissenschaftliche Schriften mit Zeichnungen des Autors.* Ed. Ruth Schneebeli-Graf. Berlin, 1983.

———. *Werke in zwei Bänden.* Ed. W. Feudel and Ch. Laufer. Munich, 1982.

Cipolla, Carlo M. *Geld-Abenteuer—Extravagante Geschichten aus dem europäischen Wirtschaftsleben.* Berlin, 1995.

Claudius, Matthias. *Asmus omnia sua secum portans oder Sämmtliche Werke des Wandsbecker Boten.* Vol. 1. Gotha, 1879.

Corino, Karl, ed. *Genie und Geld: Vom Auskommen deutscher Schriftsteller.* Nördlingen, 1987.

Coulmas, Florian. *Language and Economy.* Oxford, 1992.

Curtius, Ernst. *On the Religious Character of Greek Coins.* London, 1870.

Curtius, Ernst Robert. *European Literature and the Latin Middle Ages.* Trans. Willard R. Trask. Princeton, 1967.

Daemmrich, Horst S., and Ingrid G. Daemmrich. *Themen und Motive in der Literatur.* Tübingen, 1995.

Dante. *Dante's Inferno: The Indiana Critical Edition.* Trans. and ed. Mark Musa. Bloomington, Ind., 1995.

Dascal, Marcelo. "Language and Money—A Simile and Its Meaning in 17th Century Philosophy of Language." *Studio Leibnitiana* 8, No. 1 (1976): 187–218.

Deleuze, Gilles, and Fèlix Guattari. *Anti-Oedipus: Capitalism and Schizophrenia.* Trans. Robert Hurley, Mark Seem, and Helen R. Lane. New York, 1972.

Derrida, Jacques. *Given Time: I. Counterfeit Money.* Trans. Peggy Kamuf. Chicago, 1992.

———. *The Post Card: From Socrates to Freud and Beyond.* Trans. with intro. and notes Alan Bass. Chicago, 1987.

———. *Specters of Marx: The State of the Debt, the Work of Mourning, and the New International.* Trans. Peggy Kamuf. Intro. Bernd Magnus and Stephen Cullenberg. New York, 1994.

———. *Speech and Phenomena and Other Essays on Husserl's Theory.* Trans. David B. Allison. Preface Newton Garver. Evanston, Ill., 1973.

Detering, Heinrich. *Das offenbare Geheimnis—Zur literarischen Produktivität eines Tabus von Winckelmann bis zu Thomas Mann.* Göttingen, 1995.

Diagonal. Zum Thema: Geld. Ed. K. Sturm. Journal of the Universität-Gesamthochschule Siegen. Siegen, 1991.

DiPiero, Thomas. "Buying into Fiction." *diacritics* 18, No. 2 (1988): 2–37.

Dobras, Werner. *Plaudereien vor dem Bücherschrank.* Lindau, 1979.

Donne, John. *The Sermons of John Donne.* Vol. 10. Ed. E. M. Simpson and G. R. Potter. Berkeley, 1962.

Dumas, Alexandre. *The Count of Monte Cristo.* 2 vols. Ed. Ernest Rhys. London, 1949.

Dürrenmatt, Friedrich. *The Assignment, or, On the Observing of the Observer of the Observers.* Trans. Joel Agee. New York, 1988.

Eichendorff, Joseph von. *Memoirs of a Good-for-Nothing.* Trans. Bayard Quincy Morgan. New York, 1968.

Engelhardt, Michael von. *Der plutonische Faust—Eine motivgeschichtliche Studie zur Arbeit am Mythos in der Faust-Tradition.* Basel, 1992.

Engert, Rolf. *Silvio Gesell in München 1919—Erinnerungen und Dokumente aus der Zeit vor, während und nach der ersten bayerischen Räterepublik.* Hannover-Münden, 1986.

Erasmus, Desiderius. *The Collected Works of Erasmus: Poems.* Trans. Clarence H. Miller. Ed. Harry Vredeveld. Toronto, 1974.

Erbes, Volker. *Die Spur des Schwimmers—Roman.* Frankfurt am Main, 1991.

Escherig, Manfred. "Bei der Betrachtung einer Dollarnote." *Diagonal. Zum Thema: Geld.* 125–30.

Ferlinghetti, Lawrence. "Oral Messages." In *A Coney Island of the Mind.* Norfolk, Conn., 1955. Rpt. 1958. 47–74.

Fetzer, John. *Clemens Brentano.* Boston, 1981.

Feuchtwanger, Lion. *Gesammelte Werke.* Vol. 14. Berlin, 1985.

———. *Pep: J. L. Wetcheek's American Song Book.* English version by Dorothy Thompson. New York, 1929.

Feyerabend, Paul. *Against Method.* 3rd ed. London, 1993.

Flaubert, Gustave. *Madame Bovary.* Trans. Francis Steegmuller. New York, 1993.

Fohrmann, Jürgen. "Über das Schreiben von Literaturgeschichte." In *Geist, Geld und Wissenschaft—Arbeits- und Darstellungsformen von Literaturwissenschaft.* Ed. Peter J. Brenner. Frankfurt am Main, 1993. 175–202.

Fontane, Theodor. *Delusions, Confusions.* Trans. William L. Zwiebel. In *Delusions, Confusions and the Poggenpuhl Family.* Ed. Peter Demetz. New York, 1989.

———. *A Man of Honor.* Trans. E. M. Falk. New York, 1975.

Forget, Philippe, ed. *Texte und Interpretation.* Munich, 1984.

Fortunatus. In *Bibliothek der frühen Neuzeit—Romane des 15. und 16. Jahrhunderts.* Ed. J.-D. Müller. Frankfurt am Main, 1990. 383–585.

Foucault, Michel. "The Discourse on Language." In *The Archaeology of Knowledge; and The Discourse on Language.* Trans. A. M. Sheridan Smith. New York, 1972.

———. *Les mots et les choses.* Paris, 1966.

Franck, Georg. "Aufmerksamkeit, Zeit, Raum." In *Zeit-Räume: Raumzeiten—Zeiträume.* Ed. Martin Bergelt and Hortensia Völckers. Munich, 1991.

Frank, Manfred. *Conditio moderna.* Leipzig, 1993.

———. *Das kalte Herz—Texte der Romantik ausgewählt und interpretiert von Manfred Frank.* Frankfurt am Main, 1981.

———. *Die Unhintergehbarkeit von Individualität—Reflexionen über Subjekt, Person und Individuum aus Anlaß ihrer "postmodernen" Toterklärung.* Frankfurt am Main, 1986.

Franklin, Benjamin. "Advice to a Young Tradesman." In *The Writings of Benjamin Franklin.* Vol. 2. Ed. Albert Henry Smyth. New York, 1907. 370–71.

———. "The Way to Wealth." In *The Writings of Benjamin Franklin*. Vol. 3. Ed. Albert Henry Smyth. New York, 1907. 417–18.

Frenzel, Elisabeth. *Motive der Weltliteratur*. Stuttgart, 1980.

———. *Stoff-, Motiv- und Symbolforschung*. Stuttgart, 1978.

Freud, Sigmund. "A Case of Paranoia Running Counter to the Psycho-analytic Theory of the Disease." In *Standard Edition of the Complete Psychological Works of Sigmund Freud*. Vol. 14, 261–72.

———. "Character and Anal Erotism." In *Standard Edition of the Complete Psychological Works of Sigmund Freud*. Vol. 9, 167–76.

———. "Fetishism." In *Standard Edition of the Complete Psychological Works of Sigmund Freud*. Vol. 21, 152–57.

———. *Jokes and Their Relation to the Unconscious*. In *Standard Edition of the Complete Psychological Works of Sigmund Freud*. Trans. and ed. James Strachey. With a biographical introduction by Peter Gay. 24 vols. New York: Norton, 1989.

———. "Negation." In *Standard Edition of the Complete Psychological Works of Sigmund Freud*. Vol. 19, 235–42.

———. "Neurotic Mechanisms in Jealousy, Paranoia and Homosexuality." In *Standard Edition of the Complete Psychological Works of Sigmund Freud*. Vol. 18, 223–34.

———. *The Standard Edition of the Complete Psychological Works of Sigmund Freud*. 24 vols. Trans. under the general editorship of James Strachey, in collaboration with Anna Freud. London, 1975.

———. *Totem and Taboo*. In *Standard Edition of the Complete Psychological Works of Sigmund Freud*. Vol. 13: 1–162.

Freytag, Gustav. *Debit and Credit*. Trans. L. C. C. New York, 1858.

Friedrich, Inge. Semiotische Thematisierung der Problemfelder des Geldes. Diss. Stuttgart, 1980.

Fuchs, Peter. "Vom schweigenden Aufflug ins Abstrakte: Zur Ausdifferenzierung der modernen Lyrik." In *Reden und Schweigen*. Ed. P. Fuchs and N. Luhmann. Frankfurt am Main, 1989. 127–77.

Gehlen, Arnold. *Man: His Nature and Place in the World*. Trans. Clare McMillan and Karl Pillemer. Intro. Karl-Siegbert Rehberg. New York, 1988.

Geld—Gestern und heute—Eine Dokumentation über Geldwesen und Währungen in der Bundesrepublik Deutschland. Graz, 1967.

Gephart, Irmgard. *Geben und Nehmen im "Nibelungenlied" und in Wolframs von Eschenbach "Parzifal."* Bonn, 1994.

Gerloff, Wilhelm. *Die Entstehung des Geldes und die Anfänge des Geldwesens*. Frankfurt am Main, 1947.

Gernhardt, Robert. *Weiche Ziele—Gedichte 1984–1994*. Zürich, 1994.

Geulen, Eva. "Adalbert Stifters Kinder-Kunst—Drei Fallstudien." *Deutsche Vierteljahrsschrift* 4 (1993): 648–68.

Geyer, Dietrich. "Gewalt in der postkommunistischen Welt." *Osteuropa* 43, No. 11 (1993).

Giddens, Anthony. *The Consequences of Modernity*. Stanford, 1990.

Glauser, Friedrich. *Matto regiert*. Zurich, 1986.

Goethe, Johann Wolfgang. *Elective Affinities*. In *Goethe's Collected Works*. Vol. 11. Trans. Judith Ryan. New York, 1988.

———. *Faust*. In *Sämtliche Werke*. Vol. 7/1–2. Ed. A. Schöne. Frankfurt am Main, 1994.

———. *Faust I & II*. In *Goethe's Collected Works*. Vol. 2. Ed. and trans. Stuart Atkins. Boston, 1984.

———. *Goethe's Plays.* Trans. Charles E. Passage. New York, 1980.

———. *Hamburger Ausgabe in 14 Bänden.* Munich, 1981.

———. *Poetry and Truth.* In *Goethe's Collected Works.* Vol. 4, and vol. 5: 522–605. Trans. Robert R. Heitner. Intro. and notes Thomas P. Saine. New York, 1987.

———. *Roman Elegies and Venetian Epigrams: A Bilingual Text.* Trans. L. R. Lind. Lawrence, Kans., 1974.

———. *Scientific Studies.* In *Goethe's Collected Works.* Vol. 12. Ed. and trans. Douglas Miller. New York, 1988.

———. *Selected Poems.* In *Goethe Edition.* Vol. 1. Trans. Michael Hamburger, David Luke, Christopher Middleton, John Frederick Nims, and Vernon Watkins. Boston, 1983.

———. *Werke.* 142 vols. Weimar, 1887–1919.

———. *West-Eastern Divan.* Trans. J. Whaley. London, 1974.

———. *Wilhelm Meister's Apprenticeship.* In *Goethe's Collected Works.* Vol. 9. Ed. and trans. Eric A. Blackall. New York, 1989.

———. *Wilhelm Meister's Journeyman Years or The Renunciants.* In *Goethe's Collected Works.* Vol. 10. Trans. Krishna Winston. New York, 1989.

———. *Wilhelm Meisters Wanderjahre.* In *Sämtliche Werke.* Vol. 10. Ed. G. Neumann and H.-G. Dewitz. Frankfurt am Main, 1989.

Goethe, Johann Wolfgang von, and Friedrich Schiller. *Correspondence between Goethe and Schiller 1794–1805.* Trans. Liselotte Dieckmann. New York, 1994.

Gombrich, Ernst H. *Aby Warburg: An Intellectual Biography.* Leiden, 1970.

Gotthelf, Jeremias. *Geld und Geist oder die Versöhnung. Ausgewählte Werke in 12 Bänden.* Ed. W. Muschg. n.p., 1978.

———. *Wealth and Welfare.* Trans. Howard Fertig. London, 1876. Rpt. 1976.

Goux, Jean-Joseph. "Banking on Signs." *diacritics* 18 No. 2 (1988): 15–25.

———. *The Coiners of Language.* Trans. Jennifer Curtiss Gage. Norman, Okla., 1984.

———. *Freud, Marx—Ökonomie und Symbolik.* Frankfurt am Main, 1975.

Granta. Thema: Money. No. 49 (Fall 1994).

Greenblatt, Stephen. *Marvelous Possessions: The Wonder of the New World.* Chicago, 1991.

Gumbrecht, Hans Ulrich, and Karl Ludwig, eds. *Materialities of Communication.* Trans. William Whobrey. Stanford, 1994.

———. *Paradoxien, Dissonanzen, Zusammenbrüche—Situationen offener Epistemologie.* Frankfurt am Main, 1991.

Günther, Horst. "Voltaire wird wieder jünger." *Freibeuter* 62 (December 1994): 3–10.

Habermas, Jürgen. *The Philosophical Discourse of Modernity.* Trans. Frederick Lawrence. Cambridge, Mass., 1987.

———. *The Theory of Communicative Action. Vol. 1: Reason and the Rationalization of Society.* Trans. Thomas McCarthy. Boston, 1981.

Halbach, Wulf R. "Simulated Breakdowns." In Gumbrecht and Ludwig, eds., *Materialities of Communication.* 335–43.

Hamacher, Werner. "Faust, Geld." *Athenäum* 5 (1995): 131–88.

Hamann, Johann G. "Vermischte Anmerkungen über die Wortfügung in der französischen Sprache" (1761). In *Sämtliche Werke.* Ed. J. Nadler. Vienna, 1950.

Hartmann, Günther. *Die Ruine im Landschaftsgarten—Ihre Bedeutung für den frühen Historismus und die Landschaftsmalerei der Romantik.* Worms, 1981.

Hart-Nibbrig, Christiaan L. *Übergänge—Versuch in sechs Anläufen.* Frankfurt am Main, 1995.

Haubrichs, Wolfgang. "Glück und Ratio im 'Fortunatus'—Der Begriff des Glücks zwischen Magie und städtischer Ökonomie an der Schwelle der Neuzeit." *Zeitschrift für Literaturwissenschaft und Linguistik* 13 (1983): 28–47.

Hauschild, Jan-Christoph. *Georg Büchner—Biographie.* Stuttgart, 1993.

Hegel, Georg Wilhelm Friedrich. *Lectures on the History of Philosophy.* 3 vols. Trans. E. S. Haldane and Frances H. Simson. New York, 1955.

———. *Logic.* Trans. William Wallace. Foreword J. N. Findlay. Oxford, 1975.

———. *Phenomenology of Spirit.* Trans. A. V. Miller. Analysis and foreword J. N. Findlay. Oxford, 1979.

———. *Werke in 20 Bänden.* Ed. K. M. Michel and E. Moldenhauer. Frankfurt am Main, 1971–79. Rpt. 1986.

Heidegger, Martin. "The Age of the World View." Trans. Marjorie Grene. In *Martin Heidegger and the Question of Literature: Toward a Postmodern Literary Hermeneutics.* Ed. William V. Spanos. Bloomington, Ind., 1976. 1–15.

———. "The Anaximander Fragment." In *Early Greek Thinking,* trans. Krell and Capuzzi. New York, 1975. 13–58.

———. *Being and Time.* Trans. John Macquarrie and Edward Robinson. New York, 1962.

———. *The End of Philosophy.* Trans. Joan Stambaugh. New York, 1973.

———. *The Essence of Reasons.* Trans. Terrence Malick. Evanston, Ill., 1969.

———. "Logos (Heraclitus, Fragment B 50)." In *Early Greek Thinking,* trans. Krell and Capuzzi. 59–78.

———. *Nietzsche.* 4 vols. Trans. David Farrell Krell, Joan Stambaugh, and Frank A. Capuzzi. San Francisco, 1961.

———. "The Thing." In *Poetry, Language, Thought.* Trans. Albert Hofstadter. New York, 1971. 163–86.

———. "Die Zeit des Weltbildes." In *Holzwege.* Frankfurt am Main, 1963. 69–103.

Heine, Heinrich. *French Affairs.* In *The Works of Heinrich Heine.* Vol. 7–8. Trans. Charles Godfrey Leland. London, 1893.

Heinrich, Klaus. *Arbeiten mit Ödipus—Begriff der Verdrängung in der Religionswissenschaft.* Basel, 1993.

Heinsohn, Gunnar. *Privateigentum, Patriarchat, Geldwirtschaft—Eine sozialtheoretische Rekonstruktion zur Antike.* Frankfurt am Main, 1984.

Heinze, Theodor T. "Verdammte Wirklichkeit—Zur Kartendunst zwischen europäischer Antike und American Express." *Paragrana—Internationale Zft. für Historische Anthropologie* 3 (1994): 335–46.

Henkel, Arthur. *Entsagung—Eine Studie zu Goethes Altersroman.* Tübingen, 1964.

———. "Traum und Gesetz in Kleists 'Prinz Friedrich von Homburg.' " In *Der Zeiten Bildersaal—Studien und Vorträge.* Stuttgart, 1983. 133–56.

———. "Die 'verteufelt humane' Iphigenie." In *Goethe-Erfahrungen en Studien und Vorträge.* Stuttgart, 1982. 81–102.

Henrich, Dieter. *The Unity of Reason: Essays on Kant's Philosophy.* Ed. and intro. Richard L. Velkley. Trans. Jeffrey Edwards et al. Cambridge, Mass., 1994.

Hesiod. "Theogony." In *The Poems of Hesiod.* Trans. R. M. Frazer. Norman, Okla., 1983. 21–90.

Hesse, Helmut, and Otmar Issing, eds. *Geld und Moral.* Munich, 1994.

Hobbes, Thomas. *Leviathan.* Ed. C. B. MacPherson. Baltimore, 1968.

Hoffmann, Henriette. Eine Untersuchung ueber Kapital, Industrie und Maschine von Goethe bis Immermann. Diss. Vienna, 1942.

Hofmannsthal, Hugo von. *The Cavalier of the Rose.* In *Selected Plays and Libretti.* Trans.

Christopher Holme. Ed. and intro. Michael Hamburger. New York, 1963. 379–527.

———. *Gesammelte Werke in zehn Einzelbänden—Gedichte, Dramen I, 1891–1898.* Ed. B. Schoeller. Frankfurt am Main, 1979.

———. "On Transitoriness." In *Poems and Verse Plays.* 28–31.

———. *Poems and Verse Plays.* Trans. Michael Hamburger. Ed. and intro. Michael Hamburger. With a preface by T. S. Elliot. New York, 1961.

———. *Sämtliche Werke—Gedicthe 2.* Ed. A. Thomasberger and E. Weber. Frankfurt am Main, 1990.

———. "Terzinen—Über Vergänglichkeit." In *Poems and Verse Plays.* 28–31.

Hogrebe, Wolfram. *Prädikation und Genesis—Metaphysik als Fundamentalheuristik im Ausgang von Schellings "Die Weltalter."* Frankfurt am Main, 1989.

Hölderlin, Friedrich. *Friedrich Hölderlin: Poems and Fragments.* Trans. Michael Hamburger. Cambridge, 1980.

Homer. *Homer's Iliad.* Trans. and intro. Denison Bingham Hull. Chicago, 1964.

Hondrich, Karl Otto. "Wann ist eine Gesellschaft liberal? Zum Verhältnis von Mehrheiten und Minderheiten." *Merkur* 561, No. 12 (1995): 1073–83.

Hörisch, Jochen. *Die andere Goethezeit: Poetische Mobilmachung des Subjekts um 1800.* Munich, 1992.

———. "Die beiden Seiten einer Münze—Sohn-Rethels Theorie von Geld und Geltung." In Sohn-Rethel, ed., *Das Geld, die bare Münze des Apriori.* 7–11.

———. *Brot und Wein. Poesie des Abendmahls.* Frankfurt am Main, 1992.

———. "Etcetera-Typen—Der Mensch im Lichte der Literatur/Wissenschaft." In *Der Mensch—das Medium der Gesellschaft?* Ed. P. Fuchs and A. Göbel. Frankfurt am Main, 1994. 352–64.

———. *Gott, Geld und Glück—Zur Logik der Liebe in den Bildungsromanen von Goethe, Keller und Thomas Mann.* Frankfurt am Main, 1983.

———. "Herrscherwort, Geld und geltende Sätze—Adornos Aktualisierung der Frühromantik und die poststrukturalistische Kritik des Subjekts." In *Materialien zür Ästhetischen Theorie Theodor W. Adornos Konstruktion der Moderne.* Ed. B. Lindner and M. W. Lüdke. Frankfurt am Main, 1980. 397–414.

———. "Identitätszwang und Tauschabstraktion—Alfred Sohn-Rethels soziogenetische Erkenntnistheorie." *Philosophische Rundschau* 25, Nos. 1, 2 (1977): 42–54.

———. "Die Krise des Bewußtseins und das Bewußtsein der Krise—Zu Sohn-Rethels Luzerner Exposé." Foreword to Sohn-Rethel, *Soziologische Theorie der Erkenntnis.* 7–33.

———. "Die Medien der Natur und die Natur der Medien." In *Zum Naturbegriff der Gegenwart—Kongreßdokumentation zum Projekt "Natur im Kopf."* Ed. Joachim Wilke. Stuttgart, 1993. 121–38.

———. "Non plus ultra—Paul Virillios rasende Thesen vom rasenden Stillstand," *Merkur* 534–35 (September–October 1993): 784–94.

———. "Optionen der Gegenwartsliteratur." In *Literarische Moderne—Europäische Moderne im 19. und 20. Jahrhundert.* Ed. R. Grimminger et al. Reinbek, 1995. 770–99.

———. "Poesie des Geldes," *Universitas* 4 (1990): 334–44.

———. "Poetische Überproduktion," *Merkur* 471, No. 5 (1988): 433–38.

———. *Die Wirklichkeit der Medien und die medialisierte Wirklichkeit.* In *Funkkolleg Literarische Moderne 10/ Studieneinheit 29.* Tübingen, 1994.

———. *Die Wut des Verstehens—Zur Kritik der Hermeneutik.* Frankfurt am Main, 1988.

Hörisch, Jochen, and Michael Wetzel, eds. *Armaturen der Sinne—Literarische und technische Medien 1870 bis 1920*. Munich, 1990.

Horn, Hans-Jürgen. "Gold." In *Reallexikon für Antike und Christentum*. Vol. 11. Stuttgart, 1981. 895–930.

Issing, Otmar. "Aristoteles—(auch) ein Nationalökonom?" In *Vademecum zu einem Klassiker des antiken Wirtschaftsdenkens*. Ed. Bertram Schefold et al. Düsseldorf, n.d. 94–125.

Janowitz, Anne. *England's Ruins: Poetic Purpose and National Landscape*. Cambridge, Mass., 1990.

Jauss, Hans-Robert. *Wege des Verstehens*. Munich, 1994.

Jochum, Uwe. *Kleine Bibliotheksgeschichte*. Stuttgart, 1993.

Kaiser, Gerhard. *Gottfried Keller—Das gedichtete Leben*. Frankfurt am Main, 1981.

Kaiser, Gert. *Textauslegung und gesellschaftliche Selbstdeutung—Die Artusromane Hartmanns von Aue*. Wiesbaden, 1978.

Kant, Immanuel. *Critique of Pure Reason*. Unified Edition. Trans. Werner S. Pluhar. Intro. Patricia Kitcher. Indianapolis, Ind., 1996.

———. "Ideas for a Universal History with Cosmopolitan Intent." In *The Philosophy of Kant: Kant's Moral and Political Writings*. Trans. and ed. Carl J. Friedrich. New York, 1977. 116–31.

———. "Metaphysical Foundations of Morals." In *The Philosophy of Kant: Kant's Moral and Political Writings*. Trans. and ed. Carl J. Friedrich. New York, 1977. 140–208.

Kasch, Wilhelm F., ed. *Geld und Glaube*. Paderborn, 1979.

Kästner, Hans. *Fortunatus—Peregrinator mundi—Welterfahrung und Selbsterkenntnis im ersten deutschen Prosaroman der Neuzeit*. Freiburg, 1990.

Keller, Gottfried. *Green Henry*. Trans. A. M. Holt. New York, 1960.

———. *The Misused Love Letters*. In *The Misused Love Letters and Regula Amrain and Her Youngest Son*. Trans. Michael Bullock. New York, 1974. 13–94.

———. *Werke—Züricher Ausgabe*. Ed. G. Steiner. Zürich, 1978.

Kent, Robert W., and Lothar Schmidt, eds. *Geld—Aphorismen und Zitate aus drei Jahrtausenden*. Reinbek, 1990.

Kerényi, C. [Karl]. *Eleusis: Archetypal Image of Mother and Daughter*. Trans. Ralph Manheim. London, 1967.

Kirchhoff, Bodo. *Im Operncafé*. In B. Kirchhoff, *Ferne Frauen: Novellen*. Frankfurt am Main, 1986. 105–21.

Kittler, Friedrich. *Draculas Vermächtnis—Technische Schriften*. Leipzig, 1993.

———. "Fiktion und Simulation." In *Aisthesis—Wahrnehmung heute oder Perspektiven einer anderen Ästhetik*. Ed. K. Barck et al. Leipzig, 1992. 196–213.

Kittsteiner, Heinz-Dieter. *Naturabsicht und unsichtbare Hand—Zur Kritik des geschichtsphilosophischen Denkens*. Frankfurt am Main, 1980.

Kleist, Heinrich. *Heinrich von Kleist: Plays*. Ed. Walter Hinderer. Foreword E. L. Doctorow. New York, 1982.

Klinger, Cornelia. *Flucht, Trost, Revolte—Die Moderne und ihre ästhetischen Gegenwelten*. Munich, 1994.

Knapp, Georg Friedrich, and Henrik Bendixen. *Zur staatlichen Theorie des Geldes—Ein Briefwechsel 1905–1920*. Ed. K. Singer. Basel, 1958.

Kockjoy, Wolfgang. Der deutsche Kaufmannsroman—Versuch einer kultur- und geistesgeschichtlichen genetischen Darstellung. Diss. Freiburg am Breisgau, 1932.

Köpnick, Lutz. *Nothungs Modernität—Wagners "Ring" und die Poesie der Macht*. Munich, 1994.

Kracauer, Siegfried. *Theory of Film: The Redemption of Physical Reality.* New York, 1965.

Krell, David Farrell, and Frank A. Capuzzi, trans. *Early Greek Thinking.* New York, 1975.

Kretschmer, Ernst. *Der sensitive Beziehungswahn—Ein Beitrag zur Paranoiafrage und zur psychiatrischen Charakterlehre.* 1918. Rpt. Berlin, 1950.

Krieg, Peter. *Mythen der Moderne 2—Die Seele des Geldes.* Frankfurt am Main, 1990.

Kurnitzky, Horst. *Triebstruktur des Geldes—Ein Beitrag zur Theorie der Weiblichkeit.* Berlin, 1974.

Kursbuch. Thema: Korruption. No. 120 (June 1995).

Kurz, Robert. *Der Kollaps der Modernisierung—Vom Zusammenbruch des Kasernensozialismus zur Krise der Weltökonomie.* Frankfurt am Main, 1991.

Lacan, Jacques. *Écrits.* Paris, 1966.

———. "Das Problem des Stils und die psychiatrische Auffassung paranoischer Erlebnisformen" (1933). In S. Dalí, *Unabhängigkeitserklärungen der Phantasie. Gesammelte Schriften.* Ed. A. Marrhes and T. D. Stegmann. Munich, n.d. 352–56.

Langholm, Odd. *Economics in the Medieval Schools: Wealth, Exchange, Value, Money and Usury According to the Paris Theological Tradition 1200–1350.* Leiden, 1992.

Lasky, Melvin J. *Wortmeldung zu einer Revolution—Der Zusammenbruch der Herrschaft in Ostdeutschland.* Frankfurt am Main, 1991.

Lauer, Enrik. *Literarischer Monetarismus—Studien zur Homologie von Sinn und Geld bei Goethe, Goux, Sohn-Rethel, Simmel und Luhmann.* St. Inbert, 1994.

Laum, Bernhard. *Heiliges Geld.* Tübingen, 1974.

———. *Viehgeld und Viehkapital in den asiatischen-afrikanischen Hirtenkulturen.* Tübingen, 1965.

LeGoff, Jacques. *Wucherzins und Höllenqualen—Ökonomie und Religion im Mittelalter.* Stuttgart, 1988.

Lennhoff, Eugen and Oskar Posner. *Internationales Freimaurer-Lexikon.* Vienna, 1932.

Lexikon der Wirtschaftsethik. Ed. G. Enderle et al. Freiburg, n.d.

Lovejoy, Arthur O. *The Great Chain of Being.* Cambridge, Mass., 1936.

Luhmann, Niklas. "The Economy as a Social System." Trans. Charles Larmore. In *The Differentiation of Society.* Trans. Stephen Holmes and Charles Larmore. New York, 1982. 190–225.

———. "Knappheit, Geld und bürgerliche Gesellschaft." In his *Gesellschaftsstruktur und Semantik.* Vol. I. Frankfurt am Main, 1980. 186–210.

———. "Das Kunstwerk und die Selbstreproduktion der Kunst." In Hans Ulrich Gumbrecht and Karl Ludwig Pfeiffer, eds., *Stil—Geschichten und Funktionen eines kulturwissenschaftlichen Diskurselements.* Frankfurt am Main, 1984.

———. *Love as Passion: The Codification of Intimacy.* Trans. Jeremy Gaines and Doris L. Jones. Cambridge, Mass., 1986.

———. *Social Systems.* Trans. John Bednarz, Jr., with Dirk Baecker. Stanford, 1995.

———. *Die Wirtschaft der Gesellschaft.* Frankfurt am Main, 1988.

———. *Die Wissenschaft der Gesellschaft.* Frankfurt am Main, 1990.

Lukács, Georg. *History and Class Consciousness.* Trans. Rodney Livingstone. Cambridge, Mass., 1971.

Lyotard, Jean-François. *The Differend: Phrases in Dispute.* Trans. Georges Van Den Abbeele. Minneapolis, 1988.

MacLeod, Henry Dunning. *The Elements of Political Economy.* London, 1858.

Mann, Heinrich. *In the Land of Cockaigne.* Trans. Axton D. B. Clark. New York, 1929.

Mann, Thomas. *Buddenbrooks—Verfall einer Familie.* Frankfurter Ausgabe. Ed. Peter de Mendelssohn. Frankfurt am Main, 1981.

———. *Doctor Faustus.* Trans. H. T. Lowe-Porter. New York, 1992.

———. *The Holy Sinner.* Trans. H. T. Lowe-Porter. New York, 1951.

———. *Joseph the Provider.* Trans. H. T. Lowe-Porter. New York, 1944.

———. *Königliche Hoheit.* Frankfurter Ausgabe. Ed. A. von Schirnding. Frankfurt am Main, 1984.

———. *The Magic Mountain.* Trans. John E. Woods. New York, 1995.

———. *Royal Highness.* Trans. A. Cecil Curtis. Berkeley, 1967.

———. *Tagebücher 1953–1955.* Ed. I. Jens. Frankfurt am Main, 1995.

Manuel, Nikolaus. *Der Ablaßkrämer.* Ed. P. Zinsli. Bern, 1960.

Marcuse, Herbert. "Über den affirmativen Charakter der Kunst." In *Schriften.* Vol. 3. Frankfurt am Main, 1979. 186–226.

Marin, Louis. *Portrait of the King.* Trans. Martha M. Houle. Minneapolis, 1988.

Marti, Urs. *Der grosse Pöbel- und Sklavenaufstand—Nietzsches Auseinandersetzung mit Revolution und Demokratie.* Stuttgart, 1993.

Martres, Didier, and Guy Sabatier. *La Monnaie électronique. Que sais-je?* 2370. Paris, 1987.

Marx, Karl. *Capital.* Vols. I–III. Ed. Frederick Engels. Trans. Samuel Moore and Edward Aveling. New York, 1967.

Marx, Karl, and Frederick Engels. *The German Ideology: Part One, with Selections from Parts Two and Three, Together with Marx's "Introduction to a Critique of Political Economy."* Ed. C. J. Arthur. New York, 1970.

Mauss, Marcel. *The Gift: Forms and Functions of Exchange in Archaic Societies.* Trans. Ian Cunnison. New York, 1967.

McLuhan, Marshall. *Understanding Media: The Extensions of Man.* New York, 1964.

Meißner, Alfred. *Charaktermasken.* 3 vols. Leipzig, 1861–63.

Menasse, Robert. *Phänomenologie der Entgeisterung—Geschichte des verschwindenden Wissens.* Frankfurt am Main, 1995.

Merzbacher, Dieter. "Der Abendmahlstreit zwischen dem Vielgekrönten und dem Spielenden, geschlichtet vom Unveränderlichen—Georg Philipp Harsdörffers Lehrgedicht *Vom heiligen Abendmahl Christi* in einer Anhalter Akte aus dem Jahre 1651." *Daphnis* 22, Nos. 2–3 (1993): 347–92.

Meyer, Eva. *Zählen und Erzählen—Für eine Semiotik des Weiblichen.* Vienna, 1983.

Michelsen, Peter. "Diplomatik als Editionsprinzip—Zur Textgestalt des 'Faust' anhand der Ausgabe Albrecht Schönes." *Merkur* 557, No. 8 (1995): 595–706.

Modick, Klaus. *Weg war weg—Romanverschnitt.* 1988. Rpt. Reinbek, 1991.

More, Thomas. *Utopia.* Ed. Edward Sturz. New Haven, Conn., 1964.

Moritz, Rainer. "Wie schreibt man eine Literaturgeschichte? Zu stilistischen und anderen Defiziten einer Textsorte." In *Literaturgeschichte: Österreich—Prolegomena und Fallstudien.* Ed. W. Schmidt-Dengler et al. Vienna, 1995. 64–78.

Morshäuser, Bodo. *Die Berliner Simulation—Erzählung.* Frankfurt am Main, 1983.

Moths, Eberhard. "Die Preise schweigen." *Merkur* 530, No. 5 (1993): 455–62.

Mühlherr, Anna. *"Melusine" und "Fortunatus"—Verrätselter und verweigerter Sinn.* Tübingen, 1993.

Mulisch, Harry. *Die Entdeckung des Himmels—Roman.* Munich, 1993.

Müller, Adam. *Versuche einer Theorie des Geldes.* Ed. F. Bülow. Leipzig, 1931.

Müller, Rudolf Wolfgang. *Geld und Geist—Zur Entstehungsgeschichte von Identitätsbewußtsein und Rationalität seit der Antike.* Frankfurt am Main, 1977.

Münch, Richard. *Dialektik der Kommunikationsgesellschaft.* Frankfurt am Main, 1991.

Musil, Robert. *The Man without Qualities.* Trans. Sophie Wilkins. New York, 1995.

Muthesius, Volkmar. *Geld ist weder bös noch gut—Das Geld in der Dichtung.* Frankfurt am Main, 1960.

Naipaul, V. S. *Finding the Center.* New York, 1984.

Needleman, Jacob. *Money and the Meaning of Life.* New York, 1991.

Nelssons, Benjamin. *The Idea of Usury: From Tribal Brotherhood to Universal Otherhood.* Chicago, 1969.

Nestroy, Johannes. *Komödien in drei Bänden.* Ed. F. H. Mautner. Frankfurt am Main, 1970.

———. " 'Nur keck!'—Stücke 34." In *Sämtliche Werke, Historisch-kritische Ausgabe.* Ed. J. Hein and J. Hüttner. Vienna, 1989.

Nietzsche, Friedrich. *Beyond Good and Evil: Prelude to a Philosophy of the Future.* Trans. Walter Kaufmann. New York, 1966.

———. *The Genealogy of Morals: An Attack.* In *The Birth of Tragedy and The Genealogy of Morals.* Trans. Francis Golffing. New York, 1956. 147–299.

———. *Human, All Too Human: A Book for Free Spirits.* Trans. R. J. Hollingdale. Intro. Erich Heller. Cambridge, 1993.

———. "Nachgelassene Fragmente." In *Kritische Studienausgabe.* Vol. 12. Ed. G. Colli and M. Montinari. Munich, 1988.

———. *Thus Spake Zarathustra: A Book for All and None.* Trans. Thomas Common. In *The Complete Works of Friedrich Nietzsche: The First Complete and Authorised English Translation.* Vol. 11. Ed. Oscar Levy. New York, 1964.

———. *Werke in drei Bänden.* Ed. K. Schlechta. Munich, 1966.

Nooteboom, Cees. *Rituals.* Trans. Adrienne Dixon. Baton Rouge, La., 1983.

North, Michael. *Das Geld und seine Geschichte—Vom Mittelalter bis zur Gegenwart.* Munich, 1994.

Novalis. *Das philosophische Werk II. Schriften.* Vol. III. Ed. R. Samuel. Stuttgart, 1968.

Odier, Charles. "L'argent et les névroses." *Revue française psychanalytique* 2 (1928) and 3 (1930).

Oexle, Otto G. "Tria genera hominum." In *Institutionen, Kultur und Gesellschaft im Mittelalter.* Ed L. Fenske, W. Rösener, and Th. Zotz. Sigmaringen, 1984.

Ohly, Friedrich. "Zum Kästchen in Goethes 'Wanderjahren.' " *Zeitschrift für deutsches Altertum und deutsche Literatur* 91 (1962): 255–63.

Pape, Walter. "Symbol des Sozialen—Zur Funktion des Geldes in der Komödie des 18. und 19. Jahrhunderts." *Internationales Archiv für Sozialgeschichte der deutschen Literatur* 13 (1988): 45–67.

Péguy, Charles. "L'Argent." In *Oeuvres en prose 1909–1914.* Ed. M. Péguy. Paris, 1957.

Peyrefitte, Alain. *Du "miracle" en économie—Leçons au Collège de France.* Paris, 1995.

Pindar. *The Odes of Pindar.* Trans. Sir John Sandys. Cambridge, Mass., 1946.

Plato. *The Republic of Plato.* 2 vols. Trans. Benjamin Jowett. Oxford, 1936.

Pott, Hans-Georg. *Literarischer Bildung—Zur Geschichte der Individualität.* Munich, 1995.

Pound, Ezra. *The Cantos of Ezra Pound.* New York, 1950. Rpt. 1971.

Prasse, Jutta. "Kästchen." In *Phantasma und Phantome—Gestalten des Unheimlichen in Kunst und Psychoanalyse. Katalog zur Ausstellung Offenes Kulturhaus Linz.* Ed. M. Sturm. Linz, G. C. Tholen, and R. Zendron. 1995. 169–78.

Qur'an. Trans. T. B. Irving. Brattleboro, Vt., 1988.

Qur'an [*The Holy Qur'an*]. 2 vols. Text, translation, and commentary Abdullah Yusuf Ali. Cambridge, 1938.

Raitz, Walter. *Fortunatus*. Munich, 1984.

Rau, Peter. "Die Vorbereitung der romantischen Interpretation der Renaissance bei Karl Philipp Moritz." In *Romantik und Renaissance—Die Rezeption der italienischen Renaissance in der deutschen Romantik*. Stuttgart, 1994.

Reemtsma, Jan Philipp. "Kombabus." *Fragmente—schriftenreihe zur psychoanalyse*, August 27–28, 1988: 154–74.

Reichert, Klaus. *Fortuna oder die Beständigkeit des Wechsels*. Frankfurt am Main, 1985.

Renner, Rolf Günter. "Schrift der Natur und Zeichen des Selbst—Peter Schlemihls wundersame Geschichte im Zusammenhang von Chamissos Texten." *Deutsche Vierteljahrsschrift* 65 (1991).

Richter, Dieter. *Schlaraffenland—Geschichte einer populären Fantasie*. Cologne, 1984.

Ricoeur, Paul. *Le conflit des interprétations—Essais d'herméneutique*. Paris, 1969.

Rilke, Rainer Maria. *The Notebooks of Malte Laurids Brigge*. Trans. M. D. Herter Norton. New York, 1949.

———. *The Selected Poetry of Rainer Maria Rilke*. Ed. and trans. Stephen Mitchell. New York, 1982.

Rohrmann, Peter. "The Central Role of Money in the Chapbook 'Fortunatus.'" *Neophilologus* 59 (1975): 262–72.

Rorty, Richard. *Philosophy and the Mirror of Nature*. Princeton, 1979.

Rowland, Herbert. *Claudius, Matthias*. Boston, 1983.

Rubin, Miri. *Corpus Christi: The Eucharist in Late Medieval Culture*. Cambridge, 1991.

Rudolf von Ems. *Der gute Gerhart*. Ed. J. A. Asher. Tübingen, 1989.

Rühmkorf, Peter. *Lombard gibt den Letzten—Ein Schauspiel*. Berlin, 1972.

Sahlins, Marcus. *Stone Age Economics*. London, 1974.

Samhaber, Ernst. *Das Geld—Eine Kulturgeschichte*. Bayreuth, 1976.

Schade, Sigrid, Monika Wagner, and Sigrid Weigel, eds. *Allegorien und Geschlechterdifferenz*. Cologne, 1994.

Schefold, Bertram, ed. *Die Darstellung der Wirtschaft und der Wirtschaftswissenschaften in der Belletristik*. Berlin, 1992.

Schestag, Thomas. "Économie." In his *Parerga*. Munich, 1991. 160–209.

Schiebler, Ralf. "Kandinsky lockert die Deckungsvorschrift—Die moderne Kunst und der Goldstandard." *Frankfurter Allgemeine Zeitung*, April 29, 1995 (Insert: *Bilder und Zeichen*, 2).

Schiller, Friedrich. *Mary Stuart: The Maid of Orleans*. Trans. Charles E. Passage. New York, 1961.

———. *The Poems of Schiller*. Trans. Edgar A. Bowring. New York, n.d. [2nd edn.; original preface dated 1851].

———. *Werke in drei Bänden*. Ed. H. G. Göpfert. Munich, 1966.

———. [Johann Christoph Friedrich von Schiller]. *Wilhelm Tell*. Trans. and ed. William F. Mainland. Chicago, 1972.

Schily, Otto. *Flora, Fauna und Finanzen—Über die Wechselbeziehungen von Natur und Geld*. Hamburg, 1994.

Schlaffer, Heinz. *Faust II—Die Allegorie des 19. Jahrhunderts*. Stuttgart, 1981.

———. "Knabenliebe—Die Geschichte der Liebesdichtung als Vorgeschichte der Frauenemanzipation." *Merkur* 577, No. 8 (1995): 682–94.

———. *Poesie und Wissen—Die Entstehung des ästhetischen Bewußtseins und der philologischen Erkenntnis*. Frankfurt am Main, 1990.

Schlegel, Friedrich. *Jenaer Vorlesung über Transcendentalphilosophie*. In *Kritische Ausgabe*. Vol. 12. Ed. Ernst Behler, J.-J. Anstett, and H. Eichner. Munich, 1964. 1–106.

———. *Philosophical Fragments*. Trans. Peter Firchow. Foreword Rodolphe Gasché. Minneapolis, 1991.

———. "Über die Unverständlichkeit." In *Kritische Ausgabe*. Vol. 2. Ed. Ernst Behler, J.-J. Anstett, and H. Eichner. Munich, 1967. 363–71.

Schmidt, Max. *The Primitive Races of Mankind: A Study in Ethnology*. Trans. Alexander K. Dallas. London, 1926.

Schmitt, Carl. *Political Theology: Four Chapters on the Concept of Sovereignty*. Trans. George Schwab. Cambridge, Mass., 1985.

Schmölders, Günter. *Einführung in die Geld- und Finanzpsychologie*. Darmstadt, 1975.

———. *Gutes und Schlechtes Geld—Geld, Geldwert und Geldentwertung*. Frankfurt am Main, 1968.

———. *Psychologie des Geldes*. Munich, 1982.

Schnack, Ilse. *R. M. Rilke—Leben und Werk im Bild*. Frankfurt am Main, 1973.

Schöne, Albrecht. "'Auf Biegen und Brechen'—Komparative Motivgeschichte als vergleichende historische Verhaltensforschung." In *Akten des VIII. internationalen Germanistik-Kongresses*. Vol. I. Ed. E. Iwasaki. Tokyo, 1990. Munich, 1991.

———. *Götterzeichen, Liebeszauber, Satanskult—Neue Einblicke in alte Goethetexte*. Munich, 1993.

Schreker, Franz. *Der Schatzgräber—Oper in einem Vorspiel, vier Akten und einem Nachspiel*. Vienna, n.d. [1985].

Schulze, Gottlob Ernst. *Aenesidemus oder über die Fundamente der von dem Herrn Professor Reinhold in Jena gelieferten Elementarphilosophie*. Ed. A. Liebert. Berlin, 1911. Rpt. 1972.

Schurtz, Heinrich. *Grundriss einer Entstehungsgeschichte des Geldes*. Weimar, 1898.

Schwanitz, Dietrich. *Systemtheorie und Literatur—Ein neues Paradigma*. Opladen, 1990.

Schwarz, Fritz. *Segen und Fluch des Geldes in der Geschichte der Völker*. 2 vols. Bern 1931, 1933.

Schwendter, Rolf. "Geld und Subkultur." *Diagonal. Zum Thema: Geld*. 277–81.

Schwitzgebel, Helmut. "Gustav Freytags 'Soll und Haben' in der Tradition des deutschen Kaufmannsromans." *Gustav-Freytag-Blätter* 24 (1981): 3–11, and 25 (1982): 3–13.

Sédillot, René. *Muscheln, Münzen und Papiere—Geschichte des Geldes*. Frankfurt am Main, 1992.

Seitter, Walter. *Menschenfassungen—Studien zur Erkenntnispolitikwissenschaft*. Munich, 1985.

Seneca. "De vita beata." In *Philosophische Schriften—Lateinisch und Deutsch*. Vol. 2. Ed. M. Rosenbach. Darmstadt, 1995.

Shakespeare, William. *Merchant of Venice*. Ed. Louis B. Wright. New York, 1957.

Shell, Marc. *Art and Money*. Chicago, 1995.

———. *The Economy of Literature*. Baltimore, 1978.

Simmel, Georg. *The Philosophy of Money*. Trans. Tom Bottomore and David Frisby. London, 1978.

———. "Die Ruine." In his *Philosophische Kultur*. Potsdam, 1923. 135–43.

Sloterdijk, Peter. *Critique of Cynical Reason*. Trans. Michael Eldred. Foreword Andreas Huyssen. Theory and History of Literature 40. Minneapolis, 1987.

———. *Thinker on Stage: Nietzsche's Materialism*. Trans. Jamie Owen Daniel. Foreword Jochen Schulte-Sasse. Theory and History of Literature 56. Minneapolis, 1989.

——. *Weltfremdheit*. Frankfurt am Main, 1993.

Sohn-Rethel, Alfred, ed. *Das Geld, die bare Münze des Apriori*. Berlin, 1990.

——. *Intellectual and Manual Labour: A Critique of Epistemology*. Trans. Martin Sohn-Rethel. London, 1978.

——. *Soziologische Theorie der Erkenntnis*. Frankfurt am Main, 1985.

——. "Zur kritischen Liquidierung des Apriorismus—Eine materialistische Untersuchung." In his *Warenform und Denkform*. Frankfurt am Main, 1978. 27–89.

Sonnemann, Ulrich. *Negative Anthropologie—Vorstudien zur Sabotage des Schicksals*. Reinbek, 1969.

Staiger, Emil. *Die Zeit als Einbildungskraft des Dichters—Untersuchungen zu Gedichten von Brentano, Goethe und Keller*. Munich, 1976.

Steiner, George. *Real Presences*. Chicago, 1989.

Stemmler, Theo. "Ein Hymnen-Test." *Die Zeit*, October 1, 1993.

——. *Stemmlers kleine Stil-Lehre—Vom richtigen und falschen Sprachgebrauch*. Frankfurt am Main, 1994.

Stifter, Adalbert. "Abdias." In *Brigitta; with Abdias, Limestone, and The Forest Path*. Trans. and intro. Helen Watanabe-O'Kelly. London, 1990.

Stoker, Bram. *Dracula*. Ed. and intro. Maurice Hindle. New York, 1993.

Strauß, Botho. "Anschwellender Bockgesang." In *Deutsche Literatur 1993—Jahresüberblick*. Ed. F. J. Götz et al. Stuttgart, 1994. 255–69.

Strecker, Bernhard. "Geben und Nehmen—Oder die Korruption in den Tiefen der Menschheit." *Kursbuch* 120 (1990): 1–8.

Tacitus. "Germania." In *Tacitus: Historical Works*. Vol. 2. London, n.d. 307–43.

Taubes, Jacob, ed. *Der Fürst dieser Welt—Carl Schmitt und die Folgen*. Munich, 1983.

Thalmayr, Andreas. *Das Wasserzeichen der Poesie oder die Kunst und das Vergnügen, Gedichte zu lesen*. Ed. Hans Magnus Enzensberger. Nördlingen, 1985.

Theunissen, Michael. "Begriff und Realität—Hegels Aufhebung des metaphysischen Wahrheitsbegriffs." In *Denken im Schatten des Nihilismus (Festschrift für W. Weischedel)*. Darmstadt, 1975. 164–95.

——. *Negative Theologie der Zeit*. Frankfurt am Main, 1991.

——. *Sein und Schein—Die kritische Funktion der Hegelschen Logik*. Frankfurt am Main, 1978.

——. *Selbsverwirklichung und Allgemeinheit—Zur Kritik des gegenwärtigen Bewußtseins*. Berlin, 1982.

Theweleit, Klaus. *Male Fantasies*. Minneapolis, 1987.

——. *Männerphantasien*. 2 vols. Frankfurt am Main, 1977.

Tholen, Georg C., and Michael O. Scholl, eds. *Zeit-Zeichen—Aufschübe und Interferenzen zwischen Endzeit und Echtzeit*. Weinheim, 1990.

Thomson, George. *Die ersten Philosophen—Forschungen zur Altgriechischen Gesellschaft II*. Berlin, 1974.

Timm, Uwe. *Headhunter*. Trans. Peter Tegel. New York, 1994.

Vak, Karl. "Unterwegs zum abstrakten Symbolsystem Geld." In *Kursbuch neue Medien—Trends in Wirtschaft und Politik, Wissenschaft und Kultur*. Ed. Stefan Bollmann. Mannheim, 1995. 301–12.

Valéry, Paul. *Monsieur Teste*. Trans. Jackson Mathews. New York, 1947.

Veblen, Thorsten. *Theorie der feinen Leute—Eine ökonomische Untersuchung der Institutionen (1899)*. Frankfurt am Main, 1993.

Vernon, John. *Money and Fiction: Literary Realism in the Nineteenth and Early Twentieth Centuries*. Ithaca, N.Y., 1984.

Vief, Bernhard. "Digitales Geld." In *Ästhetik der elektronischen Medien*. Ed. F. Rötzer. Frankfurt am Main, 1991. 117–46.

Volney, Constantin François. *The Ruins, or, Meditation on the Revolutions of Empires and the Law of Nature*. Peter Eckler edn., 1890. Rpt. Baltimore, 1991.

Voltaire, François Marie Arouet de. *Philosophical Letters*. Trans. Ernest Dilworth. Indianapolis, Ind., 1961.

Wagner, Falk. *Geld oder Gott—Zur Geldbestimmtheit der kulturellen und religiösen Lebenswelt*. Stuttgart, 1984.

Wagner, Richard. *Götterdämmerung* Libretto. Georg Solti. Vienna Philharmonic Orchestra. Trans. G. M. Holland. LP. London Records, 1965.

Warburg, Aby. *Heidnisch-antike Weissagung in Wort und Bild zu Luthers Zeiten. Gesammelte Schriften*. Vol. 2. Leipzig, 1932.

Watzlawick, Paul, Janet Helmick Beavin, and Don D. Jackson. *Pragmatics of Human Communication: A Study of Interactional Patterns, Pathologies, and Paradoxes*. London, 1968.

Weber, Max. "Asketischer Protestantismus und kapitalistischer Geist." In his *Soziologie, Weltgeschichtliche Analysen, Politik*. Ed. Johannes Winckelmann. Stuttgart, 1956. 357–81.

———. "Protestant Asceticism and the Spirit of Capitalism." In *Weber: Selections in Translation*. Ed. W. G. Runciman. Trans. Eric Matthews. Cambridge, 1978. 138–73.

———. *The Protestant Ethic and the Spirit of Capitalism*. Trans. Talcott Parsons. Foreword R. H. Tawney. New York, 1958.

———. *Die Protestantische Ethik*. Ed. Johannes Winckelmann. Gütersloh, 1991.

———. *Wirtschaft und Gesellschaft*. Tübingen, 1972.

Weber, Wilhelm. *Geld, Glaube, Gesellschaft—Vortrag G 239 der Rheinisch-Westfälischen Akademie der Wissenschaften*. Opladen, 1979.

Wegner, Gottlieb. *Liberis et libris sacerdotum oratio, Vulgo Dicterio, Priester hinterlassen nur Bücher und Kinder/opposita*. Leipzig, 1967.

Weimar, Klaus. *Geschichte der deutschen Literaturwissenschaft bis zum Ende des 19. Jahrhunderts*. Munich, 1989.

Weimer, Wolfram. "In Zukunft zählt die Zahlungselektronik—Zur Geschichte und Gegenwart des Papiergeldes." *Frankfurter Allgemeine Zeitung*, June 16, 1990: 13.

Weinmann, Barbara. *Studien zur Gebrauchssituation früher deutscher Druckprosa—Literarische Öffentlichkeit in Vorreden zu Augsburger Frühdrucken*. Munich, 1982. 151.

Weinrich, Harald. "Münze und Wort." In *Festschrift für G. Rohlfs*. Halle, 1958.

Weinreich, Otto. *Nachwort zu Aristophanes: Sämtliche Komödien*. Zürich, 1968.

———. "Seltsame Liebespaare—Ein Beitrag zur Personalmetapher von Krations bis Arno Holz." Afterword to Aristophanes, *Werke*. Ed. L. Seeger. Zürich, 1968.

Weis, Heinz. *Iocosa*. n.p., 1939.

Weiß, Christoph. " 'Gestaltung des unmittelbaren Greifbaren'—Lion Feuchtwanger und sein Roman 'Erfolg' im Kontext der neuen Sachlichkeit." In *Neue Sachlichkeit im Roman—Neue Interpretationen zum Roman der Weimarer Republik*. Ed. S. Becker and Christoph Weiß. Stuttgart, 1995. 314–32.

Weissberg, Liliane. "Gedanken zur 'Weiblichkeit'—Eine Einführung." In Liliane Weissberg, ed., *Weiblichkeit als Maskerade*. Frankfurt am Main, 1994. 7–33.

Wellershoff, Dieter. "Frauenfeind und Dr. Krebs—Über Namen." *Merkur* 513, No. 12 (1991): 1113–25.

Werber, Niels. "Von Feinden und Barbaren—Carl Schmitt und Niklas Luhmann. *Merkur* 558–559, Nos. 9–10 (1995): 949–57.

Widdig, Dietmar. " 'Tägliche Sprengungen'—Elias Canetti und die Inflation." *Merkur* 548, No. 11 (1994): 985–97.

Winthrop-Young, Geoffrey. "Undead Networks: Information Processing and Media Boundary Conflicts in *Dracula*." In *Literature and Science*. Ed. D. Bruce and A. Purdy. Amsterdam, Ga., 1994. 107–30.

Wörterbuch der deutschen Volkskunde. Oswald A. Erich and Richard Beitl. Stuttgart, 1981.

Wunderlich, Werner, ed. *Der literarische Homo oeconomicus*. Bern, 1989.

Zelle, Carsten. "Moneten, Moral und Motivation—Johann Gottlob Krügers Beitrag zur Psychologie des Geldes in der Frühaufklärung." *Diagonal. Zum Thema: Gelt.* 251–59.

Zimmermann, Johann Georg. *Memoire an Seine Kaiserkönigliche Majestät Leopold den Zweiten über den Wahnwitz unsers Zeitalters*. Ed. Ch. Weiß. St. Ingbert, 1995.

Zola, Emile. *Money*. Trans. Ernest A. Vizetelly. Dover, N.H., 1991.

Zöller, Sonja. *Kaiser, Kaufmann und die Macht des Geldes—Gerhard Unmaze von Köln als Finanzier der Reichspolitik und der "Gute Gerhard" des Rudolf von Ems*. Munich, 1993.

INDEX

Abdias (Stifter), 245–49
Der Ablaßkrämer (The Indulgences Peddler) (Manuel), 25
Absolute, the, 138, 245
Abstraction, of money, 182, 185, 186–87, 189, 191, 194
Academe: homosexual latencies, 121–22; as mother, 120–24; sexlessness, 125–26; women in, 126
Adelberts Fabel (Chamisso), 242–44
Adorno, Theodor W., 195, 292n. 12; on Benjamin's commodity-fetish, 208–9; "On the Fetish Character in Music," 201; on Goethe, 209; *Minima Moralia*, 171, 185; reaction to Sohn-Rethel, 199–200
Advertising, 155
"Advice to a Young Tradesman" (Franklin), 130
Aesthetic code, 35, 250
Aesthetic of existence (*Daseins-Aesthetik*), 157
Agrippa, Menenius, 117, 118
Albee, Edward, 174
Allegory, 37, 205–6. *See also* Benjamin, Walter
Allen, Woody, 11

Alma mater, 122, 123
Anagram poem, 34–35
Anal imagery, and money, 94–95
Analytic linguistic theory, 30
Anna Karenina (Tolstoy), 174
Antigone (Sophocles), 294n. 1
Anti-Oedipus: Capitalism and Schizophrenia (Deleuze and Guattari), 58
Antiphilus of Byzantium, 123
Antiutopians, 177
Aquinas, Thomas, 103, 105, 130
L'Argent, 223
Aristophanes, 101
Aristotle, 105
Army: homosexual latencies, 121–22; as mother, 120–24
Arnim, Achim von, 212–13, 221, 281
Art: function of, 30; and money, 177–78; system of, 31
Assignats, 71, 155, 197, 212
Association of the manifold, 187, 188
Audio-visual media. *See* Electronic media
"Aufrichtigen Gesellschaft von der Tannen" ("Upright Society of the Firs"), 42
Augustin, Ernst, 18

Aurea catena Homeri (anonymous), 246–48, 250
Auto-da-Fé (Canetti), 174, 177
Ayrer, Jacob, 265

Bachofen, Johann Jakob, 194
Balzac, Honore de, 277
Banknotes, 59–64, 71, 213; in *Faust*, 108–9; German, 63–64, 65–66; Swiss, 60; U.S., 60–63
Bankruptcy, 79
Banks, 142–46, 196, 305n. 33
Baroque allegory, 206
Baroque period, 195–96
Bataille, Georges, 154
Baudelaire, Charles-Pierre, 213, 214
Baudrillard, Jean, 58, 70
Becher, Johannes R., 261
Becker, August, 194
Becker, Thorsten, 195
Being and Time (Heidegger), 132
Benjamin, Walter, 28; on acceleration of time, 144; on Adorno, 199; on allegorical character of society of commodities, 200–202, 203–8, 213; definition of allegory, 204, 270; interest in Baroque, 37, 195, 265; *Passagen-Werk*, 144, 202, 209, 213; on philosophical truth, 36, 37; reaction to Sohn-Rethel, 200; "Socrates," 194; on tragic drama, 206; *Zentralpark*, 202
Berlin, wie es weint und lacht (Kalish), 269
Berliner Simulation (Morshäuser), 198
Bildungsroman, 221
"Blood money," 281
Bloy, Léon, 129
Blumenberg, Hans, 181
Body of Christ, 118
Book-money, 69
Book of Life, 43
Book of the World, 41, 43
Books: generation of, 123–24; metaphor of, 50–53
Börne, Ludwig, 298n. 32
Der böse Geist Lumpazivagabundus oder Das liederliche Kleeblatt (Nestroy), 157–58
Brant, Sebastian, 43, 44

"Bread and Wine" (Hölderlin), 28, 236
Brecht, Bertolt, 166–68, 274, 294n. 12
Brentano, Clemens, 242, 315n. 3
"The Bridegroom" ("Der Bräutigam") (Goethe), 156–57
Brocke, Barthold Heinrich, 45
Buddenbrooks: The Decline of a Family (Thomas Mann), 267–70
Die Bürgschaft (Becker), 195
Burke, Kenneth, 307n. 15
Burns, Robert, 72
Butler, Samuel, 25, 26, 176–77

Canetti, Elias, 309n. 18; *Auto-da-Fé*, 174, 177; *Crowd and Power* (*Masse und Macht*), 185; *The Torch in My Ear*, 288n. 14
Capital, 129
Capital-life insurance, 128–29, 133
Cassirer, Ernst, 204, 290n. 47
The Cavalier of the Rose (*Rosenkavalier*) (Hofmannsthal), 133–37, 139
Caves, 94–95
Celan, Paul, 28, 238–40, 285–86, 305n. 22
Celebrity, 197
Center, source of, 241–50
Chamisso, Adelbert von: *Abelberts Fabel*, 242–44; dramatization of the Fortunatus story, 216–20, 227–28, 249; on functional primacy of money, 161–62, 222; *Peter Schlemihls wundersame Geschichte*, 127, 128, 165; *Poetisches Hausbuch*, 164–65
Changing talers, 107
"Character und Anal Erotism" (Freud), 94
Chargaff, Erwin, 56
Child-book metaphor, 123–25
Children vs. money, 91–92
Chobham, Thomas von, 105
Christian Directory (Baster), 130
Church: homosexual latencies, 121–22; metaphor of the militia, 118; as mother, 120–24; ontosemiology of Communion, 22, 25
Churchill, Winston, 178
Cipolla, Carol M., 164

Claudius, Matthias, 46–47, 49
Codes, 35; aesthetic, 35, 250; genetic, 56; of love, 172; monetary, 152
Coins, 213; of antiquity, 64, 194; and Communion wafers, 27, 291n. 54, 291n. 62; invention of, 193
Collin, Matthäus von, 313n. 9
Commodities, 183; allegorical character of society of, 200–202, 203–8, 213
Communal economy, 193
Communication, 30–31, 292n. 14, 296n. 2
Communion, Holy, 23, 195–96, 197; allusions to in *Dracula*, 319n. 16; and coins, 27, 291n. 54, 291n. 62; ontosemiology of, 22, 25
Comparative literature, 293n. 34
Consciousness, effects of money-code on, 191
Copernicus, Nicolaus, 185
Corporate bodies, as mothers, 119–24
Council of Lyon, 24
The Counterfeiters (Gide), 72, 106
Counterfeit money, 252
"Counterfeit Money" ("Fausse monnaie") (Derrida), 59
The Count of Monte Christo (Dumas), 68
"Cover," 13–14, 288n. 10
Credit cards, 65
Crime and Punishment (Dostoyevsky), 80
Critique of Pure Reason (Kant), 150, 180, 184, 186–90
Cross of the present, 136
Crowd and Power (Masse und Macht) (Canetti), 185

Dadaism, 178
Danae motif, 93, 103
Dante, 106, 278
Darwin, Charles, 185
Dasein (existence), 161
Death, 132–33
The Death of Money (Kurtzmann), 284–85
Deconstruction, 267; of meaning, 230; of money, 251–60; money as incarnation of, 59
Deficiency. *See* Scarcity
Dekker, Thomas, 221
Deleuze, Gilles, 58, 195

Delusions, Confusions (Irrungen, Wirrungen) (Fontane), 78–79
Derrida, Jacques, 58, 59, 207, 228, 316n. 17; "Counterfeit Money" ("Fausse monnaie"), 59; *Economimesis*, 59
Detering, Heinrich, 227
Devotion (Die Widmung) (Strauß), 226
Dickens, Charles, 91–92
Differentiation of subsystems, 170, 171, 174
Dingsymbol, 173
"Dinks," 92
"The disconcerted communication" ("die verdutzte Kommunikation"), 31
Discourse: order of, 253; primary vs. secondary, 221; secondary, 224–26
Doctor Faustus (Thomas Mann), 130–31
Dollar bill, 61–63
Donne, John, 288n. 10
Dostoyevsky, Fyodor, 80, 91, 121
The Double, 234
Dracula (Stoker), 276, 282–84
Dumas, Alexander, 68, 298n. 32
Dürer, Albrecht, 221

Economimesis (Derrida), 59
Effi Briest (Fontane), 174
Ego, 187
Eichendorff, Joseph von, 153, 237
Einstein, Albert, 138
Elective Affinities (Goethe), 37, 124, 203, 211
Electronic banking, 65
Electronic media, 22, 23, 55, 197
Electronic money, 68–69
Ems, Rudolf von, 163–64
Die Entdeckung des Himmels (Mulisch), 284
Enzensberger, Hans-Magnus, 144–46, 318n. 18
Equivalents: money-mediated exchange of, 169–78, 192–93; pre-monetary, 192–93
Erasmus, Desiderius, 41–42
Erbe, Volker, 299n. 37
Erewhon, or, Over the Range (Butler), 176–77
Erzählungen und Spiele (Newmann and Varnhagen), 242

Eternity, doubt of, 131
Excess, of money, 153–58
Exchange, 170, 186–87, 190
Exégèse des lieux communs (Interpretation of Platitudes) (Bloy), 129
Exposé zum Plan einer soziologischen Theorie der Erkenntnis (Sohn-Rethel), 152

"Faust, Geld" (Hamacher), 214
Faust I (Goethe), "Walpurgis Night" scene, 95, 96–99
Faust II (Goethe), 11–12, 32, 97; as allegory, 213; assignats, 11–12, 14; homosexual reproduction of money, 98, 107–11, 227; Masquerade scene, 153–56; origin and propagation, 95–96; Sir Greed, 111–13
Federal Republic of Germany, 195
Fellow Culprits (Die Mitschuldigen) (Goethe), 51, 115
Ferlinghetti, Lawrence, 62–63
Fetish, 183, 201, 203, 204–5, 207, 208–9, 311n. 19
"On the Fetish Character in Music" (Adorno), 201
Feuchtwanger, Lion, 47, 49
Fichte, Johann Gottlieb, 181
Film, 55
The First Philosophers (Thomson), 181
Flaubert, Gustave, 79–80, 174
Fontane, Theodor, 298n. 32; Delusions, Confusions (Irrungen, Wirrungen), 78–79; Effi Briest, 174; A Man of Honor, 120–21
Fonteyn, Bernard, 221
Forgery, 66, 72
Forster, Georg, 274
Fortunatus theme, 16, 17–18, 92–93, 195, 220–22, 249, 277
Foucault, Michel, 58, 195, 253, 290n. 47
Foundations of Transcendental Philosophy (Wissenschaftslehre) (Fichte), 181
Franc, 178
Frank, Manfred, 310n. 30
Franklin, Benjamin, 130
French Affairs (Französische Umstände) (Heine), 66–67, 68
French literature, money in, 71–72

Freud, Sigmund, 94, 125, 185; "Character und Anal Erotism," 94; essay on negation, 148; the fetish, 205; gold and feces, 94; "a good joke," 295n. 23; Interpretation of Dreams, 125; "Neurotic Mechanisms in Jealousy, Paranoia and Homosexuality," 121
Freytag, Gustav, 80
Fridolin, Stephan, 16

Galileo, 196
Gehlen, Arnold, 148
"Das Geld" ("The Money") (Enzensberger), 144–46
"Geldkunst" ("The Art of Money") (Walch), 45
Geld und Geist (Wealth and Welfare) (Gotthelf), 80, 255–58, 259
Generalizable media, 149–50
Genetic code, 56
George, Stefan, 224
Georgics (Virgil), 61
German banknotes, 63–64, 65–66
German Democratic Republic, 81, 195, 273; national anthem, 261–63, 317n. 1; secret service, 267
German Federal Bank, 151
The German Ideology (Marx), 207
German literary criticism: avoidance of money, 18–21
German literature: resistance to conversion from God to money, 26
German Romantics, 177
German unification of 1990, 195
Gibertius, Johannes, 221
Gide, André, 72, 106
The Gift (Essay sur le don) (Mauss), 192, 193
Gift-exchange, 193
Godwi (Brentano), 242
Goebbels, Joseph, 225
Goethe, Johann Wolfgang, 225–26; allegorical late work, 209–15; "The Bridegroom" ("Der Bräutigam"), 156–57; child-book metaphor, 124–25; Elective Affinities, 37, 124, 203, 211; experiences with ruins, 266; Faust I, 95, 96–99; Faust II,

Goethe, Johann Wolfgang (*continued*)
11–12, 32, 95–96, 97, 98, 107–13,
153–56, 213, 227; *Fellow Culprits*
(*Die Mitschuldigen*), 51, 115; *Goetz
from Berlichingen with the Iron Hand*,
211; hands motif, 211; key motif,
113–16; letter to patron, 21; little
box motif, 116; money = blood
metaphor, 280; *Poetry and Truth*
(*Dichtung und Wahrheit*), 116, 124,
247; psychosexual and historical
theory of money, 95–116; reason
for end of symbol, 214; *Venetian
Epigram*, 16; *Wilhelm Meister's
Apprenticeship*, 19–21, 101, 172, 174;
Wilhelm Meister's Journeyman Years,
210–13
Goetz, Rainald, 29
*Goetz from Berlichingen with the Iron
Hand* (Goethe), 211
Gold, 94, 177
"The Golden Pot" (Hoffmann), 242
Gotthelf, Jeremias, 80, 255–58, 259
Goux, Jean-Joseph, 71
Grabbe, Christian Dietrich, 298n. 32
"Grabschrift eines Reichen" ("Rich
Man's Epitaph") (Logau), 43
A Grammar of Motives (Burke), 307n. 15
Greenblatt, Stephen, 26–27
Der grüne Heinrich (*Green Henry*)
(Keller), 80
Guattari, Felix, 58
Der Guote Gêrhart (Gerhart the Good)
(Ems), 163–64
Gutenberg Galaxy, 55, 65, 75
Gutes Geld (Augustin), 18

Habermas, Jürgen, 30, 191, 204, 292n.
12, 310n. 30
Hamacher, Werner, 214
Hamann, Johann Georg, 58, 251–52
Handke, Peter, 29, 153
Harvey, William, 280
Headhunter (*Kopfjäger*) (Timm), 18, 60
"Heads or tails," 13
Hegel, Georg Wilhelm Friedrich, 148,
208, 222, 266; formula of identity
and difference, 170, 186; on
Germans and money, 19; on Kant,

182, 184, 190; on money code, 164;
Phenomenology of the Spirit, 254;
"rose in the cross of the present,"
136; "take and give," 254
Heidegger, Martin, 179, 208; *Being and
Time*, 132; criticism of gossip, 224,
225; on meaning, 230; on
modernity as the first age of
worldview, 54; Nietzsche
reconstruction, 235–36; on
obliviousness of being, 193
Hein, Christoph, 34
Heine, Heinrich, 66–67, 68, 86, 274,
298n. 27
Heinrich, Klaus, 125
Heinrich von Ofterdingen (Novalis), 243
Henrich, Dieter, 187
Heraclitus, 193–94
Hermeneutists, 28
Hermlin, Stephan, 272–73
Hesiod, 123
Historical consciousness, 274
Hitler, Adolf, 267
Hobbes, Thomas, 118, 279, 280, 309n.
15
Hoffmann, E. T. A., 242
Hofmannsthal, Hugo von, 72–75,
195–96; *The Cavalier of the Rose*
(*Rosenkavalier*), 133–37, 139;
"Verse, auf eine Banknote
geschrieben" ("Verses Written on a
Banknote"), 72–75
Hölderlin, Friedrich, 28, 236, 285
Holy Communion. *See* Communion,
Holy
The Holy Sinner (Thomas Mann), 104,
241
Homer, 150, 247
Homosexual latencies, of institutions,
121–22
Homosexual reproduction, of money, 98,
107–11, 227
Horace, 42
Hugo, Victor, 298n. 32
Human, All Too Human (*Menschliches,
Allzumenschliches*) (Nietzsche), 229,
234–35, 237

Ibsen, Henrik, 174

"Ich trink Wein" ("I Drink Wine")
(Celan), 285–86
The Idea of Usury (Nelssons), 302n. 34
"Ideas for a Universal History with
Cosmopolitan Intent" (Kant), 81
Ihara Saikaku, 106
Iliad (Homer), 247
Illusions perdues (Balzac), 277
Im Operncafé (Kirchhoff), 18
Indifference, 170, 171
Indulgences, 49
Inferno (Dante), 106
Infidelity, 171
Inflation, 197, 288n. 14, 298n. 25, 309n.
18
Ingeborg Bachmann Competition, 29
Institutionalized worldviews, 148–50
Institutions: corporate, as mothers,
119–24; as obsessive-compulsive
macroneuroses, 149
Interest, prohibition against, 103–8, 112,
302n. 24
Internationalization, 90, 293n. 34
Interpretation, conflicts of, 35
Interpretation of Dreams (Freud), 125
Interpretive sociology, 30
Intersubjectivity, 192, 197
Ion (Plato), 35
Islam, 104–5

Japanese language, 105–6
Jaspers, Karl Theodor, 204
Jodl, Friedrich, 162

Kalish, David, 269
Kalldewey Farce (Strauß), 226
Kant, Hermann, 29
Kant, Immanuel, 81, 266; absolute, 138;
concept of the apriority, 192;
Critique of Pure Reason, 150, 180,
184, 186–90; on equivalence, 171;
"Ideas for a Universal History with
Cosmopolitan Intent," 81; problem
of actual existence of God, 190;
"Synthesis des Mannigfaltigen," 23;
Table of Categories, 150, 179, 184,
189; theory of schematism, 189–90
Karl V, 104
Kasseler Fortunat, 221
Kästner, Hannes, 16

Keller, Gottfried, 80, 180, 181, 183; *The
Misused Love Letters* (*Die
Mißbrauchten Liebesbriefe*), 77,
82–89, 91, 125, 276; *The People of
Seldwyla* (*Die Leute von Seldwyla*), 82
Kirchhoff, Bodo, 18
Kirchwege, Anton Joseph, 247
Kittler, Friedrich, 284
Kleist, Heinrich, 29, 265–66
Die Kommandeuse (Hermlin), 272–73
Koran, 104
Kracauer, Siegfried, 55
Kraus, Karl, 224
Kretschmer, Ernst, 82
Die Kronenwächter (Arnim), 221, 281
Krüger Johann Gottlieb, 45
Kurtzmann, Joel, 284–85

Lacan, Jacques, 58, 205, 267
In the Land of Cockaigne (*Im
Schlaraffenland*) (Heinrich Mann),
98, 276–77
Language, 251–54; of commodities, 203;
inflation, 223–26; limitations of,
253; and money, 58, 251–54, 258,
259, 316n. 3
Law, John, 71, 280
Law's reforms, 197
The Legend of the Grand Inquisitor
(Dostoyevsky), 121
Leibniz, G. W., 309n. 15
Lessing, Gotthold Ephraim: *Minna von
Barnhelm*, 169, 171, 175; *Nathan the
Wise*, 24, 169, 171, 175
"Letter of Lord Chandos"
(Chandosbrief) (Hofmannsthal),
141
Leviathan (Hobbes), 118, 279, 280
Life insurance, 127–28
Literary history: defusion of paradoxes,
32–33; as the history of problems,
28–38
Literature: and cover, 17–18; disruption
of accepted communication, 28–30;
double status, 18; interweaving of
words and things, 24; knowledge of,
36–37; money in, 18, 44–50, 70–76,
147–58; and paradoxes, 31–35;
self-definition, 274; superfluity, 27

Little box motif, 213
Locke, John, 58, 309n. 15
Logau, Friedrich von, 43, 44
Love, code of, 172
Love as Passion: The Codification of Intimacy (Luhmann), 174
Löwenhalt, Jesajas Rompler von, 42
Luhmann, Niklas, 30, 33, 174, 190, 197, 267
Lukács, Georg, 180, 183, 208, 236, 310
Luther, Martin, 281
Lyotard, Jean-François, 162

Madame Bovary (Flaubert), 79–80, 174
The Magic Flute (Mozart), 272
The Magic Mountain (Thomas Mann), 43, 162, 270
Magic philology, 202, 203, 209
Mahmoody, Betty, 29
Mann, Heinrich, 98, 276–77
Mann, Thomas, 43, 105, 162, 276, 318n. 4; *Buddenbrooks: The Decline of a Family*, 267–70; *Doctor Faustus*, 130–31; *The Holy Sinner*, 104, 241; *The Magic Mountain*, 43, 162, 270; *Royal Highness (Königliche Hoheit)*, 276, 277–82
A Man of Honor (Fontane), 120–21
Manuel, Niklaus, 25
The Man without Qualities (Musil), 37–38
Maori, 192
Marin, Louis, 291n. 54
Marquand, Odo, 250
Marriage, 174
Marx, Karl, 107, 180, 237, 266; on capitalistic modernity, 208; on fetish, 205; *The German Ideology*, 207; McLuhan's critique of, 298n. 33; theory of fetishism of commodities, 183, 203
Mattenklott, Gert, 227
Mauss, Marcel, 192, 193
Mautz, Kurt, 34
McLuhan, Marshall, 69
Media: generalizable, 149–50; ontosemiological major, 23, 55, 178, 191, 196, 284. *See also* Electronic media
Media technology, 284

Mei$ner, Alfred, 237
Memoirs of a Good-for-Nothing (Aus dem Leben eines Taugenichts) (Eichendorff), 153
Mensch, 50
The Merchant of Venice (Shakespeare), 24, 107, 169, 171, 174–75, 195
Metaphors, 52, 245
Metaphysics, and metaphor, 245
Michelsen, Peter, 109–10
Military. *See* Army
Minima Moralia (Adorno), 171, 185
Minna von Barnhelm (Lessing), 169, 171, 175
The Misused Love Letters (Die Mißbrauchten Liebesbriefe) (Keller), 77, 82–89, 91, 125, 276
Mnemosyne project, 37
Modernity, 12–13, 104, 271; characterization by Goethe and Benjamin, 214; leftist critique of, 223; money as "God term" of, 46, 144, 168, 221–23; paradoxes of, 31; reactionary critique of, 223–24; scarcity of time and money in, 131, 140
Modern literature: money motifs and problems, 165, 168; observation of the ir/rationality of money, 169
Modick, Klaus, 29
Monetary code, 152, 191
Monetary coverage, 14–16
Money: and anal semantic field, 94–95; and art, 177–78; attempts to negate, 150; authority of, 15, 53; blood and, 43; change of form, 64–65; vs. children, 91–92; collapse of the medium of, 197; conflict with religion, 25–26; "continuous cohesion," 82; in contrast to books, 50–52; counterpart to death, 133; deconstruction of, 251–60; deflation of, 66; electronic transfer, 68–69; excess of, 153–58; function, 17, 113–15; illusion of, 65; im/materiality of, 64–70; indifference of, 256; insubstantiality of, 132; and interest, 103–8, 112; ir/rationality, 169, 173; and

language, 58, 258; and legibility of world, 54, 55–57; literary critique of, 18, 44–50, 70–76, 147–58, 294n. 1; metaphor of the circulation of, 281; and modernity, 46, 221–23; as ontosemiological major medium, 23, 55, 178, 191, 196; paradoxes of, 222; pentecostal spirit of, 254–58; phallic power of, 92–94; and philosophy, 180–98; procreational power, 98, 103, 105–6, 107–11, 130, 169, 227; relationship of the sexes to, 102–3; relationships established by, 79–90, 169; revolts against, 194–95; scarcity of, 53, 151–53, 169, 253; secondary vs. primary status, 221–22, 257; semantic poverty, 53, 168, 176; speechlessness, 177, 221, 249; and spirit, 289n. 30; surplus value, 59; suspicion of, 14–15; and time, 127–33, 137–42, 169; and validity, 179–98

The Money (Zola), 67–68, 72

"Money-adventure" stories, 164

Money and Fiction (Vernon), 71

Money = blood metaphor, 280

More, Thomas, 294n. 10

Morgenblatt für gebildete Stände, 161

Morgenröte (Nietzsche), 237

Morshäuser, Bodo, 198

Mother Right (Das Mutterrecht) (Bachofen), 194

Mothers, corporate bodies as, 119–24

Les mots et les choses (Foucault), 58, 290n. 47

Mozart, Wolfgang Amadeus, 272

Mulisch, Harry, 284

Müller, Adam, 222, 256, 258–59

Müller, Heiner, 28, 274

Müllner, Laurenz, 162

Musil, Robert, 37–38

Myth, 203

Naipaul, V. S., 205

Napoleon oder die Hundert Tage (Grabbe), 298n. 32

Nathan the Wise (Lessing), 24, 169, 171, 175

Nature, reading of, 55–57

Nazism, 271

Negation, 148

Nelssons, Benjamin, 302n. 34

Neo-Marxism, 204, 208

Neoplatonism, 247

Nestroy, Johann, 77, 151, 157–58

Neue Lehre von den Gemütsbewegungen (Unzer), 45

Neumann, Wilhelm, 242

Neurosis, 149

"Neurotic Mechanisms in Jealousy, Paranoia and Homosexuality" (Freud), 121

New Media. *See* Electronic media

Nibelungenlied, 163

Nietzsche, Friedrich, 182–83, 271, 273; critique of money, 237–40; *Human, All Too Human (Menschliches, Allzumenschliches)*, 229, 234–35, 237; on Kant, 181–82, 184; *Morgenröte*, 237; platonic chrematophobia, 237–40; on Platonism, 233–35, 238; *Thus Spake Zarathustra*, 234; *The Wanderer and His Shadow*, 228–36

Nooteboom, Cees, 284

The Notebooks of Malte Laurids Brigge (Die Aufzeichnungen des Malte Laurids Brigge) (Rilke), 138–42, 144

Not without My Daughter (Mahmoody), 29

Novalis, 58, 180, 181, 183, 221, 243

"Nur keck!" (Nestroy), 77

Odyssey (Homer), 150

Ofterdingen, Heinrich von, 242

The Old Curiosity Shop (Dickens), 91–92

Oneness, 217

Ontology, 22

Ontosemiological major media, 23, 284

Ontosemiology, 22–23; monetary, 23, 55, 178, 191, 196

Opus mago-cabbalisticum (Welling), 247

Order of discourse, 253

Ovid, 123–24

Paper money. *See* Banknotes

Parsons, Talcott, 23

Parzival (Wolfram von Eschenbach), 163

Passagen-Werk (Benjamin), 144, 202, 209, 213
Passion, 171
Paul, Jean, 28
Paul, Saint, 118, 119
Peirce, Charles Sanders, 204
Penthesilea (Kleist), 265–66
The People of Seldwyla (*Die Leute von Seldwyla*) (Keller), 82
Pep: J. L. Wetcheek's American Songbook (Feuchtwanter), 47–48
Peter Schlemihls wundersame Geschichte (Chamisso), 127, 128, 165
Phallic power, of money, 92–94
Phantasus (Tieck), 242
Phenomenology of the Spirit (Hegel), 254
Philology, 35, 203; magic, 202, 203, 209
Philosophical criticism, object of, 36–37
Philosophical hermeneutics, 30
Philosophical Letters (Voltaire), 25–26
Philosophische Lexikon (Walch), 45
Philosophy, and money, 180–98
Philosophy of Symbolic Forms (Cassirer), 290n. 47
Pindar, 123
Plato: *Ion*, 35; *Republic*, 117–18, 233; *Symposium*, 101
Platonism, 233–35, 237–40
The Pleasant Comedie of Old Fortunatus (Dekker), 221
Pleonasm, 86
Pliny the Elder, 42
Pluto, 97
Plutus, 154, 155
Poetics. *See* Literature
Poetisches Hausbuch (Chamisso), 164–65
Poetry and Truth (*Dichtung und Wahrheit*) (Goethe), 116, 124, 247
Polis, 117–18
Politics of confession, 81
Poor Richard's Almanac, 130
Popper School, 35
Portrait of the King (Marin), 291n. 54
Post-metaphysical era, 236–37, 238, 250
Postmodernism, 56, 92, 271
Post-Romanticism, 245–49
Poststructuralism, 58
Potlatch, 154, 192
Pound, Ezra, 106–7

"Preface on Money" (Krüger), 45
Primary and secondary: discourses, 221; distinction between, 234; Dracula and, 282; literature, 36, 220; money and, 221–22, 257; shadow and, 229
Primary interpretations, 148
Pringsheimer, Katja, 281
Promises, 255
Promissory notes, 142–43
"Psalm" (Celan), 305n. 22
Psychoanalysis, 313n. 12
Purchase, 186, 187–88

Raimund, Ferdinand, 313n. 9
Von realer Gegenwart (*Of Real Presence*) (Steiner), 224
Realism, 178
Realistic literature, 77, 245, 274
Real Presences (Steiner), 224–26
Real socialism (*Realsozialismus*), 271
Rée, Paul, 125
Referential orders, 271
Reformation, 49
"Reichtum in Armut" ("Wealth in Poverty") (Löwenhalt), 42
Relational mania (*Beziehungswahn*), 82, 169
Religion, 24–26
Religious affiliation, 80–81
Republic (Plato), 117–18, 233
Rieter, Sebald, 16
Rilke, Rainer Maria, 29, 153; *The Notebooks of Malte Laurids Brigge* (*Die Aufzeichnungen des Malte Laurids Brigge*), 138–42, 144
Ring, symbol of, 171–75
The Ring of the Nibelungs (Wagner), 169, 171, 176
Ritter der Tafelrunde (Hein), 34
Rituals (*Rituelen*) (Nooteboom), 284
Roman Elegies (Goethe), 211
Romanticism, 221, 222–23, 242, 244–45, 249–50, 273, 313n. 12
Rorty, Richard, 191
Rousseau, Jean-Jacques, 309n. 15
Royal Highness (*Königliche Hoheit*) (Thomas Mann), 276, 277–82
Rühmkorf, Peter, 50
Ruin and ruins, 261–75

"Die Ruine" (Simmel), 317n. 2

The Ruins, or, Meditation on the Revolutions of Empires; and The Law of Nature (Volney), 274–75

Rushdie, Salman, 29

Sachs, Hans, 220

Sahlin, Marcus, 193

The Satanic Versus (Rushdie), 29

Saussure, Ferdinand de, 58, 267

Scarcity: of goods, 152; of money, 151–53

Schematism, 189

Schiebler, Ralf, 177–78

Schiller, Friedrich, 26

Schlaffer, Heinz, 226

Schlegel, August Wilhelm, 313n. 9

Schlegel, Friedrich, 150, 177, 222, 223, 242

Schmidt, Max, 193

Schmitt, Arno, 28

Schmitt, Carl, 224, 225

Schöne, Albrecht, 96, 100, 101, 109–10, 293n. 34

Schulze, Gottlob Ernst, 182, 309n. 12

Schwanitz, Dietrich, 175–76

Scriptural revelations, paradox of, 52–53

Scrooge McDuck, 93–94

Secondary: discourse, 224–26; growing domination of, 271; literature, 36, 220; shadow as, 229

Self-consciousness, 185, 193

Semiology, 22

Seneca, 42, 179

Shadow, theme of the, 228–40

Shakespeare, William: *The Merchant of Venice*, 24, 107, 169, 171, 174–75, 195; *Timon of Athens*, 195, 207, 302n. 34

Ship of Fools (Brandt), 44

Signified and signifier, 195–96, 202, 204

Simmel, Georg, 81–82, 180, 183, 265, 317n. 2

Simrock, Karl, 161

Simulation: and money, 70; theory, 208; of worldviews, 54

Sinn und Seiendem, 22, 27

Slums, 90

Socrates, 180

"Socrates" (Benjamin), 194

Sohn-Rethel, Alfred, 152, 180–81, 184–86, 192, 197–200, 208, 312n. 32

Soll und Haben (Debit and Credit) (Freytag), 80

"Song of the Stimulating Impact of Cash" ("Lied von der belebenden Wirkung des Geldes") (Brecht), 166–68

Sonnemann, Ulrich, 149

Sophocles, 294n. 1

Source of the center, 241–50

"Speak, You Also" ("Sprich auch du") (Celan), 238–40

Speech, 177

Speechlessness, of money, 177, 221, 249

Speed, Albert, 267

Die Spur des Schwimmers (Erbe), 299n. 37

Staatssicherheitsdienst (Stasi), 31, 267

State, metaphor of body, 117–19

Stegmayer, Matthäus, 313n. 9

Stein, Gertrude, 58

Steiner, George, 217, 220, 224–26

Stifter, Adalbert, 245–49

Stock exchange, 66–70, 299n. 37

Stoker, Bram, 276, 282–84

Storytelling, 195, 248

Strauß, Botho, 226

Strauß, Franz Josef, 121–22

Strindberg, August, 174

Structural linguistics, 58

Suetonius, 123

Symbol, 204, 205

Symbolic uni/formi/ty, 36

"Symbolon," 32

Symposium (Plato), 101

Synesius, 124

"Synthesis des Mannigfaltigen" (Kant), 23

Synthetic judgments, 186, 187

Systems, 35

Systems theory, 23, 37, 49, 174, 197

Table of Categories, 150, 179, 184, 189

Tacitus, 190–91

Telegraph, 298n. 32

Theory of relativity, 138

"The third elegy, against a greedy rich man" (Erasmus), 41–42

Thomasius, Christian, 44
Thomson, George, 181
Thus Spake Zarathustra (Nietzsche), 234
Tiberius, 42
Tieck, Ludwig, 221, 242, 249, 313n. 9
Time: insubstantiality of, 132; and
    money, 127–33, 137–42, 169; and
    risk, 142; sale of in the form of
    labor, 131
Time banks, 143–44
Timm, Uwe, 18, 60
Timon of Athens (Shakespeare), 195, 207,
    302n. 34
"To My Friends" ("An die Freunde")
    (Schiller), 26
The Torch in My Ear (Canetti), 288n. 14
"To sing everyday" ("Täglich zu singen")
    (Claudius), 46–47
Totalitarianism, 267, 274
Totalitarian literature, 266–67
Tower of Babel, 252
Transcendental philosophy, 223
"Transcendental poetry," 242
Transcendental subjectivity, 242; and
    money, 180, 181, 190, 191, 192, 208
Transmission, 248
Transubstantiation, 217
Tristia (Ovid), 123–24
Truth, 253, 254
Tucher, Hans, 16, 289n. 26

Uhland, Ludwig, 249, 313n. 9
Understanding, 30–31
Unzer, Johann August, 45
Usury, 103, 104, 105
Utopia (More), 294n. 10

Valéry, Paul, 309n. 15
Varnhagen, Karl August, 242
Venetian Epigram (Goethe), 16
"Vermischten Anmerkungen über die
    Wortfügung in der französischen
    Sprache" (Hamann), 251–52
Vernon, John, 71
"Verse, auf eine Banknote geschrieben"
    ("Verses Written on a Banknote")
    (Hofmannsthal), 72–75
Versuche einer neuen Theorie des Geldes
    (Müller), 256

Virgil, 61, 123
De vita beata (Seneca), 179
Volney, Constantin François de, 274–75
Voltaire, François Marie Arouet de,
    25–26
Vorwort zu einer Grammatik der Biologie
    ("Introduction to a Grammar of
    Biology") (Chargaff), 56

Wackenroder, Wilhelm Heinrich, 221
Wackernagel, Wilhelm, 161
Wagner, Richard, 172; *The Ring of the
    Nibelungs*, 169, 171, 176
Walch, Johann Georg, 45
Walt Disney, 93
The Wanderer and His Shadow
    (Nietzsche), 228–36
War, 154, 271
Warburg, Aby, 37
"The Way to Wealth" (Franklin), 130
Wealth, 154
Wealth and Welfare (Geld und Geist)
    (Gotthelf), 80, 255–58, 259
Weber, Max, 130, 259
Weg war weg (Modick), 29
Welling, Georg von, 247
Who's Afraid of Virginia Woolf (Albee),
    174
Wilhelm Meister's Apprenticeship
    (Goethe), 19–21, 101, 172, 174
Wilhelm Meister's Journeyman Years
    (Goethe), 210–13
Willehalm von Orlens (Ems), 163
Without Feathers (Woody Allen), 11
Wittgenstein, Ludwig, 148, 218
Wolf, Christa, 29
Wolfram von Eschenbach, 163
World, and money, 41–57
World market, 89
Worldviews, institutionalized, 148–50
Wörterbuch der deutschen Volkskunde, 107
Writing, 35
"Wunder über Wunder" (Arnim),
    212–13

Zentralpark (Benjamin), 202, 213
Zola, Emile, 67–68
Zöller, Sonja, 163

Books in the Kritik: German Literary Theory and Cultural Studies series

Walter Benjamin: An Intellectual Biography, by Bernd Witte, translated by James Rolleston, 1991

The Violent Eye: Ernst Jünger's Visions and Revisions on the European Right, by Marcus Paul Bullock, 1991

Fatherland: Novalis, Freud, and the Discipline of Romance, by Kenneth S. Calhoon, 1992

Metaphors of Knowledge: Language and Thought in Mauthner's Critique, by Elizabeth Bredeck, 1992

Laocoon's Body and the Aesthetics of Pain: Winckelmann, Lessing, Herder, Moritz, Goethe, by Simon Richter, 1992

The Critical Turn: Studies in Kant, Herder, Wittgenstein, and Contemporary Theory, by Michael Morton, 1993

Reading After Foucault: Institutions, Disciplines, and Technologies of Self in Germany, 1750–1830, edited by Robert S. Leventhal, 1994

Bettina Brentano-von Arnim: Gender and Politics, edited by Elke P. Frederiksen and Katherine R. Goodman, 1995

Absent Mothers and Orphaned Fathers: Narcissism and Abjection in Lessing's Aesthetic and Dramatic Production, by Susan E. Gustafson, 1995

Identity or History? Marcus Herz and the End of the Enlightenment, by Martin L. Davies, 1995

Languages of Visuality: Crossings between Science, Art, Politics, and Literature, edited by Beate Allert, 1996

Resisting Bodies: The Negotiation of Female Agency in Twentieth-Century Women's Fiction, by Helga Druxes, 1996

Locating the Romantic Subject: Novalis with Winnicott, by Gail M. Newman, 1997

Embodying Ambiguity: Androgyny and Aesthetics from Winckelmann to Keller, by Catriona MacLeod, 1997

The Freudian Calling: Early Viennese Psychoanalysis and the Pursuit of Cultural Science, by Louis Rose, 1998

By the Rivers of Babylon: Heinrich Heine's Late Songs and Reflections, by Roger F. Cook, 1998

Reconstituting the Body Politic: Enlightenment, Public Culture, and the Invention of Aesthetic Autonomy, by Jonathan M. Hess, 1999

The School of Days: Heinrich von Kleist and the Traumas of Education, by Nancy Nobile, 1999

Walter Benjamin and the Corpus of Autobiography, by Gerhard Richter, 2000

Heads or Tails: The Poetics of Money, by Jochen Hörisch, translated by Amy Horning Marschall, 2000